History's Lost Moments
Volume V

The Stories Your Teacher Never Told You

Tom Horton

Order this book online at www.trafford.com
or email orders@trafford.com

Most Trafford titles are also available at major online book retailers.

© Copyright 2014 Tom Horton.
All rights reserved. No part of this publication may be reproduced, stored in a retrieval system, or transmitted, in any form or by any means, electronic, mechanical, photocopying, recording, or otherwise, without the written prior permission of the author.

Printed in the United States of America.

ISBN: 978-1-4907-4470-4 (sc)
ISBN: 978-1-4907-4469-8 (e)

Library of Congress Control Number: 2014914926

Because of the dynamic nature of the Internet, any web addresses or links contained in this book may have changed since publication and may no longer be valid. The views expressed in this work are solely those of the author and do not necessarily reflect the views of the publisher, and the publisher hereby disclaims any responsibility for them.

Any people depicted in stock imagery provided by Thinkstock are models, and such images are being used for illustrative purposes only.
Certain stock imagery © Thinkstock.

Trafford rev. 10/08/2014

 www.trafford.com

North America & international
toll-free: 1 888 232 4444 (USA & Canada)
fax: 812 355 4082

Contents

300. Carolina Mavericks In Texas 1
301. Jefferson and The Idea of Separation of Church and State 4
302. The Private Lives of General George E. Pickett, C.S.A. and
     LaSalle Corbell 8
303. Honoring the Washington Light Infantry On Their 203rd Anniversary 12
304. Marie Laveau, The VouDou Queen of New Orleans 16
305. Calculating The Wages of Sin In Antebellum Charleston 20
306. Young Jim Edwards Served In The Merchant Marine in WW II 23
307. Kreutner's Snee Farm Swim Team Among Elites 28
308. The Centennial Conference of A.M.E. Palmetto Conference 33
309. Finding History and Adventure On Old U.S. Highway 1 36
310. Jenkins Orphanage Band's 105th Anniversary 40
311. New South's Origins Owe Much To University of North Carolina 44
312. A 1780s Quaker Family Survived Two Years Captivity By Indians 48
313. In The Company Of Heroes With Medal of Honor Recipients 52
314. What Became of Those Unvanquished Confederate Generals? 56
315. Money Man of the American Revolution Was Haym Solomon 59
316. Burrsylvania and the Principality of Aaron I 63
317. A Salute To The Carolina Upcountry 67
318. Goodbye Milton Friedman, Hello Disaster Capitalism With
     Naomi Klein 70
319. It's An Honor To Vote In S.C. First Congressional District 74
320. Anthony Kennedy's Seat On Supreme Court Once Belonged To
     John Rutledge 78
321. The Events Leading To Osceola's Death At Fort Moultrie 82
322. Carolinians Who Did Not Celebrate Secession 86
323. The Story Behind Those Currier and Ives Prints 90
324. Christmas In Charleston 75 Years Ago 94

325. Murder on Charlotte Street 75 Years Ago 98
326. Historically Significant Santee River Plantations Lost Forever In 1939 101
327. Battle of New Orleans Was America's Greatest Military Victory 104
328. John Blake White's Painting of Marion Depicts Faithful Servant,
     Oscar 108
329. There's More History In Awendaw Than Meets The Eye 111
330. C.D. Bull and Sons: At $1.69 a Pound, Cotton is King Again! 114
331. Mount Pleasant Businessman Has Keen Interest In Bell-Ringing
     Tradition 118
332. A Walk Around Charleston In February 1811 122
333. Exposing the Origins of Old Glory's Stripes 126
334. Not All of SC's Heroes Hailed From Charleston 129
335. Fanny Trollope's Book On Early American Manners Outraged
     Our Ancestors 133
336. South Carolinians At The Alamo 137
337. Commencement At Willington Was SC's Grandest Annual
     Academic Occasion 141
338. Remembering That Incomparable Carolina Teen, Eliza Lucas 145
339. Lincoln Sent Hoodwinking Hurlbut as Envoy to Charleston in 1861 149
340. Recalling Fort Sumter Centennial 50 Years Ago (1861) 153
341. Abolitionist William Lloyd Garrison Was Keynote Speaker at
     Fort Sumter in 1865 158
342. The Carolinian Who Became Governor of Antigua 162
343. Recalling the Night the U.S.S. Hobson Went Down 166
344. Yankee Generals Fared Well After War 170
345. A Brief History of Apocalyptic Events 174
346. It's Hard To Say Good Bye To Alex's 178
347. Touring Charleston Back in 1912 181
348. June 6th Belongs to the Rangers Who Scaled Pont-du-Hoc in 1944 185
349. Make Kansas City One of Your Destinations This Summer 189
350. This Past Sunday Was the 146th Anniversary of Juneteenth 192
351. Charleston During the French Revolution 196
352. Finding a Sunken Steamboat Buried in a Cornfield in Kansas 200
353. July 13 Marks 148th Anniversary of Worst Riot in American History 204
354. Honoring Duportail and L'Enfant for Their Dogged Defense of
     Charleston, 1780 208
355. Headmaster Jaycocks Recalls Life on the Savannah and Cape
     Romain Refuges 212

356. Kershaw Folks Believe There's Gold Beneath Snowy Owl Road 216
357. Oldest Continuing School Board In Country Taps Former
     Moultrie News Editor 220
358. French Botanist Andrae Michaux Was 241 Yesterday 224
359. Lincoln - McClellan 1864 Presidential Campaign Secured the Union 228
360. War Brings Out Best and Worst of Character Traits 232
361. Why Southerners Had Affection For Lehman Brothers 236
362. Reliving The Early Days of the Brokers Who Started Goldman-Sachs 240
363. Citadel Alum James Lide Coker's Business Empire Began With
     Rural Store 244
364. Father of Southern Textile Industry Was Carolinian William Gregg 247
365. Carolina Tycoons of Industry and Commerce Noted in Hall of Fame 251
366. Uncovering History At Hughes Lumber On Mary Street 255
367. Has Charleston Become a Playground for the Rich? 260
368. Best Book For October Evenings Is Jackpot By Jason Ryan 263
369. Laying Bare the 150 Year-old Hammond-Hampton Feud 267
370. Did Your Grandmother Go To Memminger? 271
371. What We Don't Know About History Can Hurt Us -- Bretton Woods 276
372. Charlestonian Was Acquaintance of Edgar Degas in New Orleans 280
373. Why Southern Men Approve of the Poetry of William Butler Yeats 284
374. The Citadel Paradigm Appreciated 288
375. What Happened to Puritan John Winthrop's "City Upon a Hill" Idea? 292
376. Carolina Should Boast of its Connection With Locke 296
377. How a Group Called "The Inquiry" Shaped American History 300
378. Did Wilson's White House Physician Exceed His Authority? 304
379. Tragic Upstate School Fire Gave Us Fire Codes and Fire Drills in 1923 308
380. Ex-Slave Harriet Tubman Led Union Raid on the Combahee in 1863 312
381. Saluting the Palatines' 300 Years in South Carolina 316
382. The Luces of Mepkin Were No Ordinary Couple 320
383. South Carolina Native Was Life Magazine's Founding Editor 324
384. Urban Graffiti: Criminal Act or Pop Art? 328
385. South Carolina Scalawags -- Scoundrels or Political Progressives? 331
386. The Road To Utopia Begins At Number 2 Meeting Street 335
387. The Tales They Tell About Horrell Hill 339
388. Stateburg's Angelica Singleton Was America's First Lady, 1839 - 1841 342
389. The Charleston Side of the Landmark Hayne - Webster Debate 346
390. Mount Pleasant's Earliest Known Historic Site Is 203 King Street 350
391. From St. Philip's Street to Schloss Cecilienhof 354

392. Hamburg, Germany Has Played a Key Role in Charleston History 358
393. Much of Charleston's German Population Hails From Berlin 362
394. Vienna, St. Petersburg, Berlin, and Hamburg Once Were
     Thriving S.C. Towns 366
395. Retired Physician Receives Honor from SC Medical Association 370
396. Lordy, Lordy, Travis Jervey Is 40 374
397. The Powerful Intellect of James McBride Dabbs 378
398. Charleston Port of Call for Wallenius-Wilhelmsen M/V *Turandot* 382
399. The H & R Sweet Shop on Royall Avenue Turns 65 This Month! 386
400. Anderson County Native Jack Swilling Founded Phoenix, Arizona 390
401. Charleston Native Managed Kansas City's Famous Savoy For
     Nearly 50 Years 394
402. Earthen Mound Was Holy Ground For Santee Tribe 398
403. The Eastern Cougar Does Inhabit South Carolina 401
404. Cowasee Basin Is Much More Than a Floodplain Forest in the
     Midlands 404
405. Grandest Home Site in South Carolina Is Atop Cook's Mountain 407
406. Reverend Woodmason's 1762 Account of Upcountry Woes 410
407. How Cully Cobb Helped Transform the South 414
408. Why The Progressive Farmer Launched Southern Living Magazine 418

*To the Glory of God, Amen.
This volume of History's Lost Moments is dedicated to
Millie Bull Horton
Soulmate, best friend, and proofreader.*

Carolina Mavericks In Texas

"Mama, Don't let your sons grow up to be cowboys." Remember that old tune by Johnny Paycheck?" Most South Carolinians will never know what it's like to roam the range rounding up strays and fighting off cattle rustlers. Our days of singing "Home On The Range" ended 200 years ago. One former Charlestonian, Sam Maverick (d. 1870), however, has left an indelible mark on American history as well as the list of colloquial expressions indigenous to our land.

Sam Maverick, lawyer, land speculator, cattle rancher, and a pioneer of the Texas Republic, would no doubt have made his mark as a South Carolinian had he not argued with the Nullifiers in 1830. Opposing the Calhoun faction in South Carolina was the kiss of death for an ambitious man in the Upstate. Maverick's story is typical of both South Carolina and Texas in the 1830s. Quite a number of hotspurs migrated west as depleted soil here produced less and less wealth for expanding families.

In Texas the local historians regale eager listeners with tales of men like Maverick who came out in a covered wagon with little to no knowledge of how to survive in the wild west. South Carolina hadn't experienced an Indian raid in 3 generations. War-painted savages turned out to be the least of the worries for Carolinians migrating west. Sam Maverick's stubborn demeanor would combine with that curious quality the his name has become synonymous with -- a glorious independent cussedness that drives rule-followers mad.

We hear the expression "he's a maverick" quite often in political discussions. John McCain relished the euphemistic label. However, few around here these days know that the original maverick was a Charlestonian, a son of an importer, who grew up on the lower peninsula until the embargoes associated with the War of 1812 dried up foreign trade.

Samuel Augustus Maverick probably would have lived his life out in the Carolina Lowcountry had not the War of 1812 forced his father, the elder Samuel Maverick, to seek another venue for commerce. Perhaps he would have joined Judge James Louis Petigru in opposing the Ordinance of Secession. We'll never know because the train of events that'd lead him west and away from Carolina forever occurred when the Maverick family left Charleston and moved to the idyllic upstate village of Pendleton.

Details are sketchy, but old man Maverick must have done rather well as a merchant in Pendleton. Quite a few prominent families were in the area -- John C. Calhoun, Robert Anderson, Benjamin Cleveland, John Moffet, etc. According to old land deeds, Maverick, Sr., owned farm land in three states when he died. There must be more than a coincidence in the fact that the elder Maverick was wed to the daughter of Revolutionary War Brigadier General Robert Anderson, and he relocated to her hometown when financial reversal beset him in Charleston.

Young Sam Maverick was packed off to a private tutor in Ripton, Connecticut, at age 18 (1821). A year later young Maverick of Pendleton was hobnobbing with the scholars of Yale. He took his degree in just under three years and was known as quite a classical scholar. When Maverick was accepted to read law under the tutelage of Henry St. George Tucker of Virginia there was scarce a Carolinian other than Calhoun who could be his equal in academic credentials. Tucker was a Madison-appointed federal judge in Virginia, and double-degreed from the prestigious College of William and Mary.

Old Revolutionary War soldiers in the Pendleton District were ardent Union men and supporters of Jackson in the 1828 Nullification -- much to the chagrin of John C. Calhoun, so-called "Father of the Nullification Doctrine." Outspoken young Maverick got himself into a bitter S.C. House race in 1830. One story says that even Maverick father and son were on opposing sides of nullification. The South Carolina General Assembly used secret ballot in the 1830 election to name James Hamilton of Charleston as governor. That act incensed the Anti-Nullifiers. The tension of the times swayed the younger Maverick to quit the state to seek his fortune elsewhere.

For a few years Maverick operated a gold mine in northeast Georgia were John C. Calhoun was an investor. His father gave him land and slaves with which to become a gentleman planter. With a name like Maverick, it's unlikely that Sam could be content to practice law in rural Georgia and supervise a plantation. Wanderlust took hold of the man who would help make Texas great. There was another interlude of two years on family lands in Alabama, but Texas fever was white-hot with the rumors of impending war with Mexico.

Maverick arrived just before the siege of Bexar, now known as San Antonio. He got trapped behind the lines, and for a few days he feared for his life.

Maverick's diary provides the best eyewitness record that Texas historians have of that early battle for Texas independence.

Sam Maverick was most likely the best educated pioneer in Texas in the mid-1830s. Yet, it was a man's quickness with a Colt pistol that profited him more than his knowledge of torts. The former Carolinian enlisted with the militia and battled Comanche and Mexicans, highway gangs and horse rustlers. He sent back to Alabama for a certain pretty 18-year-old young lady, Mary Ann Adams to come be his wife in this exciting new territory. Mary Ann Maverick's personal diary is one of the earliest records of Texas frontier life from a woman's perspective. Sam Maverick was an intimate, and sometimes an opponent, of the likes of Sam Houston and Stephen Austin. Maverick purchased over 35,000 acres of farm and ranch land in Texas, and the unbranded cattle that roamed on his land were disdainfully referred to as "Maverick's" by the more knowledgeable ranchers. When Texas seceded, Sam Maverick had harsh words for his native South Carolina and even harsher words for his adopted state of Texas for following South Carolina's lead. Today the legacy of Sam Maverick belongs totally to Texas, and Charleston barely recalls that one of her sons helped to win the West.

Jefferson and The Idea of Separation of Church and State

The two things we are taught never to bring up at a dinner party are religion and politics. So, rambling on about separation of church and state while munching *hors d'oeuvres* is a good way not to get invited back. As we celebrate our nation's 234th anniversary it's good to reflect upon just what Jefferson must have been thinking when he penned those words, "Congress shall make no law respecting an establishment of religion, or prohibiting the free exercise thereof..."

Is it significant, or not, that Jefferson wrote the words "separation of church and state," rather than phrasing it "separation of church from state?" To this question we may find some understanding, if not clarification, by looking back at the times when the First Amendment was written.

No doubt, Thomas Jefferson was our young nation's finest legal mind. That's why he was appointed to be our Minister to France in 1787. He was a widower grieving for a wife who'd died in childbirth and his friends felt that a change of scenery would do him good. However, the loss of the lanky redhead's political acumen was profound during that long, hot summer of the Constitutional Convention.

While Jefferson savored the last heady moments of the French Enlightenment before the cataclysm and the fall of the Bastille, James Madison and the rest of the Founding Fathers were hammering out the compromises that we know as The Constitution.

Try to imagine Jefferson's fascination as he read through the Constitution for the first time in his apartment in Paris. He had to admire the concise phraseology of his friend Madison.

When Madison asked for Jefferson's opinion, the Charlottesville lawyer quipped some things needed to be worded more precisely. The first point that Jefferson hammered home was the role of government and religion. "Congress shall make no law respecting an establishment of religion, or prohibiting the free exercise thereof . . . ."

These words of the First Amendment were quickly endorsed by Madison and the Founders. Citizens first heard all of this on September 25, 1789, and became part of the law of the land on December 15, 1791.

For almost 219 years one group or another has found reason to challenge these words of the First Amendment. Some challengers fault the Amendment for not going far enough in restricting religious expression on the part of government. When Jefferson wrote his addendum to the Constitution, it was a generation prior to the religious fervor associated with the Second Great Awakening. Great preachers such as Alexander Campbell, Charles Finney, and Barton Stone were not then household names. The trend toward Baptist and Methodist denominations in the southern Piedmont was just beginning.

Where did the Founders stand on matters of religion? None was an Evangelical as we know the term. James Madison chose to attend an evangelical Episcopal Church in his later years. Thomas Jefferson's personal feelings toward Christianity resemble what a modern-day professor of philosophy might espouse, but he asked that an Episcopal clergyman conduct his funeral.

John Adams was a member of the liberal wing of the Congregational Church -- the wing that opposed the Great Awakening by evolving into the Unitarian Church.

Benjamin Franklin was brought up Episcopalian. He was invited by Jediadiah Andrews to become a Presbyterian and he did so for 5 straight Sundays, but soon embraced Deism. Unlike his friend Tom Paine, Franklin never sought to "wither Christianity by ridicule or bludgeon it to death by argument."

George Washington was a lifelong Episcopalian. Of the founding fathers, 28 were Episcopalians, 8 Presbyterians, 7 Congregationalists, 2 Lutherans, 2 Dutch Reformed, 2 Methodists, 2 Roman Catholics, 1 unknown, and only 3 were deists--Williamson, Wilson, and Franklin.

When Jefferson read the Constitution for the first time, his mind must have wandered back to the many volumes he possessed in his library at Monticello. He recalled a volume entitled *The Two Treatises On Government* by the 17th century English philosopher, John Locke. In Locke's theoretical musing known as the "social contract," the government lacks any authority with regard to individual conscience -- and this implies religion. For Locke, the basic natural right of man was his freedom of religious thought and practice. In 1690 this was radical thinking. However, 100 years later and 4000 miles westward, the idea was taking root in the colonies. Jefferson was aware of Maryland's 1649 Act of Religion -- the world's first religious toleration act.

Roger Williams disagreed that the colonies enjoyed religious freedom as Williams was forced to flee Puritan Massachusetts for safety in Rhode Island. The Baptists of Rhode Island developed the most open colony as far as religious rights are concerned.

A walk around Philadelphia, the second largest city in the British Empire revealed to any observer the wide-open nature of religion. Apart from Philadelphia's Christ Church Episcopal where many of the Founding Fathers worshipped regularly, there was St. Mary's Catholic Church, a Jewish synagogue, Congregational Meeting Houses, Shaker and Quaker Establishments, the Unitas Fratrum of Moravians, Schwenkfelders, Mennonites, Dutch Reform, and Anabaptists. The Pennsylvania Quaker movement had been so strong prior to the Revolution that Pennsylvania had been forbidden to organize a state militia. Jefferson didn't need a Ph.D. in politics to know that a law granting preference to any one faith would be disastrous.

Thomas Jefferson reread the proposed constitution, all 4,434 words, and he thrust a quill into a nearby ink well to dash off another 483 words. Scholars believe them to be the finest words ever penned by an American -- the Bill of Rights.

Just a year prior to the Constitutional Convention, Jefferson and Madison had collaborated on a landmark freedom of religion law in Virginia. Interestingly enough, the words we hear today, "separation of church and state," appeared, not in the First Amendment, but in an 1801 letter to the Danbury Baptists of Danbury, Connecticut. Jefferson used that phrase, it is believed, for the first time. Jefferson also coined the phrase "a wall of separation between church and state" to connote the strong legal language defending the principle. Franklin had earlier used the weaker words, "a line of separation between church and state."

John Quincy Adams, our 6th president, in an oration to the inhabitants of Newburyport, Massachusetts, on July 4, 1837, best stated our religious attitude in these words:"Why is it that, next to the birthday of the Savior of the World, your most joyous and most venerated festival returns on this day? Is it not that, in the chain of human events, the birthday of the nation is indissolubly linked with the birthday of the Savior? That it forms a leading event in the progress of the gospel dispensation? Is it not that the Declaration of Independence first organized the social compact on the foundation of the Redeemer's mission upon earth? That it laid the corner stone of human government upon the first precepts of Christianity, and gave to the world the first irrevocable pledge of the fulfillment of the prophecies, announced directly from Heaven at the birth of the Savior and predicted by the greatest of the Hebrew prophets six hundred years before?"

If Jefferson were here today, he'd note that John Quincy Adams made those remarks as private citizen Adams and not as President Adams. That great statesman-philosopher, Jefferson, asked that just three personal accomplishments be engraved upon his tombstone: the Declaration of Independence, the Virginia Freedom of Religion Act, and the establishment of the University of Virginia.

The Private Lives of General George E. Pickett, C.S.A. and LaSalle Corbell

Tabloids have been a staple of journalism for as long as anyone can remember in Britain and America; the prurient interests of the people demand it. Editors of muckraking rags reap the riches associated with this low order of the fourth estate.

McClure's Magazine flourished briefly as a platform for the literati -- Mark Twain, Jack London, Arthur Conan Doyle, etc., before the yardbirds of yellow journalism captured its soul. From the 1890s until its demise in 1929, McClure's was the province of the "poison pens." Ida Tarbell, Lincoln Steffens, and Ray Stannard Baker were some of McClure's best "rakers" -- or writers. Anyone who had an axe to grind could submit to the ten-cents-a-copy monthly periodical.

Sally Ann (LaSalle) Corbell Pickett, widow of the immortal C.S.A. General George E. Pickett Gettysburg, needed money in 1908, so she sold her collection of love letters. Since LaSalle Corbell was the 18-year-old bride of the 38-year-old, Pickett, the old letters fetched a handsome sum -- even though General Pickett had been dead for 33 years. McClure's Magazine proved the hottest topic at the 45th anniversary of the Gettysburg battle.

The Bitter War of Disunion had but few moments of pomp and glamour amidst the gore and destruction of the southern way of life. However, a genuine love story will out no matter the circumstances -- and such was the nature of tender, young LaSalle and her cavalier, George Pickett.

Old letters can build quite a story, even when none of the responses are known to the reader. LaSalle Pickett did not have to invent her letters as popular novelists did -- she had real ones from a legendary general who was twice her age when he penned them. The enthusiastic public caused McClure's to sell out each month during the serialization.

Widow Pickett decided to publish after her last surviving child died. What if she embellished the truth a bit in the preface? After all, her late husband's reputation had been bandied about maliciously by veterans of both sides of the North-South war. Pickett's famed charge at Gettysburg on July 3, 1863, represented the high-water mark of the Confederacy. The fact that this charge failed to hold its objective has been the subject of finger-pointing and innuendo. Following Lee's retreat back into Virginia, the dashing cavalryman who epitomized the South's version of Prince Rupert, took leave to wed his beautiful sweetheart in what must have been the most romantic moment of the war.

While Pickett waited with his division under the shade of trees fringing the wheat field that fateful afternoon at Gettysburg, Confederate Colonel Porter Alexander opened up a barrage of artillery with over 150 big guns aimed at Cemetery Ridge a mile and a half distant. In the heat of that battle with the acrid smoke of the guns clouding the field, Pickett sat astride his war horse, Old Black, and penned what he thought would be his last-ever letter to his fiancee´.

"Our line of battle faces Cemetery Ridge. Our detachments have been thrown forward to support our artillery which stretches over a mile along the crests of Old Ridge and Cemetery Ridge. The men are lying in the rear, my darling, and the hot July sun pours its scorching rays almost vertically down upon them. The suffering and the waiting are almost unbearable. . . . My brave Virginians are to attack in front. Oh, may God in mercy help me as he never helped before! I have ridden up to Old Peter [General Longstreet]. I shall give him this letter to mail to you if ---. Oh, my Darling, do you feel the love of my heart, the prayer, as I write that fatal word?"

"Now I go, but remember always that I love you with all my heart and soul, with every fiber of my being; that now and forever I am yours -- yours, my beloved. It is almost 3 o'clock. My soul reaches out to yours -- my prayers. I'll keep up a *skookum tum tum* [Chinook word for brave heart] for Virginia, and for you my Darling. Your Soldier."

Pickett survived the battle unscathed, but two of his three brigade commanders, Garnett and Armistead, were killed, while the third, Kemper, was badly wounded. However, a division commander normally directed the battle from a position in the rear. Detractors alleged that Pickett sought shelter in a barn during the 30 minute assault. Defenders maintained that he actually led his men until urged to pull back. The army was well aware that Pickett was smitten by a pretty girl, and some suspected that the General determined then and there that he'd be among the survivors that day.

No one labeled her a liar, but LaSalle took literary license with the facts. She claimed in the preface to her McClure's piece that she was a mere slip of a girl, age 15, when "my Soldier," as she referred to Pickett, swept her in his arms in their wedding at St. Paul's Episcopal Church in Petersburg. "God Bess you! My son was with you at Gettysburg," was the whispered greeting LaSalle heard from several women wearing black. Pickett's family was an old Virginia clan that dated back to the 17th century. They claimed cavalier status from the English Civil War, and George was determined to perpetuate that ideal -- in his appearance with perfumed ringlets down to his shoulders -- and in his bold and reckless disregard of danger. As a lieutenant he'd been the first American over the parapets of the citadel in the Mexican War.

Who cared that Pickett was the "goat," or bottom man in the West Point Class of 1846? Her soldier's best friend at The Point had been George B. McClellan, and the Union general they called "Little Mac," had graduated number 2. The two men, though fighting on opposite sides, remained best friends.

Her soldier had little time for a honeymoon as he was a major general in command of a division in Longstreet's Corps. Since the War devolved around Richmond after the repulse at Gettysburg, LaSalle's soldier often slipped in for a romantic rendezvous at their rented house in that city. A month after J.E.B. Stuart and Wade Hampton's stunning defeat of Judson Kilpatrick's cavalry at Buckland Mills, October 19, 1863, Mrs. General Pickett informed her husband that she was expecting their first child. The battle that was celebrated in Richmond as "the Buckland Races" was a total rout for the North.

Letters reveal that when George E. Pickett, Jr., was born and the news reached Union lines three loud cheers from the enemy were raised in honor of Pickett and bonfires were lit. Under a flag of truce, a Union officer brought a package containing a baby's silver service engraved "To George E. Pickett, Jr., from his father's friends U.S. Grant, Rufus Ingalls, George Suckley." Such is the West Point camaraderie that even in the midst of a civil war the bonds of classmates remain unbroken.

The General's wife tells how after the fall of Richmond and the Union army had entered the city that her door bell rang. Standing there was a tall and very sad-looking man -- President Abraham Lincoln. He had stopped by to see the infant son of his dear friend, General George Pickett.

Following the war, the Picketts fled to Montreal where they lived for a while as exiles in the famed St. Laurent Hotel. The General rejected the offer of the Khedive of Egypt to take over command of his army on the Nile. President Ulysses S. Grant entertained the Picketts several times in the White House after he, Pickett, declined to be nominated for governor of Virginia. Eventually George Pickett accepted a directorship of a New York life insurance company office in Norfolk. Their two sons enrolled in V.M.I., and Lasalle expected to live out her life with her dashing general, but he contracted scarlet fever and died on July 30, 1875 at age 50.

LaSalle Corbell Pickett took it upon herself to represent General Pickett and the South at the annual Gettysburg Battle reunions. She became the grand dame of the battlefield on those days and was cheered by Union men and Confederates alike. Her husband's love letters can be found in *The Heart of A Soldier* (1913; reprinted 1995).

Honoring the Washington Light Infantry On Their 203rd Anniversary

"The weakest of all weak things is a virtue that has not been tested in the fire," so says sage Mark Twain in "The Man That Corrupted Hadleyburg." The men of the Washington Light Infantry (W.L.I.) down through the years recall the words "Valor and Virtue," to be the motto emblazoned on their flag and engraved on their hearts. As one of the nation's oldest militia companies, the W.L.I. traces its origin to June 22, 1807, as our new nation was severely tested by Great Britain in what is known as the *Chesapeake - Leopard* affair. The British warship *H.M.S. Leopard* in waters off Norfolk, Virginia, ordered the *Chesapeake*, James Barron, commanding, to prepare to be boarded and searched for contraband. When the American ship refused, the British fired several volleys in rapid succession. In the rain of grapeshot and canister, three Americans were killed and a score were wounded. Haughty jack tars of the Royal Navy clambered aboard the Chesapeake and ordered the crew to muster for interrogation. Four crewmen were jerked out of the lineup and taken back to the *Leopard* under the charge of being British Navy deserters.

American anger was at fever pitch, yet the Nation was practically impotent to defend itself against aggressors. President Jefferson decried the incident and prepared to resort to diplomacy and the court of world opinion. In Charleston the citizens were indignant that Commander Barron hadn't defended his ship to the last man and gun of them. Red-blooded men across the new republic determined to add teeth to the diplomatic efforts. Slogans such as "Remember the *Leopard*!" appeared on handbills and even on ribbons in ladies' hair.

On July 17, 1807, scores of Charleston men enrolled in a new militia company formed for defending our country should the *Chesapeake* affair widen to become another war with Britain. Jefferson's diplomacy merely forestalled the inevitable as war between Britain and the United States erupted in 1812 due to continual harassment of our cargo ships.

Though the W.L.I. saw only guard duty and patrols along the coast during the War of 1812, it did see lively action during the Seminole War and the Mexican War. The real test of the W.L.I's mettle came, however, in 1861 when South Carolina seceded and the call came from Montgomery, then the Confederacy's capital, for South Carolina to send her fair share of soldiers to Virginia. The men of the W.L.I. assumed, as did other local militia units, that their duty would be confined to defending our coast. Had it not been for a priest, a young South Carolina College (now U.S.C.) graduate, and a Broad Street attorney, this grand old organization might have sat out the War guarding the sea islands.

The 32-year-old priest of the Church of The Holy Communion, Reverend A.T. Porter, was walking across Washington Square in May1861, when Thomas M. Logan, age 20, ran to catch up with him. Porter served as chaplain to the W.L.I. and young Logan, just graduated from South Carolina in Columbia, wanted to bend his ear about an urgent matter. The W.L.I. had recently met for drill, and the men voted not to deploy to Virginia. Porter had opposed secession and feared the consequences of a Union invasion of the South, but he listened to Logan's plea for help in finding someone of courage and ability to lead at least a token company of the W.L.I., Charleston's elite rifle company, to the war's centerstage in Virginia. Former Congressman James Chesnut had recently assured everyone here that there'd be no war. So certain was he that the North was bluffing, Chesnut said he'd personally drink all of the blood shed in this war.

Porter inquired who else felt the way that Logan did, thinking that perhaps there were dozens of men eager to deploy. "William Dotterer, Theodore Klink, and myself" came the reply from Logan. That evening at the chaplain's home on Spring Street, the roster of the W.L.I. was divided into sections and Logan, Dotterer, Klink, and Porter set out on foot making calls on the ranks of the W.L.I.. Most men seemed willing to consider going to Virginia if the right man could be found to lead them. But who among the members could command them in battle if war actually came?

Benjamin Jenkins Johnson of Christ Church parish was the name that many of the ranks agreed upon. Once again Logan prevailed upon Porter to travel by ferry to Haddrell's Point, hire a buggy and ride the 16 miles up the King's Road to Johnson's plantation.

Ben Jenkins Johnson greeted his old friend warmly and invited him for dinner, knowing all the while that Porter had not ridden out just to speak pleasantries. Later, the dishes were cleared, and Johnson asked the reverend to lead the family in evening prayers. It was after 9 P.M. when Johnson and Porter discussed the reason for the visit. Johnson begged time to consider, but he gave Porter his pledge the next day. With a light heart the chaplain retraced his steps and met Logan at the Market Street wharf. The deal had been struck -- the W.L.I. had their leader, and Charleston would be represented at Manassas. The next evening Ben Johnson waited outside the W.L.I. armory on Wentworth Street as his name was put into nomination by Logan. The thundering applause told him that the vote had been unanimous. Johnson was ushered in with Dotterer, Logan, and Klink flanking him. However, when Johnson came to the podium to address the men who'd unanimously elected him their captain, he held up his hand for silence. Reaching into his coat, Johnson pulled out a telegraph that he'd just received that very day from Wade Hampton in Columbia. Hampton promised Johnson a Lieutenant Colonel's commission if he'd sign with Hampton's Legion. The W.L.I. members were shocked and demoralized, and many voted to discontinue the idea of deployment.

The next day Logan met Porter on Broad Street near the corner of Meeting, and the chaplain was commiserating with the disappointed Logan. Just at that moment James Conner, one of the city's eminent attorneys stepped out of his office and headed up Broad Street where he encountered Porter and Logan. "That's the man!" shouted Porter. "That's the man we have been searching for. Why didn't we think of him ahead of all the others?" Catching up with Conner, the reverend and the young militiaman put the question to the astonished lawyer. "Will you command the W.L.I. if the vote is unanimous?" blurted the chaplain. The rest of the story is the foundation of legend.

As Richard Schreadley recounts in *Virtue and Valor: The Washington Light Infantry in Peace and War* the men of the W.L.I. mustered for service in Virginia in June of 1861 wearing black felt hats looped up on the left side with the Palmetto cockade attached. The company was attached to Hampton's Legion and was in the thick of the fighting between the Henry and Robinson houses on Friday afternoon, July 19, 1861. Through the din and smoke of battle the Captain Conner and the men of the W.L.I. probably heard the hoarse voice of Colonel Thomas Jonathon Jackson imploring his Virginians, "There's [General] Bee standing like a stonewall. Let us determine to die here, and we will conquer!" An instant later Bee fell mortally wounded. Benjamin Jenkins Johnson of Mount Pleasant was killed a few yards away. Colonel Wade Hampton was wounded but refused to leave the field. Reverend Porter assisted the surgeons in bringing the dead and wounded from the ongoing battle.

No longer was the war about bluffs and bluster or fancy uniforms and parades. Conner became Major General Conner and received a wound that cost him a leg at Cedar Run. Theodore Klink was killed. Thomas M. Logan, who'd been an eager youth at the war's beginning, became the Confederacy's youngest general. Dotterer was killed at Drewery's Bluff in 1864. Many other men of the W.L.I. also gave their lives in this war.

The W.L.I. aided in the healing of hard feelings by accepting the invitation proffered by President Hayes to march in the nation's centennial of 1876 held in Philadelphia. Today, 134 years later, the Washington Light Infantry is a patriotic organization unaffiliated with the active-duty military. Its membership is composed of veterans and descendants of some of the original members.

Marie Laveau, The VouDou Queen of New Orleans

Poor New Orleans. For all the misfortune that has befallen The Big Easy and the white sand Cajun coast, they can blame it on Mother Nature -- La Nina. They can blame the Republican president or the Democrat mayor. They can blame Katrina, BP, or El Nino. But they can't blame Voudou priestess Marie Laveau. For once in the old city's history, the sorceress isn't defending against accusations of malevolent rituals or evil incantations. From 1820 'til 1900 Crescent City citizens -- Cajuns, Creoles, Caucasians, and Africans alike -- gave Madame Laveau wide berth along Canal Street when she promenaded with her retinue of courtesans. So many bizarre occurrences have been attributed to Madame Laveau that researchers have no way of separating what is fact and what is legend about her colorful life. Contemporaries told of spells being cast that caused men to go insane or become demon possessed. People thought that Marie Laveau could control the weather and that she could cause men and women to become sterile just by a stare. Others maintain that she was just an eccentric whose ancestral mix of African, Creole, and Caucasian cultures had produced in her one of those rare combinations of old world mysticism and new world savvy.

New Orleans jazz musician John Rebennack, alias "Dr. John, the night tripper," sings a song to the notorious woman's memory entitled "Marie Laveau."

> "*Now there lived a conjure lady, not long ago,*
> '*In New Orleans, Louisiana, -- named marie Laveau.*'
> '*Believe it or not, strange as it seem,*
> '*She made her fortune selling voodoo, and interpreting dreams.*'

Fitting the facts together as biography is a challenge for even the most fastidious researcher, for some locals in New Orleans still maintain that the whole story of this spirit world woman is just a legend -- that Marie Laveau is a compilation of several women who practiced herbal medicine with incantation in the French Quarter during the mid-19th century. Yet another sordid tale says that Marie was a prostitute who cast more than romantic spells upon her gentlemen clients.

Before "Dr. John" penciled his "Marie Laveau" lyrics, rock musicians had already drummed out a 1960s rhythmic hit entitled "The House of The Rising Sun." It's a haunting ballad made popular by singers such as Eric Burdon of the British Blues-Rock band "The Animals" and Los Angeles' Whiskey A-Go-Go" nightclub singer, Johnny Rivers. No one knows for sure who wrote the song, but refrains from the current version have been around New Orleans for decades. The focus is an opium den and brothel that stood on Conti Street in the French Quarter until it was razed after World War II as a vermin-infested public health hazard. Scholars who delve in the social history of New Orleans believe that Marie Laveau may have been a popular "lady of the evening" at the tawdry establishment -- or more likely, that she may have been its owner and madame at one time!

Close your eyes and you can hear in your mind Eric Burdon's gravelly, whiskey-throated voice belting the words:

> *"There is a house in New Orleans,*
> *They call the Rising Sun.*
> *And it's been the ruin of many a poor boy*
> *And God I know I'm one."*

Comically, some sources call Marie Laveau a strikingly beautiful woman whose charms were strictly of an esoteric nature. Others say she was a bent-over old woman with a crooked nose and eyes as black as coal. Most sources agree that this woman whose celebrity status was recounted in faraway places such as the nation's capital, San Francisco, and New York was a mulatto whose mother, Marguerite Darcantrel, had been a free person of color that had had to flee Haiti during a slave uprising. Laveau's father is believed to have been New Orleans cotton factor Charles Laveau. The liasion that produced the infant named Marie is believed to have been one of the numerous gentleman-mistress relationships that existed in New Orleans in the 19th century. Whatever the case, Charles Laveau left a dowry for Marie as if she had been his legitimate daughter. That's where the story grows vague. One account maintains that Marie used her dowry to establish New Orleans' grandest brothel -- one that even the river boat captains advertised on the way downriver.

Where did the stories of Marie Laveau being a voudou sorceress originate? Speculation has it that Marie's religious heritage was a peculiar blend of French Catholicism, superstition born of illiteracy, and Haitian voudou. Marie was of a racial mix known then as a quadroon, and many of these women possessed a mysterious beauty that men found alluring. Often the quadroons set themselves apart from other persons of color. In New Orleans there were quadroon cliques that were quite prosperous and sophisticated in the mid-19th century.

City records reflect that Marie Laveau had a Catholic wedding performed by Pere Antoine in Saint Louis Cathedral. Her beau was another quadroon, Jacques Paris. Paris wasn't in the picture for long because Marie took a lover by the name of Louis Christophe Dumesnil de Glapion. Numerous children were attributed to this unblessed union; however, locals believe the de Glapion liaison was a cover for the occasional off-spring that crop up with "ladies of the evening." One of her daughters she christened as Marie Laveau II, and for this reason the tales of the two women morph into one thread that runs almost the entire span of the 19th century. Marie II is reported to have been even more notorious than her mother in all of her endeavors, carnal and spiritual.

The story goes that Marie Laveau became a hairdresser to fashionable ladies in the French Quarter and that the clients confided in her their joys and concerns. Armed with the confidences of so many well-connected women, a whispered word from Marie could cause jitters down on the New Orleans Cotton Exchange. Marie may have delved a bit in midwifery also because quite a few society mavens called for Marie and her bag of assorted herbs, roots, bark, bones, and powders. But it was the eerie incantations that she mumbled -- unearthly sounds that did not seem to emanate from a human -- that convinced the townsmen that she belonged to the underworld.

Together the two Maries sort of hijacked the "Feast of St. John" away from the Catholics and turned it into a Laveau mystical ceremony that had hues of Catholicism and the saints as well as seances with the underworld. Lake Ponchatrain was the site of numerous St. John Feasts, Laveau style. The feast date is always June 24 and its pre-Christian origins lie rooted in summer solstice pagan ritual. Devout Catholics shuddered at the popularity of Laveau's voudou carnival atmosphere profaning their own Holy Day. However, Marie Laveau maintained that she was just as devout as her critics.

A notable source cites that as thousands ringed the outdoor festival site "a cauldron boiled with water from a beer barrel, into which went salt, black pepper, a black cat, a black rooster, various powders, and a snake sliced in three pieces representing the Trinity." Naked girls danced provocatively and many townsmen stripped and danced with them. Marie would don a black cape and preach a sermon that seemed quite inappropriate to those who remained sober.

The fact that Marie kept a rather large pet snake named Zombi as a household companion just made tongues wag even more. The name "Zombi" celebrates a west African god of the underworld. The daughter Marie was quite clever in marketing her mother's skills in casting all manner of spells, hexes, and trances. Even at the time many believed the pair to be hucksters who raked in enormous profits from the illicit trade in prostitution, raw opium, and blackmail. Ill-gotten profits, they say, were then pumped into legitimate enterprises such as the hair salon, a hotel, and the stock market. Some say that Marie ran an informal lending agency that financed quite a few businessmen who'd gambled away their family fortune at the roulette tables.

When Marie Laveau finally died in 1881, at approximately 90 years of age, she had an elaborate funeral procession that rivaled anything in the Mardi Gras tradition. Her sepulcher in Saint Louis Number 1 has become a rendezvous for practitioners of the occult. Little artifices of the voudou religion such as candles, strange emblems, and chicken bones deface the tomb.

Marie II either drowned on Lake Ponchatrain in a hurricane or died in the city in 1918, take your pick. In the years that Marie Laveau I thrived amidst the seamy underside of New Orleans' rich, multi-racial culture, she met and entertained the likes of Vice-President Aaron Burr, the Marquis de Lafayette, Pierre Gustave Toutant Beauregard, and French General Humbert. Charleston had no one like her at all -- except perhaps the infamous Grace Piexotto.

Calculating The Wages of Sin In Antebellum Charleston

Charlestonians of olden times boasted of their virtues and published their dueling code of honor to the world; however, the same Charlestonians cultivated their vices discretely behind closed doors -- doors of notorious establishments located on Fulton, West, and Beaufain Streets in what was known as the City's tenderloin district until the late 1950s. Too bad that a dandy such as James Boswell didn't leave us a diary of Charleston's "dark side" the way that descriptive essayist did of 18th century London. Fortunately, we have a resident expert on the seamy side of old Charleston's history. Mark Jones, local author and carriage tour guide, published a book a few years ago through History Press entitled *Wicked Charleston: The Dark Side of the Holy City* (2005). Mark's book makes an excellent airline read as it moves the reader from one tawdry scene to another in a manner that would have had Boswell and Samuel Johnson giddy with delight.

What makes port cities so sensual -- that's the enigma of travel. Around the globe inland cities appear pious and productive while coastal baronies languish in debauchery. The quays and grog shops of London, Bristol, Portsmouth, and Liverpool were the models for Charleston's early waterfront. The seagoing men of a dozen foreign ports brought a worldliness here, not to mention a profane nature, that was seldom seen elsewhere south of New York. Jones's Wicked Charleston does justice to the unflattering behavior of some of our colorful ancestors who trod these cobbled stone streets and inhabited these pastel, stuccoed mansions.

In one memorable chapter, "Sodom and Gomorrah of the South," Jones tells of the Methodist bishop, Francis Asbury denouncing "drinking, smoking, card playing, [and] sexual debauchery of the vilest kind" during his stay here. Asbury actually referred to Chareston as the "Sodom and Gomorrah of the South," according to Jones.

The chapter on lusty Charleston goes on to describe our city as a popular stopover for traveling troupes of actors back when people associated with the theater universally enjoyed a dubious reputation. Actresses particularly were frowned upon for their often lewd performances on stage and their loose behavior about town.

One company of players well-known here in the 1790s was the French acrobatic company under the direction of Alexander Placide. Jones tells us that this unique group of ballet dancers, gymnasts, and high-wire artists performed at a French-language playhouse located on the west side of Church Street and that several sexual scandals occurred here involving these celebrated performers. Placide's claim to fame was a "pleasure garden" he named Vauxhall located on the northeast corner of Broad and Legare Streets -- presently the location of the Cathedral of St. John the Baptist. Patterned after the infamous Vauxhall park in London, the park allowed patrons to enjoy music amidst exotic surroundings lit with brightly colored lanterns. What went on in Vauxhall "stayed in Vauxhall."

Jones's best story, however, is the tale of Grace Piexotto, the Madame of the "Big Brick," Charleston's most notorious house of ill-repute. With so many foreign sailors in town and a high number of well-off, indolent young gentlemen, brothels flourished here from the time of the City's inception. Some of these dens of iniquity were mere taverns with client rooms upstairs. However, several of these houses of assignation served a well-heeled clientele, and that was the case with Grace Piexotto's parlor.

Jones tells us that Piexotto was an 18th century Charlestonian who, as a child, had witnessed a speech made by George Washington during his 1791 visit to Charleston. One version of Grace's story portrays her as the daughter of the music leader at Beth Elohim Synagogue, but that has never been verified. Legend has it that Grace plied her trade in the evening pleasure industry, and that she was so successful that she built her own establishment in 1852.

From New Orleans to Mobile, from Savannah to New York the crews of cargo vessels headed straight to the lounges that their depraved nature craved from long weeks at sea. Few port cities possessed a fine, freestanding, brick hotel built exclusively by a madame for the evening pleasure trade. Down on Fulton Street today you can walk by the imposing edifice where alluring young women hailed passers-by from the windows as recently as the 1950s. Before the building was renovated as an office it had a brief history as a jazz night club, and it produced the "feel of New Orleans" as much as any place on the eastern seaboard possibly could.

Grace Piexotto knew that her upper-crust patrons desired privacy and refinement, and she delivered on both accounts. Her girls were well-mannered, stylish, and amiable conversationalists for the southern aristocratic gentlemen who came up Beresford Street (now called Fulton) in custom-made carriages. Downstairs there were parlors where guests could read the latest newspapers and magazines while they enjoyed brandy and a cigar. Upstairs Grace offered well-upholstered bedrooms for more intimate conversation. The Brick was not an establishment for the lowborn in the antebellum era. For 50 years the so-called "carriage trade" of red-light industry did their business there. The expansion of the naval shipyard in the 1930s did change the nature of the flesh trade downtown, however.

An excerpt from a piece Mark Jones wrote about Grace Piexotto's establishment states, "If you couldn't pay--well Grace would just see to it that you didn't come back. In fact, brazen Grace Piexotto was so upset by students from the College of Charleston that she wrote the faculty of the college a letter asking them to keep their students away from her establishment." He goes on to say that city officials never bothered Grace's business, probably because these officials were patrons themselves.

The old madam became wealthy and influential. Piexotto was the model of discretion, and she became a confidante of notable Charleston men. Grace kept their secrets well and carried them with her to the grave. Margaret Mitchell even used Grace as the model for the fictitious character, Belle Watling, in her novel, *Gone With The Wind*. Jones recounts that when Piexotto died it was the Unitarian Church on Archdale which came forward to offer her a decent burial. Every other church in downtown Charleston was in fear that the madam desired their divine services as her last request.

No Charleston gentleman dared attend the funeral rite of the famous madam, but curiously, the funeral procession included dozens of empty carriages -- carriages of the rich men who had been her faithful patrons. It is said that Grace's funeral procession was second only in size to that of John C. Calhoun.

In the late 1940s and early 1950s Charlestonians shopping at the nearby Colonial grocery store (site of the Canterbury House), or Al and Bella's corner store got an eyefull of pulchritude adorning the open windows of the Big Brick. The adjoining streets often had Lincolns and Cadillacs double-parked as early as noon. By the end of the 1960s the trade in prurient pleasure had moved up on the Charleston neck leaving only The Big Brick as a reminder of what used to be. Read Mark Jones's book, Wicked Charleston, for dozens of other delicious stories about the City's past -- or better yet, take his carriage tour for a firsthand account!

Young Jim Edwards Served In The Merchant Marine in WW II

If it's true what the old proverb says, that "character is forged on the anvil of adversity," then our former governor James Burrows (Jim) Edwards certainly went out of his way to acquire for himself an extra measure of adverse experiences. By all accounts the young man who'd eventually garner more prestigious honors than just about anyone in our state's history was too young in 1944 to be drafted -- and exempt for being underweight.

Ordinary Seaman Edwards, quartermaster on the *S.S. George Washington*, was the first earned distinction for the man who'd later win acclaim as James B. Edwards, D.M.D. (1955 - present); Senator James B. Edwards of the S.C. legislature (1972-1975); Governor James B. Edwards (1975-1979); Secretary of Energy, Reagan Administration James B. Edwards (1981-1982); President James B. Edwards of the Medical University of South Carolina (1982-1999); and most recently, namesake for the James B. Edwards College of Dental Medicine (2010), James B. Edwards School, and James B. Edwards Park of Mount Pleasant.

Jim, his school teacher parents, and siblings moved to Mount Pleasant in 1938 from Saint Andrews parish, Charleston. Coincidentally, Jim grew up being good friends with Arthur Ravenel, later state senator and Congressman Ravenel. These two men had much interaction in forming the Republican party in Charleston in the 1960s.

The most memorable moment of his adolescent years here in Hungryneck, as he proudly recalls it, was the meeting of his future bride at the corner of Venning and Simmons Streets when she was 12 years old and he was thirteen. Ann Darlington, he remembers as if it were just yesterday, was a cute little blue-eyed blonde with a turned-up nose -- and all business with her school-crossing guard's sash. Ann's father was a Yale-educated engineer associated with the building the hydroelectric plant at Pinopolis, and the family lived on the harbor in the Old Village next door to the present Edwards home. Ann's mother suffered from a severe cardiac disorder and in those days of no air conditioning the harbor breezes aided her comfort. Edwards recalls graduating from Moultrie High School in 1944, the first class to go all four years there. He and his best friend, Ashley Utsey, were "champing at the bit" to do their part in the War. Ashley's father was the overseer for the vast Guggenheim estate that stretched from Daniel Island to Cainhoy. Years later Jim Edwards would serve on the Guggenheim Foundation board of directors when Daniel Island was sold to private developers.

Being the son of dedicated teachers, young Jim dutifully followed his parents' wishes that he go to the College of Charleston and get his degree before enlisting in the military. However, just a semester into his degree the man who would set the world on fire academically a few years later withdrew failing. By his admission he had no interest then in studying; he just wanted to do his part. Yet, getting in the service underage and 5 pounds underweight was no snap. Try as he might he could not gain the weight to get him to the minimum 130 pounds.

Back in 1944 security was tight at Fort Moultrie, but not so tight as to preclude an eager young man from volunteering to serve his country in the motor pool. So, almost within sight of his boyhood home, Edwards began serving his country. Soon the service, pressed for able-bodied men, had him onboard navy tugboat L78 towing targets for the 155 mm guns of the 263rd Coastal Artillery to have live-fire target practice. It was adventurous, but Jim Edwards wanted blue water and convoy duty.

Friend Ashley Utsey had little problem with the recruiters, but Jim Edwards ate a dozen bananas and strapped lead weights to the inside of his legs beneath his trousers -- not realizing that he'd have to undress to be weighed. The astonished corpsman said, "Son, I guess if you want to get in that badly, I'll waiver you." So, it was on to Merchant Marine Boot Camp at St. Petersburg, Florida, for the two boys from Mount Pleasant.

By 1944 the United States and her allies had lost 177 ships sunk by German submarines in the South Atlantic. Nearly 500 ships total had been sunk off the coast from Nova Scotia to the Gulf of Mexico. The Merchant Marines had the highest percentage casualty rate of any branch until the Marines surpassed them at Okinawa. There were no inessential lessons taught at St. Petersburg boot camp in 1944. Everything a seaman needed to know -- hawsers, lifeboat drill, how to man a 50-caliber machine gun, or a 20 mm cannon, as well as the eternal job of the sailor -- how to swab decks and chip and paint.

No one can ever say that Jim Edwards didn't work his way from ground up -- his first job on a Liverpool-bound hospital ship, the *USAHS Dogwood*, was scrubbing pots and pans in the galley. He says that to this day he's still the best pot and pan scrubber anywhere around. The *Dogwood* brought the wounded from the European theater back to the States. Jim relates that he was profoundly touched by what he saw on those Atlantic crossings. Young men barely older than himself were missing legs, arms, eyes -- one had been run over and crushed from waist down by a German panzer tank. This was March of 1945, nine months after D - Day.

Thanks in part to the vigilance of the U.S. Navy's antisubmarine patrols, there were few German craft still active in the North Atlantic by 1944. Admiral Middleton Read, U.S.N., a Pocotaligo native, commanded the Atlantic fleet; however, he never gained the fame of the Pacific fleet commanders since the British had already severely crippled Hitler's fleet by the time we joined the war. By late 1944 convoy duty had become almost routine with just a few calls to General Quarters on any given crossing.

The only hostile action Edwards personally witnessed during the war occurred as his ship, the *George Washington*, was on the *Wesser River* leaving Bremerhaven when in the distance off their bow, the U.S. Army transport ship *Edmund B. Alexander* hit a mine and its passengers, most nurses headed for Port Said, had to be evacuated to Edwards' ship. By that time, Edwards was 3rd Mate and enjoying some of the privileges of rank at sea. He spent quite a bit of time on the bridge of these ships acquainting himself with navigation and ship operations.

By his calculation, Jim made 11 round trips, 22 crossings of the Atlantic, and he hasn't had any desire to take a luxury cruise since. He shipped out on a number of ships, one of which was the *USAHS Dogwood*, a converted Liberty ship. He sailed on the *George Washington* for several voyages to Bremerhaven and Le Harve.

Shortly after the war's end, Edwards helped ferry German and Italian prisoners back to their homeland for repatriation. There were huge P.O.W. installations located in Charleston and Berkeley counties, and a large one near Florence. The return voyages brought the victorious American troops home -- often to ticker tape parades in New York City where even the Andrews sisters would ride a boat out to greet the returning heroes as they entered the harbor amidst tugboats sending spumes of water in the air. As the Merchant Marine ships ferried the P.O.W.s to Germany, the prisoners had to do menial chores such as chipping and painting at sea under the supervision of the Merchant Mariners and the Armed Guard. Jim struck up conversations with a number of these soon-to-be-liberated prisoners. He recalls a conversation: "You know, we Germans are superior fighters to you Americans. We outfought you every time.

When we shot down a plane or crippled a tank, there were always five more to take its place. That's why we didn't whip you." Those words helped form a part of Jim Edwards' political outlook -- that America must always maintain a strong military industrial complex and a strong national defense.

Some of the happy duty Jim remembers is making several "warbride runs" from Liverpool New York to bring back young women, some of whom were pregnant, who'd been betrothed to American soldiers stationed abroad.

After the war, Jim's ship was overseas loading army vehicles aboard the *George Washington*. He heard a voice that sounded familiar. An American army captain curtly yelled up, "Hey, you "so-and so's," don't bang up my jeep!" Jim looked down over the deck and hailed, "Who's that hollering about a jeep!" "What d - - - difference does it make to you who I am!" came the reply. "Steve Darlington, is that you?" retorted Edwards. It was his future brother-in-law, Ann's brother and fellow Mount Pleasant native. They had quite a reunion. The decorated Army infantry officer and the merchant marine loaded the jeep onboard and headed into town to celebrate.

Post war found the College of Charleston full of veterans -- all dedicated scholars pursuing an education with all the maturity that only wartime can give a young male. Arthur Ravenel, Jr., Jim Edwards, and Biemann Othersen were just a few of the names we recall from those times. Edwards pursued a double major of chemistry and biology and he remembers fondly the excellent professors he had -- Askew, Clements, Cook, Donahue, Jennings, and Toal.

To make ends meet since the Merchant Marines did not get the G.I. Bill, Edwards sought part-time work as a licensed relief officer on ships entering Charleston harbor. One summer he shipped out on a cargo ship to Rouen carrying coal under the Marshall Plan. When the ship docked, the French stevedores went on strike and so did the rail and truck lines. American ships, American coal, all delivered free to France -- and there was no one to off-load! That summer Jim had a grand tour of the countryside including a Bastille Day in Paris. He barely made it back to school by September!

Edwards made more spending money by serving as officer of the watch at night on merchant ships docked at the port. Law required that a licensed officer be on duty at all times. Since the crew enjoyed liberty in the evenings, there was always a slot for Jim to go aboard and study in the captain's quarters until 0700 hours the following morning when he'd drive back to the College. Even though it was the officer's cabin that he occupied, the ship's electricity was switched off at night thereby forcing him to do his studying by candlelight.

The most unusual part-time job Jim Edwards ever had was during the summers of 1947 and '48. He heard that Santee-Cooper planned to replace its earthen dam with rip-rap and that the granite stones were to be ferried from Columbia to Pinopolis using landing craft as barges. Jim, Ashley Utsey, and some friends had the necessary experience to operate these flat-bottomed, shallow-draft craft.

The pay was 10-cents a ton plus $35 a trip -- good money for those days. A barge could carry 260 tons of rock and Jim says that they tried to make three trips a week. The river with its lakes made for about a hundred miles of navigation. Their plan was to load before dawn near the quarry and wait for the Lake Murray dam to release water downstream from its hydroelectric facility. That tide of water floated the heavy landing craft over shoals near Cayce. An old-timer with a moonshine still below Columbia would flag down Edwards and the barge would tie up at a stump. The old man sold them his "White Lightning" corn whiskey for $2 a quart. That homemade liquor and the fish they "borrowed" from local traps made the downriver voyages pleasant. The hairy part of the voyage was the low-rail trestle near Rimini when the river was high. Of course, there were no markers, buoys, or lights on the river then.

Sixty years have passed and the ordinary seaman-turned oral surgeon-turned elder statesman of South Carolina still savors the out-of-doors and getting together with his very active family. "We've had a wonderful time," remarks Ann Edwards as she and Jim pause to reflect.

Kreutner's Snee Farm Swim Team Among Elites

Been to a Snee Farm swim meet lately? If not, schedule yourself an evening next June and stroll amidst the hundreds of youthful aquatic competitors, savor the sweet smell of hotdogs and chlorine. Revel in the sounds and sights that subsist exclusively in the domain of summer. Something so special is going on betwixt the pines and clubhouse complex that sooner or later the national media is bound to pick it up. You see, the Snee Farm Swim Team has just successfully defended its Coastal Carolina Aquatic Association championship -- better known as CCAA -- for the 22nd consecutive year!

Sure, quite a few athletic clubs have put together a string of wins. Harvard's wrestlers slammed down their 23rd regional championship. A few miles away the Williams College thinclads sprinted to their 22nd in a row league title. La Salle College High School owns a 22 year swim team record in the Philadelphia Catholic League. And the winningest tradition of any program in the country belongs to Indian River Community College in Ft. Pierce, Florida -- they've won 36 back-to-back swim and dive competitions in the National Junior College Athletic Association -- NJCAA. Yet, what makes Snee Farm's Swim 22-year streak unique is that they've won 21 of their titles under the same coach -- Jason Kreutner.

Coach Kreutner is not one to toot his own horn when it comes to his accomplishments; however, his assistant coaches and swim team participants are eager to praise his leadership style. Jason Kreutner was just 18 and barely out of Porter-Gaud when he helped coach Snee Farm to its first league title. That was back in 1989 when George H. W. Bush was president. Danny Ford was still coaching at Clemson.

What's Jason Kreutner's secret? As coach he welcomes approximately 190 youngsters each year ages 4-18, many of them siblings of older children who've been swimming competitively on his team for years. Jason's own daughter, Kessler, was on the team this year. How does any one person go about organizing, coaching, mentoring, and developing a winning strategy for this diverse an age group -- and win consistently in a highly competitive league of 24 teams? "Create the conditions where the kids will want to succeed," says Jason emphatically.

Kreutner credits his older brother Erik with providing the framework for his own coaching philosophy. Growing up in Creekside in the 1980s, Jason, Erik, Kara, and Kevin Kreutner spent their summers competing at the pool. Erik, in 1987, took on the task of turning around a 1986 team that had gone winless. Three years later, Jason stepped into the leadership role.

When asked about his coaching style which centers heavily around mentoring and motivating, Jason emphasizes that his young charges learn the value of deferring pleasure for long-term gain. He is constantly building for the future -- investing in the slower swimmer who will likely mature in two or three years.

The Snee Farm Swim Team web site states that the team won championships in the 1970s and '80s, but the victory in 1985 came at a costly price and disrupted the longstanding traditions of the team. Overzealous team organizers used special "summer club memberships" that year to bring in fast swimmers from other areas -- to the detriment of good sportsmanship values as well as to the neighborhood kids. In 1987, Erik Kreutner was hired to recenter the program and return it to its roots of neighborhood competition. Jason Kreutner took over the program in 1990 and built upon brother Erik's foundation. Jason evolved as a coach over the years, and in the mid-'90s focused on training the older swimmers in his program into hands-on role models. On any given summer day Snee Farm's team practice consists of little groups of youngsters paying rapt attention to an older mentor. It's abundantly clear that the winningest swim coach anywhere around this region has devised a method to build character traits such as determination, self-sacrifice, personal discipline, and team spirit. Many times over the years Snee Farm has come back to win big after initially being down in the rankings. Jason attributes the team's resilience to the character of his swimmers.

One assistant coach who competed 12 years for Snee Farm is local Mount Pleasant resident David Thomas, 2010 graduate of the College of Charleston. I caught up with David by cell phone this week as he is doing work for the National Park Service out in Utah. Of Coach Kreutner, David says "He's probably the humblest person I've ever met. He's always honest and upfront with us." David Thomas is a natural athlete who ran track and played soccer at the Academic Magnet High School before becoming a miler and 8 K man on the College of Charleston Cougar Track team. However, it was his 12 years as a swimmer that shaped much of his competitive spirit as well as philosophy of life.

David recalls being outscored by Coosaw Creek Swim Team in a key match and hearing Coach Kreutner above the din of the crowd saying, "Hey guys, you've got to pep it up and swim better than you ever have before!" He says that as corny as it sounds, that when Jason says that, every swimmer reaches deeper to find power to swim faster.

As to his future, David Thomas wants to follow the example of Coach Kreutner and go into teaching and coaching. "He's helped me more than just about anyone I know. Every job I've ever gotten, Coach Kreutner has written recommendations for me and made phone calls. He's definitely shaped who I am today."

Kreutner says, "David is the epitome of the Snee Farm team. He is a gentleman, a team player, and he's ultra-competitive." "One thing to remember," Jason reminds, "is that these kids come together as a team for two months out of the year. Few of them swim year round. They move on to play other sports in the fall and spring. Yet, in the summer all of their focus and intensity is on making Snee Farm the best team in the league."

Walking around the Snee Farm Country Club, one would expect to see a trophy wall containing the dozens of championship awards that the swim team has garnered over the last couple of decades. That is not the case, however. The trophies are tucked away in the attic, for Coach Kreutner wants his team humble and always mindful of the work ethic that has brought success to approximately 1500 swimmers before them. When you swim for Snee Farm, you know what is expected -- hard work, tremendous self-discipline, and teamwork -- there are no superstars, and there's no gloating over victories.

When asked if he ever has a problem with pushy parents who try to insist that their child swim in a key event, Jason responds, "No. We have a culture here that the parents embrace. They know and trust the system, and they respect my judgment and let me do my job."

Chelsea Joyner is another of Jason Kreutner's proteges. She and her older sisters, Lindsay and Lisa, grew up spending their summers competing in league meets at Snee Farm. Now a sophomore at the University of Georgia, Chelsea considers Kreutner "almost like a second father to me." She began swimming with the team at age 5 and was at the pool cheering on her sisters practically from birth. Since 2007 Chelsea has served as coach and mentor for ages 6 and under, a role that she cherishes. One of her young swimmers this year was Jason and wife Tasha's own daughter, Kessler, age 5.

Like David Thomas, Chelsea echoes the idea of teammates coaching the younger ones. She remembers looking up to Kelly Vance and Kelly Kiggans as two older swimmers who really inspired her to excel. "Jason's technique," says Chelsea, "is to teach the older swimmers and younger coaches how to teach. He's really good at that." As for coaching from the sidelines, "Coach Kreutner always has his eye on us. When we are on the blocks just before a start, he makes a point of calling each of us by name and telling us good luck. That little moment means so much," says Joyner, the former Porter-Gaud head cheerleader and "Race For The Cure" fundraiser.

"He instills pride in us," says Chelsea. "We won the Good Sportsmanship Trophy again this year as well as the League Championship. The Sportsmanship trophy is a huge thing for us, for he instills that in us at every practice and meet. We always stay late to help clean up not only our side, but the other side as well. Being courteous and supportive of the other teams is something he emphasizes daily."

Can Snee Farm ever be beaten in a championship meet? Some opponents roll their eyes and lament that it'll never happen. However, Jason Kreutner says with a laugh that it will happen. He says, "Coosaw Creek trounced us in the regular meet this summer, and it was a tremendous accomplishment to beat them in the league championship." David Thomas remarked that it basically comes down to the relays, and that is where the swimmers get their extra adrenaline. "They look at Jason and they know what a fierce competitor he is, and what a great swimmer he is and has been, and they know they have to dig down deeper and give some more for the team." There's definitely an inner feeling motivating these kids, a feeling that "we can't be the ones to break the chain," though Kreutner seldom brings up the matter of championships.

For Coach Kreutner, giving a hundred percent, never giving up, being "in it to win it," is a personal way of life. Following graduation from Porter-Gaud, Jason pursued the USC Honors College's most difficult degree (Baccalaureus Artium et Scientiae) and a history M.A. at Emory University. He's taught history at Heathwood Hall Episcopal School in Columbia, Porter-Gaud School, and Charleston Collegiate School. He's been Dean of Students in all those schools, as well as Chairman of the History Department at Porter-Gaud. For the last three years, Jason Kreutner has served as Headmaster of a school he founded, University School of the Lowcountry, located on the campus of Hibben UMC on Coleman Boulevard in Mount Pleasant. It's a co-educational, non-sectarian, non-profit independent school geared to high-achieving students who learn three global languages and take weekly field trips to explore the world outside the classroom.

All the while, Jason continues to produce championship teams who demonstrate the highest level of character and citizenship at the pool where he has spent every summer since 1986. I predict that this is a story that is headed for national prominence.

The Centennial Conference of A.M.E. Palmetto Conference

For those of us old enough to remember a half century ago, there was absolutely nothing so spiritually uplifting as driving by an old A.M.E. church, remote on some rural road, and hearing the praise of the choir as those old-time hymns and spirituals wafted through the summer night air. *Can't you hear it now, "Get you ready, there's a meeting here tonight. Camp meeting in the wilderness / There's a meeting here tonight. I know it's among the Methodists. There's a meeting here tonight."* Sweet, soul-searching music it was, sung as only an A.M.E. gospel choir can sing. Well, brothers and sisters of the old time faith, there's a meeting here in Mount Pleasant this week, and it's the old-time A.M.E. religion borne from the struggles of Freedmen making a go of life during reconstruction times. Drive six miles up the old King's Highway, U.S. 17, to the intersection of S.C. Highway 41, and you'll see that the rustic little church in the wildwood has blossomed into a glorious, modern house of worship known to all of us in the community as Greater Goodwill African Methodist Episcopal Church. Under the leadership of the Reverend Herbert L. Temoney, B.A., M. Div., the congregation of Greater Goodwill is hosting the 100th anniversary meeting of the Palmetto Annual Conference with pastors, delegates, and observers coming from Lake City to Little River to lower Charleston county. Bishop Preston Warren Williams, II, shepherds this vast flock of believers as they wrestle with weighty issues such as how the church should respond to inequities in healthcare and the shortage of jobs. On Wednesday, August 25, there'll be the divine service of ordination -- of ministers, elders, and deacons, followed by the charge of the Great Commission -- "Go ye therefore into all the lands and proclaim the gospel."

Since John Wesley preached in this area more than 220 years ago, adherents to Methodism have united their hands and their feet with their faith. "Be ye doers of the Word, not hearers only," is more than scripture; it's a creed of sorts. This notion of the gospel is that of an outreach ministry to all in need.

Greater Goodwill A.M.E. Church, located at 2818 Highway 17 North, has been a refuge for believers as far back as the 1880s, and perhaps a lot longer than that. When that dual-lane thoroughfare was still a graded dirt road in the 1930s a white frame sanctuary, no more than 25 x 40, stood on this site. Back then it was the Reverend C.S.J. Molette who ministered to these congregants who live between 5 Mile and 10 Mile, now known as Awendaw.

Though the African Methodist Episcopal denomination owes much of its doctrine and governing structure to the Methodists who formed in the years following the Great Awakening, there's a distinct African heritage that unites its members which dates to 1787 when Richard Allen and Absalom Jones led a walkout of the African contingent from the Philadelphia Methodist Conference. This brazen move was a response to an ugly incident where kneeling black men were bodily dragged by white members away from an area of the church designated as all white.

Realizing then that the type of equality that the framers of the Constitution were cobbling together up the street in Independence Hall would not likely be extended to persons of color, Allen and Jones broke away from Methodism *per se* and formed the African Methodist Episcopal (A.M.E.) denomination. The singing and the preaching were powerful instruments for conversion. By the 1850s the A.M.E. had reached the Pacific coast and included members of all races, as it does to this day.

The eminent North Carolina jurist, Augustus White Long, writes of the 19th century Methodists, "Next to the Roman Catholic, the Methodist is probably the best organized church in the world. Its machinery runs smoothly and effectively. Its government is rather aristocratic and its discipline rigid -- more rigid perhaps than the discipline of the Roman Catholic Church." Long goes on to say, "If the government of the latter [Catholic] was modeled after that of the Romam Empire, it may be said that the machinery of the Methodist Church took its form from the ideas of government prevailing in England in the time of the [Hanoverian] Georges. If so, both churches are a living proof that new wine may be put into old bottles provided the bottles are of good quality."

Both the Methodist and the African Methodist Episcopal denominations have come a long way from when Bishop Francis Asbury rode circuit in the Carolinas with Reverend Harry Hoosier, "Black Harry," as his minister to the free blacks and slaves.

The apostolic structure of the A.M.E. church is evident in the succession of bishops descending from Bishop Allen and his renown Bethel A.M.E. Church dating to 1794 in Philadelphia. Richard Allen was a man suited to his times.

He'd been a slave in Delaware prior to the Revolution, and as a free man in Philadelphia at the time of the Constitution's implementation throughout the seaboard states, Allen boldly petitioned the Pennsylvania Supreme Court for the right of his black Methodist congregation to co-exist with the various all-white churches in Philadelphia. The decision of the Pennsylvania court is one of the early landmark cases for civil rights in America. In this week's Palmetto Conference, one of the men's choirs is known as the "Sons of Richard Allen."

If you look closely at the emblem of the A.M.E. Church you'll notice an anvil placed on top of a cross. Of course, it symbolizes Richard Allen's blacksmith shop in Philadelphia where he and Deacon Absalom Jones organized the A.M.E. denomination. It's quite possible, and it would be ironic if proved, that Allen's blacksmith shop shod the horses of the delegates to the Constitutional Convention.

By the 1850s the religious movement begun by Allen and Absalom Jones had spread into Canada under the dynamic leadership of A.M.E. Bishop Morris Brown. By 1891, Bishop Henry Turner carried the A.M.E.'s unique Christian worship into Liberia where former slaves from Virginia and Maryland had been liberated and resettled by the James Monroe administration seven decades previously. Today you'll find the A.M.E. Church functioning amidst the strife in Sierra Leone and all the way into old Swaziland and to some extent even in Zimbabwe -- all from the original efforts of Henry Turner, whom some theological scholars refer to as the "Black Apostle Paul."

When so many of the old-line denominations in the U.S. are declining in membership and diminishing in the exercise of moral and spiritual authority, it's refreshing to witness the filled-to-capacity edifices of the A.M.E. denomination. From Friendship to Greater Zion to Greater Goodwill, the faith is alive, the hymns o praise are sung with enthusiasm and passion. Preaching is still that old-time gospel and you'll hear many an "Amen" and "Thank you, Jesus." That old spiritual, "There's a Meeting Here Tonight," could easily be rephrased to close with this refrain appropriate to the conference that Bishop Williams and Reverend Temoney are conducting here this week: "There's fire in the East, there's fire in the West. There's a meeting here tonight. I know it's among the A.M.E. There's a meeting here tonight!"

Author's Note: I owe a special debt of gratitude to Emma Williams of Greater Zion A.M.E. Church for her help in acquiring information for this story.

Finding History and Adventure On Old U.S. Highway 1

When breezes bearing fall's first hint whisper "Get thee gone," and you wonder where a weekend's adventure can be found on a shoestring budget, ponder no further. Point the Urban 4-wheeler north and mate-up with Old U.S. Highway 1.

You'll discover more nostalgia, more colonial heritage, and more Mom and Pop diners than you'll meet with in the entirety of the uninteresting interstate freeways combined!

Next year marks the 100th aniversary of Old Number 1, the highway that Model-T motorists knew then as the Old Atlantic Highway. Henry Flagler, the real-estate and railroad tycoon, buttonholed congressmen to build the highway just about the same time that Henry Ford made the automobile affordable. By default the two men became the godfathers of modern tourism. In the early days of motoring, drivers donned goggles and dusters to shield themselves from the elements. The road ahead unfolded at an easy pace and a farmer's cow was no serious obstacle in the road. Rural Americana waved and received a blast from the side-mounted brass horns. Where has all of the sentimentality of motoring gone? Why is getting there none of the fun?

Backroads went the way of filling stations and tourist courts. When cruise-control became a standard feature on even the economy cars, Americans took to the freeway where a mile's worth of scenery flashes by in less than a minute. We traded adventure for predictability, and high-speed comfort suffices for the thrill of discovery. It's not that the Kangaroo at Exit 32 doesn't have charm and a host of quality-assured treats and conveniences. There you'll find Kenyan roast coffee fresh brewed, frankfurters flown in from Chicago, and sparkling restrooms verified as clean by someone with initials of RJH. Quick stops on the interstate do not equal the slower-paced charm, however, of dining at the historic Wilcox Inn in Aiken or selecting whole hickory-cured hams and stone-ground grits at Four Oaks Farms in Lexington -- both easy stops along U.S. Highway 1.

Lunching at The Roost in Bethune overlooking Old Number 1 is something even Charles Kuralt never got around to, nor did he get to savor the authentic German cuisine at Oskar's in Cheraw.

Blame it on cruise control, blame it on speed dial, accuse our hyper, self-obsessed culture, yet the truth lies within us -- we've lost our sense of touch and smell and taste for anything that's not prepackaged for ease and convenience. The pre-interstate roads linked real people who bonded in meaningful ways with the passing motorists, often building up relationships with travelers over the years.

U.S. 1 unfolds as an open book -- a hefty volume with 15 chapters -- measured not in pages, but in miles, 2930 miles---- one chapter for each state it bisects and one for the great federal city, Washington, D.C. Begin at mile marker zero in Key West, very near Papa Hemingway's favorite hangout, Sloppy Joe's. Each chapter of the old road has a nickname bestowed by locals -- such as Atlantic Highway along the Florida coast. The same asphalt stretch assumes the identity of "Dixie Highway" in South Georgia. In South Carolina it's Old Number One, and by the time it winds its way into Virginia, the by-now-familiar pavement becomes the Jeff Davis Highway. In the interest of sectional unity, the portion of the thoroughfare that rolls through Massachusetts and on into New York is known by locals and old-timers as The Lincoln Highway.

Nowhere does Old Number One teach us more history than it does in the Cavalier state of Virginia. Petersburg, Richmond, Fredericksburg, and Alexandria stretch out before you with the same topography that all the historic personages from the past would still recognize -- no 50 foot flyovers, no dizzying cloverleafs. You can pull over whenever a historic marker or interesting view catches your fancy. For miles this stretch of road was known in Virginia as the Boydton Plank Road. The Confederate battle of Burgess Mill south of Petersburg is known alternately as the Battle of Boydton Plank Road.

South of Alexandria and north of Fairfax in the rolling hills of Virginia, we encounter a stretch of U.S. 1 that's four-laned with a generous median, all a concession to the burgeoning suburbs that have sprung up since World War II. Still visible, though, are the elevated concrete railroad trestles that date to the WPA program in the 1930s. These icons of a bygone era were guarded night and day in the early 1940s by an army infantryman with a bayonet fastened upon his M-1 rifle. In those days America feared sabotage of its primary arteries for troop and material movement.

A small sign along this Fairfax to Alexandria stretch of what Virginians still proudly refer to as the Jeff Davis Highway denotes that the motorist is intersecting with Telegraph Road. Civil War buffs know that this was one of the most fought over roads in the conflict. Douglas Southall Freeman, in his three-volume account entitled Lee's Lieutenants, mentions Telegraph Road no fewer than 13 times. After detouring just a short way into that ancient byway you imagine you hear the thunderous hooves of Stuart's or Sheridan's cavalry causing the loamy earth to tremble once more.

Another obscure marker along Number 1 near Fort Belvoir notes that Colonel George Washington and General Edward Braddock rode side-by-side along here as the mighty British army headed toward the Monongahela and Fort Du Quesne. Braddock's engineer corps cut with axes a wide swath for the Army to bring up its caissons and supply wagons. That road, known still as Braddock's Road, intersects Old Number 1 just a few miles below Telegraph Road. Braddock didn't know that he was riding into an ambush -- an ambush that'd leave him dead on the field and his French and Iroquois adversaries jubilant. Young Washington must have figured right there and then that the mighty British were mere mortals who knew not the ways of wilderness fighting in the New World.

Fort Belvoir is the headquarters for much of the U.S. Army's supply corps. The name Belvoir dates back to the enormous plantation once owned by Lord Thomas Fairfax, 6th Baron Fairfax of Cameron. The officers club at Fort Belvoir is a stately colonial-looking mansion perched on a 70-foot high bluff overlooking the Potomac. The "O" Club sits approimately where Lord Fairfax's grand Tudor - styled hall once stood. The Club pays homage to the former dwelling a magnificent Tudor hall complete with a hammer beam ceiling and enormous fireplaces. Thomas Fairfax sublet his grand estate in Virginia to his cousin, William Fairfax on condition that William collect the rent from the numerous tenants as well as port customs for the Crown.

The Fairfaxes were the most aristocratic family in North America, and their nearest neighbors were the Washingtons. William Fairfax had a beautiful 15-year-old daughter, Anne, who was a bit of a flirtatious girl for her era and a scandal occurred at the local parish church with the young curate, Charles Green, just arrived from England. Details are scarce as would befit a lady of Anne's standing, but a parishioner witnessed something untoward occurring between the priest and the teen, and immediately it was announced that Anne Fairfax was engaged to Lawrence Washington, a houseguest of the Fairfaxes. Obviously, the hasty plan was designed to save the reputation of Anne. She soon went upriver to Lawrence Washington's new plantation home that was named Mount Vernon in honor of Royal Marine Captain Lawrence Washington's commanding officer in the British navy.

Today, Pohick Parish Church sits quietly by Number One just as it has for the past 270 years. Six miles farther up the road, past modern fastfood franchises such as Roy Rogers and Hardees, one can see the site of the old John Carlyle House (c.1750) where four New England governors came south to meet with Virginia Governor Dinwiddie over the pressing problem of the French presence in Pennsylvania. That congress is noted as the first grand collaboration of the colonies prior to the events leading to the Revolution.

If your budget allows, historic Number 1 will carry you through Philadelphia and skirt New York City as you head to Fort Kent, Maine -- a place once known as Fort Kent Blockhouse in the "Aroostook War" -- an undecalred border dispute between America and Britain in 1838. However, that's a story for another day.

Jenkins Orphanage Band's 105th Anniversary

As we read this article there's high drama occurring in a meeting between Palestinians and Jews in the White House Oval Office. Our President is hoping to be a factotum of the peace process. "Blessed are the peacemakers," says the Lord, "for they shall be called the children of God" (Matthew 5:9). Many dramas have unfolded over the years in the office of the President. There are some that we wish *Life Magazine* had been there to record, and there are some that we'll be happy for *Time* to forget. A poignant moment that has been lost to history will regain currency thanks to local attorney Thomas Tisdale republishing the Reverend Doctor Anthony Toomer Porter's memoirs, *Led On! Step By Step* (c. 1902; 1967; 2010). In Porter's memoirs of Charleston in the aftermath of the Confederacy, there's an incident that occurs in President Andrew Johnson's office that bears directly upon Charleston and -- ultimately, upon the emerging jazz age of the 20th century. The White House is no stranger to curious guests, cap in hand, asking favors. However, Republican President Andrew "Andy" Johnson must have rubbed his eyes in disbelief in the autumn of 1866 when in walked the perfect odd couple, Union Army General O.O. Howard, Director of the Freedman's Bureau, and, the Episcopal priest and former Confederate chaplain, Anthony Porter of Charleston.

In 1866, with passion still intense from the war, there could have few visitors more odd than O.O. Howard, implementor of the "20 acres and a mule" program that Sherman devised for the freedmen of the conquered South and Charleston aristocrat, Anthony Porter. To southerners, that odious 20-acre federal giveaway came at the expense of southerners whose property had been seized for nonpayment of taxes. For many of these southerners the tax issue was made contemptible by the nonexistence of greenback currency circulating around these parts. Paying taxes in Confederate bonds or currency wasn't an option. Reverned Porter's private residence on the corner of Spring and Rutlege Avenues had been seized by the Freedmens' Bureau, so Porter and Howard were not destined for immediate friendship in 1866. Yet Howard could not have been more cordial to Porter when he heard of the reverend's intentions. The same was said for General Sherman and a host of other federal officers who'd put down the southern effort for independence.

Admittedly, Porter looked the part of planter -- white hair and goatee, Charleston drawl, and courtly manners. Yet, that clerical collar seemed far less threatening than the Confederate captain's uniform he'd worn with the Washington Light Infantry, a part of Hampton's Legion, at battles such as Manassas and Secessionville. When Johnson heard his visitor's unusual request, he could hardly believe his ears. Reverend Porter from the Church of the Holy Communion in downtown Charleston wanted federal aid for the start up of a school exclusively for the children of recently freed black families in Charleston. Imagine Johnson's shock. In 1866 there were still reports circulating of guerrilla bands of ex-Confederates plundering post offices, banks, and trains in the southwestern territories. Porter's request was the first glimmer of hope that Andy Johnson saw in the reform of the Old South.

The embattled president, even then in a struggle against the radical members of his own party, mumbled something, wiped his eye, and reached for his checkbook. Johnson handed Porter a personal bank draft for $1000 ($14, 475 in 2009 inflation estimation). Gratified beyond belief, Porter hurrried to Union Station where the telegraph office was and wired Charlestonian John Hanckel, to purchase immediately the old mariner's hospital, a bombed-out structure near the county jail on the Charleston's west side. The first school in the South to be established by whites primarily for the newly free African-American children was this institute focusing upon elementary education for offspring of former slaves.

That afternoon in downtown Charleston when the telgram came over the wire, a hurried meeting was called by Episcopal Reverends C.C. Pinckney, Christopher Gadsden, former Confederate States Treasurer George Alfred Trenholm, businessman E.L. Kerrison, and planter Thomas W. Porcher -- all members with Porter on the Board of Missions for establishing schools in war-torn Charleston.

The Mariners Hospital on 20 Franklin Street was one of architect Robert Mills's noble creations. It was an antebellum Charleston landmark, but the Federal bombardment had left the building with huge gaps where shells had dropped through and exploded. It'd take many thousands of dollars, but friends that Porter made in New York, Boston, Philadelphia, Washington, D.C. and even as far away as London, contributed to this humble Episcopal priest who felt profoundly the call for healing ministry. In New York, Porter preached at Holy Trinity, Brooklyn, and a bewhiskered fellow approached him after the sermon and said, "I am Captain Worden who fought the Monitor against the Merrimac in Hampton Roads." Worden opened his wallent and gave all of its contents to Porter for use with the new Charleston school. He continued to be a donor to this worthy cause.

Another New York donor who shelled out personal money for a school that'd educate black orphans and indigents was the prominent New York financier, A.A. Low. Reverend Porter preached at Trinity Cathedral in New York and the vestry passed the collection plates for a special offering to aid the enterprise. And to think that all of this happened less than one year after General Joe Johnston surrendered the last of the Confederate Armies at Goldsborough and Bentonville in April, 1865! Low said to Porter on the way out of the church, "Sir, you and your sermon have accomplished what bullets could not." The "school for the colored children," as it was referred to then, operated from 1866 through 1870; that was when South Carolina reentered a period of insurrection, chaos, and bloodletting over resistence to the repressive reconstruction policies. Porter was preaching on Sunday mornings at the Church of the Holy Communion on Ashley Avenue and in the afternoons he preached at St. Marks on 16 Thomas Street. The latter was an Episcopal mission to the Freedmen. The so-called "colored school" became an affiliation of St. Marks, but the furor surrounding radical reconstruction brought down, at least temporarily, the best intentions of good northerners and southerners in the wake of the war.

Porter worked indefatigably to establish a trade school for the training of women in textile arts and a school for orphaned white children. The great moment of resurrection for the "colored school" that became the famed Jenkins Orphanage came in the 1890s when a black minister, Reverend Daniel Jenkins, pastor of St. Marks, determined to revive the school effort of a generation earlier. Following the same footsteps of praying, pleading, planning, and implementing that had worked for Porter, Jenkins gradually built the orphan school that today proudly bears his name.

Jenkins could not wrest money out of northerners and southerners quite as quickly as had Reverend Porter, but that was because of the bitterness surrounding the contested presidential election of 1876. Jenkins, no musician himself, had a stroke of genius when he decided that the best way he could think was to form his young male students into a kind of pop-orchestra and ask passers by for donations. Graduating Citadel cadets gave their old uniforms for the band members to wear. Music instruments were donated, some by Siegling Music Store on Broad Street, and the little sidewalk band made its debut on street corners from King to Calhoun.

At first, the music was tin-pan quality, but with some instruction, the budding musicians hit their stride. Boys and girls danced a favorite dance they called the "black bottom" to accompany the jazzy tunes, and by the time the Jenkins Orphanage Band played the Cotton Club in Harlem a few years later, that dance had been renamed "The Charleston."

Freddie Green of Count Basie's Band, was an alum of the Jenkins Orphanage Band, as was Claddys "Jabbo" Smith, who played with Duke Ellington. Another jazz great who got his start here was William "Cat" Anderson who performed with Claude Hoskins, Doc Wheeler, and Duke Ellington. There were many other musicians who played for quarters along street corners here, but the real story lies in the hundreds of young men and women who got another chance at life thanks to men of great faith and determination -- men such as Reverends Anthony Porter and Daniel Jenkins.

New South's Origins Owe Much To University of North Carolina

Can the leopard change his spots? Can the songbird learn new tunes? These sayings have been with us for centuries. Our beloved state has long been known as the Hotspur State perhaps after Sir Henry Percy "Harry Hotspur," 1st Earl of Northumberland. In Shakespeare's *Henry V*, Harry "Hotspur" Percy was a rival of young Prince Hal, the future King Henry V. The two youthful noble men fought a sword duel and Hal ran Hotspur Percy through with his broadsword. "Oh Hal, Thou have robbed me of my youth," whispered Percy. "Oh Percy, thou art dust and food for . . . food for worms, Brave Percy," lamented Prince Hal. Reverend William Percy settled in Charleston in 1775 and married into the prominent Elliott family. Yet, despite the number of prominent offspring from that auspicious union, it's doubtful that one Percy descendant could sway a whole state to tempestuousness. As far back as 1754, Benjamin Franklin caricatured South Carolina as the rattles on his famous "Join, Or Die!" rattlesnake cartoon depiction of the colonies' disunited posture in the face of renewed French and Indian threat. Historians agree that S.C. was boisterous long before the troubles leading to 1776. A hundred and fifty years after the War of the Confederacy, historians also agree that two-score of hotheads on each side propelled us into the dreaded cauldron of civil war.

Overlooking William Lowndes Yancey of Alabama and Edmund Ruffin of Virginia, the bulk of the southern fire-eaters were South Carolinians. The bitterness of reconstruction and the aftertaste of a decade of carpetbagger / scalawag government hardened most South Carolinians' hearts to reconciliation. Alas, like poor Percy, 1st Earl of Northumberland, the prospects for our state became food for worms for many decades following that unpleasantness.

Not so for the Old North State, as North Carolina was referred to by our citizens in antebellum days. For whatever it's worth in looking back, the North Carolina veterans and sons of the veterans of Lee's army sought solace in academia -- some who'd had a classical education prior to the War became professors of Greek or Latin or Mathematics. The two universities, UNC and Trinity, reopened to several dozen poor scholars in the 1870s. The men who matriculated at those institutions were first among those who forged the attitude known now as the "New South."

Men such as Edwin Alderman, Walter Hines Page, Dick Reynolds, and Augustus White Long sprang from the soil of central or eastern North Carolina, each in his own way to champion a new vision for the Old South. The University of North Carolina at Chapel Hill and Trinity College, the precursor of Duke University, became the bastions of intellectualism in the 1880s that they'd been destined to become prior to the strife that had torn the nation asunder.

Chapel Hill in the 1870s possessed one store, Long and McCauley General Mercantile Company, and a tobacco warehouse owned by W.T. Blackwell. New Hope Chapel still sat on top the little hill that gives the town its name. Both Confederate General Joe Wheeler and Union General Tecumseh Sherman had left their unwelcome imprint upon this rural community.

For a decade or so the only intellectual fervor heard within 10 miles of the crossroads was the gathering of men around the potbelly stove of the Long and McCauley Store. Sometimes the Methodists waxed fervently about politics and reform. However unadorned this cracker-barrel environment may have appeared from the outside, the ideas that were taking form in the hearts of the men wearing overalls were anything but ordinary.

Edwin Anderson Alderman was born in Wilmington one month to the day after the firing on Fort Sumter in 1861. As a youth he watched the blockade runners steal in and out of city wharfs. When his family heard that the university at Chapel Hill was reopening in 1875, the teenager Alderman walked the 130 miles through all kinds of weather to get there. Lee's words to the Richmond press following Appomatox were not universally taken to heart by all southerners. "The war was an unnecessary condition of affairs, and might have been avoided if forebearance and wisdom had been practiced on both sides. We failed, but in the good providence of God apparent failure often proves a blessing." More North Carolinians appeared ready to put the past behind them by 1875 than did the citizens of the deep south.

"There's a lot of poor teaching going on inside these walls," were the words Augustus White Long overheard as he sat on the steps of Old East in the 1870s. However boring or pedantic the teaching may have been, the University of North Carolina came closer to the postwar ideals espoused by Robert E. Lee than did any other southern university of the postbellum years. Alderman distinguished himself by becoming the only student of his time ever to win the oratory medal of the Dialectic and the Philanthropic literary societies. Alderman became president of UNC, his Alma Mater, at age 35, and then president of Tulane at age 40.

However, Alderman's greatest achievements in academia came as president of the University of Virginia, an honor he achieved by age 44. Alderman Library is named there in his honor. The University of Virginia gained national prominence under Alderman's leadership, and Andrew Carnegie was a frequent visitor to the campus as well as benefactor. Perhaps Alderman's greatest moment in the spotlight occurred when he was asked to give the eulogy for former President Woodrow Wilson before a joint session of Congress in 1924.

As classmates watched in awe at UNC's commencement, the class scholars delivered silver-tongued addresses before the state's dignitaries and the visiting throngs. In Alderman's class there were numerous young men of ambition and Locke Craig, future governor of the state, was not the least of them. Locke Craig practiced law in Asheville before ascending to the governor's mansion on the coattails of Woodrow Wilson's election to the White House in 1912. Wilson, another voice of the New South, never broke with the North Carolina friends he'd made in the years he'd spent at Davidson College.

Augustus Long, a native of Chapel Hill, was a year or two behind Alderman, Craig, and the host of UNC alums that went forth in the early 1880s to rebuild the shattered image of the Old North State. Augustus Long, orphaned son of a Chapel Hill merchant, studied classics and rose to become a professor of literature at Wofford College, Johns Hopkins, and finally at Princeton University. In his memoirs, *Son of Carolina* (1939), Long details interesting accounts of Princeton president Woodrow Wilson in the years prior to the great man's entry into politics.

Augustus Long impressed another North Carolinian, Walter Hines Page, when he, Long, was editor of the UNC student newspaper. Page, a newspaperman, came to UNC to teach a course and met Long, thus beginning a long friendship. Page grew up in Cary, near Raleigh. His father, a Confederate veteran, owned and operated the only hotel in Cary -- a town that was known then for mule traders and tobacco auctions. Walter Hines Page had graduated from Trinity College and used his writing skills to start several reform - oriented newspapers as well as the progressive Watauga Club. The Watauga Club emphasized the theme that the South must shed its old ways of thinking and adjust to the new industrial world. One of the Club's vocal members was Dick Reynolds who later became better known as R.J. Reynolds.

Woodrow Wilson appointed Walter Hines Page to be the Ambassador to the Court of St. James, and Page used his position to promote progressive-leaning southern men to careers in the foreign service. There were forward-thinking men in other southern states. Jabez Lamar Monroe Curry of Georgia championed public education throughout the South. Henry Grady of Atlanta promoted the ideals of the New South in his newspaper empire. Stephen Dill Lee, former general of the Confederacy, also looked to the new ways, but the vanguard of new thinking in the South owed much of its origin to the graduating classes of UNC immediately following reconstruction.

A 1780s Quaker Family Survived Two Years Captivity By Indians

Ever wonder what it was like on the American frontier in the 18th century? If you were a fan of actor Fess Parker, movie icon of the 1950s and '60s -- the man who played Davy Crockett and Daniel Boone for Disney -- then you already have an appreciation for the romance and adventure associated with those bygone days.

The frontier was the incubator of so many American ideals -- ideals ranging from our love of firearms to our cherished rights of unfettered speech and worship. However, the frontier days brought agony, suffering, and horror to many colonials as their culture clashed with the various Indian tribes who were here first.

One Mount Pleasant family, however, doesn't have to go any further than the 150-year-old, leather-bound volume of its ancestors' two-year ordeal of captivity by savage Mohawk and Cayuga Indians. Cameron Burn of the Old Village in Mount Pleasant is a direct descendant of Benjamin and Elizabeth Gilbert, 18th century Quakers of Bucks County, Pennsylvania. For Cameron and his family, all they have to do to commune with the triumphs and tribulations of their ancestors is to flip through the yellowed pages of *A Narrative of the Captivity and Sufferings of Benjamin Gilbert and His Family Who Were Taken By The Indians In The Spring of 1780* (John Richards, publisher, Philadelphia 1848). Fourteen members of the Gilbert clan were forcibly removed in 1780 from their rural Pennsylvania cabins and forced into a brutal captivity whereby they were led overland 200 miles through dense wilderness to a Cayuga encampment near Niagara on the Canadian border.

The little book of 240 pages of memoirs is rare enough that the park rangers at Old Fort Niagara, located where the Niagara River joins Lake Ontario, had never heard of it when the Burns family apprised them just a few years ago. The memoirs of the Gilbert family -- all of whom miraculously survived the 26 - month ordeal -- except the patriarch -- reads like something historical fiction writer Kenneth Roberts might have written -- *Northwest Passage* (1937), *March To Quebec* (1938), etc. How ironic that the Mohawks chose to sweep down upon a settlement of Quakers situated in the forest north of Philadelphia at dawn on Tuesday morning, April 24, 1780. Those descendants of William Penn's followers were the least aggressive white people the red man had ever dealt with.

As pacifists, the Quakers took no side in the Revolutionary War, yet they were drawn into the hostilities when Patriot General John Sullivan of New Hampshire led a punitive raid against the Five Nations of the Iroquois. Sullivan's 4000 men swept down the Delaware River Valley torching Indian settlements left and right. One village laid waste was called Coreorgonel, not far from Ithaca, New York. The surviving warriors fanned out in every direction to extract a terrible revenge, and that is the genesis of the sad story of the peace-loving Gilbert family.

Sullivan was a rough-natured man and his cruelty made for a nightmarish outcome. When he'd been a practicing attorney in Portsmouth, he'd been a party to so many foreclosure lawsuits that he'd almost been run out of town. As a commander of infantry he was known to use up his soldiers and horses in a careless manner. So, when ordered to suppress the Iroquois allies of the British, he made no inquiry as to which Indian settlements fit that order and which didn't.

Fourteen members of the Gilbert family, ranging in age from Benjamin, Sr., at age 70, to granddaughter Elizabeth Peart, age 9 months, were dragged from their cabins at daybreak by whooping, tomahawk-wielding savages who were painted in a hideous manner to heighten their terrifying demeanor. Curiously, these Indians all bore Christian names -- the leader of the Cayuga was Rowland Monteur, the half-breed son of a French trapper and an Indian squaw. John Monteur, John Huston, John Huston, Jr., Samuel Harris, and John Fox, were also part of the raiding party. The Indians set fire to the cabins and barns, and they destroyed the livestock. Farm tools, silverware, and blankets were the booty that the prisoners had to carry on their backs as they were led by the neck with ropes. All travel was through the uncharted wilderness, and the Gilberts wore the scant bed clothing that they'd been taken in.

When grandfather Gilbert stumbled to the ground, the savages raised tomahawks and threatened to dispatch him right there in front of his wife and children. The captors showed no mercy and made it plain that they planned to kill the men and make the women and children their slaves. When teenage mother Elizabeth Peart grew faint and struggled to carry her crying infant, the savages forbade the others to assist her, and they threatened to kill the baby. The party of Quaker captives was separated into two bands and each was hustled off northward through the woods along different routes. The Indians told the captives that their friends in the other group had been killed. Cayuga and Mohawk warriors cut their captive's hair with hunting knives, leaving just a ragged tuft. Then they painted the men and women's faces black or red, or a combination of black and red. Black meant that the captive was to be left for dead if he or she collapsed. Red meant that the captive was of value and would be adopted into a tribe somewhere. A combination of red and black meant that they hadn't made up their minds one way or the other. The captives made a hideous appearance to each other -- exhausted, tattered clothing, and blood trickling down their faces.

The memoirs of the Quaker family of Byberry, Pennsylvania, are today one of the best surviving sources of life among the northern Indians at the time of the American Revolution. We can understand their culture so much better now that we can see their behavior through the eyes of educated settlers who spent years amidst them -- albeit unwillingly. The Indians lived from hand to mouth. When the corn was harvested, they feasted until it was gone. Never did they consider rationing it through the winter. In lean times they dug roots and ate berries -- or they went hungry.

These peace-loving Quakers clung to their religious faith through their harrowing captivity. Occasionally, they glimpsed another family member in an encampment they passed. It was customary as the band of captives trudged through an Indian settlement that the Indian women, children, and old men rushed out of their wigwams and beat the prisoners in retaliation for the battle losses suffered by their tribe. Many times the blows were severe enough to leave the recipient unconscious. In that event, another captive had to bear the injured one while enduring more lashes and blows.

Upon reaching the Niagara area, the various British forts offered the prisoners hope of eventual freedom. Old man Benjamin Gilbert expired during the captivity, and the British prevailed in getting him a burial rather than having his body dumped into the Niagara River. British officers even succeeded in buying some of the captives and keeping them in the fort until the War ended.

Gradually, one by one, with the exception of their deceased patriarch, the clan reunited in the British garrison. With the cessation of hostilities, the Gilberts began their 200-mile journey home. In characteristic Quaker manner, the survivors gave thanks to their Creator, and they maintained steadfastly that the Indian men never once attempted to take advantage of the captive women.

The story of the Gilberts occurred simultaneously with the surrender of Charleston in 1781 and the famous guerilla-war excursions of Francis Marion and Thomas Sumter. If you wish to read the complete story of this family's incredible escape from brutal captivity, Google Books has scanned the entire text on-line.

In The Company Of Heroes With Medal of Honor Recipients

Last Friday Porter-Gaud and Charleston Day students were honored to be in the company of a hero. 1968 Medal of Honor recipient James A. Taylor Major, United States Army, retired, delivered a stirring address that will long be remembered by those present. Taylor, who received his award for valor during the height of the Vietnam conflict, made an appeal to the assembled youth to rally around the virtues that have made America great -- teamwork, responsible citizenship, and stepping forward when our country calls. The thunderous ovation indicates how these traits are making a comeback.

Anyone who has heard these soldiers, sailors, and airmen speak knows that these brave men seldom dwell upon their own courageous deeds, but rather, they deliver motivational talks that compel every man to do his duty, and every woman, too. Major James A. Taylor spoke of his own high school days in San Francisco during the 1950s as a star athlete who was suspended for violating team rules. It was the toughest discipline he'd ever had to endure, but he fulfilled Coach Bob's demands for regaining his playing status the following year. That deep-cutting lesson stayed with Taylor in his army years. In Que Son, Republic of Vietnam, in 1967, First Lieutenant Taylor of the 1st Cavalry Regiment, Americal Division, was cut off and surrounded by Viet Cong forces, Taylor's instincts and self-discipline enabled him to rescue men from burning vehicles, call in an air strike, and arrange for the air evacuation of his wounded -- all while coordinating a counterattack against the enemy. None of these facts were part of Major Taylor's address to the students, however. Teens and adults alike respond well to the wisdom of their elders when they know the words come from someone who's earned the right to be listened to.

There's been a gathering this past week of heroes, and suddenly Mount Pleasant is a destination point for reunions of the bravest of the brave. That grey hull carrier with CV-10 emblazoned on her bow has brought this town more glory than all our politicians and ballplayers combined. And few halls in the world contain as much military history as does that Medal of Honor Museum located on the hanger deck. It's a tour destination that should be on every red-blooded American's travel agenda.

Many recall that in the mid-1980s South Carolina native, Vietnam war Medal of Honor recipient CPO James Elliott Williams, USN, was the man most instrumental in getting the Medal of Honor Museum and Society to move here from New York. Famed aviator and fellow Medal of Honor winner Jimmy Doolittle held a reunion of his Tokyo Raiders here aboard the Yorktown. Most of those brave airmen have since passed on, but Mount Pleasant is on the map because of that warship and museum.

Where else can one find such history as the stories of heroism in the face of adversity -- of men locked in desperate combat and prevailing over great odds? Thankfully, our military has fought for great ideals to prevail rather than for national glory or fortune. No doubt that is the reason for two grand museums dedicated to the courageous ones who are awarded the Medal of Honor. Of course, there's the Medal of Honor Museum aboard the aircraft carrier Yorktown at Patriot's Point here in Mount Pleasant, and there's an equally fine one in Chattanooga. One of the legion of stories to be found in the Medal Museum involves the eight medals won by South Carolinians in World War I. There's no better place to learn of their heroism than right here at Patriot's Point.

South Carolina's eight Medal of Honor winners from the First World War? Only 53 years had elapsed between Appomattox and Woodrow Wilson's "War To End All Wars." Not only were the memories of Sherman's march to the sea still fresh, but so was the evidence visible -- especially in the upstate of South Carolina where chimneys stood where fine homes once had. Carolina's sons rallied to the red, white, and blue during the Spanish-American War in 1898, and it was no surprise when France was overrun by the Kaiser, that our boys joined the chorus of Doughboys singing "Lafayette, We Are Here!"

Our state had a population of approximately 1.6 million inhabitants in 1918 and we had 8 medal of honor winners -- the highest percentage per capita of any state in the Union. New York, by comparison, had a population of 5.6 million then, and 16 of their brave men won medals. For Carolinians, the grandest medal story involves Richmond Hobson Hilton of Westville, just a couple of miles due north of Camden.

Hilton's birthplace was just a mile or two from where Baron de Kalb was mortally wounded, August 19, 1780, while fighting for the patriot cause in the Battle of Camden. Richard H. Hilton's grandfather had served gallantly as a corporal in Company "G," 2nd S.C. Volunteers, Kershaw's Regiment, in the Confederacy. As compelling as that military lineage is, it gets even more interesting. Richmond Hobson Hilton was born soon after the Spanish-American War ended, and the newspapers of the day were flush with stories of the sons of ex-Confederates who distinguished themselves under Old Glory's banner. Navy Lieutenant Richmond Hobson, an Alabama native, won the Medal of Honor for heroism at Santiago Harbor. Hilton's parents thought that the Richmond Hobson name just suited their newborn son. For those who believe that names can have prophetic powers, Richmond Hobson Hilton became the only namesake of a medal recipient to win the Medal of Honor. Douglas MacArthur is the only son of a medal recipient also to receive a Medal of Honor.

Nineteen-year-old Sergeant R.H. Hilton, Company M, 118th Infantry, 30th "Old Hickory" Division, exhibited "Conspicuous Gallantry and Intrepidity in Action At the Risk of Life Above and Beyond the Call of Duty" on October 11, 1918, near Brancourt, France. The citation presented by President Wilson to Sergeant Hilton at a White House ceremony, states, "While Sgt. Hilton's company was advancing through the village of Brancourt it was held up by intense enfilading fire from a machinegun. Discovering that this fire came from a machine gun nest among shell holes at the edge of the town, Sgt. Hilton, accompanied by a few other soldiers, but well in advance of them, pressed on toward this position, firing with his rifle until his ammunition was exhausted, and then with his pistol, killing 6 of the enemy and capturing 10. In the course of this daring exploit he received a wound from a bursting shell, which resulted in the loss of his arm."

Sergeant Hilton distinguished himself in the highest tradition of gallantry of the United States Army. He died at age 34 due to the complications associated with his war wounds. A plaque honors Hilton in the foyer of the South Carolina Capitol.

It's not known if former Medal of Honor winners had gatherings such as the one we just experienced in Mount Pleasant this past week, and it's not known if Hilton ever met his fellow South Carolinians who also won the famed medal during that "war to end all wars." It would have been a grand gathering of gallant men if it ever occurred -- Army Lieutenant James C. Dozier of Gallivant's Ferry, Army Sergeant Gary Foster of Inman, Army Sergeant Thomas Lee Hall of Fort Mill, Army Corporal James Heriot of Providence, and Army Corporal John Villepigue of Camden -- all men of the famed 30th "Old Hickory" Division.

Since not a single African-American was awarded a Medal of Honor during the First World War, President George H.W. Bush changed that record by posthumously awarding Anderson County native, Corporal Freddie Stowers, the prestigious honor 73 years after the event of his valor. Corporal Stowers' sisters received his medal. The citation reads: "Corporal Stowers, a native of Anderson County, South Carolina, distinguished himself by exceptional heroism on 28 September 1918, while serving as a squad leader in Company C, 371st Infantry Regiment, 93rd Infantry Division. His company was the lead company during the attack on Hill 188, Champagne Marne Sector, France, during World War I. A few minutes after the attack began, the enemy ceased firing and began climbing up onto the parapets of the trenches, holding up their arms as if wishing to surrender. The enemy's actions caused the American forces to cease fire and to come out into the open. As the company started forward and when within about 100 meters of the trench line, the enemy jumped back into their trenches and greeted Corporal Stowers' company with interlocking bands of machine gun fire and mortar fire causing well over fifty percent casualties. Faced with incredible enemy resistance, Corporal Stowers took charge, setting such a courageous example of personal bravery and leadership that he inspired his men to follow him in the attack. With extraordinary heroism and complete disregard of personal danger under devastating fire, he crawled forward leading his squad toward an enemy machine gun nest, which was causing heavy casualties to his company. After fierce fighting, the machine gun position was destroyed and the enemy soldiers were killed. . . . ."

Medal of Honor winners, from the living recipients such as Major James A. Taylor and Mount Pleasant resident Major General James E. Livingston, U.S.M.C., continue to teach us the lessons of duty, honor, courage, and self-sacrifice. Their deceased comrades still teach us by their example.

What Became of Those Unvanquished Confederate Generals?

Remember what Douglas MacArthur said to the cadets up at West Point in 1964 -- that "Old soldiers never die . . . they just fade away." An eyewitness to that speech remarked that MacArthur spoke in the mess hall as the cadets ate the noon meal, and that the old general droned on for a long time provoking some rather irreverent remarks from the Corps. Not to contradict General MacArthur and what has turned out to be one of the greatest of American addresses -- but quite a few old soldiers have bent their spears into pruning hooks, metaphorically. Approximately three-hundred Confederate generals survived the War, and with a few notable exceptions, most became quite productive in the civilian sector. In fact, their postwar productiveness invites us to ponder what might have been if saner heads had prevailed in 1861.

"Marse Robert," the affectionate name for Lee bestowed upon him by his soldiers, set the example of postwar reconciliation. Despite the anger and hard feelings and despite the refusal to reinstate confiscated property and the denial of the rights of citizenship, Lee advocated reunification under the red, white, and blue banner. He set an example of honorable post-war service by accepting a low-paying position but high-profile post as president of Washington College in Lexington, Virginia.

One of the most unusual postwar careers of a former Confederate general was that of York, South Carolina native, D.H. Hill. This hard-fighting general who won laurels at Gaines Mill, Sharpsburg, Fredericksburg, Gettysburg, the Wilderness, and Petersburg, was appointed by President U.S. Grant as our Minister to Turkey. Hill was also the bother-in-law of the deceased Thomas J. "Stonewall" Jackson. Oddly enough, Grant and Sherman had almost as many ex-Confederate generals for friends after the war as they had from the Union. Perhaps the ties that many of these old soldiers had from their days at West Point helped to begin the reconciliation process.

In the era of the Confederacy, it was routine for southern legislators to wrangle commissions from their peers as colonel or brigadier general of state militia. Some of these popularly elected generals succeeded in the field once the bullets began to whine -- sometimes they were miserable failures. Milledge Luke Bonham was one of the political generals from South Carolina. Bonham was all thunder and lightning prior to Fort Sumter, and shortly afterwards, he led a regiment at the battle of 1st Manassas. Bonham's best work, however, was serving in the Confederate infrastructure -- as wartime governor of S.C. in 1863-'64 and in the Confederate Congress in Richmond. Bonham resigned from the Congress and returned to his home state to lead a brigade against Sherman in that general's famed "march to the sea." Bonham lived prosperously for 35 years following the war by reviving his law practice and becoming a railroad commissioner.

A lesser-known Carolinian was General John Bratton, C.S.A., of Winnsboro. Bratton was a country doctor and a gentleman planter prior to the War. He became the fighting physician in the 1860s; Bratton commanded Jenkins' Brigade and Fields' Division at Petersburg and Appomattox. He was at "the Crater" when all Hades broke loose and men, horses, and cannon went flying fifty feet in the air. After the War Bratton settled back into his prewar life and even ventured into state politics.

Porter Alexander is another name familiar to Civil War buffs. As a colonel he commanded more than 160 pieces of artillery in the ferocious bombardment of Union General Meades's position on Cemetery Ridge prior to Pickett's charge on that blistering hot and fateful Friday afternoon, July 3, 1863. Alexander had grown up on a plantation near Washington, Georgia, in sight of the Savannah River. Following the War, he toyed with the idea of accepting a general's post offered by the government of Brazil, but he chose instead to teach mathematics at South Carolina College -- now USC. Alexander was a mathematical wiz in the engineering program and graduated near the top of his West Point class in 1857. He got the professorship when another Confederate icon of the state, A. C. Haskell, commander of the 7th South Carolina Cavalry, turned it down. Alexander stayed at Carolina from 1866 through 1872 -- a time when just fifty-seven students were enrolled and the university president made just $1000 yearly salary.

Because it appeared that South Carolina College would not survive the era of reconstruction, Alexander left and pursued engineering and management offers in Charlotte. President Cleveland sent him to arbitrate a border dispute between Costa Rica and Nicaragua in 1887. While deployed, Alexander surveyed and laid plans for a deep water canal that our government proposed digging across Central America. Alexander's proposal was "Plan B" if the present-day Panama Canal of later years had not come to fruition. He died in Savannah in 1910 and was remembered as one of the country's great engineering minds.

Ellison Capers was likely the last Confederate officer to be appointed to the rank of general, and he had barely six weeks to wear the rank of brigadier before he was captured at Bentonville in April 1865. Capers was a 1857 graduate of what is now known as The Citadel and he became an Episcopal priest following the War. In 1894 Ellison Capers was made bishop of South Carolina, and in 1904 he became Chancellor of The University of The South at Sewanee. This native son died in 1908, and The Citadel honored him a few decades later by naming the liberal arts building on the new campus for him.

One of Robert E. Lee's closest associates during the war was General William Nelson Pendleton, an artillery commander and a classmate of Lee and two other Confederate generals, Joseph E. Johnston and John B. McGruder. McGruder, hero of the Peninsula Campaign against McClellan, was Pendleton's roommate.

Pendleton became an Episcopal priest seven years after leaving the Academy, and he became rector of Grace Church in Lexington, Virginia, a charge that he kept until the outbreak of hostilities in 1861. Having been expertly trained as an artilleryman the priest followed the caissons to war. He commanded the famed Rockbridge Artillery, a unit that fought throughout the Shenandoah Valley under Stonewall Jackson. Pendleton's battery of guns was code-named Matthew, Mark, Luke, and John for the four gospels. It was Pendleton who was Porter Alexander's artillery superior at Gettysburg.

When Lee surrendered at Appomatox, General Pendleton rode back to Richmond with his commander. It was Pendleton who urged Lee to accept the offer of the presidency of Washington College -- the least lucrative offer of the many that General Lee received from around the South. Lee set the example for his fellow southerners by emphasizing faith, scholarship and civil pursuit. Robert E. Lee's career as a college president lasted a mere five years. The great man died shortly after presiding at the vestry meeting of Reverend Pendleton's Grace Church in Lexington on Wednesday afternoon, September 28, 1870. An hour later Lee sat at his dining room table in the president's house on the campus of Washington College (now Washington and Lee) and bowed his head to say grace. He opened his lips to pray but no words came -- and the old soldier expired.

Lee's old classmate and comrade in arms presided at the funeral service. Pendleton continued in his labors for the Lord until he, too, succumbed thirteen years later.

Money Man of the American Revolution Was Haym Solomon

Fighting a war with weapons and tactics is one matter; financing a war is a different business. Not only does an army travel on its stomach, but it also marches on shoe leather. Kings and dictators confiscate what their armies require. Lincoln used inflation and high-interest Yankee bonds to bankroll Hooker, Burnsides, Meade, and Grant. When Robert E. Lee's Army of Northern Virginia invaded Maryland and Pennsylvania, they paid for what they requisitioned -- with worthless Confederate dollars.

No American commander had a worse time financially than did George Washington, and no American congress has ever dithered and dallied as did the Continental Congress when the topic of war funding was broached. As Washington waged a war of attrition against the well-funded British military, he had to fret over how to make his payroll and how to pay his army's creditors.

In defense of Congress, Robert Morris was the official financer of the revolutionary army; however, it was New York immigrant Haym Solomon, a Polish Jew, who produced the money miracles when General Washington was in dire straits. Robert Morris was a native of Liverpool who came out to the colonies as a 13-year-old lad accompanying his tobacco merchant father. In time Morris became as shrewd a trader as any in Philadelphia and he caught the eye of newspaper "magnate-turned-revolutionary - Benjamin Franklin." Morris, Franklin, and George Washington were bound by the ideals of liberty and severance from British rule. Furthermore, the three men were members of the fraternal and secretive order of Free Masonry.

When George Washington won an unexpected victory over British forces at Princeton in January 1777, Parliament sanctioned more soldiers for British Generals Clinton and Cornwallis, but it also authorized covert financial shenanigans against the fledgling rebels -- subterfuge such as counterfeiting colonial paper money and discrediting American envoys in Holland and France.

Their plan was to cause Washington's army to mutiny from lack of pay and necessities.

Since Philadelphia was a city rife with Tory sentiment, the Continental Congress despaired of conducting any secret negotiations. A select committee of men known only within their own circle made the financial arrangements for the struggling American army. So perilous was the status of the army that often their existence was a day-to-day affair.

George Washington was almost as adept as a spymaster as he was at fighting the war of attrition. The great commander had a system for planting incorrect information on the status of his army to confuse his British pursuers. The Culper Ring in New York was one of many such disinformation ruses. Nathan Hale was a part of this ring, as was the mysterious Agent 355, believed to be a young woman who moved easily within the circle of British Major John Andre and other notables.

Because Robert Morris was constantly under surveillance, Washington resorted to someone of lower profile whom he could trust. One of Washington's youngest staff officers was Lieutenant-Colonel Isaac Franks, a son of the senior partner of the import-export firm of Levy-Franks in Philadelphia. Isaac Franks was barely out of his teens, yet he was forage master for Washington's army that lay encamped about Long Island. When Robert Morris found it nearly impossible to coerce financial contributions from the states for the war effort, Isaac Franks suggested that Washington contact his -- Franks' -- brother-in-law, the currency broker, Haym Solomon. In the hard war years that followed George Washington ordered his private couriers more than once to "Send for Haym Solomon."

Haym Solomon was a 36-year-old Polish Jew who'd immigrated to the colonies just one year prior to the outbreak of hostilities in 1776. Before the year was out, Haym Solomon had established himself in the import-export trade along New York's waterfront and he'd become a part of the John Lamb Sons of Liberty circle in that city. Lamb was one of the most zealous anti-British men on the continent -- years earlier his father had been deported to the colonies from London as a common thief. However, John Lamb was the catalyst for revolution among the business elites of the colony's leading port. Lamb kept up an active correspondence with hard-core revolutionaries such as Samuel Adams, Aedanus Burke, Patrick Henry, Richard Henry "Lighthorse Harry" Lee, and Charleston's Christopher Gadsden.

Solomon proved his worth as a spy for Washington as well as a finance man. On several occasions Solomon was captured by the British and he used his commanding knowledge of European languages to talk his way, or bribe his way out of prison. Reputedly, he persuaded over 500 Hessian soldiers to desert the British cause for the American side. There are so many legends circulating about Haym Solomon that it is difficult to discern the facts. He did have contact with the Dutch Jewish community on St. Eustatius in the Caribbean, and that settlement of traders was one of the main suppliers of French-made rifles and other war materiel to the patriots. When the British got too hot on Solomon's trail of colonial intrigue, he moved his operations to Philadelphia. Solomon was known to run a private bank and investment brokerage from the back room of Philadelphia's London Coffee House. Here he sold commercial paper, shares in trading ventures, and he made personal loans to the Declaration Signers from his accumulated fortune.

In 1781 George Washington received word that a large army under the command of the Count de Rochambeau would be able to coordinate one brief campaign with the patriot forces. That was when Washington determined to strike a desperate blow against Lord Cornwallis who was encamped close to the Chesapeake awaiting the British fleets of Admirals Graves and Rodney to evacuate his forces to New York.

Robert Morris and Haym Solomon went into overdrive to produce the finances to supply Washington and his allies in the costly venture of moving south toward Yorktown. Philadelphia had probably never seen such wheeling and dealing, and some fantastic schemes were devised to deceive the ever-present Tory spies that hung about the London Coffee House.

What's interesting to us in the Lowcountry is that Daniel deSaussure of Charleston was in 1781 a member of the financial cartel in Philadelphia that included Robert Morris and Haym Solomon. DeSaussure, a wealthy Carolina merchant, had studied in Switzerland, and so had Solomon. Some years later Daniel deSaussure became the president of the Charleston branch of the (1st) Bank of the United States located on the corner of Broad and Meeting Streets, now City Hall. At one juncture in the 1781 Yorktown financing, Haym Solomon ran afoul of even the lax colonial codes of financial propriety and was implicated in a $50,000 securities fraud. It was a critical moment in the funding of the patriot forces, and, for a while, it looked as though Solomon would be imprisoned by his own people as a huckster. Robert Morris sprang to the rescue and somehow got the tables turned on Haym's accuser and had that man arrested instead. At that point, Solomon threw his own fortune into the army's fund plus he sold another $20,000 in securities -- enough to purchase the critical supplies for Washington's army to move 200 miles south.

Of course, Washington and Rochambeau trapped Cornwallis at Yorktown. One of the ironies for the British was the fact that British Admiral George B. Rodney was too late arriving on the scene. He took a detour to destroy the Jewish settlement at St. Eustatius that had been supplying the colonists with weapons. Rodney burned their settlement, destroyed their small synagogue, and separated families and dispersed the St. Eustatius Jews all over the Caribbean as retribution for their aiding the American rebels.

Regrettably, Haym Solomon died shortly after the Revolutionary War, probably of tuberculosis contracted while a prisoner of the British in New York. He died penniless, having donated everything that he owned to the patriot cause. Attempts to receive restitution from congress fell on deaf ears, partly because it was all that Congress could do to pay a token pension to the soldiers.

During the war there were anti-Semitic cries raised against Haym Solomon and some of the other Jewish patriots who assisted in the financing of the cause. Solomon's 1781 Philadelphia newspaper editorial "I am a Jew" became one of the most eloquent pleas for religious understanding ever printed. The words, "I am a Jew; it is my own nation; I do not despair that we shall obtain every other privilege that we aspire to enjoy along with our fellow-citizens," have been cited in numerous patriotic essays.

Some admirers claim that Haym Solomon helped pen a draft of the Constitution before he died. Others claim that he and Morris devised the dollar sign, a clever reduction of the two marble columns entwined in ivy that are found on the 18th century Spanish-milled silver dollar known as the real, or pieces of eight. Some conspiratorial theorists believe that Haym Solomon was part of the shadowy Illuminati group that sought the overthrow of monarchs and the subsequent establishment of a one-world government.

No conspiracies have been pinned on the patriot Haym Solomon. Solomon is a true Son of Liberty, and in 1975 the U.S. Postal Service issued a stamp in his honor.

Burrsylvania and the Principality of Aaron I

Cable News arrived two centuries too late. Instead of droning on endlessly about the stimulus and which candidate can exaggerate more during our silly season, pretend what it would have been like to have had cable way back when -- for instance, like when our vice-president was on the lam from shooting the former secretary of the treasury and he attempted to set himself up as a king in the Southwest! In the early days of the republic, we had some ripping stories.

Two-hundred years ago this grand republic was nothing like what it is today. We had 17 states by the 1804 election, and back in those days the Wild West was the region of the Mississippi Valley. The fundamentals of what we call "Americanism" had not hardened into the core of unquestionable truths that we take for granted today. America was like wet cement -- great men desired to write in broad strokes across its surface.

In Europe Napoleon was completely redesigning the political landscape according to his own vision. Bonaparte toppled kings and potentates -- replacing them with minions of his own choosing. In the winter of 1803 the little big man Napoleon negotiated the sale of 820,000 square miles, or approximately 525 million acres, in the heartland of North America to the United States government for 60 million francs, or 3 cents per acre. In today's currency that equals 11.2 million dollars. Our population was under 6 million people, and just one in twenty over here lived in an urban setting. Quite a few Americans dreamed Bonapartist dreams on this continent.

Americans call it the Louisiana Purchase, but in actuality, it was a Napoleonic Yard Sale. In March 1804, the funds were transferred, and a Jefferson-led America had rolled the dice boldly, waging over 11 million dollars to double the nation's land mass. The total revenue of the government was just over 12 million dollars at the time. In a roundabout way the U.S. treasury funds for the Louisiana Purchase ended up financing Napoleon's Wars of the Third Coalition -- Wertingen, Ulm, Austerlitz.

The Third Coalition was pained at the American enthusiasm for doing a mutually beneficial financial deal with its nemesis. The armies of Britain,

Austria, Russia, and Sweden were strewn across Europe like so many balls on a pool table. The Battle of Austerlitz where Bonaparte routed the superior forces of Austria and Russia was such a master stroke of military genius that the tactics are still standard fare for cadets at West Point, St.Cyr, and Sandhurst today.

As Napoleon redrew the map of Europe and the idea of Manifest Destiny had not yet taken hold of the American psyche, many men schemed of founding their own dynasties a la Bonaparte. Even Daniel Boone and his son, Dan Morgan Boone, made a gargantuan land deal with Spain -- only to have Spain transfer the land out from under them to France. Then three weeks later, France sold the land to the Federal government in Washington. For a brief time Boone was commandant, more like lord, of a fiefdom the size of the duchy of Cornwall. Americans' dreams were limited only by their imagination in the early 1800s.

Article III, Section 3 of our constitution boldly states that territories are under the jurisdiction of Congress, and it clearly lays out the procedure for acquiring statehood. Though the Constitution was only 20 years old, Aaron Burr put the ideals of his own peers and associates to the gravest of tests. Burr proceeded with his Grande Scheme to defraud the U.S. of much of its new acquisition. With Jonathan Dayton, his college chum from Princeton, Burr set off on an odyssey down the Ohio River that still has historians scratching their heads in disbelief.

Burr had just killed Alexander Hamilton in a duel at Wehawken, New Jersey, just across the harbor from New York. It was the final episode in a long, bitter feud between the two patriots. Hamilton had thrown support to arch-rival Jefferson to break the 1800 Presidential election deadlock. The "Revolution of 1800," witnessed the House of Representatives having to horse-trade a victor out of a 63-63 electoral tie between Aaron Burr and Thomas Jefferson. Hamilton angered Burr by persuading fellow federalist Congressman James Bayard of Delaware to switch his vote in the controversial election. Hamiliton said, "There is no doubt that upon every virtuous and prudent calculation Jefferson is to be preferred. He [Jefferson] is by far not so dangerous a man and he has pretensions to character." Of Burr, Hamilton stated publicy, "If we have an embryo-Caesar in the United States, 'tis Burr."

There are darker rumors afloat, as well. It was whispered after the duel that Hamilton had made some disparaging remarks about Burr's unusually close relationship to his [Burr's] daughter, Theodosia Burr Alston -- the wife of South Carolina Governor Joseph Alston. The Alstons lived in Charleston and at their plantation on the Waccamaw River near Georgetown.

Burr was unquestionably the best pistol shot in America -- at least his friends proclaimed him to be. Hamilton misfired and Burr drilled him through the abdomen -- insuring that the death would be certain and painful. However angry Burr was, the former vice-president knew that his political career in the United States was over for ever. Yet a new political career even greater than being president of a paltry republic might be awaiting him in the American West.

Jonathan Dayton, a wild and ambitious Princeton dropout from New Jersey was Burr's sole confidante in the hasty flight from justice in the Hamilton duel. Dayton had been a revolutionary war soldier at age 15. He'd served as clerk of the fledgling House of Representatives at age 21, and he'd lied about his age when he ran for Congress in 1791. The Constitution maintains that one must be 25 years of age in order to serve in congress. It appears that Dayton was merely 22 at the time.

Just how much Burr revealed to young Drayton as they floated on a barge down the Ohio River is uncertain. Everywhere they stopped Aaron Burr was recognized as a man of authority. Word of his murderous duel had not preceded him, so he basked in the glory of being a former Revolutionary War colonel, a V - P, and son of the late president of Princeton University, then known as the College of New Jersey. If that weren't enough glory for one man, remember, too, that his grandfather was Jonathan Edwards, the most famous evangelistic preacher in America until the heyday of Billy Graham. Burr persuaded simple farmers of the Ohio Valley to follow him to a rendezvous of glory at the mouth of the Mississippi. Many followed in his wake and some even went on ahead of him -- not knowing for certain what was to occur.

At Blennerhassett Island in the middle of the Ohio River, Aaron Burr tipped his hand, so to speak, to wealthy Irish immigrant Harmon Blennerhassett. Herman Blennerhassett had emigrated from Ireland with an idea of setting himself up as a lord of a kingdom in this new world utopia. Even Jonathan Dayton became suspicious of their conversation. Burr had a great amount of money with him -- some of his funds had been entrusted to him by his son-in-law, Joseph Alston of Charleston. Burr bought 40,000 acres across the river from Blennerhassett, supposedly as a staging area for future operations.

As the flotilla of pseudo-conspirators made their way toward the Mississippi delta and the newly acquired city of New Orleans, it was clear that most in the rag-tag operation thought they were going to slaughter pirates or Spaniards or Mexicans, and gain for themselves plunder and free land. Only Burr and perhaps Blennerhassett knew for sure.

Upon arriving in New Orleans Burr went into hasty consultation with U.S. Army Governor - General James Wilkinson. Did Burr know already that Wilkinson was in the secret employ of Spanish agents who conspired to get the Napoleonic lands back? No one can be sure. Popular legend has it that in a New Orleans Catholic church, seated in the rear row as Franz Lizst's Mass in C-Minor was performed, Wilkinson and Burr whispered inaudibly. Each man thought he had the other man's pledge. A month later when Wilkinson turned Burr in to the U.S. government for treason against the United States, the sorry saga became a "he said, he said" affair. Wilkinson's aide was Colonel William C.C. Claiborne of Virginia. Claiborne became suspicious of Burr as soon as the ragtag flotilla reached New Orleans. The Burr operation looked like a band of filibusterers perhaps on their way to Cuba. Cliborne sent secret messages to President Jefferson.

To save his own hide from betrayal by Burr, Wilkinson betrayed Burr first. In the long extradition trip to the federal court house in Richmond, Aaron Burr spent at least one night in the county jail of Chester, South Carolina. At the trial, which was tailor-made for television if only it had existed, many witnesses fretted over what testimony to give. Even Andrew Jackson had had long conversations with Burr during this bizarre eight-month adventure. In the end, Burr's close political ally, Chief Justice John Marshall, ruled "inadequate evidence for conviction" on the charge of treason.

Burr's daughter, Theodosia disappeared with much money and her father's personal papers during this intense drama. Apparently, she was on her way to Richmond to console him when her ship foundered off Hatteras.

Burr left the country and lived abroad, probably trying to curry some favor with Napoleon. A few years later the broken man returned to America and married former brothel owner, Madame Eliza Jumel, one of the wealthiest people in New York. Madame Jumel was beautiful and as refined as a woman in her position could be -- she, herself, was also the daughter of a prostitute. Burr died leaving the most bizarre legacy of any American ever. Blennerhassett's mansion was sacked by the Ohio militia, but Blennerhassett lived to become a major speculator in lands and commodities. Burr's associate Jonathan Dayton was honored by having Dayton, Ohio, named for him. Did the two men, Burr and Dayton, plan to establish Burrsylvania as the testimony against Burr charged--and did Burr plan to set himself up as king? Cable news would have had a field day.

A Salute To The Carolina Upcountry

Getting away for a Fall weekend is a Carolina Lowcountry tradition that dates back to the Model T. Point that Tin-Lizzy north by northwest to Highway 11 and you will be rewarded with an artist's palate of color from hardwoods we hardly know in this coastal plain. You'll renew your reverence for the Divine, and somewhere along the way you'll gain a new appreciation for a completely different side of old Carolina. It's about time that we Lowcountry raise a toast to our cousins in the upstate.

Where'd the angst originate that propels the oft referred to Lowcountry / Upcountry rift? One fellow whose business it is to know such arcane stuff believes the origin to be rooted in the courthouse rather than the church sanctuary or the legislative hall. Long before political matters divided Carolinians and before the two Carolinas, North and South, were established, there was the irksome issue of having to travel to Charleston to record a land transaction -- or any other legal record. Charleston's first brush with tourism probably came with the discovery that inns, taverns, stables, and even brothels flourished during the seasons when the courts were in session.

We Charlestonians lost our monopoly on all things legal in the 1780s when Patrick Colhoun --yes, he spelled it that way -- brought an armed upstate militia to the corner of King and Broad to demand that our legislature move to the center of the State. Fortunately for us, the ancestors of the secession fire-eaters kept a cool head and didn't press the matter. These country boys had just run Cornwallis out of the state and they were in no mood to quibble with men who wore lace collars and sipped tea. Besides, the whole backcountry was still under arms in the command of that fighting Presbyterian elder, General Andrew Pickens. The reign of the City of Charleston had run its course -- 1680 to 1790.

Three-hundred feet of altitude definitely gives a different perspective on things. The air is different, the sky is more blue, the nights are cooler, and even the birds sound different. The average altitude of a location in upstate South Carolina is slightly more than 300 feet above sea-level. We Lowcountry lovers must subtract 250 to 290 (feet) from the average. Does altitude make a difference in health and attitude? Some sociologists believe that it does.

Dig down a hundred feet in our coastal soil and you'll be lucky to find grey marl. Almost anywhere in the Upstate where wells are dug, the drill needs an industrial diamond bit to chew through granite. It'd take a geologist to describe how drinking water bubbling up through marl differs from water coming through granite fissures. Our kin in the Upcountry tell us they have iron in their physical constitution and that they drink it in daily through their tap water. What that theory implies about us, I do not know.

Our worship roots lie in the Episcopal tradition while theirs are Southern Baptist, or Methodist. When they were clogging on the front porch we were Dirty Dancing at the Ocean Drive Beach pavilion. When they sneaked a beer into the dorm at college, the Lowcountry boys produced labels obtained from the Red Dot store. However, Beach Music united us briefly in the early 1960s.

The Upstate has its own ways of thinking and doing things. They always have. When we had pink brick imported from England in the early 1700s and slate quarried from Wales for our roofs, they had roughhewn timber cabins with deer or bear hides curing on the outside walls. When we drank Madeira they sipped applejack. When we went to war our uniforms looked European. They shunned uniforms; instead the colonial fighters from the Upstate wore buckskin or a rough fabric known as linsey-woolsey. When wronged in the city our men sought legal counsel -- even way back in the 1700s. When wronged in the crossroad they reached for their blade. No one in colonial South Carolina knew the differences of the two sections better than did William Henry Drayton, William Tennent, and Richard Furman. Those men ventured into the high hills of Carolina on the eve of the Revolution to persuade the backwoodsmen to enlist their aid in the defense of Charleston. Of course, it was Moses Thomson's legendary Raccoon Company from the Congarees that defended Breach Inlet on June 28, 1776.

Today, the Upstate boasts a lower unemployment than we do, and their literacy rate is higher on average. They went to Germany and recruited BMW. We went to Seattle and won Boeing. They have Clemson, we have The Citadel and MUSC. A nuclear reactor at Oconee generates electricity for thousands while we rely upon hydroelectricity. They have the Greenville Symphony Orchestra directed by world-famous Maestro Edvard Tchivzhel. In fact, their symphony performed Beethoven's Fifth on October 26th to a packed concert hall at the Peace Center. We have classical music, also, and Sirrus Radio still charges about what a year's balcony subscription used to cost when we had the beloved Charleston Symphony.

When our section boasted of 4 signers of the Declaration, the folks of the Upcountry were more interested in the new ironworks of Solliman Hill and William Wofford. Rice planters like Isaac Hayne invested in the Hill ironworks. Indeed, it was one of the first over-the-counter stocks traded in the state. The Tyger River mills were know far and wide for the quality of their flour in the 1740s. Theirs was the benchmark standard for Carolina cooks. Coming into modern times the Upstate produced J. Strom Thurmond and he gained national acclaim for his accent. Charleston produced Jimmy Byrnes, but he soon claimed Aiken as his residence, and then Spartanburg. In recent years we prided ourselves in Fritz Hollings and Burnet Maybank. They put Dick Riley in the governor's mansion. We countered with Jim Edwards. They partied when Jim Hodges of Lancaster became governor. We rejoiced when Mark Sanford was sworn in. The beat goes on and on. There's a method in our madness, I'm sure.

When newspapers ruled the current events scene, it was Tom Waring of the *News and Courier* who presided over the state's unofficial college of editors. It was Waring who did much to persuade Thurmond to switch parties in 1964. *The State* soon gained regional notice under the very able William D. "Bill" Workman.

When radio talk shows began in the 1950s and 1960s, nowhere in South Carolina had a conservative voice on the air comparable to the persuasive and erudite Frank Best, Sr., of WDIX in Orangeburg. His weekly radio editorial helped put Floyd Spence into Congress for the Second Congressional District. Spence became Chairman of the House Armed Forces Committee when the Republicans swept the elections of 1995.

In the all-important measure of pulchritude the Upstate has won hands-down in the number of crowned Miss South Carolina contestants. We have Jane Jenkins of John's Island, who won in 1979. Crystal Garrett and Jessica Eddins, both Lowcountry natives, have helped towards evening the score by winning the crown in 2007 and 2003, respectively.

We will continue to tussle with the Upstate over spending measures in the Legislature. Clemson will always have the best chance of any state school of winning a national championship, Gamecock baseball not withstanding. We'll disagree forever on highway funding and the need for two medical schools, but one thing is forever engraved in stone -- the Carolina Upcountry is the place to be for leaf season in the Fall!

Goodbye Milton Friedman, Hello Disaster Capitalism With Naomi Klein

So what's to become of Middle America since the darling of the new left has co-opted the longtime icon of the conservative right? If you're a follower of blogs that cater to social justice and progressive politics, that's precisely what has happened. Naomi Klein of the Canadian Centre for Policy Alternatives (CCPL) is clever, cute, and quick to poke a humorous jab at conservative theorists and pundits. For those who came of age between Pearl Harbor and the Tet Offensive, the political landscape has experienced more upheavals than Edward Craven-Walker's legendary lava lamp. Since the heart of most meaningful political disputes these days is fundamentally economic in nature, it stands to reason that an assault on conservative economic guro Milton Friedman is akin to a lunge for the jugular of the middle-class mindset.

If one has lived on the right side of the political divide for any time at all, he or she owns a copy of Free To Choose, the 1980 New York Times Best Seller written by Nobel Prize economist Milton Friedman. Friedman's office at Swift Hall, East 59th Street, University of Chicago was ground zero for Reaganite conservatives. Even today a group photo of Friedman with fellow economists Stigler, von Hayek, Fogel, Becker, and Posner comes close to rivaling the famed 1985 Chicago Bears "Black and Blues Brothers" poster.

Free To Choose (1980) did for conservative thinking in America what Betty Crocker did for baking brownies. Friedman possessed all the acumen necessary to condense complex quantitative theorems and convey them in layman's terms. For a few years Friedman's office was just a few feet away from that of his left-of-center colleague, Paul Samuelson. The most brilliant of the "right" and the "left" free market thinkers shared the same elevator, copier, secretary, coffee pot, and restroom. Both Friedman and Samuelson were Nobel Laureates. However, The University of Chicago has had no fewer than 85 Nobel Laureates associated in one way or another with its various departments. Yet, no scholar gained favor more among conservatives more so than Friedman. Today, Friedman is being picked apart by the "new left." His essays on the national economic response to catastrophic disasters is providing fuel for left-wing think tanks such as Klein's CCPL in Montreal.

When Hurricane Hugo pounded down upon the Louisiana coast, Milton Friedman was quoted as saying, "Freedom as the ultimate goal and the individual as the ultimate entity in the society." After a crisis has struck, a new administration has some six to nine months in which to achieve major changes; if it does not act decisively during that period, it will not have another such opportunity." According to Klein the hurricane that flooded New Orleans unleashed a Pandora's box of "new right" policy initiatives. From Chapter 20: "Disaster Apartheid" of her book, *Shock Doctrine*, Klein lashes out at Friedman: "In [an] editorial written only a few months after Hurricane Katrina hit, Milton Friedman states that the storm gave New Orleans 'an opportunity to radically reform the educational system' and called for replacing the public school system with an unpopular voucher program." Klein accuses Paul Teller of the Congressional House Republican Study Committee of circulating a petition in the aftermath of Katrina for "Congress to withdraw tariffs on Canadian lumber and [to allow] drilling in the Arctic National Wildlife Refuge" -- things that "have nothing to do with Hurricane Katrina," but everything to do with enhancing the Republican national agenda.

When Milton Friedman wrote his highly acclaimed *Capitalism and Freedom* published by the University of Chicago Press in 1962, Americans had two years earlier by narrow margin elected Kennedy, the brash Bostonian progressive, over the oft-time stodgy California moderate, Richard M. Nixon. To our north, the Canadians were crippling the governmental grip of their Progressive Conservative Party led by Prime Minister John George Diefenbaker. Social progressivism much like the post-World War II European model of politics was making creditable advances upon middle-class thinking in North America.

Friedman's 1962 Capitalism and Freedom book tour became something akin to an evangelical movement among conservatives in the heartland and deep south. Friedman was acclaimed on southern campuses as a harbinger of the new-styled second wave of modern conservative thought. Young, crewcut college males wearing blazers and the narrow necktie of the era posed with the forty-something Friedman to proclaim that Kennedy-style liberalism would most certainly be challenged in the coming national election of 1964.

Part of Friedman's sizzling success on his campus tour was his dry wit and ability to turn a phrase of his opponent to his own calculated advantage. For example, on page 5 of Capitalism and Freedom the eminent Chicago professor co-opts the word "liberal," devalues it in its contemporary 1960s context, and redirects his readers to the etymology of the phrase. The term "liberal" derives from 14th century France and means literally "befitting free men, noble, generous," from liberalis "noble, generous." Friedman had a way when speaking to large audiences to curl out the word "free" as if mocking the numerous restraints then being imposed on business and society by the democratic majority. The Goldwater movement was sparked, in part, by the Midwest book tour made by Friedman on sabbatical from the University of Chicago Economics Department in 1962.

The tragic event that occurred in Dallas on November 22, 1963, did not leave our nation leaderless, but both parties were at a loss as how to proceed in the aftermath of JFK's assassination. The Kennedy domestic agenda was in shambles and so were his foreign policy initiatives. Lyndon Johnson began to lean heavily on former "whiz kid," Cal Berkeley and Harvard Business school standout, Robert McNamara. "Mac," as his colleagues at Ford Motor Company called him when he was CEO, had almost been fired for being the only man who voted against going into production with the Edsel automobile. When the Edsel automobile failed and Mac's own pet project, the Falcon, succeeded beyond dreams, the Democratic pols in Washington called the Ford executive into their inner-circle to be a catalyst for something relatively new -- a policy "think tank."

Seeing that two can play this game, Milton Friedman privately encouraged prominent political conservatives to finance so-called "think tanks" to counter the anti-capitalist ideals of the social progressives. The Hoover Institute, the American Enterprise Institute, and, most notably, the Heritage Foundation came into their own following the 1964 defeat of Barry Goldwater.

Though Goldwater was blown away in the electoral count, 486 to 52, conservatives across America were amazed at their first-ever attempt to compete on a national ticket. The Friedman conservatives looked at 1964 as a superb start of something noble and imminently possible in the future. Hollywood political activist Ronald Reagan gave a stemwinder speech for Goldwater at the Cow Palace convention center in San Francisco, and everyone knows the rest of that story.

Since quite a portion of the American progressive agenda of the 20th century hails from Bismarck's policies in the newly unified Germany of the 1870s, it is conceivable that the Friedman idea of developing contingency economic policy plans came from studies of the Bismarck era. The German military developed the general staff and command concept in the age of Bismarck. When some unexpected calamity occurred on Germany's border, the Kaiser had a plethora of options preconfigured and push-button ready. In fact, the general staff concept aided the idea of blitzkrieg in warfare as much as did the railroad and the telegraph. Applying the aggressive, yet highly efficient German ideal to politics may have be Milton Friedman's grand legacy.

A leading automotive insurance company has employed an effective advertising campaign featuring the "Life comes at you fast" series of everyday commuter mishaps. The ads portray the need for the consumer to have preexisting plans for an emergency. Naomi Klein, the much adored and highly effective spokesperson of the "New Left" has returned the favor to the late Milton Friedman for hijacking the "liberal" idea. Klein has seized upon Friedman's phrase, "freedom as the ultimate goal and the individual as the ultimate entity in the society," and redirected it to the political left as a battering ram against conservative ideology and as a way of fighting fire with fire.

Naomi Klein's book, *The Shock Doctrine: The Rise of Disaster Capitalism* (Holt: c. 2007) exposes what Klein believes to be sinister manipulation of catastrophic events by conservatives. Her other books Fences and Windows (2002) and No Logo (2000) are both unabashed criticism of "run-wild capitalism" in a deregulated market. Klein's message is enhanced by her winsome looks and wit; however, in defense of Friedman, she seldom connects with the blatant failure of many of the new left's high-cost social policies in Europe.

It's An Honor To Vote In S.C. First Congressional District

This Is Not Your Father's First Congressional District. The clock has chimed another hour. And so it goes every two years in this great country. Remember Ben Adler? He used to write for Newsweek when that periodical was a newsstand staple. Today, Adler writes for a host of syndicated outlets: Politico.com, Atlantic Monthly, Columbia Journalism Review, to note a smattering of the outlets for his well-turned phrases. Recently, the S.C. 1st Congressional District race caught erudite Ben's attention enough for him to remark: " . . . the ability of South Carolina's white Republicans to get behind a black candidate, even a conservative one, may strike some political observers as remarkable, particularly because South Carolina is arguably the most unlikely of all Southern states to host such a racial breakthrough."

Welcome to a rapidly changing New South. The popular black businessman Tim Scott handily defeated a field of seven candidates in our recent congressional race, and then he cruised to a run-off win over his friend Paul Thurmond. This congressional contest may have been the most civil election contest anywhere in the country. Before this recent election there were 39 black members of Congress. Today, there are 42, and the South produced two of the new black members. Allen West of Florida's 22nd Congressional District will be joining Tim Scott as another of the newly elected black Republicans. Like Scott, West has a powerful success story of his own.

West and Tim Scott are already the toast of the Republican party Congressmen gathering at L'Enfant Hotel and the Capitol Club in downtown D.C. As a highly-decorated Army officer who saw service in Gulf War I, West was forced out of the military and fined $5000 when it was learned that he had violated articles 128 and 134 of the UCMJ, the Uniform Code of Military Justice. When a prisoner was brought in for questioning about Iraqi army units still operating on Colonel West's perimeter, he clammed up and wouldn't divulge a thing. West pulled his pistol and fired a round over the Iraqi's head.

At that moment the detainee cooperated fully. Helicopter gunships came in and destroyed the enemy units that were in position to ambush West's convoy. Colonel West, now Congressman-elect West (R-Fla.), told the military court prior to his 2002 dismissal from active duty, "If it's about the lives of my men and their safety, I'd go through hell with a gasoline can." Ninety-five members of Congress, mostly Republicans, signed a petition in support of him -- to no avail. Allen West's 22nd Florida Congressional District stretches from West Palm Beach to a few miles below Boca Raton. That was Republican territory in the divisive presidential race of 2000. Tim Scott's district reaches from Kiawah Island to North Myrtle Beach. A quick look at the 2000 S.C. Congressional districting map makes us wish we could have been a fly on the wall observing how the back room pols went about drawing up districts 1, 2, and 6. The House seat that Tim Scott will occupy in just 49 days dates to March, 1789. That was when the old 13 original states mapped out their congressional districts. Our state's population was 249,000 and we were allowed 5 congressional seats. Each congressman represented approximately 50,000 citizens. Today the number 12 times greater. S.C.'s First District seat was initially occupied by the staunch pro-Washington supporter, William Loughton Smith. Besides being one of the founders of the Federalist party, Smith was also an ardent pro-slavery man -- one of the Charleston men who were prepared to derail the new constitution unless it contained phrases that'd preserve the "peculiar institution," as slavery was referred to in polite circles.

Charleston aristocrat planter-lawyer William Loughton Smith brought the same type of credentials to our first Congress that Tories in London's House of Commons possessed. Like the Tories, Smith had been educated at Westminster and the Middle Temple of the Inns of Court in London. Going them one better, Smith had pursued additional academic work at the University of Geneva. Prior to his election to Congress, an honor accorded him by the state legislature, not the voters directly, William Loughton Smith had served in the state house and as warden (mayor) of the City of Charleston.

In the 18th century a Congressman's pay was essentially an honorarium instead of a salary. Wealthy men were expected to give of their time in service to the country. For the first few decades the country avoided the "career politician" syndrome even though a few families, such as the Adamses, did seem to linger a long while in public service. The idea prevailed of good men being summoned by the call of their country. Power through tenure arose during the Jacksonian era.

Congressman William Loughton Smith's Tory counterparts in the House of Commons were almost like hereditary peers of the realm. Their families dominated a constituency and a seat regularly passed from father to son, or at least to a man that was acceptable to the dominant family. Herberts, Pelhams, Duncombes, Sandys, Barings, and Peels aplenty crop up for 150 years running in British parliament. That practice never took root on our side of the Atlantic for, even in Charleston, there was enough wealth and difference of opinion to contest every biennial congressional election.

The life-stories of the thirty-five men and one woman who have represented the coast in the S.C. 1st Congressional District render a wonderful insight into the evolving nature of this great republic. The First District of this state is one of the oldest districts in the federal system. The original boundaries were configured by men who had hammered out the Constitution and campaigned for its ratification by a reluctant upstate.

The old first districts of the original 13 states are unique political entities within our grand federal scheme. Virginia's First Congressional District reaches from Aquia Harbor on the Chesapeake to Gloucester Point. Williamsburg, Fredericksburg, and Jamestown are among its principal townships. Mount Vernon is included, as is Stratford, the ancestral home of the Lees. Pennsylvania's First District includes Philadelphia, Chester, Darby, and Yeadon -- the core of the colonial state that gave rise to Franklin. Massachusetts' First District was drawn far to the west of its principal city of Boston. Fisher Ames of Dedham was the leading man in the state at the time. He'd surpassed Sam Adams in influence. The old first districts of the original 13 states are of interest to history lovers on election nights.

As long as American politics was dominated by strong-central-government Federalists, Charleston lawyers filled the billet. Thomas Pinckney and Thomas Lowndes represented us up until the age of Jefferson. With Jefferson's agrarian-based politics our district witnessed a political change. Robert Marion, a planter from St. Stephen and cousin of Francis Marion, became the democratic-republican Congressman from the 1st District. The democratic-republicans were the forerunners of the modern Democratic party and their Charleston meeting place was upstairs at 235 Meeting Street -- now a popular barbeque eatery.

Langdon Cheves, Henry Middleton, and Charles Pinckney of Snee Farm held the 1st District seat until the age of Jackson. Andrew Jackson's election in 1828 changed the face of politics forever in this country and the Jacksonian Democrat was a new breed never seen before in the annals of democracy. Joel

Poinsett was that new man for the 1st District, and he and Mendel Rivers of the 20th century are the most significant men to hold this particular office.

Henry Laurens Pinckney, son of Charles Pinckney, was elected to Congress from here on the Nullification Party ticket in 1833. He served two terms and opposed the policies of Jackson even to the point of advocating secession. Hugh Swinton Legare, a Charleston lawyer, writer, and the greatest classical scholar of his time in this country, campaigned and won the seat back for the Democrats in 1837.

John McQueen of Society Hill represented us at the time of secession, and he continued by representing this district in the Confederate Congress. He was the first graduate of U.N.C.-Chapel Hill to hold high office in South Carolina. Ben Franklin Whittlemore, a carpetbagger from Massachusetts, was our Congressman during Reconstruction, and he was the first republican to hold the office. In the 1960s the Charleston Republicans had to overcome the stigma of this era in order to win their initial local races.

Tim Scott stands on the shoulders of giants -- men such as Turner Logan, Democrat representative, 1921-1925; Thomas McMillan, Democrat, 1925-1939, and a lawyer, professional baseball player, and baseball coach at The Citadel; and a host of fine representatives including the great L. Mendel Rivers, Mendel Davis, Tommy Hartnett, Arthur Ravenel, Jr., Mark Sanford, and Henry Brown. Clara Gooding McMillan, widow of deceased Congressman Thomas McMillan, served this district in Congress from 1939 to 1941.

Ben Adler's remarks about South Carolina politics and our own Tim Scott reflect how far we have come in two centuries of biennial elections. He's the 36th elected representative to serve the district in its 222 year history, and he's the second African-American to hold the office. Joseph Hayne Rainey, a barber and former slave from Georgetown, served the district as a Republican during Reconstruction. We wish Tim Scott and the entire 112th Congress success with the myriad of problems that beset us.

Anthony Kennedy's Seat On Supreme Court Once Belonged To John Rutledge

What a blessed thing it was that historians left out the "begats" when they chronicled who succeeded whom in those august chambers United States Supreme Court. Back in July, 2009, Nick Summers created a very clever chart for Newsweek entitled. "Who Died And Made You Supreme Court Justice?" Summers' labors constitute one of the year's few journalistic highlights for that money-losing periodical. What catches the eye of the Charlestonian, however, is that, from John Rutledge's swearing in as the fifth and final justice of the Supreme Court in 1789, no fewer than 12 successor justices in 221 years have presided from his spot on the high bench -- Anthony Kennedy occupying it at the moment.

Nick Summers' clever chart gives us succession at a glance, but it cannot give perspective. The history of our top court and its personnel gets bottom drawer billing in American history texts. In Great Britain, until a couple of generations ago, those privileged to get an education read lengthy excerpts from the four-volume set, The Lives of the Chief Justices of England by Lord Campbell. Instructors in England's finest schools found a way to work into their lectures readings from Campbell's ten-volume set of The Lives of the Lord Chancellors and Keepers of the Great Seal Until the Reign of King George IV. Thomas Acre, Sir Edmund Coke, Thomas Erskine, John Philpot Curran -- the list of legal notables hailing from Inner Temple and Middle Temple is legion. This ancient legal institution was the entity that ruled on the legality of William and Mary's reign in 1688. No doubt the American colonials who were educated here rubbed shoulders with the finest lawminded men in western civilization. Yet, with all its heraldry, high-drama, and consequence, there are few who can make sense of the complex renderings that proceed from court chambers. And the evolution of the law is less known among us than, say, the evolution of the amoeba.

For historians and the general public alike, reading court history is akin to learning to appreciate dry burgundy wine. The trick with both is to make it a regular part of your diet. We, who make up the area which once was known exclusively as Christ Church Parish, should be aware that one of the five original justices on the bench of that first high court session in the Fall of 1789 was our John Rutledge.

Rutledge was the last one of the five to be nominated by President Washington, though all five names went to the Senate for confirmation over a ten-day period. Though he was the final name, Rutledge possessed on paper, at least, the most impressive credentials -- for he alone had been educated as an English barrister twenty-five years prior at the Middle Temple of London, one of the famous Four Inns of Court that have trained English jurists since the Middle Ages.

Forget not that Rutledge had served as governor of this state during the darkest days of the American Revolution -- part of that time hiding out in the Orangeburg area between the old Bruce house on Russell Street and sometimes astride his horse deep in the morasses of nearby Bull Swamp. It wasn't for nothing that the man was known affectionately as "the dictator" by patriots following the successful conclusion of the War. And, like so many of the Founding Fathers, he paid dearly to a pillaging British army for his political beliefs. Rutledge coordinated with Generals Greene, Marion, Sumter, and Pickens from his saddle, and the governor's office was wherever his saddlebags rested.

Justice John Rutledge became Chief Justice John Rutledge in 1795 when our nation's first chief justice resigned in order to accept his election as governor of New York. Rutledge had resigned his seat on the high court just three years after his swearing in. There was very little to do on the high bench -- the court heard just nine cases in its first session. The man who at age 21 had represented Christ Church parish in the colony's Provincial Assembly returned to his home state to become chief justice of the South Carolina Supreme Court, as it was a court of greater importance in the early days of the Republic.

In Rutledge's day, the rights of man was a battle cry heard from here to France. However, the underlying truth was that rights were determined by propertied men, and no type of revolution could derail that apparent natural right. John Rutledge saw no contradiction between slavery and the Bill of Rights. From his youth he had witnessed men of wealth and influence aspire to serve the new republic in every capacity. A letter in the Charles Cotesworth Pinckney collection dated 1753 shows just how important London culture was to the Carolina Lowcountry. Here are a few of the Charleston families Pinckney discusses as having sons boarding in English schools: Izard, Rutledge, Middleton, Drayton, Lynch, Grimke, Trapier, Heyward, Moultrie, and Hume. Others such as Fayssoux, Chandler, and Harris were at Edinburgh, and Bull had a son pursuing medicine in Leyden. This type of elite education was not rampant across the colonies, however.

John Rutledge's associate justices were well-versed in law even though none had had the advantages abroad that the Charlestonian's wealth had afforded him. John Jay, age 44 at time of selection, was Washington's pick as the first chief justice. He was the son of Huguenots and he grew up in Rye on the Hudson, above New York. Jay's education was at King's College, now Columbia University. As with the other justices, his judicial interests centered on the protection of property rights.

James Wilson, one of the first associate justices, was born near Saint Andrews, Scotland. He was a true "child of the Scottish Enlightenment" and a devoted political disciple of David Hume. Wilson was 45 when he was called to the bench. He'd read law under the tutelage of fellow Declaration signer, John Dickinson, a man only ten years Wilson's senior. James Wilson was one of those brilliant attorneys for which the expression "you'll need a Philadelphia lawyer" was coined. Poor fellow, he was actually thrown into debtors' prison for a while --as was our own General Moultrie! Wilson died on a visit to Edenton, North Carolina, right up the coast from us. Wilson got his great wish to bring Baron Montesquieu's "separation of powers" concept into being. French aristocrat Montesquieu's radical for the times book, The Spirit of The Laws (1748), theorized the political integrity that would arise from splitting a monarch's power into three separate but equal branches--executive, legislative, and judicial. Of course, Louis XV was not amused. Montesquieu's book was the most consulted reference book during the Constitutional convention in 1787.

William Cushing and John Blair round out the famous five first justices of the U.S. Supreme Court. Cushing, of Massachusetts, was the only one of the first five to stay on the bench for any length of time. John Blair, Jr., of Williamsburg, Virginia, was the most renowned of the legal scholars on the bench in the 18th century. Before ascending to the top court which sat for a year in New York and then a decade in Philadelphia prior to relocating permanently in the District of Columbia, Blair founded the College of William and Mary and served as its first president. The Supreme Court lagged in equality with the other two branches of government, as every school child does know, until the landmark case, Marbury

v. Madison U.S. (1 Cranch) 137 (1803) was cleverly used by Chief Justice John Marshall to develop the process known as judicial review.

John Rutledge was chosen as a recess appointment for chief justice of the court when Jay left to serve as governor of New York in 1795. However, Rutledge was not confirmed by the Senate. Reasons of mental instability were rumored about Washington, D.C. Rutledge suffered bouts of severe depression that may have been associated with the death of his wife a few years earlier. Oliver Ellsworth succeeded to the post in his stead.

Anthony Kennedy's Seat On Supreme Court Once Belonged To Our John Rutledge By using the Nick Summer Newsweek (July 20, 2009) guide to the justices of the Court, we see that John Roberts holds down the seat first occupied by John Jay of New York. Sonia Sotomayor sits on the bench once occupied by legal scholar James Willson of Virginia. William Cushing's seat is held by Stephen Breyer. Blair's seat is now John Paul Stevens' and, of course, Anthony Kennedy has the Rutledge slot. The sixth seat was inaugurated with Thomas Todd in 1807, and the number seven justice was created with John McKinley in 1837. Stephen Johnson Field made eight members in 1863. The ninth was Joseph Bradley in 1870. Franklin Roosevelt's attempt to pack the Supreme Court with more justices in 1937 never got off the ground.

The Events Leading To Osceola's Death At Fort Moultrie

"Cast a cold eye on Life, on Death, Horseman pass by." So reads the epitaph of William Butler Yeats's gravestone in Drumcliffe, County Sligo, Ireland. He's the 1923 Nobel-prize winner for literature and the guardian of Ireland's soul. With just a little imagination it's possible to visualize W.B. Yeats having been a kindred spirit to the dusky savage, Osceola, who lies buried beneath the walls of Fort Moultrie. If time and circumstance had brought these two visionaries into the same orbit, who knows but that Yeats would have penned those immortal words for a tragic patriot of another romantic lost cause -- the Seminole Nation of North Florida.

If ever there was an honorable foe worthy of our blood and steel, it was the Seminole chief, Osceola. That dark-skinned, wily native is remembered as one of the U.S. Army's most formidable opponents. No matter how many soldiers were sent to capture him, Osceola eluded his pursuers the way a deer leaves hounds befuddled in the swamp. Finally, an elaborate ruse was concocted to capture him, and Fort Moultrie was chosen as the most secure stockade to hold this rebellious Seminole in December of 1837.

Who was this natural-born leader who toyed with his white tormentors the way that a ferrel cat terrorizes its prey? Like many radicalized males, Osceola renamed himself with a *nomme de guerre* that suited his militaristic calling. The mixed-blood man was named "Billy Powell" when he was born in 1804 in Tallassee, Alabama. Almost everyone in Tallassee was of mixed blood -- Creek, Seminole, Muscogee, Spanish or English Caucasian, or African. There was hate aplenty in southern Alabama in 1804. The Creek nation split into two hostile factions. Runaway slaves were tracked by white bounty hunters, and only a generation earlier the Spanish had supplied rifles to the inhabitants for the purpose of making war on the colonials. Billy Powell never trusted white Indian traders and he despised the agents sent out by the Great White Father in

Washington. Powell assumed the ominous-sounding native name, "Osceola," literally translating as "black drink shouter."

There was one Indian trader in whom Osceola did have confidence -- his own grandfather, William Powell, an English trader. Osceola's mother was herself part white. Her grandfather supposedly was Peter McQueen, a Scottish Indian trader active in the Alabama region since the 1790s.

Other than the usual suspect trade deals that the Indians received from the white traders, the time of troubles that culminated in the Seminole Wars had its origin in what is known as the Yazoo Land scandal -- a particularly sad era in Georgia's early statehood. Thousands of acres of Georgia, Alabama, and Mississippi pine barrens land were sold to southern speculators, frequently by quasi-land agencies who lacked authority to sell. Quite a few of South Carolina's most prominent families made huge profits from their purchase of tens of thousands of acres at pennies an acre. The U.S. Supreme Court had to step in and adjudicate an ugly matter in a landmark case known as *Fletcher v. Peck* (1810). The high court of John Marshall, in a rush to "sanctify legal contracts," granted legitimacy to some of the most corrupt political dealings in our country's history.

The native-Americans, already distrustful of the expanding white population, had further reason to be wary. British slave traders along the West Florida to Alabama coast supplied the Chickasaws with weapons, thereby giving them the upper hand among the natives. In return, the Chickasaws rounded up healthy males from the rival Seminole and Muscogee factions and turned them over to the British to be sold into slavery. The early English settlers of Charleston used the same method of exploitation to eradicate the native population. From the settlers' point of view, it made good sense to aid the Indians in their deadly rivalries. From 1750 to 1820 the Indian population of the Southeast dropped dramatically from internecine warfare, white man's diseases, and from their being sold into slavery as far away as the Caribbean Islands.

"Yazoo lands" speculation fever was still rife when Andrew Jackson became President in 1828. Native American religious belief did not countenance the idea of private land ownership by anyone. To a man the chiefs misunderstood the whole notion of land speculation and the concept of property rights. To them, the Great Spirit owned the land and humans were tenants for the Great Spirit. In 1823 the John Marshall court in the case *Johnson v. McIntosh* ruled that Americans could not enter into land dealings with Indians. The case may read to a Caucasian like a landmark decision full of legal merit, but to the Indians -- particularly those of the Southeast -- the *Johnson v. McIntosh* case was "bunkum." The Indian was to be shoved about the country from wasteland to swamp at the leisure of fat, corrupt land agents. Andrew Jackson's military commanders in the Florida / Alabama corridor did little to dispel the notion.

The idea of resistance to white authority seems to have originated with the Scots Indian trader, Peter McQueen, a kinsman of the halfbreed Billy Powell. Powell began using the militant name "Osceola" around the time that he became a leader of several hundred Seminoles and runaway slaves who moved southeast into the Florida panhandle and away from the Yazoo squabbles.

Most estimates give Osceloa effective command of no more than 200 to 350 warriors, and many of these were what the whites derogatorily called "renegades."

Yet a finer swampland fighting force probably never existed on American soil. Armed by covert Spanish agents with the best rifles in the world, these native men were as elusive as shadows in the forest. They chose not to fight whenever they could negotiate a land compromise that they could live with. In fact, U.S. Army Generals Clinch, Gaines, and Jesup praised Seminole chieftains such as Holatamico, a.k.a. Billy Bowlegs, Coacoochee, a.k.a. Wild Cat, Micanopy, and Osceola as being men of their word.

From Fort Brooke in the Tampa area to Fort Gadsden on the Apalachicola River, Seminoles, white settlers, and the U.S. Army coexisted for lengthy periods between their flare-ups of the early 19th century. They purchased tobacco, tools, and corn from the company store that was annexed to each fort. Of course, when the shooting started it was duly noted that the clerks in the company stores were shot multiple times whereas one bullet and a tomahawk blow dispatched the others.

Osceola never admitted to knowing much English -- he carried on monosyllabic conversations with high-ranking army officers, and they respected him as a man of his word. Osceola was a family man, husband to two beautiful wives simultaneously, Indian fashion. One wife was half-African. He doted on his children and dressed his strikingly pretty daughters in bright colors. Often, Osceola acted as quasi-legal counsel for his tribesmen in their dealings with whites in central Florida and the panhandle region. He always knew more than he let on, and it is suspected that his English was far better than anyone knew.

One white man that Osceola respected almost as a brother was army lieutenant John Graham, a 21-year-old West Point graduate stationed at Ft. Brooke. Graham spoke the Seminole-Creek dialect and bought presents for Osceola's children thereby gaining the confidence of the great warrior. Graham was impressed with Seminole civilization and its basic decency to humanity of all rank and station. Only when much provoked would the Seminole strike back. And when he did strike, it was all steel and fury with no mercy. The young officer was West Point Class of 1834. Underclassmen that he would have held rank over included the future Union generals Meigs and Meade, and the Confederate generals Bragg and Early. The Seminole Wars and the resulting Indian removal to the west disheartened Lieutenant Graham such that he left the Army for civilian pursuit.

President Jackson ordered the Indians to be removed and directed the U.S. Army to "assist" the tribes in their overland journey to Oklahoma. Osceola, Micanopy, and Billy Bowlegs respectfully declined Jackson's offer of land in Oklahoma. Jackson called for troops, and South Carolina sent more than her share to the Florida panhandle. Runaway Gullah slaves fell in with the Seminoles and together made a formidable force of savvy swamp fighters. The Indians lured the U.S. Army into terrain favorable to their type of warfare, for the Indian feared the heavy cannon of the army. Malaria, heat stroke, snakes, and Indians took their deadly toll. Every attempt to kill or capture Osceola failed until General Thomas Jesup came up with the ruse to call for a ceasefire and to have the head men of both sides meet in a neutral field. Ordinarily, Osceola would have been wary, but this time he let his guard down and trusted his white foe for once. It was a fatal error for the proud leader of the Seminoles. In the summer of 1837, Osceola and eleven of his family and entourage were brought to the Sullivan's Island stockade. The back of Seminole resistance was broken, and the pitiful band of Indians was herded west.

Proud Osceola, decked in his regal splendor of bright Spanish silk tunics and leather leggins, was a guest in at least one dinner party on Queen Street. He let out a war whoop that frightened that whole end of town, however. Osceola contracted scarlet fever and died on January 30, 1838, within weeks of arriving here. His grave outside Fort Moultrie reads "Osceola, Warrior and Patriot." Any Irishman can see why W.B. Yeats would have championed Osceola and the Seminole cause!

Carolinians Who Did Not Celebrate Secession

So says the Good Book, KJV: *For by wise counsel thou shalt make thy war: and in multitude of counsellors there is safety* (Proverbs 24:6). One hundred and seventy of the most respected men in South Carolina inked their names to the Ordinance of Secession in Charleston 150 years ago this month. Noble, Wardlaw, and Cauthen stood for secession from the Upstate; Quattlebaum, Wannamaker, and Keitt from the Midlands; Rutledge, Simons, Hayne, McGrath, and McCrady were chief among the Lowcountry signers.

Was there wise counsel in the act of secession? Historians are finding evidence that secession fever, which had lain dormant in the state since 1830, kindled into a blue flame overnight following the surprise election of Abraham Lincoln on the upstart Republican ticket. Maxcy Gregg, an ardent secessionist who later gave his life to the cause of the Confederacy, remarked that he never debated whether secession was expedient, but rather whether it was right.

Who were the voices of dissent, if not reason? South Carolina may have been the Hotspur State, our coast was home to fire eaters, but when all was said and done on December 20, 1860, the date of secession, there were many who feared that we had crossed the Rubicon with our rupturing the republic. Far from siding with the New England Republicans, the S.C. Unionists were men cast in the Jeffersonan-Democrat mold. To them -- lawmakers James Lawrence Orr and Benjamin F. Perry; federal judges James Louis Petigru and George S. Bryan; and local merchant, Jacob Schirmer, among others -- the grand old agrarian republic envisioned by Thomas Jefferson was the grandest vision of the Founding Fathers. The S.C. Unionists could not shatter the Jeffersonian ideal. They had no love for the New England Republicans and little cooperation even for Northern Democrats.

As the sesquicentennial of the North-South War looms on the horizon noticeably less attention will be paid to the foot-draggers than to the fire eaters. The Upstate produced most of the Union men. Though slavery predominated beyond the coastal parishes, it was not of the grand plantation scale of the

Charleston-Georgetown-Beaufort Plutocrats. Slavery above the Fall Line more often than not consisted of ten African men and white man stripped bare to the waist working in a field. The white man owned the Africans, yet labored alongside them. That scene was seldom played out on coastal plantations where hundreds of slaves were controlled by a caste of overseers.

Unionist Benjamin Perry defended both slavery and the Union in a famous speech given at the National Democratic Convention at South Carolina Institute Hall in Charleston in April 1860. Perry, a grandson of one of Patriot General Pickens' Revolutionary War partisans, believed that secession would do more harm to the institution of slavery than the two-thirds majority Congress could ever do. Democrat Perry could not have foreseen the southern delegate walkout and the subsequent six-way split of the remaining party delegates over the issue of popular sovereignty. The low-man on the balloting, ironically, was Jefferson Davis of Mississippi.

Stephen Douglas, the little "steam engine in britches," arrived in Charleston from Chicago as the man to beat in that national Democratic convention in April 1860. But, as balloting went on in Charleston, nationally - prominent men who held moderate views and certainly favored reconciliation -- men such as Senators James Guthrie of Kentucky and R.M.T. Hunter of Virginia -- were relegated to the political sidelines as the more extreme candidates predominated -- Stephen Douglas of Illinois for the National Democrats and John T. Breckenridge of Kentucky for the breakaway Southern Democrats. Even so, pro-Union Democrats were numerous in South Carolina, particularly in the Anderson, Pickens, Greenville, and Spartanburg area. That area had been hardcore Whig country during the Revolution. Those were the men who had defeated Bloody Ban Tarleton and Major Pat Ferguson. No one could question their patriotism or their courage.

Such a defender of the Union was Pickens native Perry that he once fought a duel and killed a man during the great Nullification Crisis of 1832. Perry killed Turner Bynum, editor of the pro-Calhoun, pro-Nullification Greenville Sentinel, on a secluded island in the Tugaloo River. Perry at the time was editor of the rival newspaper, The Greenville Mountaineer. When all of Perry's efforts to halt secession failed, he threw himself into what he knew early on to be the forlorn cause of the Confederacy. President Andrew Johnson appointed Perry, because of his known loyalty, to the office of governor during the federal occupation of 1865.

Federal judge James Louis Petigru was the state's most well-known and most tolerated Unionist prior to the War. From his law office on St. Michael's

Alley Petigru would venture forth into Meeting and Broad Streets during the jubilation and bell ringing that accompanied the secession rallies. He'd been a counterbalance to Nullification and Disunion here in the 1830s. Now the great jurist was weary and despondent for the future of the Founding Fathers' noble experiment. "My Countrymen here in S.C. are distempered to a degree that makes them to a calm and impartial observer real objects of pity."

In 1860, the economic contrast between north and south was so profound that even state legislators were completely aware of the lopsided disadvantage of taking on the North in pitched battle. Could the South have been resorting to a high-stakes poker bluff with its secession act? Not hardly. Old General Winfield Scott, all 300 pounds and six feet, four inches of him realized the dreaded state of things. From his War Department in New York -- he'd despised President Franklin Pierce so much that he'd moved the War Department out of Washington -- Winfield Scott advocated an amicable splitting of the Union into quadrants. Queen Victoria had long conversations with Lord Palmerston about sending a British army to invade the North through Canada and a navy to blockade northern ports. The death wish of her beloved Prince Albert was part of the reason that she was dissuaded.

Judge Petigru and fellow judge George S. Bryan were emmisaries between the Federal government, the independent republic of South Carolina and the Fort Sumter garrison of Major Anderson in the negotiations prior to the War's start in April 1861. For a week it appeared as if bloodshed could be avoided.

Caleb Cushing, a southern-sympathizing Democrat from Massachusetts, tried to work with Carolina Unionists to prevent a war over disunion. Cushing served as chairman of the National Democratic Convention here in April 1860. When that convention broke into six factions and the southern states marched out, Cushing sided with the South and served as Chairman of the Southern Democratic Nominating Convention in Baltimore -- the one that nominated John Breckinridge. Cushing, in service to President Tyler, had been our first minister to China and had negotiated our nation's first trade treaty with that old empire. Cushing arrived in Charleston in December 1860, on the eve of secession and went to his hotel on Meeting Street amidst the hoopla of jubilation over the done deed. There in the famed old Charleston Hotel a fare thee well occurred among men who loved the Union more than its various sections. Cushing quietly returned to the rail station on John Street for a sad trip back north.

Crossing paths with Cushing somewhere in the dark of north-south rail tracks were two men heading to Charleston -- George Salter and F.G. Fontaine.

They worked for The New York Times and The New York Herald, respectively, and they would pioneer the art of the war correspondent.

More than 10,000 bloody engagements were waged in what the South called the War Between the States. Total deaths have been estimated at one-million, one-hundred thousand. The total cost in dollars to both sides has been estimated at more than 10 billion dollars. The physical destruction of the South was beyond the ability of estimators to calculate. What price is laid on honor? Could Lincoln have achieved his goals without prompting war? Could southern secessionists have been pacified? History says, "No!" What is it that we celebrate now? Valor? Courage in the face of long odds, or the efforts of the peacemakers?

The Story Behind Those Currier and Ives Prints

Say the word "Americana" and what comes to mind? For some it's a picture of a tightlipped George Washington peering toward you from a one-dollar bill. For others it's ol' Abe Lincoln, the rail splitter from Illinois. Midwesterners might visualize a paddlewheel steamboat plying its way down the mighty Mississippi. However, just mention the lithographic art firm of Currier and Ives and everyone's thoughts go immediately to those romanticized scenes of America's yesteryear. Remember the fruitcake that came from your Great Aunt Sal at Christmas -- neatly packaged in a tin that had a Currier and Ives winter scene embossed on the lid? You were reluctant to regift such a classic-looking container. In many ways the holidays begin each year with greeting cards and advertisements depicting nostalgic New England winter scenes from the vast Currier and Ives collection. The images we possess of our country in the 19th century were shaped almost exclusively by the New York lithographic firm of Nathaniel Currier and James Ives. Their art firm produced thousands of colored lithographs that captured every subject imaginable -- from horse-pulled sleds in the snow to clipper ships making the tea run to China.

High quality, low cost, hand-colored art prints by Currier and Ives adorned parlors, saloons, law offices, and even Victorian birdcages from Niagara Falls to Hannibal, Missouri. The life of New Yorker Nat Currier parallels the rags-to-riches tales that are so often associated with the early days of the Republic. From his three-story office on Nassau and Spruce Streets near St. Paul's Chapel and Broadway, Currier could stare out of his window at the mansion of John Jacob Astor, the richest man in the country. He recalled delivering packages to the big house when he was an errand boy for a stationery and ink shop just down the street from his print shop empire. Now, in the 1840s, Currier's wealth put him in league with the City's most powerful elites.

Born the son of a shopkeeper in 1813 in Roxbury, Massachusetts, Nat Currier had every reason to expect for himself the life of a clerk -- that is until age 15 when death struck suddenly and made him the breadwinner for his mother and younger siblings. A fortunate break came for young Currier when he gained an apprenticeship with William and John Pendleton, two fellows just down from New York to try their hand at the lithographic art form then sweeping the continent of Europe. Though he wasn't much of an artist, Nat Currier acquired the skill of preparing the limestone and cutting the scene. Between 1828 and 1830, Currier rubbed shoulders with the Pendleton brothers' close friends, the famous "Painting Peale brothers --Charles Willson and Rembrandt."

The man who revolutionized the art world also transformed the newspaper business. At just 21 years of age, Nathaniel Currier ventured into New York City virtually unknown in the world of art or business, and he established a small lithographic business of his own, intent upon selling inexpensive, framable landscapes and portraits of famous people. Three blocks away from Nat Currier's tiny office was Ben Day's daily newspaper, The Sun, an up-and-coming rival to James Gordon Bennett's New York Herald. Bennett had been a copy reader for the Charleston Courier in the early 1820s.

It would be unfair to say that Jamie Bennett brought sensationalism and tawdriness into the mainstream of daily news -- for the public's penchant for gory or salacious details had already manifested itself. However, Bennett discovered just how insatiable the public's interest was for the bizarre themes that lie beyond the tedium of national and international politics. In 1835 Bennett ran a series of stories that is now legendary in the annals of newspaper reporting -- the series is referred to as "the Great Moon Hoax." Unverified reports attributed to British astronomer Sir John Herschel claimed that powerful telescopes had confirmed that there was life on the moon. For a time The Sun was the best-selling newspaper in the world. Somehow, with Bennett's Sun, the notion that newspapers and truthfulness should go hand-in-hand evaporated with the New York morning dew. Bennett needed machinery that could churn out the printed news faster than the competition.

German industrialist Friedrich Gottlob Koenig developed a new high-speed printing press and James Gordon Bennett had to have this latest bit of technology. Venture capitalists from Wall Street stopped by to see the amazing printing presses roll out the latest evening news. Nat Currier and his coterie of *bon vivants* -- Robert Fulton, Duncan Phyfe, P.T. Barnum, Lymon Ward Beecher, Louis-Jacques Daguerre, and musician Edwin Pearce Christy ducked in often to check out operations.

A story that gripped the nation in 1835 was the May 15 Planter's Hotel fire in New Orleans. The story hopped across the nation as newspaper after newspaper copied it and posted it to their readers. The fire broke out at 2 a.m. and fifty people were buried in the collapsing building. Even though all but ten people were rescued, the horrendous fire captured the imagination of the reading public. Jamie Bennett turned to Nat Currier for an illustration -- and the rest has been history.

Currier's etched lithograph of the hotel on fire was done by staff artist J.H. Bufford with no knowledge whatever of the appearance of the Planter's Hotel or its surroundings. Bufford dutifully portrayed dozens of gawkers in the foreground and a mass of collapsed rubble that was still smouldering despite the firemen's efforts. Bennett's Sun soared ahead of its competition, and Nat Currier would soon have to take on a partner to help him keep up with the demand for prints and reprints of the young nation's epoch moments.

When Cornelius Vanderbilt's steamship The Lexington caught fire and blew up in New York harbor, the art staff at the Currier firm went into overdrive. The prints sold into the thousands across the country. The Sun featured each print on the front page.

If ever business partners were paired in heaven, then tall, slim Nathaniel Currier and short, stocky James Merritt Ives were that pair. Ives had been born on the grounds of Bellevue Hospital where his father was the business manager. Ives' education had been more complete than had Currier's, but Currier's business acumen was keener than that of Jim Ives.' Together the two lithographers expanded the business to include something entirely novel -- political campaign posters!

Currier and Ives of Nassau Street, New York, became slogan writers and poster artists for William Marcy Tweed, the "Boss" of Tammany Hall. Tweed wanted a logo for his Tammany Hall political organization, and the firm of Currier and Ives produced the famous snarling tiger design that came to represent Tammany Hall's dominance over New York City's political life for decades. The snarling tiger image came from Fire Engine No. 6 at the station where Tweed occasionally volunteered as a fireman.

In 1844, the campaign of Democratic candidate James K. Polk and running mate George M. Dallas put the Currier and Ives firm "on the map" as the premier producer of lithographic art. By 1860, the beardless Lincoln lithograph had become the bete noir of southern politicians gathered in Charleston.

Currier avoided the broiling controversy of abolitionism like the plague, however. He and Ives did one contrived scene of slave branding on the Ivory coast, and, though it sold briskly in the North, the firm's southern agents let the partners know that no such artwork would ever grace southern shop shelves. Horace Greeley, editor of the pro-abolition New York Herald stopped by often at the art factory on Nassau Street to needle Currier on the subject. The firm did do a "Darktown" series that sold well in the South after the War. That series had a famous scene of a cotton field with black men picking cotton. The lyrics to the song "Jim Crow" were written beneath the scene. The era of "Jim Crow" segregation politics supposedly gets its label from that high-selling poster by Currier and Ives.

During the Great War of the Union, Nat Currier and James Ives produced dozens of graphic images depicting battles on land and at sea. The shelling of the Merrimack by the Monitor, the charge of Pickett's men, the defense of Marye's Heights at Fredericksburg -- all were sell-outs as soon as they were released. If a scene had Confederates doing valiant things, it sold well in the South after the War. If the scene depicted the Yanks being heroic, then it was guaranteed to be on every mantel in New England.

The factory on Nassau Street employed numerous artists, engravers, and machine operators. Germans just off the boat got jobs doing background color on pastoral scenes. Young women specialized in dog, horse, or wagon sketches whereas others did only clouds or gabled roofs. The art of Currier and Ives was really an assembly line process. The most famous female artist of the mid-19th century, Francis "Fanny" Palmer got her start at Currier's emporium. George Durrie did most of the famous winter wonderland scenes. Arthur Tait did the great sporting art pictures that were so popular in gentlemen's libraries and dressing rooms. Thomas Nast, the originator of the American political cartoon, worked a stint for Currier before going on to *Harper's Weekly*. The word "nasty" was coined from his vindictive political cartoons. Nast drew the "dumb and stodgy" elephant to represent the Republicans and the crazy-stubborn donkey to represent the Democrats. He's also credited with designing the image of the modern Santa Claus.

Conflagration, death, and destruction were not the consuming themes of the Currier and Ives form, however. Steamboat races down the Mississippi, particularly the fabled race of the *Robert E. Lee* versus the *Natchez* in 1870, were coveted art pieces reproduced by the thousands and sold here and abroad. Currier retired a millionaire and gave the business to his son, Edward. The old art entrepreneur who created our image of the 19th century was often seen around his country home in Ames, Massachusetts, "flying" his buggy behind a beautiful pair of matched trotters.

Today, the corner of Nassau and Spruce Streets marks the center of the Pace University campus, just six blocks east of Ground Zero marking where the twin towers once stood. Set apart this holiday the cards and fruitcake tins you receive bearing the old lithograph images of Currier and Ives.

Christmas In Charleston 75 Years Ago

"*It was the best of times, it was the worst of times, . . .,*" wrote Charles Dickens in the opening lines of *Tale of Two Cities*. What Dickens could never have known was that his immortal lines lived again as a refrain for a description of Old Charleston as it was in the midst of the Great Depression, 1935. That Victorian author of many classics could not have known -- nor would he have cared -- that the rest of his famous quote was also deemed quite appropriate for this southern city as it struggled economically 75 years ago. The Dickens' phrase refers to Paris in the midst of civil strife. In 1935, Charleston was riding out the worst economic times since reconstruction, yet, judging from the *News and Courier,* the month leading up to Christmas was punctuated by the long anticipated announcement by Mayor Burnet R. Maybank that the Public Service Commission had chosen the contractor for the massive new Santee-Cooper Project -- a proclamation that made Charlestonians much more optimistic about the new year. The rest of that Dickens refrain reads . . . "*it was the age of foolishness, it was the epoch of belief, it was the epoch of incredulity, it was the season of Light, it was the season of Darkness, it was the spring of hope, it was the winter of despair, we had everything before us, we had nothing before us, we were all going direct to heaven, we were all going direct the other way - in short, the period was so far like the present period. . . .*" No one but the Victorian Master could have penned those lines. For any local person who read that passage in the winter of 1935, the words must have given them pause.

On the positive side, everyone that was going to lose a job in Charleston had already lost it. The local economy was on the upswing. Our country was at peace and, even though there were newspaper headlines hinting that all was not well in Europe or the Far East, we were not troubled. Germany repudiated the 1919 Versailles Agreement, reclaimed the Saarland, and introduced compulsory military service. Still, we did not fret. Mussolini's Fascist Italy invaded Abyssinia and it barely made our newspaper. However, when the "Kingfisher," corrupt Louisiana governor, Huey Long, was assassinated by Dr. Carl Weiss in the state capitol building -- that story was the talk of the town for days!

Seventy-five years ago in Charleston the weather was mild in the weeks leading up to Christmas. Cotton hit 11.36 cents per pound on the New York Commodities Exchange in November, 1935. Back in 1932 S.C. farmers were lucky to get 6.5 cents a pound for their cotton. Charlestonians were familiar then with trucks pulling cotton wagons as white blossoming fields were hand-picked by day laborers -- many of whom were descended from slaves who'd worked those same fields a hundred years earlier. With the boll weevil's arrival in 1917, the bottom completely dropped out of the cotton market in 1920, and what was left of the Old South disappeared soon thereafter.

The Fall of 1935 had been just so-so for local sports enthusiasts. One of the highlights was Porter Military Academy beating Summerville 14-12 up in Flowertown. With formations such as "the flying trapeze," The wedge," and the "triple reverse," Porter Cyclone athletes Riley, Ramsay, and Thrasher wore down Summerville's boys who were paced by the offensive running of star Teddy Limehouse. Moultrie High was one of the few teams to beat Porter that year. Coach Tatum Gressette's Citadel Bulldogs did not have their greatest year in 1935. Their hardest loss came at the hands of Furman. Furman called themselves "The Purple Hurricanes," and they handily defeated a small but scrappy Citadel team led by "Kooksie" Robinson, Art Ferguson, Ed Hall, and Crosland Croft. One of the biggest teams Citadel faced all season was Newberry. Newberry averaged just over 200 pounds per player -- 20 pounds heavier on average than The Citadel. Tatum Gressette, a St. Matthews native and brother to the late state senator Marion Gressette, had been a star on the Gamecock football team in the early 1920s. Tatum's drop-kick field goal gave USC a 3-0 win over Clemson in 1920, and Gressette captained Carolina to another win over Clemson in 1921. He passed away in 1997, four years after being installed in the USC Athletic Hall of Fame.

The newspaper ads around Christmas in 1935 were just as numerous as they are in today's newspaper -- some things never change. Paul Motor Company on Spring Street offered a new Ford coach "A" Model for just $525. The ad noted a quality used -- almost new -- Ford V-8 pick-up for $425. Prices of automobiles are approximately 40X higher in today's market, however, the average family income was about $2,300 per year in the mid-1930s as compared to an estimated $49,500 median family income today.

Back in the '30s a number of downtown businesses were owned locally by stockholders, and Christmas was a time of annual meetings and stockholder parties. These parties were greatly anticipated events on everyone's social calendar. Speisseger Drug Company of 435 Meeting Street was just one of several posting notices of the annual stockholder meeting and reception. W.L. Speisseger was president and M.H. Speisseger was secretary. Burris Chemical was one of the last of the great locally owned corporations to host a grand Christmas affair. The Hibernian Hall gala was the most coveted Christmas party invitation in town.

Prohibition ended in Charleston and everywhere else on December 5, 1933, with the passage of the 21st Amendment -- which repealed the unpopular 18th Amendment. Of course, Charleston and much of the Carolina coast had remained "open" to contraband importers. Also, quite a few entrepreneurs in the Lowcountry kept alive the "Scots-Irish Art" of distilling spirits. In fact, 11 South Carolinians pled guilty for violating federal liquor laws at the Charleston federal courthouse before Judge Frank K. Myers in the weeks between Thanksgiving and Christmas. The eleven illegal distillers hailed from Sumter, Calhoun, Richland, Lexington, and Lee counties. Popular Charleston Mayor Burnet Rhett Maybank, mayor from 1931 to 1938, allegedly remarked, "When Charleston is dry, Burnet is dry. When Charleston is wet, Burnet is wet." City Council posted a notice that horn tooters and noisy revelers would be arrested on New Year's Eve. City ordinance makers announced that they were studying Mayor LaGuardia's new noise ordinances for New York.

Charleston and the state adored Burnet R. Maybank and he became a legend in state politics. The son of two old Charleston families, his father was Joseph Maybank and his mother was Harriet Lowndes Rhett. He was a Porter Miitary Academy and College of Charleston graduate -- and a cotton broker by trade. The biggest news 75 years ago was Mayor Maybank's announcement of the engineering contract for the new Santee-Cooper Authority. It was one of the biggest construction starts in the country. Along with his duties as mayor, Maybank also served as chairman of the Public Service Commission, so he had a lot to do with the naming the New York engineering firm of Parson, Klapp, Brenkerhoff, and Douglas as the firm to build the $37.5 million hydroelectric facility. Parson, Klapp, et al., had just completed the massive Platte Valley Authority project in Nebraska when they rolled into the tri-county area.

The selection of Parson, Klapp, et al., was a smart move. The Company was founded in 1885 and they played a large role in the development of the New York subway system. They were also one of the main engineering companies selected by the government to build military facilities in support of World War I. The firm constructed the New York World Fair complex in 1939, the NORAD Defense nuclear-proof center in Cheyenne, Wyoming, in the 1960s, as well as the Bay Area Transit System in the 1970s. That renown engineering construction firm brought many talented people into the Lowcountry and they created thousands of jobs over the course of a decade. Maybank's successes as mayor of Charleston catapulted him into the governors' mansion and from there to the United States Senate.

As the year 1935 drew to a close, Charlestonians read in the paper that Assistant Secretary of the Navy, Henry Roosevelt, cousin of FDR, nephew of Teddy, was coming down to Gippy Plantation near Moncks Corner to visit his brother, Nicholas Roosevelt and to get in some duck hunting. Of course, it was Henry Roosevelt who brought news privately that the Charleston Navy Yard would be significantly expanded. Did the U.S. Navy expect another war?

The only dark note in the newspapers leading to Christmas in Charleston, 1935, was the story of the murder of a well-to-do Charlotte Street woman by her next-door neighbor in her own home in broad day light -- and in front of her children! Charleston was riveted by the details of how a ten-year-old boy fought the attacker and helped to apprehend the murder suspect. The Frances Craven homicide became one of modern Charleston's most sensational crimes. Read about it in next week's "History's Lost Moments."

Murder on Charlotte Street 75 Years Ago

No self-styled Truman Capote was around to capitalize on chronicling the cold-blooded killing of Frances Craven. Her murder on Saturday afternoon, November 9, 1935, in broad-open daylight in the parlor of her home at 59 Charlotte Street shocked staid, old Charleston. It was not until 1959 that Capote pioneered that genre of literature -- the nonfiction novel -- that elevates stark realism to the art of enriched, or embellished storytelling. Charlestonian Frances Craven, middle-aged, separated mother of three, would have shuddered at the thought of being celebrated in the macabre style of the Clutter family of Holcomb, Kansas -- the horrific crime that Capote made world-famous. Capote read about the Clutter deaths in the New York Times of November 16, 1959, and turned that midwestern crime into one of the 20th century's seminal works of literature.

Seventy-five years ago downtown Charleston was made up of a dozen intimate neighborhoods. Everyone knew everyone else and the corner grocery store ran a tab for those who came in daily for Gippy milk, Claussen's bread, and the *News and Courier*. WCSC radio played the popular new songs -- "Begin the Beguine" and George Gershwin's "I Got Plenty of Nothin.'" More locals were reading Thomas Wolfe's new novel, *Of Time And The River*, than were delving into T.S. Eliot's *Murder in the Cathedral*. The motion picture that captured everyone's attention was *Mutiny on the Bounty*.

Charleston's newest celebrities, Dubose Heyward and his New York-born wife, were spending the winter up north consulting with playwrights on the development of Porgy into the musical *Porgy and Bess*. Dubose Heyward's *Porgy* was based upon a real character who had known much of the seamy side of the upper peninsula. As with all seaport cities Charleston was no exception when it came to homicides and vice. The Craven murder, however, struck a nerve downtown. This lady was one of the respectable middle-class residents in a rather fashionable, trouble-free neighborhood.

Before the Craven murder story broke, the buzz in Charleston centered about whether the new noise ordinance would ban the street venders' songs.

"Swimps, I got 'em c-o-l-d," or *"News and Cou-ri-er"* were morning chants as the barrow venders, the ice man, and flower ladies made their daily rounds. The last vestige of this quaint Charleston disappeared in the mid-1950s. Though Charleston possessed 18th century moss, and wisteria adorned Barbadian dwellings by the score, and its populace spoke a beautiful, but almost unrecognizable dialect of the King's English, the ghastly violence of its day-to-day life was all too evident at Old Roper's emergency room on Lucas Street.

Frances Craven was DOA when the ambulance delivered her to the emergency ramp of Old Roper even though the medical interns who staffed the facility worked feverishly to revive her. When the story unfolded of what had occurred just a few blocks away on Charlotte Street, even the locals who were accustomed to a high level of crime were horrified.

Coroner John P. Deveaux declared that Craven died instantly of a bullet that entered the side of her head and exited through her neck. Since it didn't appear that robbery was a motive and there was no forced entry to the dwelling, the shooting did not match the profile for downtown Charleston.

Meanwhile, on the portico of 59 Charlotte, Police Lieutenant Joseph Wise was gathering crime scene evidence and interviewing eyewitnesses. The suspect, Eugene Lewis Pop, age 42 of 225 Hill Street, Charleston, had been apprehended in the basement of a building at the Old Citadel on Marion Square. The stocky, redheaded Pop was as cool as a cucumber when taken into custody. As he joked with the arresting officers, the suspect claimed he'd shot the unarmed woman in self-defense. Pop even asked one of the officers for a plug of chewing tobacco. He said that he was returning a borrowed picture to Mrs. Craven and that all of a sudden the woman started throwing pots and pans at him. At the scene of the crime, bystanders told a different story. They said that there was a long-standing pattern of Pop annoying and pestering Mrs. Craven.

The old multi-storied house on Charlotte Street was home to half a dozen people, most of whom had been witness to the murder. Mrs. Eugenia Rumpel, a live-in friend of Daisy Craven -- sister of the victim -- told police that she heard a ruckus downstairs at approximately 3:45 P.M. that Saturday afternoon. She said she ran downstairs toward the sound of shouts in the parlor but fled in another direction when she heard shots fired.

"Mama's shot," cried Violet Craven, the fifteen-year-old daughter of the victim. After a brief struggle another shot was fired and Daisy Craven fell to the floor with a gunshot to the mouth. Daisy had struck Pop with a bottle as he knelt down at the body of Frances. From the hallway dashed 10-year-old Bobby

Craven with an ice pick, and he chased Pop out of the house and into Charlotte Street.

Lieutenant Wise of the C.P.D. was informed by eyewitnesses that Bobby Craven did indeed chase the suspect from the house and that next-door neighbor Michael Altine came out of his home brandishing a double-barreled shotgun. Altine quickly surmised what was occurring and joined the chase on Elizabeth and Henrietta Streets as Pop bounded past Stevens's Corner Grocery and around the corner.

Altine fired at Pop as he and Bobby ran along Henrietta Street. Pop turned and fired back at his pursuers. But Altime had fired high in an attempt not to hit children who were playing in the street. The fleeing suspect ran through traffic toward Meeting Street and eluded his pursuers. He was captured without struggle in an abandoned building at the Old Citadel.

If the story has a hero, it is the 10-year-old Bobby Craven who chased the murderer for a half-mile through Charleston streets wielding an ice pick and dodging sporadic gunfire.

Eugene Lewis Pop avoided the State's electric chair and pleaded self-defense. For the rest of Pop's story, read Murder and Mayhem in the Holy City by Michael Patrick Hendrix. Number 59 Charlotte Street was eventually razed to make way for the parking lot located behind the now-empty Federal Office Building on Meeting and Charlotte Streets. Altine's house disappeared at the same time.

The obituary for Frances Craven mentioned her survivors being her sister-in-law, Daisy Craven, her daughter Violet, who was wounded in the attack, her son, Bobby, and "a daughter, Claire Ringling, who'd just married a member of the circus last Thursday."

Historically Significant Santee River Plantations Lost Forever In 1939

Who can deny the greater good that has come from damming and flooding the Santee River -- especially when the hydroelectric plant helped us to win World War II. Today, at least 165,000 customers in three rural counties get low-cost electricity from those huge turbines. And don't forget that the Charleston Air Force Base is one of Santee-Cooper's biggest customers. Lakes Marion and Moultrie make beautiful recreation centers for the Lowcountry and together they yield more than 450 miles of freshwater shoreline. While the lakes are home to the magnificent painted bunting, bald eagles and ospreys, 12-foot alligators, and the world record landlocked bass, the locals remember back 75 years when a boat trip down the Santee River took you by the most historic antebellum plantation homes of the Old South. "You must pay the price if you wish to secure the blessing," so said our seventh president, Andrew Jackson. Jackson wasn't contemplating internal improvements when he said these words, but rather his own political advancement. However, Jackson, the Hero of New Orleans and the man they called "Old Hickory," would have known fleetingly of these Santee plantations. The big houses usually faced the river with their backs to the wagon road leading from Charleston to the Congarees -- a route Jackson took in 1781.

In the 18th and early 19th centuries the lower half of South Carolina was organized around the Anglican parish system. Church affairs and political, as well as legal business, were dependent upon the parish structure. The headwaters of the Santee flowed through upper St. John's Parish, Berkeley where dozens of Huguenot families carved country estates out of the wilderness. Today, this historic district has much of its acreage submerged 30 to 60 feet beneath the waters of Lake Marion as the Santee Dam and Spillway have effectively blocked the river's flow southeastward.

The most representative of the upper St. John's plantations now submerged is Springfield, part of the estate of Revolutionary War captain, Thomas Palmer. The captain had been an aide to Francis Marion in the War. Marion, of Pond

Bluff Plantation, was a near neighbor and the two men shared agricultural interests. Palmer was one of the earliest planters to develop what became known as Santee long-staple cotton, a much-valued fiber that was second only in value to Sea Island long-staple. This country gentleman was one of the founders of Pineville, a truly aristocratic little domain in the coastal plain of upper St. John, Berkeley. The Gourdins, Porchers, Gaillards, and Palmers established an academy, a library, literary society, and Episcopal Chapel there amidst longleaf pines and cotton fields.

By 1820 Springfield was home to another generation of Palmers -- Joseph, the son of Thomas, and Joseph's bride, Elizabeth Catherine Porcher, of nearby Peru Plantation. Mexico and Peru plantations date to the earliest decade of the 19th century and may reflect the South's desires to annex those domains as part of an ever-burgeoning agricultural republic. Joseph Palmer built the big house that became well-known in the region for its grand hospitality. Joseph's son, also named Joseph, studied medicine and converted the three-story mansion into a medical office in the mid-1800s.

Edward Palmer, the third generation to own the old place, forewent his final year at Porter Military Academy in 1897 to take over the family farm. He introduced Angus and Jersey cattle and made the formerly abandoned fields productive again -- that is until the land was condemned by the right of eminent domain in 1937.

According to Douglas Bostick in his book Sunken Plantations: The Santee-Cooper Project (History Press, 2008), Leize Palmer Gaillard, sister of Edmund Palmer, wrote, "How long will Springfield remain in its setting of oaks, sycamours, cedars, walnuts, holly and crepe myrtles -- each with their long streamers of Spanish moss? Who can tell! Progress, the insatiable monster, demands that all that area of St. John's, Berkeley, with its beautiful homes and historic associations, be submerged by the muddy waters of the Santee." Bostick's book is invaluable in the insight it gives through old pictures and the collected lore of this antebellum kingdom that has disappeared as though it were another Atlantis.

Belvidere Plantation also disappeared beneath the cappuccino-colored waters of Lake Marion -- a man-made body of water that is 9 miles across at some points. The British army's Colonel Alexander Stewart certainly remembered Belvidere Plantation, for that was the site of his Waterloo. He lost 45% of his 2000 man force in the Battle of Eutaw Springs. The property belonged to Captain James Sinkler, of St. Stephen's Parish. The Sinklers were cotton planters on a grand scale, and their thoroughbred stables were known from here to Virginia. The Belvidere Jockey Club was part of the circuit for South Carolina's blue bloods. From the porch of Belvidere, the family heard the bombardment of Ft. Sumter. Four years later they saw the glow of Columbia burning. The plantation never passed out of Sinkler hands in 171 years -- and it was never out of cultivation until the day when the work crews knocked down the old place in 1938.

Pond Bluff was Francis Marion's plantation high up the reaches of the Santee River. The British kept the place under surveillance during the Revolution, but the cagey Swamp Fox was much too wise to be taken in his own lair. Bostick mentions in his book that this was likely the place where Marion went to give his broken ankle time to heal. We recall that he jumped from the second floor of Alexander McQueen's home on the corner of Tradd and Orange Streets. Marion jumped because the custom of the time was for the host to lock the guests in until all of the alcohol was consumed. The Patriots surrendered Charleston during the time of Marion's convalescence at Pond Bluff, and thus one of America's greatest patriots was able to renew resistance to hated British authority. Pond Bluff burned in 1816, but its replacement and its original outbuildings passed into ownership of Colonel Keating Lewis Simons, a friend of the Marion family.

In 1939 the Simons family still owned this historic old property that had belonged to the Swamp Fox and the Santee Indians prior to the coming of the white man. Joseph Simons fought the Santee-Cooper Authority legally for years in a futile effort to derail their right of eminent domain. When all failed, Simons entered his home one last time on Friday, July 7, 1939, and put a pistol to his head and pulled the trigger. Simons is buried in an old family plot that the engineers allowed to become an island in the midst of Lake Marion.

Progress is not without its price. When we switch on our lights in the morning, when we drive on the cross-town thoroughfare, cruise up the broad, endless interstate, or water-ski across Lake Moultrie, we must remember that someone had to be forced or coerced from their familiar and beloved surroundings.

Battle of New Orleans Was America's Greatest Military Victory

Put yourself in Ned Pakenham's boots for a moment, if you can drift back 196 years through the mist of time. Forgive Sir Edward (Ned) Michael Pakenham, GCB (The Most Honourable Military Order of the Bath), must have confused our Andrew Jackson and his Tennessee backwoodsmen with Jed Clampett and the Beverly Hillbillies. It was a fatal mistake to underestimate frontier American genius, and that miscalculation cost Pakenham his life, and it forfeited Britain's last opportunity to regain her former American colonies.

The Battle for New Orleans, which concluded its nine months of chessboard maneuvering 196 years ago (January 1815) this week, was a classic David slays Goliath epic drama. British General Pakenham, brother-in-law to the Duke of Wellington, victor over Napoleon's armies on a dozen hard-fought fields such as Salamanca, the Pyrenees, and Toulouse, will get his own comeuppance against defiant ragamuffins toting Kentucky long rifles firing volleys from an embankment of hastily thrown earth and cotton bales -- known forever on the outskirts of New Orleans as the Rodriguez Line.

Balladeer Johnny Horton put it best about Jackson's rout of Pakenham in his ripping 1959 country-music hit:

> We looked down the river and we see'd [sic] the British come.
> And there must have been a hundred of' 'em beatin' on the drum.
> They stepped so high and they made the bugles ring.
> We stood by our cotton bales and didn't say a thing.

When Americans fought the British, the historians had to toss military resumes and conventional explanations out the window. Wondering just who in creation was Andrew Jackson must have been the mindset of the self-assured, 36-year-old Major General Pakenham as he gazed across the boggy bayou at 3000 scruffy-looking soldiers.

Jackson's resume would not have been impressive to a British lord, but it was respectable enough by early American standards. By age 48 he'd been attorney general of Tennessee, a Congressman, and a United States senator. We can reckon that the Battle of Horsehoe Bend and the Battle of Burnt Corn on the Tallapoosa would have meant nothing to a Knight of the Order of the Bath. Those two fights against the Creek Indians in Alabama had taught Old Hickory a lot about warfare. Yet, true grit and raw courage often united with frontier cunning in the early days of this republic. Plus, Jackson was plenty motivated from the Brits' recent torching of the White House and the new Capitol.

Jackson had some personal reasons, too, for evening the score with the Empire. As a fourteen-year-old lad up in the Waxhaws of upper South Carolina, he'd sassed a British officer during the American Revolution. That officer gashed him on the side of his head with a saber, leaving a four-inch calling card for Jackson to remember him by. Jackson's mother died in Charleston, possibly of contagious disease contracted while nursing patriot soldiers. She lies buried in an unknown grave somewhere on what is now the College of Charleston campus.

Just four months prior to the New Orleans battle that settled old debts and established this country as a nation not to be trifled with, that most belligerent of Englishmen, Admiral George Cockburn, sacked Washington and sent President Madison and Congress ignominiously fleeing.

No historian describes the 1815 debacle in Washington scene better than does Holmes Alexander, the 1960s syndicated newspaper columnist and author, in his book The American Talleyrand (1935).

"Admiral Cockburn tramped up the steps of the deserted Capitol, seated himself in the Speaker's chair and heaved his spurred heels to the desk where War Hawk Mr. Clay's gavel had so often rapped a house to order."

"Shall this harbor of Yankee democracy be burned?" he is said to have bawled. "All for it will say 'Aye.' The ayes have it," and so the multi-tiered Capitol went up in flames and a day later the charred but gutted masonry structure looked more like a mausoleum than a seat of government. If that wasn't enough to get a red-blooded American's fighting spirits up, then what Cockburn did next surely was!

In the same hour that the British admiral applied the torch to the nation's new capitol building, he rode down the Avenue to the White House and strode across the Turkish carpets with his muddy boots, sat down in James Madison's chair at the head of the elegant table in the dining room, and ordered the servants to bring him the dinner they had prepared to serve the president of the United

States. Holmes Alexander states that Cockburn devoured the meal and then consigned the White House to the same fate as he'd ordered for the Capitol.

These were perilous times for the Union, 196 years ago this week. While the great British warships rode at anchor in the Potomac and had their guns leveled at the City, Cockburn and his officers took up residence for a few days in the hotels and inns that had recently served as the Washington abodes for pro-war men, John C. Calhoun, Henry Clay, William Lowndes and Langdon Cheves of Charleston, and Felix Grundy of Tennessee. The Redcoats made ribald fun of every aspect of our struggling democracy.

Nearby, Dolley Madison, the First Lady, was left to her own devices to find safety and shelter from the invasion. President Madison and Secretary of War Monroe hastened to the nearest United States Army outpost at Bladensburg, six miles from the City. Dolley disguised herself as a gypsy woman and knocked on a farmhouse door. It was the servant and soldier bodyguard that gave her identity away. The irate farm woman was so disgusted at Madison and his "War Cabinet" that she hollered, "Mrs. Madison, if that's you come on down and get out! Your husband's got mine out fighting, and d - - - you, you sha'nt [sic] stay in my house. So, get out!" Dolley Madison had fled the White House with the Gilbert Stuart canvas of George Washington tucked under her long skirts.

Fortunately, the British warships moved on to Baltimore and bombarded Fort McHenry for 25 continuous hours. Lieutenant Colonel George Armistead of the United States Army made a name for himself in defying Cockburn's determined fleet. Francis Scott Key penned some pertinent poetry while being detained aboard Cockburn's flagship during the bombardment of the Fort.

When news reached Madison that a sizable British force was sailing along the Gulf Coast with the Mississippi as its likely objective, there was much consternation within the President's cabinet as to who could lead an army quickly to Louisiana. There were too few federal troops near New Orleans to make a stand. If Britain gained a foothold along the Mississippi River, they'd re-established their authority on this continent, and we would say goodbye to the idea of Manifest Destiny.

As irony would have it, sly young Martin Van Buren, a state senator in New York, had a dinner party for his friend, patron, and some say, his true father, the recently pardoned Aaron Burr. The topic of New Orleans came up and Burr, unhesitatingly, said that no other man than Jackson could muster an army large enough and get it in position in time to thwart the Brits. Van Buren communicated the information up the chain of command since Burr, was still *persona non grata* due to his own suspected treasonable behavior. Secretary of

Monroe was not impressed with Jackson since Old Hickory had helped Burr by providing a fleet of boats to carry Burr's fellow adventurers to New Orleans. But in this crisis, Monroe had to act fast, and Jackson was the default selection.

Peering out over cotton bales stacked along the so-called Rodriguez Line on a cold, foggy Sunday, January 8, 1815, Andrew Jackson could see little to nothing of the 10,000 red coated men maneuvering a mile and a half from where he planned to win a great victory -- or die upon the ramparts. He could hear the shouted commands and the drum rolls as subalterns put the regiments in battle formation.

Jackson had enlisted a nest of pirates under the command of Jean Lafitte to bring up cannon and gunpowder from their stronghold at Barataria Bay. The general himself was suffering from an illness like colitis and many of his men were poorly fed, unpaid by Congress, and limited to a few rounds of ammunition apiece. But, despite being outnumbered almost three to one, all wanted revenge for the burning of the nation's capitol.

Meanwhile, at the Ursuline Chapel in downtown New Orleans, dozens of nuns of the Religious Congregation of Mary Immaculate Queen and a priest led Catholic faithfuls in a mass praying for deliverance of their fair city. It'd take a miracle they knew, for Jackson and his Tennessee Militia did not look like much of a match for the British regulars who'd already bested several of Napoleon's grand armies in Spain and beyond.

Just as a Holy Communion had been completed, a man burst in the chapel door shouting, "Jackson's victorious! The city has been saved!" Many attributed a miracle to the saying of the rosary that day. Somehow that morning the fog parted in time for Old Hickory to see the enemy's formations and their plan of approach. For some inexplicable reason they were headed straight for a boggy patch that would slow their progress immeasurably. Jackson had time to reposition his own troops and to give that famous order,"Don't shoot till you see the whites of their eyes." Nine months of chess-board-styled jockeying of armies came to a brutal and dramatic conclusion in the span of two hours.

General Pakenham went down early pierced by numerous musket balls as the sharp-eyed backwoods marksmen picked off the officers quickly. What had been a sure bet for Britain's reestablishing a presence in North America became instead, the making of an American legend -- the wizened, white-haired old man who would give us Jacksonian Democracy and order the South Carolina Nullifiers back into line. It may be America's finest moment, that victory on January 8, 1815.

John Blake White's Painting of Marion Depicts Faithful Servant, Oscar

There's something special about John Blake White's 1836 oil painting of Francis Marion, the Swamp Fox, inviting a British officer to dinner; there's something so special that does not exist in any other historical paintings of Carolinians during the Revolution. This 175-year-old oil canvas hangs in the United States Capitol, somewhere in a senate office hallway. White's painting is one of the most valuable art pieces in existence depicting our state's illustrious history.

Can there be any greater compliment to an artist than to have his works displayed in the halls of Congress? This unique artwork depicting General Marion is irreplaceable in its value to South Carolina and its citizens for a number of reasons. The artist grew up on White Hall plantation five miles northwest of Pinopolis and painted Marion from memory. John Blake White was 14 when Francis Marion died. It's doubtful that any other sketch of the fiery little Huguenot is more accurate than this one by a man that knew the general, and the artist's father, Blake Leay White, was a lifelong friend of Marion. The painting was completed in 1836, forty-one years after Marion died.

Another very important aspect of this dramatic scene from the Revolution is the depiction of Marion's orderly, a slave named Oscar. Thanks to some very good detective work by Tina C. Jones of the American Historical Interpretation Foundation, Inc. in Rockville, Maryland, art historians are now convinced that the African man baking potatoes in the campfire is Oscar Marion, the great General's boyhood playmate and personal servant. Ms. Jones had been interested for years in the genealogy of the Oscar Marion line, and in the process of her research, she confirmed that she is a descendant of this African-American patriot. We can presume that if the artist painted Marion from memory, that it's likely that White did an accurate portrayal of Oscar, too. The two men, Francis and Oscar, were approximately the same age and size. Oscar, who was at Marion's side, would have been privy to so many unspoken things. His awareness of the daring exploits of Marion's men during the darkest days of the war was, no doubt, passed on to his progeny.

When White commemorated Marion in 1836, the country was salving its wounds from a contentious five-way presidential election that had resulted in a win for the New York Democrat, Martin Van Buren. Yet, in what may be our nation's most bizarre political union, an inland corridor stretching from Savannah and Charleston northwest to the shore of Lake Michigan voted the Whig ticket -- a ticket that split the Old South like a wedge and resembled the War-Hawk movement of two decades earlier. Perhaps in an attempt at healing the political divide, White produced art themes that united us.

White's painting of Marion in the Carolina swamps inspired a contemporary painter, William Tylee Ranney of New York, to memorialize Marion and his men, including faithful servant Oscar. Ranney's work, Francis Marion Crossing the Peedee," shows a flat-bottomed ferry boat crowded with partisans and horses midstream in the Great Peedee. It's obvious that Ranney took his inspiration for Marion's countenance and that of Oscar from the White canvas that had been produced 14 years earlier. Interestingly, the only man doing any physical labor in either painting is the black man, Oscar. In Ranney's masterpiece, Oscar is pulling hard on the steering oar.

Artist, John Blake White, grew up in the wilds of the upper reaches of the Santee River. The plantation where he was born, White Hall, is submerged under Lake Moultrie. In colonial and antebellum times White Hall was the site of a thriving plantation and a well-known tavern located between the Santee River and the Congaree Road. The tavern was at a veritable cross-roads of the Revolution in the South. Both Marion and Sumter had rendezvous there and redcoats such as Tarleton, Ferguson, and Rawdon knew the place well. General Nathanael Greene bivouacked his army near there after the Battle of Eutaw Springs. As a boy, White grew up amongst the legendary men who'd salvaged the South from the clutches of Cornwallis.

Surnames such as Cordes, Couturier, Gaillard, Goudine, Lynah, Marion, Simons, Singleton, and Taylor abound on property deeds in the vicinity of White Hall. It's possible that White received his primary education at the well-known Pineville Academy in that area. As the son of a prominent planter, White was privileged to have the social contacts in Charleston and Columbia. He read law for a few years in Columbia but departed the country for England with noted artist, Washington Allston of Waccamaw Parish.

The South Carolina Historical and Genealogical Magazine of April 1942 devotes a portion of that issue to excerpts from the "Diary of John Blake White."

While abroad traveling with Allston and studying portrait art, White met many notables, one of whom was Jerome Bonaparte, brother of the emperor. Though he was already a creditable portrait painter, young White determined while in London that he would concentrate his artistic talent on recreating historical scenes from his native state's past. He mentions in his diary that "I should immediately return to Carolina and enter my name as a student."

The educational attainments of John Blake White reflect the ambition of our state's aristocratic men of the 19th century. He completed his work at Carolina and read law in Charleston, the city where he attained prominence at the bar. Yet before he had even attained his 30th birthday, White had completed two of his canvas masterpieces -- "Battle of Eutaw Springs (1804)" and "Battle of Fort Moultrie (1806)." His "Battle of New Orleans" in 1816 was one of the first of great renderings of that epic American victory. And White's artistic account of Rebecca Motte urging General Marion to torch her plantation house on the Congaree in an attempt to dislodge British soldiers is a powerful statement of Carolina womanhood.

It's worth noting that White never considered art more than a diversion from his daily practice of law. He was repeatedly elected to the South Carolina legislature, and he was active in Democratic party politics until his death in 1859. White executed several excellent portraits of noteworthy Carolinians -- Charles Cotesworth Pinckney, Keating L. Simmons, John C. Calhoun, and Governor Henry Middleton. He wrote works of fiction and produced several five-act plays for the Charleston stage. "Foscari, or The Venetian Exile" (1805) and "Mysteries of the Castle" (1806) remained in print through the early 20th century.

Edward Brickell White, son of the artist, was a West Point trained army officer, engineer, railroad builder and architect. Octavius Augustus White, his other son, was a College of Charleston educated physician who served as a surgeon for the Confederacy. After the War Dr. White pioneered numerous surgical procedures in New York where he and his family relocated.

Four originals of John Blake White's art hang in various corridors of our nation's Capitol. Each depicts an aspect of our state's role in achieving independence during the American Revolution. Appropriately, one painting depicts the noble Oscar while another features a patriotic woman. Even two-hundred years ago Carolinians appreciated the contributions of all of its citizens in achieving the freedom we enjoy today.

There's More History In Awendaw Than Meets The Eye

How many times do you find that the local fellows know much more history than do the so-called experts? It happens all the time -- especially in the realm of local history. When it comes to the area north of Mount Pleasant stretching from Awendaw to McClellanville, there's no one who can match the knowledge and the story telling ability of native Tim Penninger of the SeeWee Restaurant Penninger family. Thanks to McClellanville resident and New York Times acclaimed novelist, William Baldwin, we have the book Awendaw: Tim Penninger in conversation with William Baldwin with preface by Selden (Bud) Hill (c.2008), a local history project published by the Village Museum in McClellanville.

Remember William Baldwin and his Lowcountry novel, The Hard To Catch Mercy? (c.2004, The History Press)? The man can tell a story! And when Baldwin leans back with old friends Tim Penninger and Bud Hill -- the stories roll like creek water in a summer rain. I doubt you'll ever read a better collection of local yarns than you will in this delightful book.

We know Awendaw as the frontier between us and the Francis Marion National Forest. Developers, environmentalists, and longtime residents have been having some heated discussions over this fringe of coastal plain. What's certain is that change is once more in the air, and for old Awendaw there's a good possibility that this pine barren will see enormous suburban growth once the housing and construction markets improve. Awendaw is one of the close-to pristine portions of the coastal plain that stretches 2200 miles from the New York Bight southwestward to Mobile Bay.

The small community of Awendaw stretches from a few miles west of Highway 17 all the way to Copahee Sound. The area was listed in the 2000 census as having a population of 1,195, and that census tells us that approximately 65% of the Awendaw population is African-American and 34% Caucasian. The per capita income for the town was less than $16,000 annually.

The Awendaw - Copahee area is home, also, to black bears, eagles, osprey, gators, white tail deer, boar, and an occasional Carolina cougar. Traces of a dozen or more colonial and antebellum plantations can be seen on the drive up U.S. Highway 17-North, and a few historical markers, such as the one referencing the old Wappetaw Church, entice the history lover to pause for a moment and ponder what used to be.

Thanks to Penninger, Baldwin, and Hill we have something more to go on than a few historical signs and the wind whispering through the pines. Without stealing their thunder, here are a few gleanings from the dozens of tales they recount about this forgotten nook in upper Charleston County.

Just about everyone knows that the Sewee Indians roamed this area for decades, if not centuries, before the Europeans discovered it. The Sewees are thought to have originally been associated with the great Sioux nation, or Nadowessioux as the French labeled them. Normally, the Sioux roamed the prairies west of the Mississippi, but there were pockets of Sioux-affiliated tribes in the Carolinas and Alabama. The Cheraws in the Upstate were thought to be a Sioux tribe, as well as the Catawbas. Tim Penninger tells of finding numerous arrowheads, stone axes, and bits of elaborate pottery around Awendaw. In fact, the interview that constitutes the greater part of the narrative centers around the vast array of historical objects that Tim Penninger has placed on loan to the Village Museum in McClellanville. Everything is diplayed -- from ancient Indian artifacts to colonial and revolutionary objects right down to the days when contraband whiskey and rum were stored in the area.

Although not noticeable around the Awendaw community, there are ancient shell rings in the near vicinity -- remnants of the Neolithic Age that may even predate Stonehenge as a testimony to a civilization that thrived here and vanished perhaps 6000 years ago. Awendaw's shell rings exist out in the Francis Marion National Forest as well as closer in to the coast. The rings, constructed of oyster shells, were originally 10 to 20 yards in diameter, 2 to 3 feet thick, and higher than one's head. Whether human sacrifices took place there, or sacred dances, or councils of war, no one today knows, but something very important occurred within the ring.

One day archaeologists may be able to tell us more, but Penninger relates how a few years ago an enormous shell ring was concealed during the process of cutting a new road. The ring was hastily recovered and the road was paved, and soon, only a couple of people will ever know that it existed at all.

The commercial center of Awendaw is the Seewee restaurant owned by the Penninger family and the Seewee Outpost. Nearby is the historical marker for the ruins of old Wappetaw Church -- that was the fellowship of worshipers who fled the Salem witch trials of the 1690s. Penninger tells Baldwin that quite a few families around here are descended from those New Englanders who escaped the denunciations of Salem. Whilden, Whitesides, White, and Murrell are a few of those families who relocated. Some of those families helped start the Mount Pleasant Presbyterian Church a century and a half later. Pirates are rumored to have come ashore regularly along Bull's Bay, and tales of buried treasure around Copahee have long been part of Awendaw's lore. To date, nobody knows of anyone who has ever located any pirate treasure.

For this history lover, one of the most fascinating tales of the many that are told about Awendaw is the one where Tim Penninger recounts his boyhood years spent poking around the battlefield site where Francis Marion's men met Bloody Ban Tarleton during the Revolution. Cold steel slashed against cold steel two and a half centuries ago, and Tim accidentally found a broken, rusted saber thrust into the ground unnoticed all these years! Along with that relic, which he has loaned to the McClellanville Village Museum, are British and colonial uniform buttons, coins, pipe bowls and stems, and lead musket balls.

If reading tales of local history is your idea of relaxing on wintry evenings, then look no further than Penninger and Baldwin's little treasure of tales. You'll have a new appreciation for the land and the people who dwell between the Wando and Bull's Bay. For instance, Tim tells the story of one of his great uncles who paid his own tuition to Porter Military Academy by hunting egrets near the marsh. Egret plumes were highly prized ornaments for ladies' hats and the coastal egret was almost hunted into extinction as a result; this particular young man matriculated at Porter and later earned a degree at Oxford University before coming back to teach at Porter.

In countless stories Penninger and Baldwin recreate a vivid past of the people of both races who have deep roots in Awendaw. They tell us things in the manner of two men leaning back from a fireplace recollecting what all their ancestors regaled them with when they were boys decades ago. By all means find this treasure of a book and spend some pleasant hours by your own hearth connecting with our rich past.

C.D. Bull and Sons: At $1.69 a Pound, Cotton is King Again!

You can bet your last dollar that no one around Calhoun County ever wasted time on nonsense such as "the fable of the Scythian Lamb" or better known in parts of Europe as the legend of the "vegetable wool of tartary." To those bred in the South, Gossypium Herbaceum is the dressed up name for cotton, and cotton has been part of our culture since our English ancestors brought it into this port from the West Indies sometime before 1785. A check of the commodities page in the *Wall Street Journal* reveals that cotton is at $1.60 a pound this week, and that's the kind of news that makes some old-timers' heart beat keener.

No other plant is more indicative of a region than is the lush, green and brown cotton stalk to the American South. The romance associated with this fluffy, white "vegetable wool," has intrigued historians, poets, and philosophers since antiquity. Aristotle was enamored with the legend of the "Scythian Lamb" -- that much sought creature of Tartary, a shrub-like plant that had the appearance of a lamb, yet it possessed the root system of a small tree. As he made his conquests, Alexander-the-Great was desirous of discovering this mythical, half-vegetable, half-animal creature. According to legend, the lamb's fleece could be harvested without shearing it and the creature could not bolt away. Explorers of more modern times who set out for the Caucasus Mountains hiked all the way to the Caspian Sea searching for the Scythian Lamb.

Roger Bacon, the 13th century English Franciscan friar and lecturer on Aristotelian logic at Oxford, perpetuated the ideal of the Scythian Lamb in what he more accurately defined as a "wool-bearing tree." And indeed, the cotton-wool plant was soon discovered growing wild in the Scottish highlands. Today, we know that there are more than 40 varieties of cotton plants and that the Aztecs were using the plant domestically when the Europeans encountered them in the 15th century.

By the 1880s, London botonist Henry Lee had witnessed the great textile boom that had been inspired by cotton. He'd studied the rise of the cotton-based economy of the American South and the terrible, yet glorious war that ensued from cultural division. Lee's book, *The Vegetable Lamb of Tartary: A Curious Fable of The Cotton Plant (1887)* is long out of print; however, it chronicles the thousand-year fascination that Westerners have had with a wonderful plant that in no way can be edible. Today, the magnificent cotton stalk with its crowning bolls of white wool-like fiber is experiencing a remarkable comeback as garment-makers rediscover that nothing wears better than natural fiber.

Cotton rose in popularity along the sea-island coast as indigo's market declined following the American Revolution. Most likely the plant was brought up from one of the British West Indies Islands -- Barbados, British Honduras, Jamaica, or the B.V.I. chain. The rich soil of Edisto, Kiawah, Wadmalaw, and John's Island produced the finest long-staple fiber ever encountered. Planters cleared more and more acreage for this crop that promised to enrich them beyond the grandest imagination of their forebears. The demand was made for more and more slaves from the Ivory coast. Of course, cotton's meteoric rise in the South was due to that Massachusetts Yankee, Yale-educated schoolmaster, Eli Whitney. He decided that he could improve upon the tedium of slaves' lives by inventing a mechanical device that would comb the onerous seeds from the fluffy bolls. Whitney made the upcountry, short-staple cotton a marketable commodity, and thus, the "One-Crop, King Cotton Southland" emerged in 1793, just six years after the formation of the Republic. Man's affinity for soft, affordable fabric has never slackened.

Around Augusta in the mid-19th century it was told by Augustus Baldwin Longstreet in his *Georgia Scenes* (1850) that his father, William Longstreet, invented the original cotton gin. During the experimentation process a curiously dressed woman ambled in and asked if she could examine the new machine. As the woman departed, she slipped and thereby revealed that she was actually a man in disguise. Shortly thereafter, the new media heralded Eli Whitney rather than Longstreet as the inventor of the cotton gin. The implication is that the sneaky person dressed as a woman was Eli Whitney.

American economic historian Curtis Putnam Nettles, professor at Cornell from 1945-1967, wrote in his masterwork, *The Emergence of a National Economy, 1775-1815* (c. 1977), that southern farmers became prosperous almost immediately after the invention of the cotton gin. The South produced a combined total of 3 million pounds of cotton in 1793, and by 1811 the production exceeded 80 million pounds. According to Nettles, the average price of a field slave in Charleston in 1795 was $300. By 1812, the price was stable at $550.

Just before the War of 1812 caused southern ports to cease export operations, the price of cotton was 12 cents a pound. That does not sound remarkable by today's standard, but an inflation calculator estimates that the purchasing power of 12 cents in 1812 would equal $2.03 in 2011. Of course, Britain was the great purchaser of southern cotton, and, with the Napoleonic Wars, Britain was producing uniforms for her own military plus that of the allies -- Austria, Prussia, and Russia. In fact, Britain's textile mills even produced the midnight blue tunics worn by her enemy, France!

Southerners grew more and more self-assured as their one staple crop knew no peers around the globe. From Charleston to Savannah, from Mobile to New Orleans southern gentlemen puffed on Cuban cigars and bankrolled fabulous lifestyles known by few other than the British aristocracy. Northern merchants and fledgling textile manufacturers envied the enormous financial power of the South, and southern senators such as John C.Calhoun, Robert Y. Hayne, William C. Preston, and James Henry Hammond breathed fire, brimstone, and nullification to anyone who dared dethrone King Cotton. From stormy times within the Union to the brink of disunion, the country's economic and political future centered on the multifaceted politics of cotton. On March 4, 1858, South Carolina Senator James H. Hammond stood before the U.S. Senate and made his famous "Cotton Is King" oration. "If we never acquire another foot of territory for the South, look at her. Eight hundred and fifty thousand square miles. As large as Great Britain, France, Austria, Prussia and Spain. Is not that territory enough to make an empire that shall rule the world?"

The boasts grew more intolerable and the taint of slavery rankled Puritan sensibilities, and cotton plantations went down with Dixie in the glorious and terrible War of Southern Independence.

Yet, as the *Wall Street Journal* reminds us in the article by Adam Cancryn and Carolyn Cui (*WSJ*, October 16, 2010), the South began to produce cotton shortly after Appomattox, and by 1870, the New Orleans Cotton Exchange recorded $1.70 a pound, or $28.70 in today's economy. This week the New York Commodities Exchange recorded $1.69 a pound. In Mississippi around 1863 cotton reached $1.89 a pound, and that may be the all-time price record.

Cotton production is big-time business in South Carolina again. Our state produced more than 246,000 bales at 500 pounds a bale in 2008, the last year that figures are readily available. Calhoun County alone accounted for 17%, or 42,300 bales.

On Monday of this past week the cotton growers and cotton ginners of Calhoun County and the center of the state mourned the loss of one of their own,

George Capers Bull, Jr., Mr. Bull was president of C.D. Bull and Sons, est. 1887, a cotton gin and warehouse enterprise in Cameron, S.C. George, or Josh as his Citadel Class of 1943 classmates called him, spent his whole life in the cotton business except for the three years that he served in the army in World War II. He planted cotton, graded cotton, brokered cotton, ginned cotton, warehoused cotton, and sold cotton seed and fertilizers for cotton. In 1970, George Bull served as president of the Southeastern Cotton Ginners Association, and in 1971 he was named Outstanding Ginner of the Year and was awarded the Horace Hayden Memorial Trophy for Outstanding Achievement in Cotton Ginning. He's one of the very few South Carolinians to have lived his life in the manner of his forebears dating back to colonial times in this state. I am proud to have had George Capers Bull as my father-in-law.

Mount Pleasant Businessman Has Keen Interest In Bell-Ringing Tradition

An unobservant motorist on Coleman Boulevard wouldn't have noticed, but the customers of Mt. Pleasant Radio near Shem Creek saw something odd in the parking lot during July of that scorching summer of 2007. Wray Lemke, company president, Ham-radio operator, vintage automobile enthusiast, and a novice bell-ringer at the Episcopal Cathedral of St. Luke and St. Paul on Coming Street, had rigged up a curious display on the hot asphalt. With Wray one never knows what he might be up to next. He restores vintage British automobiles, sets up elaborate ship-to-shore communication systems, and has been known to fix just about anything having more than two parts. The contraption in his parking lot looked something akin to giant soup ladles suspended from a window frame. Whatever it was, it had nothing to do with the radio business.

Nearly four years later we know that Lemke was devising an ingenious solution to a frustrating problem that the downtown Cathedral was having with its newly acquired and very costly set of change-ringing bells.

The problem, evidently never before encountered by Charleston bell towers, dealt with how to keep a bell's clapper and pin from seizing up in the oppressive humidity of a Charleston summer. The new bells rang beautifully until the hot weather settled in. Cathedral ringers despaired that their new ring of bronze bells might just be a seasonal joy.

Change ringing is different from tolling or peeling bells. Bronze bells of different size and tone are rung with the bell upside down instead of right side up. Change bells are turned in a 360 degree arc according to complex number patterns.

Lemke, a Cathedral parishioner who wandered into the bell tower on Coming Street out of curiosity, was intrigued by the mix of people and ropes in the 200 year-old bell tower of St. Luke and St. Paul. From that day in 2007, he has been a fixture in the 15 x 15 foot old-brick room with a beautiful Oriental wool carpet.

Charleston has more change-ringing towers than any other city in America. Change-ringing originated in England sometime before the defeat of the Spanish Armada in 1588. The oldest ring in England today is the one at St. Lawrence Church, Ipswich, County Suffolk. Their bells date to 1450 and are called the "Wolsey Bells" after Cardinal Woolsey. No one knows how the tradition of mounting multiple rings of bells in tall church steeples began, but it has remained largely an English custom and has become closely identified with, but not exclusive to, the Anglican Church.

Wray Lemke was relieved that the art of reading sheet music is not required for change ringers. This Greenville native, who graduated from The Citadel in 1972, discovered that the forty or so change ringers in the Lowcountry hail from all walks of life. At the Cathedral of St. Luke and St. Paul, the captain of the bell tower is the church secretary. Another ringer is a petite lady from Yorkshire who lives in Summerville. Another is a retired Air Force C-141 pilot. The bells weigh anywhere from 300 to 1650 pounds, and there are eight of them in the belfry. However, the key to ringing is stamina -- knowing the method, and keeping proper count -- not physical strength. Of course, one does not want to let a rope get wrapped around his neck. And knowing when to turn loose helps one avoid a fast ride to the top of the tower!

Since he devised a way to keep the clappers from seizing up in the humid weather, Lemke has taken it upon himself to make all sorts of repairs on headstocks and timber braces in the 120-foot tower. Bell ringers are stepping around some amazing Charleston history up in the towers of St. Michael's, Grace Church, and the Cathedral. Those bells have made Charleston special for centuries. Wray, along with Dan Beaman, Louisa Montgomery, and George Williams have been on a quest to track down the history associated with these bells.

The original Anglican Church built here in 1680, St. Philip's, had a bell, but it did not have the type of grand change ringing tower that was then being incorporated into the Christopher Wren-designed churches being built in London after the Great Fire of 1666. The first change ring anywhere around here was in St. George's Church, Dorchester, twenty miles up the Ashley River. In 1751 the prosperous planters and traders took up a collection for an octagonal bell tower, and they ordered a set of four different size and tone bells from Abel Rudhall Bellfoundry in Gloucester, England. The base of the old tower still stands today; however, the church was destroyed by the British during the Revolutionary War. St. George's Church, Dorchester, was the second church in North America to acquire a change ring set of bells. The first was the Old North Church in Boston

-- the one made famous by Longfellow in his tribute to Paul Revere's midnight ride. There are four such towers in South Carolina, all in the Charleston area, and just 48 in all of North America.

In 1815 Charlestonians undertook the building of a third grand Episcopal church that they named St. Paul's, Radcliffeborough. From the beginning it was known as the planters' church and money was no object in its construction. To quote Lemke, Beaman, Montgomery, and Williams: "St. Paul's in Charleston acquired the four bells in 1815; three of the bells were mounted in its tower as is proved by the three rope holes in the floor, still surviving. The cracked tenor was recast and given to St. John's Church, Winnsboro, South Carolina, in 1844, where it was destroyed by Sherman in 1865 when his raiders wantonly fired the church."

Around 1854 the three bells in the steeple at St. Paul's were recast into a single bell which was removed and shipped to Columbia for the Confederacy. So, change ringing ceased at St. Paul's, Radcliffeborough, until it commenced anew in 2001. By 2001, the name of the church had been changed to The Cathedral of St. Luke and St. Paul. The Confederacy called in all church bells, including those of St. Paul and St. Michael, for recasting into cannon, and the bells in Charleston were sent by rail for safekeeping in Columbia. They were never cast into cannon, however, but only stored at the statehouse. Unfortunately, the shed on the statehouse grounds where the huge bells were stored was torched by Sherman's troops 146 years ago this month.

St. Michael's Church wardens acquired the broken and charred bells that were recovered on the statehouse grounds and had them recast at the original foundry in England. It is possible that the bronze of the old St. Paul's bell is part of one of the recast bells of St. Michael's.

From 1854 until 2001 there was no change ringing at the Cathedral, though there was change ringing at St. Michael's, Grace, and Stella Maris. The millennium brought a new urge among Cathedral worshippers to renew the ancient English bell ringing tradition. A movement by the Dean of the church and parishioners made it possible to obtain 6 bells, 150 years old, from a redundant parish in England, St. Paul's. Mirfield, West Yorkshire, Diocese of Wakefield. Two more new bells were donated by generous benefactors and they were cast by Eijsbouts Foundary in the Netherlands.

Three local television stations showed film of the gigantic crane lifting the bells into place. One eyewitness recalled that a crowd of 20 people and one dog watched as the enormous bells were moved over the portico and through the Great West Doors of the Cathedral.

By Veterans' Day 2001 the grand tradition of change ringing with complex algorithmic formulae was again a part of Radcliffeborough. Rounds, Plain Hunts, Plain Bob Minor, and Grandsire Doubles are all foreign expressions to anyone but bell ringers, but their distinct chime can be discerned by any Engishman -- or native Charlestonian. Ask Mount Pleasant Radio's Wray Lemke about bells and bell towers. It's just the latest hobby that he has mastered.

A Walk Around Charleston In February 1811

"Time goes, you say? Ah no! Alas, Time stays, we go." Attribute the quote to Austin Dobson, the Victorian poet. Dobson, in his poems and essays, foreshadowed the age of literary realism -- the fictional depiction of everyday life as it really is. As winter recedes and Charleston's azaleas threaten to bud, there're a half-dozen writers researching in local libraries, culling curious bits of our past for titles they hope to publish soon. Nothing interests long suffering scholars more than probing the intimacies of colonial and antebellum life in this cobble-stoned seaport. Two-hundred years from now an aspiring novelist or historian will be noting even the random aspects of this day from the pages of our local newspaper. What's humdrum to us will charm future generations.

Featured prominently in today's newspaper are the boasts of local merchants proclaiming the quality of their wares. Of course, the paper tells of the litany of woes that have befallen us since yesterday. Solomon said it best, "What has been will be again, what has been done will be done again; there is nothing new under the sun." (Ecclesiastes 1:9; NIV). Exactly 200 years ago (1811) the waterfront along East Bay Street was a lively and colorful scene. The clerks of Moise, Sen, and Son carted bales of imported fabrics from the wharf through the streets to their store. Calico, gingham, dungaree, chintz, and khaki were among the textiles just arrived from India; however, seersucker and taffeta headlined the advertisement. Charlestonians had a flair for fashion and the "in" look for spring included seersucker. Moise, Sen, and Son offered these exclusive wares in a private sale to approved purchasers.

Meanwhile, the competition at No. 96 Church Street, Telfer, prided itself in offering "Useful and Fancy Goods" -- quantities of satin, silk, and sarsnet. American beaver fur, Welsh flannel, and worsted lambswool direct from England could be had along with ribbons in many colors. In the event that wintry winds didn't abate soon, fleecy hoisery in many colors was available from English woolen mills.

Bespoke garments in the 19th century meant that tailors often were employed by textile importers. Going to Charleston's Church Street for a fitting was as common here 200 years ago as it was for London gentlemen to call on Saville Row. Ladies were fitted by seamstresses in the privacy of their own parlors.

Macauley, Jun, and Co. of No. 18 Broad Street advertised an elegant assortment of west England super-fine cloths, single and double-milled. They announced the arrival of cashmere cloth and cord for pantaloons.

These merchants enjoyed the well-stocked shelves and the free-spending public for another six months before trade relations between Britain and America strained by war breaking out between the young republic and the Empire. By 1814 Charleston's commerce was a fraction of what it had been in 1811.

Charleston of 200 years ago was as taste conscious as we are today, yet the only eating establishment to advertise regularly was the Carolina Coffee House at Tradd and Elliott Streets. During January and February of 1811, they enticed diners with turtle soup and beef steak. An emporium known simply as No. 116 Queen Street boasted of a new arrival of 1000 pounds of cheese, 20 firkins of butter, 30 boxes of chocolate, 10 barrels of superior vinegar, 75 reams of writing paper, and 2 cases of fans.

E. Morferd of Willington and Company, 133 Broad Street, always had the latest publications together with toiletries and bottled medicines. One book that received a lot of attention here 200 years ago was The Secret History of the Cabinet of Buonaparte, including his private life, character, domestick administration, and his conduct to foreign powers together with secret annecdotes of the different courts of Europe. That ponderous title was edited in New York by Lewis Goldsmith and illustrated in New York by a gentleman just returned from France.

Goldsmith was a character of low-repute, depending upon which set of acquaintances one inquired. He was a British-born gentleman of Portuguese-Jewish ancestry, and he emigrated to France at the onset of the revolution there. Very much pro-republican in sympathy, Goldsmith became persona non grata in London -- especially when he published from Paris a pro-revolutionary journal in English. He became friends with Talleyrand and even with Thomas Paine who had joined the French Revolutionary cause. When Napoleon ascended to power, Goldsmith became a secret agent for the Emperor and was engaged in all sorts of intrigue. When Napoleon fell from power, Goldsmith returned to London from his self-imposed exile and renounced the republican ways of France, However, he had flipped his allegiances one time too many and never regained the trust of his countrymen. Nevertheless, Goldsmith's books sold quite well in America.

All of these stories appeared on the front page of The Courier, the predecessor to the Post and Courier, a newspaper that had been in circulation for 8 years by 1811. At that time there were other newspapers circulating in the city, and they all resembled broadsheets more than the newspapers of today.

Public education was in its infancy, and Charleston and the rest of the state lagged far behind New England in establishing free schools. Yet, there was a demand for accomplished schoolmasters to tutor the sons and daughters of the gentry. An ad appeared 200 years ago in the Courier stating, "A gentleman of public education and respectable connexions [sic] wishes to find employment as Instructor in a private family during the winter." Charlestonians of 1811 ate well and dressed in the finery of the latest in fashion from London and New York. They also enjoyed themselves and loved laughter and theater. "Mr. Dwyer, a celebrated comedian, arrived yesterday in the ship, Mistress, from New York. He will present an evening comedy, "John Bull," and, "The Weathercock." Doors open half past 5 and curtain rises half past 6. People of color cannot be admitted to any part of the house. Smoking in the theater is prohibited. See Mr. Mayberry, ticket agent."

In 1811 Charleston had several theaters; most of them were located on the west end of Broad Street. Plays were also performed in the long rooms of downtown taverns. An encyclopedia of London actors lists a Mr. Dwyer who began his career in Norwich and York before making his 1802 debut on Drury Lane as Balcour in "The West Indian." A few days later an advertisement featured Mr. Dwyer in "Laugh When You Can," for the next nine nights.

Charleston was a city with many medical doctors in 1811. It appears that each one concocted his own elixirs and special remedies. Thomas Peters ran an ad for his worm destroying lozenges and noted that "the medicine is mild as it is certain and efficacious in its operation." Dr. Cornwell announced that "having been burned out [he] is now recovered and [has] removed to the Bay Street just above the fish market at the corner of Hassell Street. Cornwell maintained he was prepared to deal with "all the different branches of his profession with profound secrecy in all cases that may require it." In another notice, Dr. Rogers wanted all to know of his "Efficacious Vegetable Pulmonick Detergent for consumptive, astmatick, and other afflictions."

Charleston had several slave markets for the resale of field and domestic slaves in estate liquidations. Announcements ran daily for these situations. "Negroes for sale. Mr. Payne. North side of the Exchange Building. Estate of Mr. George Lockney, Esq. 170 Negroes. Gang includes 2 drivers, mill wrights, carpenters, coopers, millers, and a shoemaker. Samuel Mutley and Thomas Naylor, Executors.

There were also frequent ads asking help in locating runaway slaves. The daily shipping news was the lead announcement in the top left corner, and often this maritime news took up a third of the front page. In February 1811 the brig Commodore Prebble, Captain James Ingley, was accepting passengers and cargo at Crafts South Wharf, John Haslet, agent. Other ships bound for Liverpool, Baltimore, Greenock, Wilmington, Savannah, New York, and Georgetown bid for fares.

Being February, it was getting close to Race Week, and all of Charleston turned out for the week-long festivities and horse races at the Washington Race Course. The Charleston Jockey Club, then the most elite in the young nation, ran notices daily. Horses arrived from Ireland and England to compete with southern thoroughbreds. Jockey Club stewards, J. B. Richardson, William Stephen Bull, Charles Sinkler, John Bond I'on, William Clement, and J.R. Pringle announced the starting times and prizes with the grand finale being the match up of the finest two-year olds in America on Friday, March 1, 1811.

Remembering past times here it's easy to recall a line by Emily Dickinson, "That it will never come again / Is what makes life so sweet."

Exposing the Origins of Old Glory's Stripes

If you're like me you cringed when the tart flubbed the "Star Spangled Banner" lyrics during the Super Bowl a week ago. Why the network executives did not ask the chorus of the U.S. Naval Academy to do the honors is beyond me -- except that star power brings in profits, whereas patriots bring only applause.

Fly it from a fifty-foot flagpole, embroider it on a sweatshirt, or emblazon it on the fuselage of a Charleston-based C-17, Old Glory is the most beautiful banner any of us know. Unlike many international flags, our fluttering icon contains no symbols of heraldry, no ancient emblems, and no dead monarch's crest. Seven red stripes alternating with six white ones and a blue field containing fifty pentagonal stars -- it's a simple design that signals fair play and the rights of man wherever it flies.

Who came up with this unique flag design? We all know that Betsy Ross stitched the first grand banner in her parlor. What many of us might not know is that Betsy, born Elizabeth Griscom, had been reared a Quaker, and when she eloped with John Ross, meeting him at a tavern in Gloucester, New Jersey, her family all but disowned her. The Quaker church dismissed her from the congregation, and she struggled as a seamstress as her husband worked in trade. Betsy Ross was a young widow when she received the flag request by a friend of the Continental Congress. John Ross had volunteered for the militia and had been killed in the explosion of an ammunition dump. The mystery of who designed our nation's flag and who ordered its construction appears to be a cleverly concealed state secret.

For decades scholars have sleuthed through the archives for evidence concerning the history of our flag's design. A hundred and forty-one years ago, a paper read before the Historical Society of Pennsylvania (March 1870), entitled *The History of the Flag of the United States* by William J. Canby of Philadelphia was published by the grandson of Betsy Ross.

In William Canby's essay he reveals the only historical tip that was known then of the flag's development. "In Dunlap's Journal of Congress, at the date of June 14th, 1777 Vol III, page 235, occurs the only scrap of official history regarding the origin of the flag of the United States yet published. In the proceedings of Congress on this page is found the following resolution: 'Resolved that the flag of the thirteen United States be thirteen stripes, alternate red and white; that the union be thirteen stars, which in a blue field, representing a new constellation.'"

It was clear by 1777 that the revolution was not going to end quickly, and the concern in the Continental Congress was that various patriot militia organizations were still carrying standards bearing the King's insignia, or even the flag of Great Britain itself, into battle against British forces. Out of a dual concern that fighting the Crown while bearing the Crown's colors might be considered a higher form of treason that insurrection, and that other patriot forces might be inclined to fire on friendly forces, it was forthwith determined to place our soldiers and sailors under colors that portrayed our new identity.

Historians have so long debated the true origins of our unique flag that even foreigners have become intrigued -- especially British historians. Sir Charles Fawcett published an essay in a British journal, The Mariners Mirror, October 1937, that supports his contention that the Americans copied the flag of the East India Company of London, then the most powerful international corporation the world had ever seen. Indeed, there is a strong resemblance between their flag of 1634 and our country's Grand Union flag of 1776.

In a carefully researched 20-page essay, Sir Charles Fawcett, an amateur naval historian, pulls together loose threads of evidence to form a case that could solve the American flag origin mystery. It appears by documented record that Lieutenant John Paul Jones ran up a red and white striped flag on the ship, Alfred, on December 3, 1775. Alfred was the flagship of the Congress Navy and was lying at anchor near Philadelphia. Four weeks later, General George Washington saluted a red and white striped banner as he assumed command of the united forces of the states at Cambridge, Massachusetts, on January 2, 1776.

As a former ship master for various British commercial interests, John Paul Jones was very familiar with the ensign of the East India Company. That London-based venture had its own navy, army, and, at times, dictated to Parliament and Crown what policies were apropos.

Imagine Ford Motor Company, Boeing, Microsoft, and Coca-Cola being combined into one monolithic entity with all of their respective tentacles of influence at the command of a handful of powerful directors. That would be the public image in Britain and abroad of the all-too-powerful East India Company. Until 1784, the directors of the Company, known to insiders simply as "The John Company," ruled India as their own domain.

Sir Charles Fawcett tantalizes our imagination with shreds of evidence that America's wiliest rebel, Benjamin Franklin, may have been behind the red and white stripe design for a much more sinister reason. In 1775 the prospect of an American victory over the British Empire was a very remote idea; therefore, why not curry favor with the East India Company directors? The Company had approximately 4 million dollars of inventory in American warehouses at the time of the patriot rebellion. It was no secret that The Company was verging upon bankruptcy in the early 1770s. Their precarious financial situation presaged the famous tea deal that so annoyed Bostonians in 1773, the year of the "Tea Party."

Could Franklin have been searching for a powerful ally with whom the leaders of the 13 North American colonies could strengthen their hand against Crown and Parliament? In those early days of rebellion, it was premature to believe that we would gain complete independence from Britain. Fawcett certainly makes a fascinating thesis that our flag was hoisted, perhaps, as an ominous warning to Crown and Parliament that we might associate with the legendary East India Company and become its domain.

By 1777, the die was cast and the colonies went their independent way -- with a lot of help from the French government. Our making the break from British rule remains to this day one of the most thrilling episodes in history. That red-and- white striped banner included a canton of blue with a galaxy of 13 stars.

Not All of SC's Heroes Hailed From Charleston

Two-hundred and thirty years ago this month the hearts of patriots quickened in conquered Charleston. For nine months the city and most of the state had been under the iron rule of Britain's Lord Cornwallis. The state's militia had surrendered with General Benjamin Lincoln's Continental Army on Friday, May 12, 1780, near where Marion Square is today. They swore never to take arms against the crown again under penalty of the hangman's noose. The quest for southern independence ended here on May 12, 1780 -- or so it seemed. New England had hopes of fighting on.

Seventeen days later, on Monday, May 29, British cavalry under the command of Lieutenant-Colonel Banastre Tarleton slaughtered more than 150 Continentals and Carolina militiamen under Colonel Abraham Buford in the Waxhaws region of upper South Carolina. The Americans died while covering the retreat of S.C. governor John Rutledge who was fleeing into North Carolina. Tarleton accused the Americans of surrendering and then opening fire on the British. Colonel Tarleton's favorite horse was shot from under him, and perhaps that's why he gave the orders for the butchering of America prisoners. The news of the massacre enraged patriotic men who'd laid down arms just days earlier.

One of the men enraged by the massacre of Buford's regiment -- a man who'd fought gallantly and surrendered on the Charleston peninsula -- was Andrew Pickens, a native of the Waxhaws. Pickens had married the daughter of Patrick Calhoun and had purchased land in the Abbeville District before the War. This brave and honorable upstate planter, an elder in the Presbyterian Church, was so outraged by the British violations of the terms of parole that he vowed to take up arms again against the detested foe.

Andrew Pickens -- the youngest of the triumvirate of Carolina militia generals, Sumter and Marion being the others -- was born in Bucks County, Pennsylvania, of Scots-Irish parentage. The Pickens surname had been anglicized from the French Picon spelling. As Huguenots, they had fled Catholic persecution in La Rochelle, with Ulster Province being their initial destination.

After settling a few years in Pennsylvania, the Pickens clan traveled the Great Wagon Road southward and settled amongst their kin in the Waxhaws. Specifically, the Waxhaws region is on the fringe of the Unwharrie Mountain range that begins on the South and North Carolina state line northwest of Lancaster and south of Mecklenburg County and Charlotte. The Waxhaws Indian tribe had been decimated by white man's diseases and then the Yemassee War of 1715. Numerous "old fields" formerly belonging to the Indians attracted the interest of this wave of tough-minded settlers in the 1740s. Names that became famous in SC history included Jackson, Richardson, Davie (the patriot general and founder of the University of North Carolina) and J. Marion Simms, the father of American gynecology.

This buckskin frontier was a haven for Scots-Irish families who, as dissenters, distrusted Anglican bishops as much as they detested the British King and Parliament. Their opinion of Charlestonians was not very high, either. The long rifle, the Bible, farm land, and freedom were their passion. They had their own peculiar recipe for distilled spirits that differed from anything coastal Carolinians ever tasted. Living on the frontier where powder and shot were scarce they developed a motto, "one shot, one kill" -- whether it pertained to a squirrel, a deer, or an Indian. The sound of an axe felling a tree was the year-round cadence to the daily chores of plowing corn and herding cattle.

Nineteen-year-old Andrew Pickens gained his first taste of warfare in 1760 when he fought in the famous Snow Campaign against the Cherokee in the upper reaches of the northwest quadrant of the state. Handsome, bold, tall, and sinewy, Andrew Pickens cut a dashing figure in his buckskin attire on the frontier. When Pickens' father died while Andrew was at a young age, the boy lost all chance of a classical education such as fellow Waxhaws native William Richardson Davie had acquired at Princeton. Andrew Pickens learned to read by repeating aloud John, Chapter 1 from the King James Version of the Bible. Being of modest disposition and a man of few words, he gained insight by being a keen observer of nature and of his fellow man.

Love at first sight occurred often on the Carolina frontier, perhaps because the population was so scattered and choices were few. Rebecca "Becky" Calhoun, daughter of Squire Patrick Calhoun of Abbeville District was about age 16 when she made Andrew her beau. Becky Calhoun, the braided raven-hair and blue-eyed beauty, was a catch for any red-blooded Carolina male. Abbeville District had great appeal to Pickens for it afforded land opportunity, Calhoun connections, and friendship with the numerous fellow Huguenots and Scots-Irish who'd immigrated to this hilly western part of the state. The wedding to vivacious Becky was a three day affair of feasts and celebrations. For decades the phrase "as grand as Becky Calhoun's wedding" was a byword for grandeur in the upstate.

Indian uprisings still plagued the upstate, so the newlyweds were forced to build a stockade fort near their home. As tension grew with Britain, the Cherokee made it their policy to remain loyal to the Crown, so there were scalping incidents and pre-dawn raids aplenty from Abbeville across to Chester. In 1776 Andrew Pickens led a detachment of upstate rangers on a retaliation raid, and he was outwitted by the wily Indians. Pickens found himself surrounded and outnumbered by at least 7 to 1. He and his men would have been wiped out had not cool-headed Pickens devised a rotating load and fire battle plan that allowed the rangers to hold off their attackers in what became known as "the Ring Fight." Eventually the Indians asked for peace. In the ensuing negotiations with the Cherokee, it became clear that they admired this tall white man very much, and they named him "Skyagunsta," a Cherokee word that means "Wizard Owl."

Skyagunsta was a nickname that Pickens relished, though most admirers around the state referred to him as "that taciturn fighting Elder," a term that paid homage to his stern religious faith and his use of scriptural quotes. When the Upstate communities viewed the 1776 struggle as a Charleston matter in which they had little interest, it was Pickens who rode from congregation to congregation to rouse the fighting men to arms. When at least half of the upstate men sided with the King, it was Pickens who stood square for American independence.

Long Canes was the name given to the region near Abbeville where the Pickens family built their home, barns, and stockade fort amidst devout pioneers with surnames of Noble, Petigru, Bowie, and Calhoun. From the days of the famous Ring Fight the Upcountry patriots wanted the 36-year-old Ranger Captain Pickens as their spokesman and leader. Pickens was a commander at the Battle at Savage's Plantation near Ninety-Six, the South Carolina equivalent of "Lexington and Concord." The Whig partisans from the Upstate were among the first to volunteer for duty against the British in Florida and Georgia. And, they rushed to the defense of Charleston when it was encircled and forced into captivity by the British General Clinton and Admiral Arbuthnot between 1779 and 1780.

Tarleton's massacre of Buford's men at the Waxhaws three weeks following the capitulation of Charleston was just one of the reasons for Andrew Pickens to negate his vow and the terms of his parole. The depredations of loyalists against patriots, known as whigs, were frightful in the Upcountry. Pickens rode to Ninety-Six where British Colonel Cruger commanded; and Pickens laid before him the reasons for his taking up arms again. So much did Cruger respect Pickens that he let Pickens pass freely out the gates and to his home without arrest.

Colonel Pickens gave payback to Banastre Tarleton at the Battle of Hannah's Cowpens on a frigid January 17, 1781. With Continentals under General Dan Morgan and Colonel John Eager Howard, Pickens' militia defeated the 71st Highlander Regiment of Foot and routed Tarleton's famed Green Dragoons. The battle gave hope to Charlestonians in captivity. Pickens was with Lighthorse Harry Lee at Haw's Creek in North Carolina, where, through a ruse, the Loyalists were cut to pieces by Patriot forces. The Fighting Elder hung his sword, pistols, and spurs above the fireplace and devoted the rest of his life to farming, the Hopewell Presbyterian Church near Pendleton, and public service to state and country. He was cousin by marriage to John C. Calhoun, and Pickens' son and namesake was governor of S.C. at the time of the firing upon Fort Sumter. The Congressional Directory cites Pickens' public service thus: "member of the state house of representatives 1781-1794; one of the commissioners named to settle the boundary line between South Carolina and Georgia in 1787; member of the state constitutional convention in 1790; elected as an Anti-Administration candidate to the Third Congress (March 4, 1793-March 3, 1795); appointed major general of militia in 1795; unsuccessful candidate for election to the United States Senate in 1797; member of the state House of Representatives 1800-1812; declined the nomination for governor in 1812; died in Tomassee, Pendleton District, S.C., August 11, 1817; interment in Old Stone Churchyard, near Pendleton, S.C."

Fanny Trollope's Book On Early American Manners Outraged Our Ancestors

Restoration playwright and poet William Congreve penned the lines, "Heaven has no rage like love to hatred turned / Nor hell a fury like a woman scorned," in The Mourning Bride of 1697. The majority of writers over the centuries have been male and their use of personification to give human traits to empires and institutions dates to the ancient Greeks. By 1828 our new republic was known far and wide as "fair Columbia," and various depictions of a toga-clad goddess defending justice and purity illustrated everything from legal manuscripts to children's books. For a foreigner to walk upon our shores, dwell amongst us, and write a book that cast aspersions on Fair Columbia's collective character and upbringing was, and still is, close kin to blasphemy. How dare Frances (Fanny) Trollope deride our young republic in her 1832 British blockbuster, Domestic Manners In America.

We're 20 decades removed from the time that 50-year-old Frances Trollope, wife of respected London barrister, Thomas Anthony Trollope, travelled to New Orleans and set out on a steamboat and coach tour of mid-America. This accomplished daughter of the Vicar of St. Michael's Church, Heckfield, Hampshire, was a sensible woman who came into her own in the literary realm when her husband's stock-market speculations destroyed the family's financial independence. March 10th marks the 231st anniversary of Frances Trollope's birth. This woman made a small fortune from her clever mockery of American manners, dress, speech, and lack of scholarly bearing. Since Frances Trollope was quite well-read for a lady of leisure in her day, it is probable that she was familiar with J. Hector St. John -- who wrote under the pen name, de Crèvecœur. This Frenchman who became an American wrote the celebrated Letters from an American Farmer (1784). Crèvecœur's collection of fictional letters of a New York farmer romanticized American life and portrayed it as an idyllic union of man in nature. No doubt this fascinating fiction inspired Fanny Trollope and then Alexis de Tocqueville to come out to the former colonies and see for themselves.

The Trollopes -- Thomas, Frances, and sons, were not idle English shopkeepers on a holiday in America. Back home in Harrow, a short distance northwest of London, the Trollopes were friends of Sir Galbraith Lowry Cole, one of Wellington's commanders in the Napoleonic Wars. The widow of the physician to Queen Charlotte of Mecklenburg-Strelitz, consort to George III, was Frances Trollope's dearest friend. They were landed-gentry and possessed the airs of English landed gentry. Alas, the Napoleonic Wars fueled a frenzy of speculation on the London stock exchanges and many of Britain's fashionable set, the Trollopes, the family of author Charles Dickens, and many others, were financially ruined in the recession following Waterloo.

Trollope men for generations had matriculated at Winchester, the hallowed hall of prep-school learning founded by William of Wykeham that dates to the 14th century. So esteemed is the academic tradition of Winchester that its alums are authorized to use the nominal letters "O.W." for Old Wykehamite," as the first distinction of nominal letters displayed after their name. Frances' husband, Thomas, and her sons, Henry, Thomas, and Anthony Trollope, all were authorized to display the coveted "O.W." distinguisher. The 700 year-old motto of Winchester is the wording of William of Wykeham's crest, "manners makyth the man." These words were more like a creed to all devotees of Winchester School and New College, Oxford, the other foundation of scholarship founded by that imminent old Bishop of Winchester.

What made Frances Trollope's aspersions even more irritating to Americans was the knowledge that she was an intimate houseguest of the Marquis de Lafayette, the hero of the American Revolution. This hero of two revolutions, the American and the French, was a well-known champion of republican ideals. However, in his daily regimen, the old Marquis demanded protocol and deference to his position. Only in America was the grand Marquis called "Citizen Lafayette."

As fortune would have it, Mrs. Trollope and her entourage, which included the noted utopian and libertine, Frances Wright of Scotland, arrived at the docks just as the city of New Orleans was celebrating the 12th anniversary of General Andrew Jackson's great victory over the British in the War of 1812. In fact, Old Hickory's forces routed the British and left dead on the field of battle the British general, Edward Pakenham, brother-in-law to General Wellington, and close friend to Trollope acquaintance, Sir Galbraith Lowry Cole, lately of Wellington's staff.

Historians suspect that Frances Trollope ventured out to America upon the urging of her friend and traveling companion, Frances Wright. The controversial

Mrs. Wright was the subject of whispers behind hand-held fans wherever English ladies congregated. Besides being a free-thinker and all that that entails, Frances Wright championed free-love, emancipation, and communal living. She purchased several thousand acres of wilderness land on the Wabash River in Tennessee with the expressed purpose of conducting a noble social experiment. Her aim was to purchase slaves, liberate them at her "Nashoba Commune," and educate them in the finest tradition of English schooling and civility. She planned to prove to the world that the African was every bit the equal of the European or the American. Fanny Trollope hoped that the Trollope boys might gain employment as instructors in Wright's bold scheme. Unfortunately, Frances Wright's utopian Nashoba scheme collapsed completely due to poor planning and insight. She ferried her freedmen to Haiti and deposited them as free citizens on that shore before going back to Scotland and taking up with Robert Owens and his bizarre New Lanark factory commune. Wright later became a foe of marriage and many other traditions of western society.

It is unlikely that Fanny Trollope had given any thought to writing for publication prior to 1828, for English ladies were expected to confine their opinions to themselves in those days. However, Fanny kept a travel diary, and she noted even the subtlest differences between the citizens of the new republic and the subjects of George IV of England.

It was clear, from her arriving in New Orleans, that America did not offer the eye-pleasing prospects of a London, a Bristol, or a Poole. Trollope's diary records her first impression thus: "I never beheld a scene so utterly desolate as this entrance of the Mississippi. Had Dante seen it, he might have drawn images of another Bolgia from its horrors. One only object rears itself above the eddying waters; this is the mast of a vessel long since wrecked in attempting to cross the bar, and it still stands, a dismal witness of the destruction that has been, and a boding prophet of that which is to come." She should have leapt for joy at the sight of land after a seven-week crossing, the last three days of which were consumed by the fright of being chased by rogue pirate ships in the Gulf!

The newspaper of the day, The New Orleans Argus dated December 26, 1827, reveals a bustling port with a decided French air about it and a saucy defiance of tradition. The paper contains notices of slaves, houses, and horses for auction. Advertisements proclaimed a new Commercial Club for gentlemen being formed by subscription. Another ad touted a grand ball at the Jackson Ball Room on Saturday night.

Immediately, the New Orleans Octaroon culture caught Trollope's sharp eye. These light-skinned young women of color who were brought up to be mistresses to Creole gentlemen. Of all the degradations of slavery in America, to Frances Trollope this Octaroon culture was the most abominable. Capping the New Orleans social scene was a yearly ball, gentlemen only, where pretty young octaroon girls were displayed for admiring men to claim. That such a culture could coexist alongside Catholicism and Protestant Christianity was unexplainable to her.

As the steamboat made its way up the Mississippi River, the coarse nature of her fellow passengers made Fanny Trollope anxious on more than one occasion. She remarks, "The gentlemen in the cabin (we had no ladies) would certainly neither, from their language, manners, nor appearance, have received that designation in Europe; but we soon found their claim to it rested on more substantial ground, for we heard them nearly all addressed by the titles of general, colonel, and major." In the new classless society that Americans were carving out of the wilderness, no man had a title, yet every man coined his own sobriquet -- becoming a colonel, a major, or captain. The rough appearance, worn clothing, and battered shoes gave the impostor away. Then, there was the universally common trait among American men of chewing tobacco and spitting -- in doors, or out. Spittoons were in every corner and ladies had to be mindful of the hems of their skirts when they walked in the presence of men.

Frances Trollope and her family dwelt among us for several years, primarily in the Cincinnati area. Occasionally, she confided to her diary praiseworthy things about Americans. We were helpful, goodhearted, frank in our discussions, and pious. Yet, it was our want of good manners and proper decorum that kept us, in her eyes, from ever being able to take our proper place at the side of Britain, France, Spain, and Holland.

An English contemporary of Frances Trollope was Harriet Martineau, a lady known in some circles as the "mother of sociology." She was a friend of John Stuart Mill, George Eliot, Charles Darwin, and Elizabeth Barrett Browning. Martineau came to America for a few years and she published a very favorable review of our people and form of government -- Society in America, 3 volumes, 1837. Her work was seen as a slap in the face to Fanny Trollope's cheeky review. Frances Trollope was in the American midwest during the ascendancy of Jacksonian democracy, one of the great leveling trends in western culture. Trollope's book, *Domestic Manners of the Americans* (1832), had a great influence upon Harriet Beecher Stowe, and Trollope's and Frances Wright's published ideas on the evils of slavery, influenced Stowe's own work, *Uncle Tom's Cabin, Or Life Among The Lowly*, published in 1852.

South Carolinians At The Alamo

"I'm determined, for one, to go with my countrymen: right or wrong, sink or swim, live or die, survive or perish, I am with them." These words were written by 26-year-old William Travis to his friend, Jim Bowie. One-hundred and seventy-five years ago this month Travis, Bowie, and 189 men died defending the Alamo from Santa Anna's force of 2400 Mexican soldiers. Of the Alamo's defenders, just 6 were native-born Texans. Sources say that 32 were from Tennessee, a few were from Pennsylvania, and about 30 hailed from England, Ireland, Scotland, and Germany. However, the South Carolinians were represented by the commander, William Travis, and four other men of steel on that bloody Sunday, March 6, 1836.

The Texas War of Independence was a bitter six-month struggle culminating in the Battle of San Jacinto, a great victory claimed by Sam Houston in April, 1836. As Houston's infantry sabered and shot the fleeing forces of Santa Anna, the victors screamed "Remember the Alamo!," "Remember Goliad!" Lyndon Johnson, himself a Texan, often used the phrases as he escalated the troop strength in Vietnam.

To President-General Antonio López de Santa Anna, the Americans who poured in to east Texas were illegal immigrants bent upon seizing his territory. To the pioneers who rode in from Alabama and Louisiana, this land belonged to the United States by right of the Louisiana Purchase -- even though the Purchase Land boundary was at least 150 miles northeast of where white ranchers were staking claims in 1836.

William Barret Travis was typical of the early 19th century upstate male. He came from good English stock. His family immigrated from Virginia and the Great Wagon Road and they stopped when they got to the fertile lands along the Saluda. The exact area was known as the Mine Creek community near Red Bank. Today, the crossroads is encompassed by the town of Saluda, but in the early 1800s the center of life there was the Red Bank Baptist Church and its dynamic pastor, Alexander Travis. This area was much inspired by the Second Great Awakening and William Travis followed his Uncle Alexander west to evangelize the Yazoo Land just opened in Alabama-Mississippi. A small Baptist was seminary opened near Sparta, probably by Alexander Travis, and young William matriculated through a few grades before signing on as an apprentice with attorney, James Dellet. Travis read law and taught school in Sparta, Alabama, until 1828 when a 16-year-old girl, Rosanna Cato, one of his students, rather hastily became his wife.

The circumstances of this marriage, William Travis was 19, are unclear, but trouble arose in the marriage shortly after they were betrothed. For a year or two William practiced law in Claiborne, Alabama, and enjoyed a happy home life with Rosanna amd their son, Charles Everett Travis. He became a captain in the local militia and seemed headed to a political career in Alabama. Yet, William deserted his bride and the legend is that she was pregnant with a child that he suspected was not his. Legend says that he killed a man and departed alone in the middle of the night. Whatever happened back in Alabama, William Travis made his way quickly to Texas. He arrived shortly after Mexican foreign minister Lucas Escalada put out the infamous "Law of April 6, 1830" which forbade anymore American immigrants coming into Texas. "The Law of April 6" ran head on into the financial might of the Galveston Bay and Texas Land Company, a real estate holding company formed in New York by partners Joseph Vehlein, David G. Burnet, and Lorenzo de Zavala. Collectively, the attitude of Burnet, Vehlein, et al, toward Escaladas was "bring it on." Other American land companies were also operating in east Texas, notably the Nashville Colony. Travis purchased a stake from Stephen F. Austin in a new township called San Felipe de Austin in May, 1830. He networked through his militia and Masonic connections and soon set up a solo law practice near Galveston Bay. Travis was 21. Travis never mentioned his problems in Alabama and no one asked. Before long he was courting a pretty daughter of pioneer stock. Like the men around him, "The Law of April 6" was their *bete noir* -- their rallying cry of disdain for Mexico. Within a year he was Lieutenant-colonel Travis and he was a leader of a popular protest movement that was arming for war with Mexico. Several accounts attribute the cause of the War for Texas Independence to Travis' continuous harangues at public meetings up and down the Texas Gulf coast. William Travis met Jim Bowie of Kentucky soon after they both arrived in the Texas borderland. The two men probably had kinship since Bowie had cousins galore in the Edgefield District back in SC. As the months dragged on, conditions between Mexico and the Americans in Texas Territory became strained. Depredations occurred where both sides claimed credit for heinous acts. By October, 1835, military engagements began all along the east Texas frontier. In Gonzalez, the Mexican Army tried to capture a fort with a cannon that the militia used to frighten away raiding Commanches. Travis' cohorts raised a white flag with a cannon barrel, a lone star, and the words "Come And Take It" emblazoned on it. After several hours of gunfire the Mexican army withdrew.

The next engagement was at Goliad, and it ended as an amazing victory for the independence-minded Texans. The only casualty was a freedman, Sam McCulloch, a former slave of George Collingsworth. His was the first blood shed for Texas Independence. At this juncture, President-General Santa Anna determined to put a stop to the insurrection caused by the "illegal Americans." He put out the word that a merciless force would sweep east Texas and that all rebels would be killed on sight. If ever a man flung down a gauntlet to answer a challenge, Santa Anna's proclamation inspired that act in William Travis. His fighting blood was up, and that was the effect upon Jim Bowie and another South Carolinian, James Butler Bonham. Bonham hailed from Saluda just as did his cousin, William Travis. Bonham had been booted out of South Carolina College (now USC) for leading a student insurrection against poor instruction and sorry food. He was close kin to the Pickens and Calhoun families, and tempestuous Bonham was known to have engaged in duels while he was in college. After reading law for a year, Bonham set up practice in Pendleton, but a fight in a courthouse where Bonham caned the opposing attorney and threatened the judge served to curtail his legal career. He became a leader in the South Carolina Nullification Crisis and was ready to fight President Jackson and the entire U.S. army over the hated tariffs. Bonham eventually drifted west where lawyers were not held to such rigid protocol in the courtroom and men could dream of land in 10,000 acre parcels.

With Andrew Jackson as president and manifest destiny as an American mindset, it is easy to understand our nation's sentiment toward "liberating" east Texas for American-styled democracy. Though, some Texians -- Americans drifting illegally into Texas -- were thinking of establishing a rival republic to the one already governed by Washington, D.C.

Santa Anna's army did as promised and rounded up American settlers and destroyed stockpiles of weapons accumulated by militia organizations. As Santa Anna's force moved closer to Mission San Antonio de Valero, the place we now know as the Alamo, General Sam Houston ordered Jim Bowie to dynamite the buildings and retreat. Bowie crumpled the letter and tossed it in the fireplace. He and Scottish-born, American Indian fighter James Neill decided to make a stand right there against Santa Anna's overwhelming force. Part of Bowie's decision was predicated upon his utter contempt for Mexican men's fighting prowess. Bowie sent word to his friend Travis to bring help.

William Travis, accompanied by his slave, Joe, and a company of heavily armed riflemen rode into the mission fort in February, 1836. They were met with raucous cheers and Travis sent word to dozens of other militia companies to call out their men and report to the Alamo. Only a few would heed Travis' pleas, however. The band known as "The Immortal 32" of the Gonzalez Rangers slipped through Santa Anna's ever tightening noose. They were the last men to reach the Alamo before Santa Anna surrounded it and demanded surrender.

As depicted in the movie, Travis drew a line in the dirt with his sword and asked men willing to stay and fight to step across it, or else flee over the wall while a chance to get out alive remained. Every man stepped across the line, including Travis' slave Joe, and another black man named Jack. The die was cast and the battle for Texas independence is part of American lore.

Davy Crockett, Jim Bowie, 28-year-old James Bonham, and William Travis, age 26, were all killed by Santa Anna's overwhelming force. Other South Carolinians that died at the Alamo were Lemuel Crawford, George Neggan of the "Immortal 32," and 20-year-old Lt. Cleveland Kinloch Simmons of Charleston. One-hundred and fifteen men perished and others died of wounds in captivity or were executed away from the Alamo. Milledge Luke Bonham, a brother of James Bonham, became one of the founders of The Citadel, a military college founded in part upon the need for defense against slave insurrection and in part as response to the Texas independence struggle.

Commencement At Willington Was SC's Grandest Annual Academic Occasion

Not a stone, a brick, a log, plank, or chimney remains to mark the site of Willington, South Carolina's nationally prominent antebellum boarding school. Only the rustling breeze through the hickory and poplar trees still whispers of the great men who were once boys together there in Abbeville District so long ago -- eight generations to be exact. It was a time when education was deemed a vital national resource, something so precious to the existence of the young republic that it was to be acquired with little regard to the cost. In fact, to be forever known as an "old boy" of Doctor Waddel's Willington was enough to set one up for a lifetime of the most elite contacts here and in surrounding states and Washington, D.C.

No Georgian columns adorned red brick lecture halls. No hallowed archways served as portals to dining or debate arenas. The modest buildings of this rustic, yet intellectually elite, campus were constructed of slabs of heart pine with floors of hard, white oak. And even as it was up at Exeter in New Hampshire, or Harrow outside London, the place rang with orations from Virgil, Ovid, and Horace. Young graduates of Doctor Waddel's famed academy headed for the elite universities in the Northeast, and they usually exempted all but the last two years of work in those august institutions. Calhoun, McDuffie, Longstreet, Crawford, Butler, Pickens, Petigru and Legare all matriculated there on the flood plain of the great Savannah River just a mile or two this side of the Georgia line.

In the early days of the state, boys fortunate enough to attend a prestigious school such as Waddel's academy were accustomed to no predetermined year-end commencement. A day in a student's life at Willington entailed translating 500 to 1000 line of one of the Latin poets and then committing the lesson to memory for the purpose of reciting if called upon. It was a rigorous curriculum equal to Eton and Harrow in England. The term was over when the masters and the head were satisfied that the year's lessons had been mastered. A month before year-end festivities, Doctor Waddel placed an announcement in the state's leading newspapers that a commencement would be forthcoming -- and what a grand occasion it was from year to year for the first half of the 19th century. Hundreds of carriages made their way to this remote section of the state to witness the latest crop of classical scholars strut their stuff in speeches, debates, and poetry recitations. It was the closest that our state ever came to the idea of *Encaenia*, the 700-year-old Oxford model of academic commencement.

The grand culmination of the academic year at Willington was a commencement week of festivities that drew parents and distinguished visitors from two states. Congressmen, governors, and senators were always on hand at Willington to meet their constituents and bathe in the glory of this backwoods republican institution. Commencement week was different from exhibition week earlier in the school year when boys would hold a public recitation of their lessons. That, too, was great entertainment, but exhibitions drew fewer spectators than did commencement.

Next to race week in Charleston this was one of the premier social occasions in the state. Commencement week was in late spring, or early summer usually, as the surrounding forest reaffirmed hope eternal with an abundance of new flora. The young Charleston student, John Bull, wrote to his mother in 1807 that "Mister Waddel had a notion of an exhibition on the last of July, but he has given it out because if the boys had to prepare for an exhibition they would not have an opportunity to prepare for examination." But when the schoolmaster determined that the time had come, sometime between May and July, row upon row of rough plank seats would be assembled in concentric circles about an elevated wooden stage. Logs laid parallel with planks placed at appropriate intervals served as seats for the ladies, while the gentlemen congregated in groups under the trees. Since accommodations in the little crossroads community were woefully inadequate for such a crush of visitors, there being but one tavern in the area, it was common practice for the boys to move out of their own boarding quarters to make room for guests, many of whom were of the fairer sex. Boys would double up or "rough it" by temporarily inhabiting the many sheds around the campus.

The first two days of commencement were always devoted to the examination of the candidates by the distinguished alumni and guests. The eminent Calhoun was almost always on hand, even after he became Vice President, as was the popular Senator Crawford of Georgia. The imposing Moses Waddel, renowned since 1807 as the "great Doctor Waddel," presided as master of ceremonies at these festive occasions much the way a nineteenth century martinet would maneuver a battalion.

When the time came for examination, it was rare that the leading political figures of the day hesitated to query the boys on the finer points of Cicero's or Thucydides' writings. The assembled visitors thrilled at the questions and prompt responses. The examination phase was taken seriously, and educated men harkened back to their school days for question topics.

Following the oral examination, there was dinner on the grounds. Picnic hampers were spread under the oaks and beech trees. Servants accompanied the well-to-do. Blushing maidens were introduced to young gentlemen scholars who were, for once, well-groomed and eager to be on their best behavior. Mothers rejoiced in the compliments their sons received from passersby. The learned Doctor Waddel no longer shunned the company of the affluent who patronized his institution and flocked to his campus for the pomp of these annual affairs. The popular Governor Mathews, who had become governor when the British vacated Charleston in 1781, had three grandsons at Willington; Senator Bibb had two brothers-in-law, and Congressman Early of Georgia had a brother there. The list of distinguished patrons of Willington was lengthy in the first two decades of the nineteenth century. One of the most notable men who came to Willington on a regular basis was William J. Hobby, the editor of the *Augusta Herald*. Hobby, as an editorialist, was one of the most respected and feared polemicists in the nation. Hobby had a son studying under Waddel. Boys of more humble background, clothed in a popular, less expensive material known as "turkey red," mingled with the sons of the powerful aristocrats.

James Lewis MacLeod, historian, states that, "Students Waddel trained at Willington headed for leadership positions in South Carolina like race horses trained for the finish line. Four elected governors of South Carolina in a row had gone to Waddel. All the speakers of the South Carolina House of Representatives from 1833 to 1847 were Waddel's students. Three United States Senators trained by Waddel went to Washington between 1820 and 1860. Three South Carolina federal judgeships in succession were filled by Willington students. One Waddel-trained Attorney General of South Carolina replaced another. In 1850 the Judge of the Court of Equity as well as the U.S. District Attorney for South Carolina had gone to Willington." The President of the Bank of South Carolina was an alumnus as were the Presidents of the Charlotte and South Carolina Railroad and the Savannah Valley Railroad. In 1857 the mayors of the rival towns of Charleston and Savannah were both Waddel-schooled. The Chancellor of South Carolina was a faithful member of the swelling alumni chorus, as was the president of the college.

The list of famous alums goes on and on. In Georgia his alumni list claimed two United States Senators, five members of the United States House of Representatives, and three governors. In Alabama, there was a United States senator, a governor, a Chief Justice of the Alabama Supreme Court, one College Chancellor, and one member of the United States House of Representatives.

The national level was not neglected either as Waddel's "old boys" (some had previously served on the state level) claimed nine governorships, three United States Secretaries of War, two Secretaries of State, one Secretary of the Treasury, and a Vice President of the United States. In the presidential election of 1824, two of the four contenders, Calhoun and Crawford, were old boys of Waddel's school. That famous election ended up being decided by the House of Representatives. Andrew Jackson claimed Waddel as his teacher when Waddel was in the Waxhaws. It is doubtful whether any preparatory school in America can lay claim to more alumni fame, especially in so short a time. Since there were no Presbyterian seminaries close by, a number of theology students were supervised in independent study with Moses at Willington. There were other academies in South Carolina, but none that approached the reputation of Waddel's. Moses Waddel's most famous student, John C. Calhoun, Vice President of the United States under Andrew Jackson, and author of the Nullification Doctrine, eulogized his former teacher thus: "He discharged punctually and faithfully the various duties attached to all his private relations. He was sociable and amiable, but not without a due mixture of sternness and firmness. As a minister of the gospel, he was pious, zealous, and well-versed in theology generally. His style of preaching was plain, simple, earnest. He addressed himself much more to the understanding than to the imagination or passions. As a teacher he stands almost unrivaled."

It appears unlikely that any academic insitution will ever again have commencement ceremonies as important to a state's social and political life as were the commencements at Willington between 1810 and 1840.

Remembering That Incomparable Carolina Teen, Eliza Lucas

Who among us was capable at age 16 of assuming the duties of our father's business and acting as head of household for an invalid parent and three younger siblings? Name a Carolinian who earned his or her way into the history books while he was still in his teens. One example might be Andrew Jackson, a raggamuffin of 13. He sassed a British officer and refused to black the man's boots, thus receiving a saber slash across his cheek. Yet another, more romantic, example is the tender story of Eliza Lucas. At the age that most girls are dreaming of their first prom, Miss Eliza, as the servants called her, was the mistress of Wappoo Plantation and two other large estates west of the Ashley River in the mid-18th century. Through her industry and devotion to horticulture, this teen dramatically altered the economy of the region with her adaptation of indigo to Lowcountry cultivation.

At the time when parents today are trusting their teen with the family sedan, Liza Lucas' father was handing over to her the reins of the family fortune. As a colonial officer in His Majesty's Britannic Army, Colonel Lucas had been recalled to active duty in Antigua -- the Lucas family home before they immigrated to Carolina. Certainly the Charles Town gentlemen must have scoffed at George Lucas entrusting his plantations to a young female member of his family rather than hiring a trustee from among the local gentry. One of those plantations consisted of 3000 acres of rice fields on the Waccamaw River, a day's sail from Charles Town. Within an hour's coach ride were the Middletons, Draytons, and Bulls of the Ashley River domains. Any would have considered it an honor to stand in for Colonel Lucas while he was serving the Crown's interests in the Caribbean. Little then did her father know that Liza would unlock the great secret to the Carolina colony's economic success for a century and a half when she successfully harvested indigo on the banks of the Wappoo.

Because the father had supreme confidence in the daughter to manage his affairs and to care for his invalid wife, we had one of the great American legends develop right here among our own people. The broadcaster-turned-writer, Cokie Roberts, features Eliza's story prominently in her bestselling book, Founding Mothers: The Women Who Raised Our Nation (Harper, c.2005). A century or more ago, local attorney and historian, Edward McCrady wrote: "Indigo proved more beneficial to Carolina than the mines of Mexico or Peru were to Spain . . . . The source of this great wealth . . . was a result of an experiment by a mere girl."

Charles Town in March 1742 was a royal province governed as an extension of King George II, then in the 15th year of his reign. Sir Robert Walpole, Sir Spencer Compton, William Pitt, Eldr., and Henry Pelham were the King's inner circle, and one, or all, of these counselors selected 42-year-old James Glen, of Linlithgow, Scotland, to execute the Crown's rule in the Province of Carolina. Glen was a lawyer and a soldier. He was best known in Carolina for prosecuting the various Indian wars and for bringing Germans over to populate new settlements such as Purrysburg, New Windsor, Amelia, Orangeburg, and Saxe-Gotha. Having been educated in the law at the University of Leyden, Glen was close to his Lieutenant-Governor, William Bull, who was also an alumnus of that famed institution -- albeit in medicine. Colonel Lucas, as part of the royal militia and constabulary in Carolina, was a supporter and loyal friend to James Glen and would have made many trips into Charles Town to confer with the Governor in his office at the Exchange. Glen would have been aware of Lucas' daughter taking the reins of the family plantations on the Wappoo.

Eliza Lucas' letter book chronicles the daily life of a genteel Charles Town family during the royal era of the colony. Eliza was born in Antigua and was educated at Mrs. Boddicutt's School in London. Like all proper ladies of her day, she spoke French fluently, enjoyed the classical music that often was performed as chamber music in Charles Town drawing rooms, and she did the requisite needlework that was both pastime and obligation of her gender. However, this young lady had a profound interest in horticulture, and it is evident in her journal and letters even before her ascension to the title of "planter" at the age of 16.

Every Carolinian maintained a herb garden, and many experimented with local plants for use as medicines, dyes and crops for export. Eliza was very familiar with the many varieties of cannabis as hemp rope was one of the colony's prime exports -- mostly to Antigua and the other British possessions in the Caribbean. Indeed, the first edition of the South Carolina Gazette in 1732 featured a lengthy column on the benefits of introducing cannabis to annual rotation of crops then being planted along the Carolina coast. Eliza was also experimenting with the "cotton wool" plant which sprouted voluntarily in Scotland and Ireland, and she had numerous schemes for pine and oak trees.

Operating a pitch and turpentine barreling business along with a facility for the making of oak barrel staves for a cooperage constituted her daily supervisions. By the time Governor Glen left Carolina, he had noted in his journal, "A Description of South Carolina" (1761), that a single slave could plant and care for two acres of indigo and that each acre could yield 80 pounds of indigo." An essay on Glen states, "in that case, with 1761 prices averaging around 3.2 shillings per pound of indigo, each indigo slave generated nearly £13 annually, roughly equivalent to $2,000 today." Eliza, by the time she reached age 21, had single-handedly altered the economic landscape of one of Britain's colonial crown jewels.

Communication with Antigua was particularly easy for the residents of Charles Town, for more ships departed for that island than any other destination save for England. And Eliza Lucas was what we'd call today "Daddy's girl." She wrote her father fortnightly, and occasionally more often. She laid out her "grand schemes" and she confided in him her cares and concerns for the plantations. Sometimes the news was not good -- an unusually cool March, 1742, had killed thousands of indigo seedlings. Worries of slave uprisings on the coast and Indian raids on the northern border kept Charles Town residents on edge. However, she kept her father abreast of the joyous things, too. Nothing was so merry as the "King's Birthnight Celebration" of November 10. Banquets, balls, illumination of houses, military parades, and the firing of the ships' guns in the harbor noted this grand event in the life of the colony. Occasionally, the great barons of the Ashley River estates would announce a "festal." In March 1742 Eliza and her mother were rowed down Wappoo and up the Ashley in their long boat to Ashley Hall, the elegant country seat of the Royal Lieutenant-Governor, William Bull. The event was a highlight of a letter she wrote to her father who was then serving as Royal Governor of Antigua.

As if Eliza Lucas did not have her hands full handling the plantation accounts and overseeing the planting and harvesting, she also received regular communication from schoolmasters in London on the progress of her two younger brothers. And she had the constant duty of seeing to the needs of her invalided mother. Where did she find the time to socialize? Gentlemen all over Charleston were desirous to dance with Eliza, to talk of crops with Eliza, or to hear her read some of her poems. It appears that Eliza Lucas was quite the "catch" if any man could get the chance to woo her. And woo her they did! Though she apparently had many suitors, Eliza chose the widowed husband of one of her dear friends -- Charles Pinckney. Pinckney was a planter nearby and had known Eliza since she was 14 -- she was 20 at the time of her wedding.

Charles Pinckney was an attorney, the first native-born attorney in the colony, and an advocate in the Court of Vice-Admiralty.

Together, Charles and Eliza Lucas Pinckney produced three children who survived to adulthood. Charles Coteworth Pinckney signed the Constitution and became a vice-presidential and presidential candidate on three occasions, and Thomas Pinckney negotiated the Pinckney Treaty with Spain, thus securing navigation rights on the Mississippi River. Their daughter, Harriott, married Peter Horry and became mistress of Hampton Plantation on a tributary of the South Santee. Eliza Lucas Pinckney never thought of herself as a feminist or pioneer for women's rights, nor did she seek fame or fortune for herself. She considered herself a servant of the Almighty and a loyal subject of the Crown. She was less attracted to the "Republic of Virtue" forming about her than were her progeny. Two-hundred and sixty-nine years ago this month, Eliza Lucas made her grand experiments with indigo at Wappoo Plantation west of the Ashley River, and by so doing, changed the economy of her region for one-hundred years to come.

Lincoln Sent Hoodwinking Hurlbut as Envoy to Charleston in 1861

Put yourself in the shoes of Charleston's Broad Street bankers and lawyers on Monday, March 25, 1861. Word of mouth spread the word that Steve Hurlbut was back! And the reason Hurlbut gave for showing his face here? According to eye witnesses at the Meeting Street Charleston Hotel where he checked in, Hurlbut claimed that he was an envoy for newly elected President Abe Lincoln. He and Massachusetts Congressman Ward Lamon were here to ascertain if South Carolina's old guard Union men -- such as federal judge James L. Petigru and Greenville attorney James L. Orr, and Judge Daniel Elliott Huger to name just a few -- could stem the tide of the fire-eater secessionists. If Abe Lincoln ever had one chance in a hundred of winning over a rebellious faction, he threw away his opportunity with his choice of sending long-time friend Steve Hurlbut into "that infernal snake pit of secession," as northern newspapermen labeled Charleston.

The Stephen Augustus Hurlbut who grew up at 8 Montagu Street in the 1830s was a clean-cut, ambitious, and popular young lad. His father, Martin Luther Hurlbut, was a New England schoolmaster who started a private school near the College of Charleston. At the time, it was the finest classical academy in the city. Headmaster Hurlbut's son was the school scholar and quite a child prodigy about town.

Martin Luther Hurlbut and his family were communicants of the Congregational Church on Meeting Street until the Reverend Samuel Gilman persuaded him to bring his family to the Unitarian Church on Archdale Street. With Harvard-trained Gilman as the minister, the Unitarian Church became the center of the Whig faction that sparred with the Nullifier faction led by the Calhoun disciples. The fact that the Unitarians were anti-trinitarian did not seem to matter much to antebellum Chalestonians. Young Hurlbut was even then aligning himself with the New England manner of thinking.

Though the senior Hurlbut took his family to Philadelphia for a year or two, he returned and took up residence at 96 Church Street and arranged for longtime family friend James Louis Petigru to take Stephen into a law apprenticeship at Petigru's law office on St. Michael's Alley. The year was 1840. Whig president William Henry Harrison died shortly after taking office. The rumor was that he was too vain to wear a hat in the frigid Washington weather on the day that he gave his inauguration address. Texas annexation was the talk of southerners everywhere. And up on Marion Square a military academy was being constructed under the auspicious name, The South Carolina Military Academy, to aid in quelling slave insurrections and Texas annexation if called upon. Hurlbut became one of Petigru's brightest legal scholars, and he revelled in the older man's Unionist, Whig views.

Upon satisfactory examination by three local attorneys, Stephen A. Hurlbut was admitted to the Charleston bar, and he hung out a shingle at No. 25 Broad Street. It wasn't long before Hurlbut took a partner, John E. Carew, into his firm, and the two handled various cases before the state and federal bench. One case in particular stands out where Hurlbut acted as agent for a widow to auction her slaves. He exacted a percentage fee for his services, an act which was standard procedure; however, in later years, Hurlbut boasted that though he endured the slavocracy of Charleston, he'd never personally profited through slave dealings. Add liar to the lengthening list of character flaws of Lincoln's envoy to Charleston in March of 1861.

As early as 1835, refugees from northern Florida's Seminole troubles entered Charleston county, and the young bloods seethed with anger that the United States military presence in Florida was not doing enough to quell the Indian uprisings. Stephen Hurlbut was an up-and-coming lawyer with political ambitions, and he decided to enlist with the city's most elite military militia company, the Washington Light Infantry, known around Charleston as the W.L.I. Jeffrey Norman Lash tells in his biography of Hurlbut (A Politician Turned General: The Civil War Career of Stephen Augustus Hurlbut, Kent State Press, 2003) that an aspiring Whig attorney named Francis Lance urged Hurlbut to join the W.L.I. Other members of the Charleston bar who had political aspirations and were desirous of a military legacy were James Taylor, William Blanding, and John Schnierle. Off they all marched to northern Florida where the men spent most of their time in garrison or on brief reconnaissance patrols. No engagements with the fierce Seminoles took place. Those Indians fought only when they could outgun, or outrun their hapless opponents. Hurlbut distinguished himself as a drill sergeant, eventually becoming a lieutenant in the W.L.I. Occasionally, he served as collation chairman when the military unit celebrated Washington's birthday, or some other notable event. He enjoyed wearing the grand uniform and parading with the unit. The official biography of the W.L.I. does not make mention of Hurlbut or Lance in its index of notables.

Military men in the city took notice of Hurlbut's martial bearing. Fort Moultrie army captain William Tecumseh "Cump" Sherman was particularly impressed with him. Their friendship was rekindled when Lincoln's government appointed Hurlbut a major general in the Union army.

In March of 1844, Stephen Hurlbut was Henry Clay's Lowcountry campaign manager and squired the Kentucky Whig Speaker of the House from speech to dinner to private time with donors. It was about this time that Hurlbut's reputation began to take a turn for the worse.

When he was not putting on martial airs with the W.L.I., Hurlbut enjoyed meeting with the New England Society and the South Carolina Society. Those prestigious organizations welcomed the handsome, smooth-talking attorney into their midst. In a matter of just three years Hurlbut became treasurer for the New England Society and was in possession of a large amount of dues money that "disappeared" in 1845. That was the year that Hurlbut's good name repeatedly came into question by his associates. He tried to borrow money from everyone he knew, and he left his legal practice unattended. Hurlbut was known to frequent taverns where whist tables were kept, and he was fast gaining a reputation as a lawyer who would rather drink whiskey and gamble than attend to business. Hurlbut was accused of cheating at cards and not paying his gambling debts. The rumor that he'd absconded with the purse of the New England Society surfaced at the time that another damning indictment forced him to leave town precipitously. Hurlbut's mentor, Judge James Louis Petigru, had a close friend in Samuel Henry Dickson, M.D., professor of medicine at the Medical College of Charleston. Dickson was a graduate of both Yale and the University of Pennsylvania, and he was one of the eminent medical minds in the country. Hurlbut did some legal work for Dickson and received a check in escrow. However, the urge to pay off gambling debts caused Hurlbut to commit fraud. He deceitfully forged Dickson's name on the check and cashed it for his own account. To make matters worse, Hurlbut contrived to do the same thing in a Savannah bank, thereby leaving Dickson, his client, liable to two unwarranted debts. Jeffrey Lash cites that Judge James Petigru advised Hurlbut to get out of town. One wonders why Charleston's most imminent legal mind did not counsel his friend and former law student to stay here and attempt to make good on his errors.

Hurlbut and his younger brother, William, took a schooner to Philadelphia. William, a protege of Samuel Gilman, the Unitarian minister, soon thereafter entered Harvard Divinity School to pursue ordination as a Unitarian minister himself. Stephen Hurlbut traveled by rail to Galena, Illinois, as far as he could go on the northern rail line. He then traveled by horse to Belvidere, Illinois, the edge of the American frontier. There he set himself up as an attorney and military authority.

Opportunism led Hurlbut the Whig to back Lincoln the Republican in 1860. One account cites that Hurlbut was able to get 12 men in Belvidere to switch their votes from Douglas to Lincoln. Whatever Hurlbut did, Lincoln was grateful, and the new president sought the former Charleston attorney out as part of the last ditch, two man diplomacy team in Charleston.

Ward Lamon and Stephen Hurlbut rolled into town on Sunday, March 24, 1861, and engaged a carriage to the Charleston Hotel on Meeting Street. The grand columns of this structure have been preserved in the architecture of the bank building that has replaced the old hotel. Thackery had stayed there. So had President Polk and Jenny Lind, the Swedish Nightingale. Word spread fast around town that the Lincoln envoys were here.

On Monday Congressman Lamon met with Governor Pickens in the privacy of Lamon's suite. Hurlbut told one former friend that he'd come to Charleston to visit his sister. Yet, he visited his old friend and mentor, Petigru, at Petigru's St. Michael's Alley office, and the old judge was incredulous that President Lincoln had sent Hurlbut as a special envoy. Meanwhile, Lamon engaged a steamboat, *The Planter*, to take him over to Fort Sumter to meet with Major Anderson. Lamon assured both Governor Pickens and Major Anderson that Lincoln would not try to resupply the fort. He also stated that Lincoln intended to pull Anderson's garrison out of Sumter. By the time Lamon reached the hotel, a lynch mob had gathered in the streets. One man had a tar and feather bucket for dealing with Hurlbut. Angry shouts from the mob caused quite a stir, and had it not been for South Carolina Congressman Lawrence Keitt being a guest at the hotel, something serious might have occurred. Keitt escorted the two republicans back to the train station and they departed forthwith.

Hurlbut was appointed a major general in the Union Army. He was known for harsh insults to African-Americans, Jews, and foreigners. President Johnston appointed him minister to Peru. Hurlbut's legacy lies in his March 27, 1861, hand-delivered message to Lincoln stating "let South Carolina make the belligerent move."

Recalling Fort Sumter Centennial 50 Years Ago (1861)

Fifty-years ago, April 12, 1961, a young physician had a day free from being on call so he accompanied his 11-year-old son to a vantage point at White Point Gardens to view the spectacle of the decade -- the centennial commemoration of the historic firing on Fort Sumter. Fifteen thousand spectators thronged the Battery and another 10,000 watched from Sullivan's Island and Fort Johnson. The weather was mild with temps in the mid-60s and a passing rain shower in midmorning threatened to put a damper on the festivities. However, by 1:30 p.m., the sun came out, as if on cue, and The Citadel bagpipers led the grand parade down King Street. As the procession approached Legerton's, the Citadel band struck up "Dixie," and throngs went wild with Rebel yells. If there was any doubt that a hundred years had made Charlestonians remorseful about "the late unpleasantness," those doubts were dashed on this Centennial Day. Amidst the pomp of the ceremonious firing at White Point, beneath the draping oaks of that hallowed ground, an 11-year-old boy gave his heart to Clio, the muse of history.

Charleston threw herself hook, line, and sinker into the centennial commemoration -- just as she'd done in the prosecution of the war, itself, one-hundred years earlier. The city wore an air of triumph and defiance. That week the *News and Courier* published columns 44 and 45 in a series entitled "The Courier at War." The columns were penned by assistant newspaper editor, Arthur M. Wilcox. These pieces on why the South fought were well-received and written from a native Charlestonian's point of view.

The Charleston of 1961 was a far different city from the metropolitan maze of cross-town expressways, overpass bridges, high-rise buildings, and interstate ramps that punctuate the peninsula. "Nothing higher than St. Philip's" was the saying of the city fathers. Telephones in the city had the prefix RA-4, or Raymond-4. Just a few years prior to 1961, it had not been necessary to use the prefix when dialing.

Everyone read the Ashley-Cooper newspaper column written by Frank Gilbreth, Jr., before going to work, and almost everyone watched Charlie Hall on WCSC-5 TV, or Ken Klyce on WUSN-2, at 6 p.m. The week leading to the re-enactment was not dominated by the talk of Fort Sumter, however. The morning paper and its rival, *The Evening Post*, featured several front-page headlines concerning the recent speaking engagement that United Nations mediator, Frank P. Graham, gave at Winthrop College in Rock Hill. A masthead editorial in the *News and Courier* portrayed Graham as "soft on communism," as a member of leftest-leaning organizations, and as an advocate of legalizing sit-in demonstrations by Negroes. Graham had been president of the University of North Carolina prior to becoming a United States senator from North Carolina and then, mediator at the U.N.

Despite the fact that Graham was a Fayetteville-native, a UNC-Chapel Hill baseball star, an Ivy-League lawyer, and a United States Marine Corps veteran of World War I, the distinguished educator was brought before the House Committee on Un-American Activities for questioning about his membership in what some termed a "Communist-front organization." Graham refused to renounce the suspect organization. When N.C. Governor W.K. Scott appointed Graham to complete the term of recently deceased Senator J. Melville Broughton, an unexpired term amounting to just a year, conservatives in North Carolina were shocked. Graham was defeated in an election bid due to a smear alleging him as pro-integration. Following Graham's speech at Winthrop, S.C. State Senator, L. Marion Gressette, proposed that Graham be barred in the future from speaking at any public institution in the state. Graham believed that the action against him was retaliation for his support of the Greensboro lunch-counter sit-ins that had taken place in February 1960.

As southern dignitaries gathered in Charleston at the Fort Sumter Hotel for a luncheon in the famed Ramparts Room with its mural of the cannonading of the fort, the rest of the city went about its everyday routine. Over at Frost, Johnson, Read, and Smith, the stock brokerage firm on the corner of Broad and Church Streets, the brokers were celebrating the NYSE striking an all-time high on the Dow Jones average -- 692 on volume of nearly 7 million shares! At the Gaud School on Broad Street, Headmaster Berkeley Grimball announced that once again the school would host the annual Gaud School Tennis Invitational -- a match that brought top male players of all ages to Charleston. John Owens of Bishop England High School, the defending male, age 17-18, was expected to enter as the tournament's top seed. Meanwhile, around the corner at 170 Church Street, Simmons Motors offered the limited production Dodge Valiant

Dixie Special, a model created by Chrysler Motor Company especially for the centennial commemoration. Lampton Motors at 4759 Rivers Avenue advertized that they, too, had a few of these special edition Dodge Valiants. Over at Fort Sumter Chevrolet on Morrison Drive, the sporty little Corvair could be had for a mere $1798.

Elsewhere in the newspapers leading up to the April 12-13 centennial, there were revealing bits and pieces of Charleston culture of a half century past. Piggly-Wiggly noted that perch fillets could be had at 39 cents a pack. Claussen's bread was 10 cents a loaf, and grits in five-pound sacks went for a quarter.

President Kennedy lamented to Howard K. Smith on CBS News that it was so easy to sell himself to the American people *via* the medium of TV, but, oh, so difficult to sell them on his ideas. Up in Orangeburg the state's junior senator, Ernest F. Hollings, turned the earth with a gold-painted shovel to begin construction on a new industrial park. He proclaimed bright days ahead for Orangeburg -- though no industry had then been recruited.

As a bonus to the local chamber of commerce, the azaleas were at their peak. Every home downtown was dressed with window boxes overflowing with lush blooms. The flower ladies and basket weavers were out in profusion along Meeting, Broad, and Church Streets as the city wore a festive air. All hotels and motels were filled and the finer restaurants -- such as the Colony House, the Harbor House, and the Fort Sumter Hotel Ramparts Room -- were booked. Guests filed in from all over the country, and historians came here from around the world.

The evening prior to the ring of guns opening fire on Sumter, there was a dinner-dance at the Nathaniel Russell House for some Charlestonians whose ancestors had been here for the original event. In hoop skirts and crinolines for the ladies and tails and cravats for the gentlemen, Mrs. Frank J. Ball, Mr. W. H. Grimball, Jr., Mrs. Henry B. Smythe, and Mr. John M. Horlbeck were pictured amidst old silver and cups of Regent's punch looking very much the part of antebellum Charleston.

The city budgeted $5,500 for a magnificent fireworks display that would last long into the evening of April 12. Adjusted for inflation, that amount would be approximately $40,000 in today's currency. Charleston Mayor J. Palmer Gaillard, Jr., coordinated the myriad of events surrounding the centennial. One of those events involved the crowning of Miss Ione Coker of Hartsville as "Queen of the Confederacy." Former Governors J. Strom Thurmond and James F. Byrnes stood with then Governor Ernest F. Hollings on a grand reviewing stand erected for dignitaries. Nearby were other V.I.P.s -- Robert E. Lee, IV and Major

General U.S. Grant, United States Army, retired, sat with P.G.T. Beauregard, IV -- all direct descendants of the terrible conflict. Rear Admiral McManes of the 6th Naval District, Charleston made an address to the assembled mass of 15,000 as several dozen television cameras rolled film.

A squabble unrelated to the Fort Sumter affair added tension to the centennial day, however. Most of the Charleston hotels and eateries catered to a white only clientele and this presented a problem to Civil War Commemoration delegations from many states outside the South. The Civil War Round Table and several other notable Civil War historical groups planned to boycott the Charleston-Fort Sumter event on the grounds of segregation -- until the Charleston Naval Base opened up Visiting Officers Quarters for the distinguished guests who refused to patronize segregated downtown establishments. President John F. Kennedy flew into Charleston aboard Air Force One and stayed in a billet not far from one he'd stayed in twenty years earlier when he'd been a naval officer stationed here.

At a centennial banquet held on the naval base, U.S. Senator J. Strom Thurmond was asked to say a few words about the firing on Fort Sumter, but the plucky senator stated that he'd prefer to speak to the need for America to maintain a strong national defense in today's world. Then there was a sharp exchange between Ashley Halsey of Charleston and a New Jersey gentleman over desegregation in the South. Frank Gilbreth, Jr., the newspaperman who penned the "Doing The Charleston" column under the pen name of "Ashley Cooper," intoned Charlestonians to act graciously and to let bygones be bygones.

As the Citadel cadets stood to their guns -- six and 12 pounders -- along the Battery seawall, the crowd cheered lustily. All morning a chorus accompanied by a symphony orchestra had been playing "Tara's Theme" from *Gone With The Wind.* Confederate flags and bunting rippled in the breeze and the sun finally broke through the dark clouds. With earsplitting explosion the number one gun spewed forth flame, smoke, and spent wadding. Then in rapid succession the other guns spoke defiance to federal authority. The cadets manned their guns with the precision and adeptness of their authentic counterparts a hundred years previously. The crowd erupted into ribald laughter as a woman's stocking blew out of a gun barrel and wafted high over the harbor. The story quickly circulated that the cadets had discovered that the black powder charges loaded more quickly if women's nylon stockings were substituted for canvas powder bags.

Finally, after appearing like a fire-breathing dragon all afternoon, old Fort Sumter began to fire back at her attackers, slowly at first, and then with alacrity. The crowd on the Battery cheered the Fort just as their ancestors had done a hundred years earlier. At least one young lad gave his heart to history and his allegiance to The Citadel that glorious day.

We learned later that the grand old historians of the Civil War Round Table did not make it to the commemorative firing on the Battery. Fred Schwengel of Iowa, David C. Mears, Ph.D., of the Library of Congress, Clyde Walton of Springfield, Illinois, and Ralph G. Newman of Chicago had purchased a rare bottle of James Hennesy and Company cognac and they fired shot after shot themselves until they, too, fell silent, as did the guns on the Battery around 9:30 p.m.

Abolitionist William Lloyd Garrison Was Keynote Speaker at Fort Sumter in 1865

If ever Charleston had a nemesis, his name was William Lloyd Garrison, and if ever a man had his say and a city had its comeuppance it was on April 14, 1865, the day Federal forces raised Old Glory again over the war-torn ramparts of Fort Sumter. No doubt, the two most polarizing characters in the era culminating in the War of the Confederacy were William Lloyd Garrison, the Boston editor of the abolitionist newspaper, *The Liberator* -- and Robert Barnwell Rhett, the Blufton, S.C. native who was the editor of The Charleston Mercury, a secessionist newspaper. April 12, 1861, was Rhett's grand triumph. April 14, 1865, was William Lloyd Garrison's moment to denounce Charleston from the parade ground of the reconquered fort where the war had begun.

William Lloyd Garrison, an intellectual who'd imbibed Quaker fundamentals, began denouncing the institution of slavery as early as 1831 in essays that he penned under pseudonyms. Words such as these inflamed southerners: "Assenting to the 'self-evident truth' maintained in the American Declaration of Independence, 'that all men are created equal, and endowed by their Creator with certain inalienable rights -- among which are life, liberty and the pursuit of happiness,' I shall strenuously contend for the immediate enfranchisement of our slave population. In Park-street Church, on the Fourth of July, 1829, in an address on slavery, I unreflectingly assented to the popular but pernicious doctrine of gradual abolition." Coming on the heels of the bitter nullification crisis, southerners were in no mood to allow Garrison's essays to circulate freely in the South. The city fathers of Columbia, S.C., offered $1,500 reward -- $35,000 in today's currency -- for information leading to the arrest of anyone circulating a copy of Garrison's *Liberator* newspaper.

Though Garrison had been writing for thirty-plus years, his hard-hitting essays all under the theme of emancipation, Robert Barnwell Rhett was agitating for southern secession. Rhett was one of the instigators of the Nashville Convention of 1850 -- a coming together of nine southern states for the purpose of countering the principles of the Missouri Compromise and the detested Wilmot Proviso, the legislation that sought to ban slavery in territories carved from the Mexican War cession.

To Rhett and his co-horts, William Lowndes Yancey of Alabama and William Porcher Miles of Walterboro, the North was determined to subdue the South through crippling economic policies -- restrictive tariffs, abolition of the slave labor system, and high interest rates for bank loans. The Nashville Convention was in many ways a Rhett, Yancey, Miles show, but the fiery speech of Langdon Cheves was the memorable moment. Cheves was the Upstate lawyer and Congressman, Speaker of the House who also served a term as president of the Second Bank of the United States. The Bank of the United States was a weak forerunner of the Federal Reserve Board. Rhett, Yancey, Miles, Cheves, and John C. Calhoun collectively became known as the Southern "fire-eaters."

Just as William Lloyd Garrison's *Liberator* was not alone in crying out for abolition, Robert Barnwell Rhett's *Mercury* had editorial company in the minded *Montgomery Mercury*, the *Tuscumbia States Rights Democrat*, the *Augusta True Democrat*, and the *Memphis Avalanche*. In the North, Frederick Douglass published his abolitionist *North Star* newspaper, and *Harper's Weekly* was another mouthpiece of antislavery. The level of vitriol in American polemics was at a sustained boiling point through the 1850s. Few editors counseled caution or moderation. The South viewed slavery as an essential aspect of its economic structure and to southerners, the real issues were unfair interest rates, manipulative legislation that favored one region over another, and unfettered trade. These later issues were points that Northerners chose to ignore.

For Rhett and his cohorts, William Lloyd Garrison was the antithesis of the Southern ideal. Southern men prided themselves on land ownership and their extensive knowledge of agriculture and livestock. To them, Garrison represented the effete, urban intellectual who was more prone to hide behind legislation and litigation. The moral points of Garrison's antislavery essays were completely lost on the fire-eaters.

As for Garrison, his view of the tart-tongued southerners was one of cold disdain. To him the South was peopled by cruel and greedy planters who would gladly wreck the Union for the sake of preserving their wealthy fiefdoms.

The historian Allan Nevins makes the point in his book, Ordeal of the Union: Fruits of Manifest Destiny: a House Dividing, 1852-1857 (Collier, 1992) that Robert Barnwell Rhett, William Lowndes Yancey, and William Porcher Miles set about as early as 1850 in Nashville to nurture a political climate in the Southern states that would lead automatically to secession when a significant event triggered it. The significant event would be the splitting of the Democratic party at its national nominating convention held, not by coincidence, in Charleston in 1860.

Garrison's *Liberator* stoked the fires of the Republican campaign of Lincoln. When Lincoln did not speak forcefully enough on immediate abolition, Garrison's paper chided him. The gulf between north and south became so embittered that ship passengers stopping in Charleston from northern ports were afraid to walk the streets. The editor of the *Evening Post* in New York wired Rhett at *The Mercury* office on Meeting Street to inquire if it would be safe for a Post reporter to travel to Charleston for the Secession Convention. Rhett wired back, "Absolutely not! He'll be tarred and feathered at the least, probably strung up." Garrison wrote of the secession, "With reasonable men, I will reason; with humane men I will plead; but to tyrants I will give no quarter, nor waste arguments where they will certainly be lost."

April 12, 1861, was a day of jubilation for Rhett and his fellow secessionists. The Confederacy was in the process of being formed through ordeal by fire. Neither Rhett nor his compatriots believed that a full-scale war would follow the forced evacuation of Fort Sumter. The South possessed pluck and bravado. The North possessed factories and an endless supply of draft-age men. The South believed that Britain would do anything to preserve its supply line of southern cotton to English textile mills. No one in Charleston foresaw Nile Valley long-staple cotton or Madras region short-staple cotton replacing British imports from Charleston, Savannah, and Mobile.

Southern valor prevailed upon many a battlefield where superior numbers of heavily armed foe were hurled back. Yet, a war of attrition was as detrimental to Davis and Lee as it would be a half century later to the Kaiser and Hindenburg. From all of this prewar vitriol 618,000 soldiers paid with their lives. Five times that number were maimed. The war was a terrible sacrifice of livestock -- 3000 horses perished just in the Battle of Gettysburg. The threat of Sherman's forces crossing the North Edisto prompted the pullout from Charleston to Saint Stephen. After four years Fort Sumter did not surrender. Confederate Captain Thomas A. Huguenin, the last southern commander of the fort, ordered the flag known throughout the South as "the Stainless Banner" to be nailed to the flag staff and the pole be swabbed with axle grease to prevent anyone from climbing to remove it. Huguenin's company of sharpshooters was quietly evacuated Friday evening, February 17, 1865. There were no cannoneers, for all the guns had been dismounted by Union fire.

Off shore Rear Admiral John A. Dahlgren's sharp observers noted the stealthy evacuation. Preparations were made for the Federal seizure of Charleston. Soon, all of the Northern newspapers were calling for a ceremonial flag raising to be held on Fort Sumter on Good Friday, April 14, 1865. Every abolitionist who could afford a steamship ticket headed for Charleston. William Lloyd Garrison was the main speaker, but he had to wait until a pale and sickly Brigadier Robert B. Anderson, U.S.A., made a brief talk commemorating the 15 weeks that he and his band of 87 soldiers held the fort in 1861. Then Anderson removed the tattered American flag from an attache case and helped secure it to the halyard. Soon it snapped proudly in the breeze and a thunder of hurrahs and cannon shots hailed the event. Garrison's speech lambasted the South so acutely that even Northerners felt that he'd overplayed the upper hand. There was no olive branch, no conciliatory gesture for the South to grasp.

On the evening of the Fort Sumter celebration a grand banquet for Northern celebrants was held in the ballroom of the Charleston Hotel on Meeting Street. Admiral Dahlgren gave the traditional toast to the President. Unbeknownst to the Admiral, President Lincoln was at that moment taking his seat in the Ford theater to have what he hoped would be a relaxing night out on the town. After all, Lee had just surrendered five days earlier and the Federals had raised the flag at Fort Sumter just hours earlier.

Robert Barnwell Rhett's worst nightmare was realized. The South's independence was nullified, the institution of slavery was ended with the 13th Amendment, and he was financially and politically ruined. Rhett had been elected to the Confederate congress and had been largely ineffective; however, he had become a major critic of President Jefferson Davis's handling of the war. Rhett eventually left the state and made his way to New Orleans.

William Lloyd Garrison ceased publication of the abolitionist Liberator newspaper and turned his focus upon a new crusade -- that of women's suffrage.

The Carolinian Who Became Governor of Antigua

Forgive us Carolinians if we pine for the grandeur of the bygone colonial days. Charles Town then was a pearl nestled between two grand rivers -- each wider than the Thames or the Tiber. There existed a peculiar order and symmetry found only where colonial establishments mirror the glory of the empire. Charles Town's first citizens were fortune seekers; but more important, they sought to create something permanent in this vast wilderness. From the 17th century this English colonial port was something apart from the balance of the Crown's far flung possessions. A dozen English-bred aristocrats carved grand baronies along these estuaries, and none can deny that they possessed a flair for boldness.

From our earliest days -- when Bay Street ended at the White Point and Dutch-gabled merchant houses fronted wharves -- there were men here who had connections in White Hall, Westminster, and the Inns of Court. Edmund Bellinger had been received at the court of Charles II prior to departing for these parts. William Percy had relatives who were peers of the realm. No Charlestonian, however, arrived with a more refined pedigree than did George Lucas, planter, Lieutenant-Colonel of a royal regiment, and, ultimately, royal lieutenant-governor of Antigua.

The Lucas family were Royalists during the English Civil War and several of the male line had fought with the Cavaliers in defense of Crown Rights and Church. Upon the triumph of Cromwell and the Parliament forces, scores of Cavaliers left England for the Caribbean fringe of the Empire -- to Antigua, St. Kitts, or Barbados. Surnames such as Lucas, Bull, and Beale can be found on old land plats of these British colonial possessions.

George Lucas sailed from London bound for Antigua, the gateway to the Caribbean, in the mid-1730s. He was accompanied by his young wife. That mountainous island with its snowy white beaches and ice blue water was known for its sugar cane. When Lucas arrived to take command of his regiment,

Antigua had been a jewel in the British crown for 105 years. Sir Christopher Codrington stationed a fleet there in 1632, and the crystal waters foamed red with the blood of Spanish, French, and Portuguese usurpers. Scores of swarthy pirates stalked the island when the British fleet weighed anchor.

Britain, more so than France or Spain, sought to establish a microcosm of the Empire in its colonies spread from Hudson Bay to Madras in India. Anglicanism was coordinated by the Bishop of London, and young clerics fresh from Oxford came out to spread the gospel. The liturgy and the Book of Common Prayer, the wig, wool sack, and the rule of English law -- these were the hallmarks of the flag that bore the Cross of St. George and the Cross of St. Andrew. Colonial assemblies elected by the large landholders allowed for local say in governance. Assemblies served as a conduit for grievances to London, and they knuckled down on the Crown's detractors. Tradition, worship, rule of law, and the contemporary fashion prevailed in the port cities of every colony. For George Lucas, the years he spent in Antigua were profitable in multiple ways. His wife bore him children -- the eldest he named Eliza. Lucas acquired a large acreage in St. Thomas Parish in the northeastern quadrant of Antigua. He acquainted himself with the culture of the growing West African slave society, and he learned the protocol of colonial politics.

Whether it was the rush to establish a cane sugar operation in Carolina or the haste to remove his sickly spouse from the tropical Antiguan climate, George Lucas relocated to Charles Town in 1738. The ease with which Lucas moved within the colonies -- acquiring land wherever he went -- bears testimony to his being the kinsman of a well-established family nestled near the seat of power in England.

It's known that in the 1720s that the Duke of Kent's oldest son was elevated by Parliament to the title of Baron Lucas and that he served in the House of Lords. Whether this man was George Lucas's father or uncle is unclear. Without a doubt, the family had the ear of the Crown and everyone else at the Court of the Hanoverians.

Lucas' lands lay west of the Ashley River. One particularly large estate was on the Wappoo. The Royal Governor of Carolina was James Glen of Scotland, and Glen welcomed Colonel Lucas to Charles Town. Soon Lucas was involved in the political and military hierarchy of the colony. He built an elegant country seat on the Wappoo and shipped his children off to boarding school in London. His wife's health revived a bit in the salt breezes here.

Carolina's purpose for being was to ship raw materials to Britain or to other colonies within the empire. In the 1740s Charles Town exported naval stores

-- timber and pitch -- to Bristol and Portsmouth, and wheat and salt pork to Antigua.

Planters were under advisement to search for new herbs for medicinal use and to plant hemp for ropemaking. In 1742 when George Lucas received communication from Spencer Compton's Whig government, successor to George Walpole, the lieutenant-governorship of Antigua had been vacant for six months due to the death of Edward Byam. Sir Edward Byam had been the royal authority in Antigua for 26 years. He had succeeded John Yeamans who'd vacated the post in 1715 to establish himself in palatial style at his Yeamans Hall plantation on Goose Creek in Carolina.

Antigua is the dominant of the Leeward Island chain. St. Kitts, Montserrat, Nevis, the Virgin Islands, and Barbuda are a few of the main islands -- all of which were major sugar producers in the colonial era. George Lucas was established as the lieutenant-governor of this important domain during the crisis known as the War of Jenkins' Ear, a 10-year naval action in the Caribbean between Spain and Britain. Though the hostility was a part of the much larger War of Austrian Succession on the European continent, this Caribbean theater began when a Spanish naval officer sliced off a British officer's ear with his saber in a dispute.

The high stakes naval strategy paid off handsomely for Britain as Admiral Edward Vernon, nicknamed "Old Grog," captured Porto Bello on the coast of Panama. That great harbor was a silver exporting center for the Spanish empire and Britain turned it into a grand gateway to lucrative trade with South America. Vernon and Fleet Admiral Sir Cloudesley Shovell were colleagues with George Lucas in maintaining the British crown's interests in the Caribbean during this expansion phase of the empire.

Lucas was instrumental in restoring order in Antigua following the savage First Maroon War, 1737-1742. The natives of the island had united with rebellious slaves to formulate a bloody rebellion that took everything two British regiments could do to subdue. Planters fled the island in droves with some heading for Carolina. There was fear that the rebellion would spread throughout the Caribbean. The most feared rebel leader was a runaway slave woman known as "Nanny Granny."

While George Lucas fulfilled his role as lieutenant-governor in Antigua, he corresponded often with Royal Governor of the Leeward Islands, Sir William Mathew, Jr. Carolinians remembered when Sir Nathaniel Johnson was governor of the Leewards in the 1680s. Since Lord Compton was ill much of the time that he was in office as the government's leading minister, Sir John Carteret conducted most of the government's business. He was the great grandson of Proprietor Sir George Carteret, and he'd inherited one-eighth of the land in Carolina. Lucas and Carteret had much in common as their Carolina land holdings almost touched.

The joy of George Lucas' week, however, was his letter to his teenage daughter, Eliza, back in Charles Town. He left her in charge of his land holdings and the proud father doted on his daughter's business acumen. It was Eliza who pioneered the bonanza export crop -- indigo. Their letters between colonial Charles Town and Antigua are among the most valuable insights historians have for this era.

Recalling the Night the U.S.S. Hobson Went Down

Dawn broke over Charleston to a partly cloudy and then a mostly sunny Saturday, April 26 fifty-nine years ago in 1952. The Azalea Festival had drawn several thousand visitors to the city and most hotels were booked. The weather was so delightful that the two harbor tour boats, *Captiva* and *Seascape*, that docked in front of the Fort Sumter Hotel were packed with out-of-towners eager to see the city from the water. Not a soul around suspected that 2000 nautical miles from here a tragedy was unfolding that would leave its mark on Charleston forever.

Even though Tuesday, April 26, 2011, was the 59th anniversary of the sinking of the destroyer-minesweeper *U.S.S. Hobson*, the worst naval disaster for our country in the Cold War, it received scant observance. On that night in 1952, through some miscommunication during a night flight exercise for the aircraft carrier *U.S.S. Wasp* battle group, the *Hobson* cut across the bow of the fast-moving carrier thereby causing that destroyer to be cut in half with 176 sailors going down with their ship. Too many years have passed and too many more pressing issues vie for our attention -- such as the price of gasoline, the deadly tornado season, and the NFL draft's impact on the Lowcountry. Thanks, however, to *Post and Courier* reporter Schuyler Kropf, the *Hobson* tragedy did warrant a front page headline this past Friday. Kropf informed us that the *Wasp* and *Hobson* survivors, including several from this area, would hold their first joint commemoration of that ill-fated event. The get-together was planned for downtown on Friday and Saturday with a ceremony at the granite obelisk marker at White Point.

There was just one television station in the state in 1952, and that was WOLO in Columbia -- so Charlestonians heard the dreadful news of the disaster on WCSC radio late Saturday evening. The story broke too late for the *News & Courier* to recall the paper from the printing press. Even so, evidently the Chief of Naval Operations, Admiral William M. Fechteler, a hero of Leyte Gulf and later head of the Navy's Bureau of Personnel, clamped a lid of secrecy on the *Wasp-Hobson* incident until facts could be determined and notification the 237 families could occur.

In Charleston, especially around the North Area as it was called before 1972, many navy and shipyard families rented small houses or apartments close to the base. Two navy chaplains, J.E. Hollingsworth, Protestant, and R.J. Walsh, Catholic, made their sad rounds. Not everyone had a telephone then, but word began to spread like wildfire by midnight on Saturday, April 26. Anxious women called the base information office all night with the pathetic words, "Is his name on the list [of survivors]?"

The year 1952 was one of the most intense years for Cold Warriors as Josef Stalin appeared to be in a "full court press" of Communist insurgency around the globe. President Harry Truman's "Containment" policy called for "toe to toe, nose to nose, eyeball to eyeball" countermeasures. Military operations, convoys, and war games were a constant reminder that the 1945 "peace" was a very fragile thing. The local newspaper had just run a story detailing "Operation Desert Rock" that elements of the 82nd Airborne were carrying out in New Mexico. A simulated, low-yield atomic bomb was "dropped" in that region, and 120 paratroopers of the 504th Regiment of the 82nd made a night drop into "enemy territory" as a practice run for what might be the real thing. Meanwhile, far out in the Atlantic, the Navy was conduction a "war game" of its own.

Essex-class carrier battle group Wasp, CV-18, was heading to the Mediterranean for an extended deployment in and around Gibraltar. While conducting aircraft launch and recovery operations in a night exercise, the *Wasp*, full throttle and bow into the wind, sliced through the hull of the Hobson which mistakenly crossed *Wasp's* path while patrolling for recovery of possible ditched aircraft. Things like this are not supposed to happen; however, wracked nerves, miscommunication, and something sailors and soldiers term "the fog of war" combine to make the unexpected commonplace. A naval court of naval inquiry later found Hobson's commanding officer, Commander W.J. Tierney, U.S.N., at fault for his ship's crossing the bow of the Wasp at that inopportune moment. Tierney went down with his ship and 176 of his crew. Sixty-one men were plucked from the stormy Atlantic on that rainy, foggy night.

Time magazine on Monday, May 5, 1952, featured a story on the worst peacetime military disaster in modern times. "She [*Hobson*] was racing along off the carrier's port quarter on "plane guard"—ready for rescue work in case a flyer missed his landing and crashed. Under the impact of the collision, the *Hobson* sank almost instantly, with many of her complement of 14 officers and

223 men asleep or helpless below." It's not known for certain, but most likely, Tierney's wife waited at quarters at the Charleston Naval Base for the chaplain's car to drive up.

Reminiscing at one of Coleman Boulevard's finest eateries on this past Tuesday evening, the 59th April 26th since the disaster, was a former Navy hospital corpsman pharmacist's mate, who was on duty at the naval hospital that fateful evening. "I remember that all of the crew members' wives who were pregnant were rounded up and brought to the hospital as a precaution," said Ira B. Horton, Jr., M.D. Horton had been recalled to active duty for the Korean conflict even though he was attending the Medical College at the time. Having previously been detailed as a hospital corpsman with the Marines in the late 1940s, Horton was eligible for recall throughout the Cold War. He later re-entered the Navy as a captain and served out his career as a physician. "Several of the women went into labor prematurely that evening," Horton recalled.

Sunday morning, April 27th, the second Sunday after Easter, also dawned clear and sunny, yet the city's mood was somber. Sailors and their families were an integral part of day-to-day life in Charleston. When the Charleston Naval Base and its companion shipyard celebrated, all of Charleston joined in. Likewise, when the Base grieved, Charleston, too, went into mourning. This was a navy town. The headlines on the Sunday edition of the *News and Courier* said it all in dramatic, bold type, "Charleston Ship Sinks, 176 Missing." Rear Admiral W.W. O'Reagan, commander of the U.S. Atlantic Fleet Mine Force, issued the frequent news updates.

The *Hobson* was a product of the Charleston naval shipyard, and its launch on September 8, 1941, saw dignitaries from around the state and nation gather at the shipyard to break the bubbly across the bow. The *U.S.S. Hobson*, DD-464 was still on shakedown cruises when the Japanese bombed Pearl Harbor. Her 12 millimeter guns assisted in the bombardment of Normandy on June 6, 1944, and she made countless trips across the Atlantic on convoy escort duty. *Hobson's* sister ship in the dry dock building stage was DD-464, the *U.S.S. Corry. Corry* was sunk by a German mine off the beach code-named Utah in the Normandy invasion. The destroyer DD-640, *U.S.S. Beatty,* also shared dry dock space at Charleston Naval Shipyard with the Hobson. *Beatty* was sunk by German aircraft off Algiers in 1943. Hobson survived the war and was outfitted with surveillance gear so sophisticated that pictures of her underway were censored by the government. Charlestonians considered these hometown ships and their crews as part of their extended family. For weeks following the tragedy, Charleston citizens saluted the Navy Shore Patrol as it cruised Market and East

Bay Streets on Saturday nights. Local sailors were invited into private homes for meals.

The weekend had begun with so much promise. The Sunday that the sad news broke across the city, a young priest was ordained by John J. Russell at St. Joseph's Church in the Diocese of Charleston. His name was Joseph Louis Bernadin, changed from the Italian spelling "Bernadini." Father Bernadin, a native of Columbia, S.C., remained in Charleston for 14 years and taught briefly at Bishop England High School before moving on. Bernadin became a cardinal in 1983, and he is reported to have aided the Reagan administration in behind-the-scenes activities in support of Pope John Paul II's relentless crusade against Communist rule in Eastern Europe.

That same weekend, acclaimed local pianist Joan Geilfuss made her concert debut with the Charleston Symphony at Memminger Auditorium. Her performance to a sellout audience included works of Bach and Haydn. In Mount Pleasant, the Moultrie Generals baseball team advanced to the state District 9 play-offs by defeating St. Paul's 10-9. Generals' slugger James Fleming hit a triple and single to score runs. The newspaper carried a picture of local beauty Miss Norma Bennett celebrating her being named the upcoming May Queen at Moultrie High.

However, the somber words of Navy Chaplain J.E. Hollingsworth summed up the feelings of everyone here 59 years ago, "Women who watch their men go down to the sea in ships now wait tearfully for a Chaplain's vehicle to drive up."

Yankee Generals Fared Well After War

Nothing succeeds like success. Everyone loves a winner. When you're hot, you're hot. Our culture, more than any in modern history, celebrates success -- and this is a good thing. Because the War of the Rebellion was so protracted and because that bitter era shaped the next hundred years of our society, it is no surprise that the victors earned places of distinction in civil life in the aftermath of 1865. Union generals were, as a rule, magnanimous in victory, and the leadership skills they'd exhibited on countless bloody fields were transformed into oratory in the courthouses, the governor's mansions, banks, and corporate boardrooms of a rapidly expanding nation.

Few commanders on either side of this bellicose affair resorted to the low art of demonizing their opponents, so the *postbellum* years witnessed quite a few incidents of former enemies helping one another after the war. True, quite a few southerners wished a hot eternity for Sherman and his staff, but most wanted to forget the whole business of war and move on to a new and better time.

Any southerner worth his ration of grits can tell you Confederate history chapter and verse in Douglas Southall Freeman's three volumes of Lee's Lieutenants. However, few sons of the soil here can cite a thing about a northern commander, and fewer still have an interest in learning at this late date. For the sake of academia and good will, here's a run down on what several of William Tecumseh Sherman's commanders did after the fray of the blue and the gray.

Hard-bitten fighters were the men chosen by Sherman to burn that broad swath to the sea in 1865. One of the Union's favorites was William Farquhar Barry, the winsome fellow who served as Brigadier General Irvin McDowell's chief of artillery at First Manassas. Barry and McDowell were classmates at West Point in the commissioning class of 1838. McDowell's career had catapulted him into a general's slot by 1861, and Barry was still a major. In that engagement both McDowell and Barry became confused over uniform colors and strange banners, and thinking they were being re-enforced, they held their fire in the face of a Confederate onslaught. McDowell's and Barry's classmate, P.G.T. Beauregard outflanked them and forced them off their entrenched position, the now famous Alexandria line. In a year Barry would be chief of artillery for General McClellan in the Peninsula Campaign, and then he held the same post for Sherman. Barry's "hot shot" rained on Atlanta's railroad warehouses and ignited a firestorm.

Following the war, Barry remained in the military and became the nation's foremost authority on ordinance. During the terrible labor riots of 1877, General Barry was summoned to Camden Station in Baltimore to quell a violent rail strike. He prudently elected not to let loose a "whiff of grapeshot" as Napoleon had done years earlier in the Vendee. Just gazing at those long barrels with prime and fuze was the catalyst for quietening the crowd. In his elder years he frequented the Army and Navy Club at 17th and "I" Streets near the White House, and it is said that he wrote his war memoirs in the reading room there amidst raucous commentary from the old soldiers who frequented that fabled spot.

What ever became of Francis P. Blair, II, the commanding general of Sherman's notorious XVII Corps? For the sake of history, we can be forgiven for raising the question. Blair's XVII Corps was Sherman's rearguard as he moved from Savannah through the Carolinas. The infamous "bummers," stragglers who looted, pillaged, raped, and burned without orders or supervision, were almost all Blair's men. Confederate General Joe Hardee, a classmate of Barry, Beauregard, and McDowell at West Point, gave chase to Blair's Corps as they crossed the Salkehatchee River and headed toward the fork of the Edisto. Hardee's men strung up every bummer they captured from Aiken to Columbia.

Blair was a Princeton man, a member of the Class of 1841. Only Princeton men know that that was the famous class that celebrated too much on the night of July 4, 1841, and nearly burned down Old North Hall. Following that riotous night of merriment, the faculty voted to dismiss the students prior to the holiday that excited such youthful exuberance. Blair became a lawyer and a midwest politician before the War, and on the eve of Fort Sumter, he organized a regiment of 1000 vigilantes known as the "Wide Awakes" and marched into Missouri to secure it for the Free Soil Unionists. To this day Blair is known as the "saviour of Missouri" for his efforts to keep it from falling into the Southern secession movement.

Following the war, Blair had a knock-down, drag-out argument with his old commander-turned-president Ulysses S. Grant. Blair had been a loyal republican since 1860, but he bolted the party and became a Democrat in an attempt to defeat Grant's presidential bid in 1868. Blair ran as Horatio Seymour's V - P on the Democratic ticket, but with southern democrats persona non grata in that election, Grant won handily. The Missouri legislature gave Blair the consolation prize of a United States Senate seat in 1872, but the old warrior-politician suffered a paralyzing stroke and was not able to serve out his term. Few in South Carolina mourned his passing in 1875. Carolinians then were absorbed in the Hampton Red Shirt Campaign to oust the carpetbaggers and scalawags who controlled state and local government.

The general most closely connected to Sherman was his former West Point roommate, George Thomas, the "Rock of Chiackmauga." This hell-for-leather general was one of the best fighters in the Union army. Born on a plantation just inside Virginia, but near the North Carolina line, Thomas grew up amidst the slave-holding aristocracy of the South. At West Point he and his roommates, "Cump" Sherman and Stewart Van Vliet, forged a lifelong friendship -- the type of bond that allowed each to know what the other was thinking during the critical battles being waged against their Confederate classmates in the War of Disunion. Both Sherman and Thomas did a military tour of duty at Fort Moultrie. Thomas was there in 1843. He probably visited the new military college that the state was establishing over on Marion Square in Charleston.

Yet Thomas was cut from a different fabric than Sherman and part of the explanation may be found in the geography of their boyhood. Thomas was a southerner through and through whereas Sherman was a midwesterner, an Ohioan. Colonel Robert E. Lee of the United States Army took Captain George Thomas under his wing as a favorite junior officer. Perhaps as Virginians they kept the same society back home. When Lee resigned his colonelcy to join the Confederacy in 1861, Winfield Scott immediately promoted Thomas to the slot Lee vacated. There had been some concern that George Thomas would "turn gray" rather than remain "blue" in his loyalty to the Union. Throughout the War General Thomas compiled a stellar record of service and, unlike Blair, Thomas tolerated no straggling or pillaging from the men in his ranks.

Following the war, Thomas' name was proffered for a Lieutenant-General's slot, but he asked that it be withdrawn. He was sent west to command a garrison of federal forces in California and collapsed and died of a stroke in 1870. The stroke may have been brought on by the anger Thomas felt over accusations made about some decisions he'd made in the war. His former friend, Union General George Schofield, had written Thomas a scathing letter full of accusations, and Thomas died while composing a reply. Though Chickamauga was the battle that earned Thomas lasting fame, the battle of Peachtree Creek near Atlanta was the fight that Thomas felt was his best set-piece action. On the "March to the Sea" George Thomas had to defend himself from Confederate

General Hardee, one of his former commanding officers in the prewar years. Southerners universally respected Thomas as a foe worthy of their steel.

One of the many sorrows associated with this tragic war was the bonds torn asunder of the "long gray line," the band of brothers in the United States Military Academy up on the Hudson. Their tragedy was in having to fire upon their own, as well as in seeing their classmates fire upon Old Glory. From the memoirs of the old soldiers, blue and gray, the battle scars healed more quickly in their ranks than did the scars of southern and northern civilian society.

A Brief History of Apocalyptic Events

Do we Americans have a "fascination with devastation" as one media pundit so aptly phrased it as cable stations switched to uninterrupted broadcast of the tornado swath cutting across Alabama? Our inability to turn away from scenes of destruction may be the reality of our coming to terms with our own mortality and the fragile nature of our existence. Man's existence is but a wisp of smoke and he is gone; so says Solomon in Ecclesiastes Chapter 4. To date 337 people died in the Alabama-Mississippi twisters and damages may top the $2 billion recorded for Hurricane Ivan in 2004. Media outlets say that the Alabama twisters that tore across four states are not our nation's worst tornado. That dubious record belongs to the storm that struck Missouri, Indiana, and Illinois on March 18, 1925. The death toll was 747 souls.

As we go about our routine here, the floodwaters of the mighty Mississippi are at an historic high -- perhaps the 500 year high. Mark Twain tells of the epic floods of his day in his autobiographical *Life on the Mississippi*. Yet, in his day news traveled slowly and live coverage was not conceivable. Video-streaming on laptops gives us a window on the worst that the world has to offer. How this virtual presence on the sidelines of horrific situations affects our collective psyche in the long run is being debated by psychiatrists and priests. In a bygone era we learned weeks or months following a cataclysm, and often the facts were reduced to statistics rather than human tales of woe.

We've seen nothing in our lifetime like the natural disasters that swept across the world before mass communication could warn people of impending danger. The worst case of natural suffering must certainly be the Great Flood of Biblical times that took everyone on earth save for Noah, his family, and his animal collection. A noted ancient history scholar, Dr. David Livingston, estimates that the Great Flood occurred sometime around 3000 B.C. -- or 5000 years ago. He conjectures that the size of the ark was commensurate with the area of 500 railroad boxcars. Even with our technology, the building of the ark and the survival of such devastation is incomprehensible to us.

Alabama's storm is the most recent natural tragedy, but even it pales in comparison with the things that have occurred in Indonesia, Mexico, Haiti, and Japan. Americans can take pride in the fact that our country has been foremost in responding with aid. Charlestonians watch those great C-17 cargo planes wing out of here bound for all points of the globe, and many times their destination has been a mission of mercy.

Would that some great world power could have harnessed human potential for the greater good in bygone eras. Here is a sample of apocalyptic events that, for lack of better description, can be filed under the insurance industry's nomenclature: "Acts of God."

Until we learn from scientists someday that meteorites knocked out all forms of life on this planet eons ago, the greatest natural tragedies short of the Great Flood have occurred in China. In the Yellow River Valley in 1887, torrential rains caused the river to overflow its banks and drown approximately one to two million people. Western missionaries in China were without adequate words to describe the misery and desolation. In 1931, it happened again and anywhere from one and a half to two million people perished in this densely populated region.

Perhaps its the high population density of the Orient. Perhaps it's the simplicity of the architecture and informality of communication, but the world's greatest disasters have beset the East with greater frequency and greater ferocity than the West.

Historians try never to be careless with statistics, but often they are callous with statistical information. Each of those Chinese sufferers died in agony and anonymity. A drought in China preceded the floods by 16 years, and that drought accounted for 9 million deaths through crop loss. The deaths were slower than those caused by rapidly rising waters, but the loss of entire cities due to starvation was beyond belief. The 19th century saw more natural disasters than did the 20th. The Irish population withered in the same manner as the Chinese during the potato famine of the 1840s. Britain's parliament dithered about the ramifications of altering the laws of supply and demand if the government sent in free food.

As tornado activity occupies our attention this Spring of 2011, let us not forget that Bangladesh had a tornado in 1989 that killed 1,300 hundred people. Pakistan had one in 1969 that killed 900. Our weather alert radios, Twitter phone messages, and television weather broadcasters have cut human losses to a fraction of what they might have been.

Nature has more tricks up its sleeve than just those involving water, or the lack thereof. Between 1300 and 1700 a vicious disease known simply as the Black Death stalked Europe, Asia, and Africa. When it abated four centuries after its initial appearance, it'd claimed the lives of 100 million people. All of human history was transformed by that deadly strain of virus. However, Spanish influenza terrified the globe on the heels of the Great War. That war took 11 million lives in a man-made debacle, but the flu killed between 40 and 80 million more from 1918 to 1920. We lost 645,000 to the illness in the States. An American soldier returning to Boston from Europe is thought to have introduced the disease here.

The Lisbon earthquake of 1775 wiped out much of one of the world's leading cities in less time than it takes to tell about it. Voltaire wrote about this event and how the life of a man was as fragile as the flickering of a candle flame. That quake influenced heavily the new thinking of the Enlightenment. Quakes can often destabilize mountain ranges and cause avalanches. Fifty-thousand Peruvians perished in 1970 in what is known as the aftershock avalanche of the Ancash Quake. Not to lessen that tragedy, Tangshan in China experienced a quake that leveled the city and claimed 242,000 souls in 1920.

However, there's more -- much more. A heat wave in Russia took an estimated 50,000 lives in 2010 and a similar heat wave killed 946 in Los Angeles in 1955. Nothing could be worse than smoldering to death in volcanic lava, but 92,000 people did just that in Indonesia in 1815. Mudslides took out 15,000 humans in Venezuela in 1999 while a wall of water known as a tsunami wiped out 242,000 folks in Indonesia in 2004. Though hard to imagine, a wildfire in Wisconsin tallied 2000 victims in 1871. We sometimes grow numb at the staggering statistics.

From hurricanes to tornadoes, earthquakes to avalanches, wildfires, volcanoes, floods, and famines, we sense that human existence is in the hands of a higher power. One can choose to be a fatalist resigned to some untimely end, or one can be a beacon of hope and caring to the most recent victims. Now that Communism has been conquered, polio eradicated, and terrorism has been dealt a death blow, it is America's destiny to lead the world in the reduction of human misery and to set the standard for compassion and care. Recently, a tractor-trailer truck departed Daniel Island loaded with disaster supplies for Alabama. I'm told that word of mouth East of the Cooper filled that truck. This past week a friend of Porter-Gaud School let it be known that he was driving an SUV to Alabama and would be happy to deliver relief supplies to the storm victims. In less than 72 hours, hundreds of pounds of food, water, linen, and baby diapers were collected by students and faculty. Around Charleston and around this great country this scenario has been repeated countless times thereby revealing once again the heart of gold that beats in the breasts those who inhabit the land of the free and the home of the brave.

It's Hard To Say Good Bye To Alex's

Where were you when you heard the sad news of Coleman Boulevard's Alex's closing its operation? Like many you may have driven past the diner and noticed the brief message on the outdoor sign, or you caught the headline on the *Post and Courier*'s website shortly after noon on Wednesday. Wherever you were it was a shock. For forty years Alex's was faithful to the breakfast crowd. In fact, it was THE place to meet for eggs anyway, a rasher of bacon, creamy grits and toast browned the way you like it.

In happier days the *Post and Courier's* Charles Williams wrote a column dated 1-19 - 2004 that was entitled "Welcome to Alex's." Looking back on that story there's a telltale hint that growing competition among moderate-priced restaurants on Coleman Boulevard was even then beginning to gnaw into the landmark business' profitability. Williams recounts the early days in the 1970s when Alex and Carol Billips opened a true old-fashioned diner in a trailer near the site where the Blue Hawaiian Restaurant had burned a year or two earlier. Since Mount Pleasant did not have a town center, Alex's unofficially served that purpose.

Alex's occupied the corner of Coleman and Live Oak Drive and in the four decades it watched over the growth of Mount Pleasant. From the large plate windows one could watch the widening of the boulevard. The awful wreck that resulted in the traffic light at the gateway to the Old Village, Whilden and Coleman, sent an automobile careening into Alex's parking lot. The taping of Alex's windows was as much a sign for us of an impending hurricane as the red flag with the black square that was run up on the pole atop the Custom House. Before on-line referrals the message board at Alex's informed you where to locate a handyman, a plumber, or a roofer. Where else could you get breakfast served 24 hours a day and see all the locals of every race, creed, and denomination? Remember the day when you could walk in the big glass door and the late J.O. Shuler was holding court among a circle of friends at the long table on the far right. That wonderful old veterinarian's cackling laugh made you feel instantly that you were among the hometown crowd. A smiling waitress would ring out, "You need a menu" even before you could slip into a booth and unfold the castoff newspaper you'd picked up on the way in. Of course you didn't need a menu. They were for out-of-towners anyway. Heck, Alex's always fixed you what you wanted anyway, regardless of whether it was on the menu, or not. Sometimes Louie, the cook, would peer through the door to see what oddball had ordered grits and tunafish or a hamburger omelet. One was never really dining alone at Alex's, for the banter from the counter kept the place cheery.

Then there was the daily intrigue of the place. More *tête-à-têtes* occurred at Alex's than anywhere in town. Hunched over coffee mugs were insurance salesmen with their client, real estate appraisers comparing notes, and loafers chewing the fat. In and out of the clusters of booths weaved Virginia or Anna, or any number of the other wait staff that stayed loyal to the place for years. Some customers came in every morning, plopped down, and soon thereafter their breakfast appeared as if by magic. They had a standing order and only Hurricane Hugo interrupted it.

Johnnie Dodds and Groggy Darby went there. So did Harry Hallman. Lawyers liked the place and so did truck drivers and stevedores. On Sunday mornings local pastors could have passed the collection plate among the booths, for the faithful fellowshipped at Alex's before, between, and after worship. The Wednesday Morning Prayer Group from Mount Pleasant Presbyterian breakfasted there every Wednesday for decades. Fishermen tanked up on corned beef hash and grits at 4 a.m. Some of them probably wished they'd had lighter fare by the time they reached the Gulf Stream. Policemen dropped in for coffee after pulling the night shift.

There probably was not another place in the county that would give separate tickets to a party of eight, but Alex's sought to be accommodating. As reporter Charles Williams remarked in his 2004 column, you went somewhere else for haute cuisine. At Alex's you got the basics served hot and fast and with genuine friendship and some good-natured banter. Tables could be rearranged to suit your impromptu community gathering. I doubt that even the White House kitchen made a better grilled cheese or hash browns and cheese omelet. And how many times did you hear the phrase, "Let's meet at Alex's."

Little old ladies felt at home confiding among tables of golfers and retired shrimpers. It was a classless place -- sort of like an Irish pub, but without the Guinness and Harp. It was the closest thing Mount Pleasant had to the legendary Cheer's bar on the television sitcom. Everyone knew your name at Alex's. There was a cast of regulars there who could have suited up for cameo appearances on a TV comedy.

Remember the day that John McCain stopped by? He was in his element amongst the blue-collar patriots he found there. Candidates of every political hue stopped by Alex's as if it were some suburban stump meeting. Lee Atwater took Strom Thurmond there several times. Since Atwater invented the Super Tuesday primary back in the 1980s, the place has hosted many of the national hopefuls. State and local vote seekers counted on a walk through for votes at election time. But, it was a tough audience, as Rodney Dangerfield used to say.

Once the breakfast crowd departed however, the last one shuffling out around 11 a.m., the lunch and dinner trade would be slim much less boisterous. Sometimes it was too hushed within those rows of booths. Even back in the good ol' days, the evening trade was lonely and the staff had time on their hands. Sometimes the television droned on inanely. Even though they cooked up the best burger and fries east of the Cooper, it was always the morning crowd that sustained the location's momentum.

True, Alex's did some goofy things -- like the daffy greeting cards by the register and those ridiculous stuffed animals in a vending machine, but you knew they were trying to make ends meet in an ever-tightening market. The constantly changing mosaic of urban dining habits, new generations of patrons seeking more exotic menus, and an ever-pinching recession that kept discretionary funds close finally did in the 40-year landmark on Coleman.

There'll always be new places opening. Laughs will resound amidst the clatter of dishes and the cry of "order up!" Yet, will those places endure for forty years? Whether your need was for a place to meet and greet, or a meat and three, Alex's was the place to be. Everyone from the United States Senator to the United States Postman felt comfortable there. To the owners and staff of Alex's, you served us well.

Touring Charleston Back in 1912

Many of us have wished that we could drift back in time to experience life as our ancestors did. Alas, we're confined to interpreting a few shards of pottery, a fragment of verse on a marble monument, or a faded letter on parchment. One avenue of time travel that is left wide open to us moderns, however, is the travel guide compiled by cities bent upon encouraging those adventuresome souls who bought our nation's first automobiles a hundred years ago.

If only the ancients had bothered to write up tourist guides for the polis. Archeologists would not have to dig those painstakingly narrow intersecting trenches looking for clues. The City Fathers of Charleston were wiser than the ancients of the polis, for in 1912, Mayor John P. Grace authorized local printing firm Walker, Evans, and Cogswell to publish a neat little volume entitled *Modern Charleston, Profusely Illustrated* with map and index, 1912.

Without a shred of modesty, the introduction states, "The South is the choicest section of the United States. South Carolina is the choicest state in the South, majestic in her history, imperial in her purposes, magnificent in her destiny." It goes on to state that, "Upon the site of Charleston the South itself was founded."

Charleston in 1912 was a city of ship masts tied at wharfside. It was full of mule drawn drays, and a handful of Model T Fords on streets paved with red brick or cobblestone. Henry Ford promised that he'd "build a car for the great multitude," and of the 300, 000 "affordable" Fords, some were seen bumping into the statue of William Pitt that was precariously perched in the center of Meeting and Broad Streets.

There's no question that Henry Ford and Henry Morrison Flagler invented tourism as we know it today. Flagler, the real estate tycoon who bought land in Florida by the square mile and sold it by the half-acre, and Henry Ford, the man who revolutionized both the automobile and the assembly line process, influenced Congress to convert the nation's graded dirt roads into macadamized highways.

Admittedly, Charleston's tourism boom began with the national attention we received from the publication of Albert Simon's and Samuel Lapham's illustrated book *The Architecture of Charleston* (1929). A few years after the innovation of the automobile made long distance travel a routine affair, Drayton Hastie, owner of Magnolia Plantation, began advertising his magnificent landscape all over. What did the earliest tourists do once they motored in from faraway destinations such as Raleigh, Richmond, and Memphis? After removing goggles, scarves, and touring caps, they headed straight for one of the city's three leading hotels -- all situated on Meeting Street. The St. John's Hotel, where the Mills House is today, was a noted landmark and its *table d'hote* was the talk of the town. Trolley cars brought guests in from Union Station located on John Street as well as from the Clyde Steamship docks. Old-timers can recall the derelict St. John's in the late 1960s, a shadow of its former glory. The once-grand domain was placed off-limits to the Corps of Cadets -- for reasons that politeness forbids detailing.

Other hotels here that attracted the automobile enthusiasts were the Charleston Hotel on the East side of Meeting and the Argyle Hotel on the corner of Meeting and Hasell. The Charleston Hotel's 18 Ionic columns towered over Meeting Street, and so much of the City's antebellum past transpired in the shadow of that three-story grand hostelry. Donald McCaig's great novel, *Rhett Butler's People* (McMillan 2007) contains several great scenes set in that classic venue.

The great West Indian Exhibition, a sort of world's fair, held here in 1901-'02 showcased our city as completely recovered from the late unpleasantness of the 1860s. Former Confederate General Stephen Dill Lee, no relation to "Marse Robert E.," touted railroad building, agricultural commerce, and tourism for this city and others of the Old Confederacy. Samuel Clemens, a.k.a. Mark Twain, and President William H. Taft made visits to this most hospitable and refined of coastal communities. Taft, a man with a hearty appetite, made several overnight visits to 116 Broad Street, then the home of R. Goodwyn Rhett, Honorable Mayor of Charleston. Rhett's cook, William Deas, whipped up a special dish for the President -- a concoction of she crab, sherry, cream, butter, and a host of secret ingredients that Deas carried with him to the grave. Charlestonians and visitors alike can enjoy the ambience of 116 Broad, though today it is known as the John Rutledge House Inn.

The Charleston Tour Guide of 1912 suggests that after checking into your hotel, you amble about King Street and enjoy the variety of shops that cater to the local gentry. "On the corner of King and Wentworth Streets is The David Outfitting Company, a Broadway store set down in Charleston." The imposing structure looked much like the Saks Department store building of more recent construction. "So high is the David standard of quality that the name is in Charleston to the men's clothing trade what Sterling is to silver everywhere." The store could be reached by telephone number 405 direct from the lobby of one's hotel.

Visitors to Charleston in 1912 were encouraged to sally forth to the M.H. Lazarus Company, "where they say that Lazarus is to hardware what Sterling is to silver." About the famed Academy of Music on King, just north of Market Street, the guide book says, "This is one of the Weiss playhouses. To the Academy come all of the high class plays booked in the South, many of them direct from New York, with metropolitan casts." You may remember the site when it was known as the Siegling Music Store at 242 King.

Louis Cohen and Company advertised itself as the John Wannamaker's Department Store of Charleston. Cohen claimed to fill every department store need in its location directly across from the Charleston Hotel. Its huge building extended from Meeting Street clear through to King Street just at "The Curve." Furs, millinery goods, shoes, handbags, sweaters and aviator caps direct from New York could be purchased at fair prices. Cohen's claimed to have parasols, stationery, floor coverings, and every kind of notion -- all available to commuters taking the Beltline Trolley.

Freyschmidt's Drug Store on King Street, just opposite Society, noted that it catered to the "Ladies' Trade." It also boasted of being a favorite with the local College of Pharmacy. Its soda fountain made all the favorite carbonated beverages the city craved, and it stayed open late to serve the patrons of the nearby Victoria Theater.

Foreign visitors to Charleston took note that the Exchange Banking and Trust Company on East Bay Street stood ready to handle all currency exchanges. "While the management has always shown evidence of sanity in method and conservatism in investment, it has not been backward in assertiveness and has always been found ready and eager to participate in the material advancement of the city."

Dining out was a matter of making reservations in the hotel or finagling an invitation in a private home. Charleston in 1912 had no shortage of saloons and bars, but restaurants were not as numerous as they are today. Getting about meant learning the trolley lines. Names such as Gadsden Loop and Schuetzenplatz Line leave us clueless a hundred years later as to their destination.

Tourists of the early 20th century appear to have been more culturally minded than our city's visitors today. The Henry Timrod monument in Washington Park attracted numerous admirers of the late poet. The Palmetto Park horse track located on the Charleston Neck was one of the most popular attractions. If you went down Market Street to Ferry Wharf, you could ride over to the Pavilion at the Isle of Palms -- the southern version of Coney Island.

Traveling back in time is great fun if you can locate a century-old tour guide. You'll discover a Charleston far different from the one you see today. You'll see why President Taft and his family came back repeatedly.

June 6th Belongs to the Rangers Who Scaled Pont-du-Hoc in 1944

"People sleep peaceably in their beds at night only because rough men stand ready to do violence on their behalf," so says sage novelist George Orwell. Never have those stark words rung more true than the early morning of Tuesday, June 6, 1944, on the Normandy cliffs of *Pont-du-Hoc*. In every desperate struggle where right and might overcome the reign of terror, there must be a corps of hardy men to kick down the tyrant's door. On D - Day that famed corps was the U.S. Army's 2nd Ranger Battalion under the command of Lieutenant-colonel James Earl Rudder, an Aggie of Texas A & M.

In the history of American men at war there are records aplenty of bloodier fights, but few approach the enormity of consequence as that of knocking out the 155 mm guns atop *Pont-du-Hoc*. Those big guns sat poised to thwart the D - Day amphibious landing, and failure to destroy them was not an option. "Wars may be fought with weapons, but they are won by men. It is the spirit of men who follow and of the man who leads that gains the victory," quipped General George S. Patton. James Earl Rudder's army rangers breached the walls of Hitler's citadel. In one hour of deadly assault those rugged young cleared the way for the allies to save western civilization from a trio of tyrants.

There's been some sort of designated ranger military unit fighting America's battles ever since the colonial wars of the early 18th century. Robert Rogers of the French and Indian War era made the military designation "ranger" synonymous with rugged courage in battles fought along Lake Champlain. When General George C. Marshall determined in 1942 that our army needed something equivalent to the British Special Air Service (S.A.S.) commandos, General Lucien K. Truscott organized the first unit and called them "rangers" in honor of Rogers' colonial frontier fighters. The letter from Truscott to Marshall was dated May 26, 1942, almost exactly 69 years ago this month.

Since Northern Ireland was a staging area for U.S. Army infantry forces in 1942, the finding of a suitable battalion chain of command was General Russell

P. "Scrappy" Hartle's assignment. Scrappy Hartle was the commander of the Army's 34th Division, the first American troops deployed to the U.K. in support of World War II. This no-nonsense general was not a West Point graduate, but rather a St. John's College, Annapolis alumni who took a commission in 1910 through Officer Candidate School. His assignments had included the Philippines insurrections, World War I combat, and chasing Pancho Villa through Texas with George Patton. Hartle was the only star-ranked officer in 1942 to have graduated from both the Army and the Navy War Colleges. He was a favorite of the enlisted ranks, for he often dismounted from his jeep to drill the troops himself, no matter if it were the firing range, the obstacle course, or close order drill.

Hartle selected Captain William Orlando Darby from his command staff to be the first ranger and to build the training cadre. Darby became the commander of the Army's first ranger battalion. The battalions began as a single company and expanded within months to full battalion size with ranger companies A, B, and C. Commando training was conducted at a top secret location near Achnacarry in the highlands of Scotland. First Battalion's baptism under fire came with the Allied surprise attack on Dieppe along the northern coast of France in August 1942. Their success in the predawn raid greatly inspired the Allies. Achnacarry was part of the traditional home of Clan Cameron, and it was known for possessing some of the most rugged terrain anywhere. The training was so brutal that a number of the recruits dropped out and several died. Today, NATO units participate yearly in a grueling commando-style, seven-mile forced march from Spaen Bridge to Achnacarry Castle. The men don full battle gear and move out double-time over the forbidding terrain -- in honor of the Rangers who scaled *Pont-du-Hoc* in June 1944. Aspiring ranger candidates were hand-picked from thousands of applications that poured in from deployed divisions. Some of the selectees did not spontaneously volunteer, however. They were notable young men with special skills who were targeted by superiors and persuaded to put their names forward for the good of the cause.

A rawboned Texan was selected to command the 2nd Ranger Battalion which consisted of Companies D, E, and F. Thirty-two-year-old Captain James Earl Rudder of Eden, Texas, was the next ranger officer picked after Darby. Rudder was a Texas A & M graduate who'd served in the Army Reserves. Rudder's prewar job consisted of teaching shop class and coaching high school football at Brady High in McCulloch, Texas. Rudder's commanders called him a "soldier's soldier from head to toe." It was Rudder who received the nod from General Eisenhower to command the critical predawn attack against the German guns atop Point-du-Hoc--a cliff commanding the landing site at code-name "Omaha Beach" on the Normandy Beach.

If ever there were a "mission impossible," then this was it -- a rocky cliff that was 80 yards straight up, guarded by vigilant and determined Germans in machine gun bunkers with supporting cannon and infantrymen lobbing grenades. Rudder's Rangers answered the challenge. The men's average age was 20. Ranger Companies D, E, and F, nicknamed "Dog," "Easy," and "Fox," spent countless hours memorizing a scale model of cliffs, bunkers, and hedgerows. They crawled over steep precipices under live fire and in all kinds of weather. Every man cross-trained so that he could do any other man's job. Rangers carried 60 pounds of battle gear, much of it ammunition. They knew that their assignment was what the army used to call a "forlorn hope," or a suicide mission. Yet, failure to knock out those German guns was not an option. Hand-to-hand fighting was expected once they negotiated the summit, and the rangers must be prepared to hurl their foe backward.

Murphy's Law states that "If anything possibly can wrong, it probably will," and that maxim held true on D-Day, June 6, 1944. In the confusion on the dark beach that was raked with enemy machine guns, a high-ranking army officer shouted through the din of battle, "What outfit is this?" A G.I. yelled back, "5th Rangers!" To this, the officer shouted, "Well then G-- D--- It, Rangers, Lead the way!" To this day that D - Day battle slogan has stuck with the rangers on countless fields of valor.

Under the most murderous fire of machine guns and German "potato-masher" grenades, Rudder's Rangers hurled grappling hooks up the side of the rocky cliffs. With grit, determination, and bloody fingers they clawed their way around dead comrades and impassable boulders. The first man on the top hurled a grenade and fired a burst of automatic fire from his submachine gun. Explosions from satchel charges and grenades made the air thick with smoke and flame. One by one the German guns went silent. Few Germans were captured as the fighting was too swift and deadly to parley. It was kill or be killed. Rudder's Rangers took heavy casualties even though their medics performed heroic service under fire. In London General Eisenhower breathed a sigh of relief when word was signaled from a British troop ship that Pont-du-Hoc was ours.

The victory of *Pont-du-Hoc* was not the single moment of valor of that long day. The paratroopers who landed behind the lines at St. Mere Eglise hours before the amphibious landings were heroes. Heroes, too, were the soldiers who waded ashore on beaches code named "Utah, Omaha, Juno, Gold, and Sword." Pilots who flew the gliders crammed with paratroopers into the hedgerows were heroes, as were the sailors who drove the Higgins landing craft onto the beaches under heavy fire and then returned for another load.

As for James Earl Rudder, he survived D-day at the summit of that rugged Normandy cliff, and later on, he lived through the Battle of the Bulge. Rudder became president of Texas A & M, and that university's elite cadet unit is called Rudder's Rangers in his honor.

No better tribute could be made than the one President Ronald Reagan made on the 40th anniversary of D - Day and the assualt on *Pont-du-Hoc*. "We're here to mark that day in history when the Allied armies joined in battle to reclaim this continent to liberty. For four long years, much of Europe had been under a terrible shadow. Free nations had fallen, Jews cried out in the camps, millions cried out for liberation. Europe was enslaved and the world prayed for its rescue. Here, in Normandy, the rescue began. Here, the Allies stood and fought against tyranny, in a giant undertaking unparalleled in human history."

Make Kansas City One of Your Destinations This Summer

Despite the uncertain economy and the high rice of gas, there's still a lot of reason to head out on the highway and see America. We're the greatest democracy on earth and we have the greatest economy. There's widespread distribution of wealth here and our splendid success over the last 200 years has manifested itself in an intriguing and delightful mix of urban and rural expression. The great American midwest provides an ideal contrast to our Old South terrain and tradition.

Steer the family land-yacht into the rapid stream of I-40 or I-64 and watch the heartland of America unfold before you. Kansas City is an ideal destination for coastal Carolinians looking for something a little different this summer. It's 1,111 miles from Coleman Hardware store if you're the kind that needs a reference point and MapQuest says you'll need about 18 hours to arrive safely by automobile. When you pull to the corner of Twelfth Street and Vine, as Wilbert Harrison's song reminds us, you'll begin to fall in love -- at least you'll fall in love with the scent of barbeque ribs smoking over the grills of the one-hundred or so eateries that bill themselves as America's best barbecue!

If you fly in to Kansas City and catch one of the convenient commuter busses into the city, you'll notice that the Kansas River is 12 feet over its flood stage. At the city bridge the Kansas River is usually 6 feet deep. It's over 18 feet at that point and still rising. Large trees complete with their root system are flooding downriver at 7 knots and slamming into barges, boats, and docks. The Kansas River flows into the Missouri River in Kansas City, and when both river systems are rising fast, as they are this month, it is a time of high anxiety -- much akin to our hurricane warning.

On the drive in you'll see a brick warehouse on the right hand side of the road near the Kansas River that dates from the 1930s. There's no sign to indicate that this was once the headquarters of the legendary Howard Hughes, the reclusive billionaire. There are so many tidbits of history lurking in the nooks and crannies of this midwestern city which some Americans desired to become our nation's capital after the bitterness of the War Between the States.

K.C., as the locals refer to Kansas City, is competing to be the culinary capital of the country. Since the place started out with a stockyard, a saloon, and a gallows 160 years ago, it has become decidedly uptown and refined in its tastes. Many travelers return saying they have been ruined for ever ordering beef steak in any other region of the country -- so acclaimed is the grain-fed beef of that grand old prairie "free state."

When Horace Greeley said, "Go west young man," he was probably talking about the great steak restaurants down by the stockyards in Kansas City. When pop singer Wilbert Harrison belted out his vocal, "Crazy Little Women in Kansas City," he probably was not referring to Kathleen Sebelius. However, we suspect he had Lidia Bastianich in mind when he crooned those lyrics. She's the Lidia of Lidia's Italian Kansas City -- one of the most famous Italian restaurants in the country -- not to mention her fame with the long-running PBS series Lidia's Italian-American Kitchen.

One of the distinctive aromas you notice quickly upon arriving in Kansas City, other than the stockyards down by the river, is the smell of coffee beans being roasted at the Folger coffee roasting center on Broadway in the Garment district. The Garment District factories have been tastefully renovated into condos and apartments. At the turn of the century most American women wore an item of apparel known as a work dress. Many of these ready-to-wear utility outfits were produced here at Jacobs Manufacturing. Sears-Roebuck marketed the no frills garment in four colors around the country.

About two blocks from the Garment District where coffee bean roasters rub shoulders with local brewmasters, you'll discover the Lyric Opera House -- a 50-year-old performing arts center that is home to the Kansas City Symphony. It's a grand stop for the traveling troupes of New York, as well. Not far away is the Crown Center, a city within a city, created by midas -touch business guru, J.C. Hall of Hallmark greeting card fame. Crown Center is one man's view 60 years ago of what the ideal inner city should be like.

The Kansas City Convention Center is the ideal political arena for hashing out who will represent our national parties in the big elections. William Jennings Bryan was selected as the Democratic nominee in Kansas City in 1900; however, the convention site that saw his nomination was across town from this one. Herbert Hoover was nominated as the Republican candidate here in 1928. Gerald Ford also received the Republican nod here in 1976.

The Populist political movement that swept the Midwest at the turn of the century was a Kansas and Nebraska idea. Throughout the South and the Midwest the poor farmers united to demand things such as the abolition of national banks, government takeover of the railroads, a graduated income-tax, and the direct election of U.S. Senators. Bryan was their man. There were as many as 45 Congressmen of the Populist persuasion as we entered the 20th century. South Carolina elected none, but our sister state to the North elected several. If you listen to their conversation and read their newspapers, the hint of populism can be detected still in Kansas conversation.

Every schoolchild should know that Kansas City was the headquarters of Tom Pendergast's political ring, a powerful political machine that was to the Midwest what Boss Tweed andTammany Hall had been to New York in the 19th century. Tom Pendergast ruled the roost in this part of the country. No one got appointed or elected without his OK. Harry Truman owed much of his early political success to Tom Pendergast's endorsement. When Pendergast was finally disgraced and packed away to Leavenworth prison for a few years, he believed that he had not one loyal friend left in the world. Vice President Harry Truman was one of the few who came to mourn Tom Pendergast at his death in 1945.

The Pendergast machine headquarters was a run-of-the-mill two story office building at 1908 Main Street, right beside the old Monroe Hotel. The phrase "1908 Main Street" was a euphemism for great political clout. All a Pendergast minion had to do was to hint that "1908 Main" wants such and such done in a hurry -- and the deed was done.

The Monroe Hotel lobby and that of the Aladdin Hotel look like something right out of the "Untouchables." You expect to see men in double-breasted suits and fedoras sitting at tables awaiting their day's orders from Tom Pendergast's precinct bosses. The Majestic Restaurant three blocks away dates to the turn-of-the-century as does the old Mulhbach Hotel. All of these places were frequented by the likes of William Jennings Bryan, Harry Truman, and Tom Pendergast. Bob Dole went there, too, albeit in a different era. At the Majestic you'll be treated to one of the finest steaks to be had anywhere. The piano player hits all the jazz notes and the old mahogany and tile decor take you back to the heady days of prohibition and speakeasies.

Don't forget the World War I museum while you're in K.C. It's so realistic that you may feel that you're in the assault at Passchendaele. It's a quick bus ride from the museum to Jack Stack's Barbeque House, but be prepared to wait in a line when you get there. If it's crowded don't fret. K.C. has over 100 barbeque restaurants. And I doubt that you'll spot anything resembling the crazy little women that Wilber Harrison sang about!

This Past Sunday Was the 146th Anniversary of Juneteenth

Just as Dad was opening yet another Father's Day present of neckties and savoring the last of the grilled burgers this Sunday, another special but less well known day -- Juneteenth -- was being celebrated across the South. For the record, Juneteenth is 43 years older as a celebration than is Father's Day. The origin of Father's Day appears to lie with Grace Clayton of Monogah, West Virginia. There'd been a terrible mining disaster and Grace wanted to honor the 210 fathers who lost their lives. The date was July 5, 1908. Calvin Coolidge endorsed the notion, the greeting card industry got behind it, and the rest is history. However, Juneteenth is a more emotional celebration -- the jubilation that accompanied the end of 300 years of human bondage in North America.

Provenance for Juneteenth betrays that it, too, is rooted in an attempt to turn suffering and injustice into healing and strength. The first Father's Day was likely in Monogah, West Virginia, coal mining country; the first Juneteenth celebration was in Galveston, Texas, cotton country. On June 19, 1865, Major General Gordon Granger of the Union army stood on the iron balcony of the Ashton Villa in Galveston and issued famed General Order Number 3 to the people of Texas.

The words of General Granger could not have come as any surprise to anyone west of the Mississippi. After all, Lee had surrendered to Grant at Appomattox 11 weeks prior, and Joe Johnston had submitted to Sherman 7 weeks prior to Granger's Federal troops landing on the coast of Texas -- arguably the Old South's last outpost.

General Order Number 3 began with the proclamation, "The people of Texas are informed that in accordance with a Proclamation from the Executive of the United States, all slaves are free. This involves an absolute equality of rights and rights of property between former masters and slaves, and the connection heretofore existing between them becomes that between employer and free laborer." Those stirring words so long in coming officially ended slavery in the Old South. Seven months later in December, 1865, the 13th Amendment made slavery a violation of the Constitution. Slavery had been just one of the causes of the great war, but it was the most divisive and emotional cause. Ironically, Ulysses S. Grant's slaves on his Missouri farm known as White Haven were not freed until January 1865, when the Missouri Senate passed a bill of manumission. Lee, by contrast, freed the only slaves in his family -- the ones his wife had inherited -- in 1863. When Granger's regiment disembarked in Galveston they encountered hundreds of former slaves who'd walked off their plantations in anticipation of freedom. However, word soon reached Granger that hundreds if not thousands of slaves were still toiling in the fields for their old overseers.

Some history buffs question whether the Federal government was in cahoots with the plantation owners in some way because the government planned to seize the cotton crop as the spoils of war. With the Confederacy a null and void state by mid-April, the overseers would have known that federal occupation of Texas was just a matter of time. When Granger made his proclamation of General Order Number 3, his couriers had assembled a great crowd of Galveston citizens to hear the general's remarks. Many in the crowd were former slaves just a week or two removed from plantation bondage. The rejoicing among the Freedmen had been anticipated by the Union army who'd closed the saloon and banned the sale of alcohol. Jubilation over freedom brought out the young and the old of the East Texas African population. Singing, dancing, clapping, waving, hugging, and a general spirit of exhilaration erupted in the streets of Galveston, and spread to the countryside.

The bond of East Texas to the Confederacy had grown strong between 1863 and 1865. The Union navy acted swiftly to blockade the port of Galveston when the war broke out, but Confederate raiders such as Raphael Semmes and others made the waters of the Gulf hot for the blockaders. Blockade runners continued to run in and out of the waterways between Galveston and Port Arthur. One of the successful blockade runners was Thomas William House, the father of President Wilson's advisor, Edward Mandell House.

Texas had been the odd fellow of the Confederacy. Its great founder and statesman, Sam Houston, had strenuously opposed secession, and only the eastern quarter of the vast state could identify with the rest of the South. A mix of complaints including defense of states rights, the defense of the institution of slavery, and the failure of the federal government to police the border with Mexico were reasons bandied about to curry favor with the cause. Texas became a supply depot and a recruiting station for the rest of the South and served the cause well until Admirals Farragut and Porter teamed up with Grant to cut the South into two parts along the Mississippi River.

Slavery in Texas was just two generations removed from the brutal land-clearing phase where so much of the inhumanity occurred that was associated with that institution. Granger, an 1845 West Point classmate of Charleston's Bernard Bee of Manassas fame, was a foe of slavery; however, he did not embrace equality between the races. Such was the condition of uncertainty that the newly freed Africans found themselves enmeshed throughout the South. Land speculators across Texas had borrowed heavily to purchase enormous tracts of woodland. Then numerous slaves were bought to clear the land and remove the stumps to make way for immediate planting. The economic panic of 1857 saw cotton piled on the wharf in Galveston, New Orleans, Savannah, and Charleston. Bankers panted for payment from the land speculators. The plantation owners panted for cotton prices to rise. The slaves just panted in the heat as they hoed a crop that was destined to rot on a wharf.

Texas Hill Country and central Texas were home to a host of German immigrants and they had little use for secession, or the Confederacy. John Bell Hood and his "gallant Texans," as Robert E. Lee so nobly referred to them, were mostly East Texans and they saved many a Confederate engagement for the Army of Tennessee and the Army of Northern Virginia. Hood had a penchant for arriving on the scene in the nick of time to make the deciding difference.

There were not many fights of consequence that occurred on Texas soil during the War Between the States. Confederate Generals John Magruder and Kirby Smith managed the keep the Yanks at bay until 1865. For that reason there were fewer slave desertions in east Texas than in the other southern states. Federal troops cut a fishhook swath through the South between 1863 and 1865 thereby liberating the Africans wherever Federals were victorious. Oddly enough, there were seldom insurrections where slaves were numerically superior.

The most notable Southern victory was brought off by Dick Dowling, an Irish pub owner who, with an artillery battery and Irish immigrants, held off 5000 Union soldiers at the Sabine Pass southwest of Port Arthur. Dowling quickly became a legend in Houston where his Bank of Bacchus pub hosted every notable Texan for years following the War. Sadly, Dowling succumbed to yellow fever in 1867, but the pub was a favorite watering hole for Texas politicians for years. Texas did not have that "fought over -- burned over" look that the other southern states had in 1865.

The June 19th celebration was short-lived as the Union soldiers put a stop to anything that resembled boisterousness. Then being suddenly free meant assuming a host of new responsibilities that the former slaves were never trained to handle. Too often they fell prey to unscrupulous men of the North and the South. Oppressive "Black Codes" and then "Jim Crow" laws replaced the shackles of slavery with a newer form of servitude.

Juneteenth became a bigger celebration with the descendants of the original slaves, and it became a way to bond over the shared experiences. It became a church service and a cookout and a time of celebration. Juneteenth disappeared for two generations because of the Great Depression and World War II, but the Civil Rights movement revived the memories. Today, Juneteenth is the sort of event "that those who know -- know, and those who don't probably never will."

Charleston During the French Revolution

Exactly 222 years ago this month something was popping in Paris, and it wasn't cork from wine bottles! Musket shots popped in the night, paving bricks ricocheted against buildings, and glass windows of shops were shattered by men wielding clubs. Even the Parisians didn't know it at the time, but a revolution was brewing. This one would be vastly different from the one that had spawned on the docks of Boston in March of 1770. Americans from New York, Philadelphia, Boston, and Charleston had intimate ties with Paris prior to the French Revolution.

Charleston and New Rochelle, New York had the largest concentration of French descendants. Historians are researching correspondence between Americans and the French to discover what influence activists from our new republic had upon the overthrow of the *ancien regime*. Charleston was a Francophile city in 1789, and not without cause. So significant was French aid in securing our independence that some leaders, notably Alexander Hamilton, fretted that French culture would predominate in our emerging republican society. At least one Charlestonian ladled rice onto his dinner plate with a serving spoon embossed with the Comte de Rochambeau's coat of arms on it. Rochambeau was the commander of the French forces at Yorktown in 1781. Others purchased furniture in the Louis XIV style. Several Lowcountry gentlemen could boast of having entertained Lafayette, de Kalb, and Pierre L'Enfant, prominent French patriots of our revolution. The elites of the Carolina coast sent their sons on the grand tour and usually that entailed a year or more in the foreign capitals, principally London and Paris. Charles Cotesworth Pinckney and his brother Thomas studied the art of war at Caen after he completed his legal studies in London. John Laurens, the gallant Charlestonian who was aide to George Washington, spent time in Paris as a young man between terms at Oxford. Numerous Americans who were fervent in the American revolution had close association with French citizens in the months leading to the fall of the Bastille.

There were at least four dozen families between Charleston and the North Santee River who had close ties with France before the French Revolution. Unlike today's postal service, the way to get a letter delivered abroad required that one read the local newspapers and note when a ship was arriving from or departing to the foreign port of interest. Le Harve was a French port of call for merchant ships serving Charleston during colonial times.

At the time of the upheaval in France, Charleston had two competing newspapers. They were *The State Gazette of South Carolina*, a semiweekly, joint effort by Peter Timothy and investor Ben Franklin, and *The City Gazette* or *Daily Advertiser*, a daily paper published by John Miller. News boys hawked the papers along Broad Street and the taverns and coffee houses along Church and Bay Streets. Ship captains could be engaged for letter courier service at Shepherd's Tavern at Broad and State Streets, or Dillon's Tavern at Broad and Meeting.

Parchments sealed with wax were hand-delivered in a tavern or at the wharf to the ship captain along with a few silver coins for his diligence. Several weeks later -- barring a disaster -- the letter made its way to its intended recipient. Historians are uncovering bundles of early American correspondence in foreign ports. It's just a matter of time before revealing aspects of Charleston commerce and social life come to light. We'll learn more about American intrigue with the French Revolution as historians scavenge archives from Normandy to the Baltic.

The national and international stories circulating in Charleston 222 years ago this month centered around two great topics of interest. James Madison proposed a raft of dramatic amendments to the Constitution which celebrated its one year anniversary as of June 1, 1789. Madison referred to the proposals as a "Bill of Rights." Of equal interest to Charlestonians was the news that French King Louis XVI was calling for a meeting of the Estates-General -- a desperate measure involving elected representatives of the clergy, nobility, and the commoners in hopes of quelling the tension in Paris. Each ship that tied up here brought fresh news from abroad to be printed in the local papers.

There's an old adage, "Rome wasn't built in a day." The obverse of that old saying might well be, "France didn't fall overnight." The *Ancien Regime* experienced so much excess, moral laxity, and corruption in the 18th century that it'd be difficult to pin the blame on church, or state, or the rigid class structure.

Americans in general, and Charlestonians especially, did encourage, aid, and abet the fall of Louis XVI's dynasty. However, it'd be a gross exaggeration to think that the French monarchy collapsed due primarily to our influence.

In this city where polite families employed a French dancing master, a fencing master, a French tutor, and a governess, one can imagine that drawing room conversation centered around the calamity in France 222 years ago this month. There was anticipation here that France would become an American-styled republic. The crusty British conservative, Edmund Burke, starkly laid out a grim rationale in his *Reflections on the Revolution in France* as to why France would not be able to duplicate the recent American experience. Tom Paine, the American revolutionary thinker who traveled to Paris to encourage the revolutionaries, gleefully rebutted Burke. Charlestonians rushed to Wells' Book Shop to purchase copies of the fiery rhetoric.

France was beset by troubles from every sector in the summer of 1789. Not the least of which was a wine vineyard disease that sank some leading wineries financially and caused the price of the basic table beverage to skyrocket. France entered into the Treaty of Eden with Great Britain in 1886. This was an ill-advised piece of diplomacy that saw Britain flood France with high-priced British goods, and, since the Brits drank Port instead of wine, they bought very little from France.

Very little cotton was imported from the Indies in 1789 due to drought, and that caused French textile factories to close and joblessness to rise. Furthermore, drought in some parts of France and flash floods in other parts led to a terrible harvest which resulted in historic food shortages.

All of the weird weather and the clumsy diplomacy might have been taken in stride by the long suffering French underclass except for the fact that this new "Age of Enlightenment" had popularized strange economic thinking. A group of intellectuals gathered in French salons to pipe-dream about "unthinkable" things -- such as accumulating personal wealth without having to seek the Crown's favor.

Francois Quesnay was one of the formulators of this clever idea that one day became known as capitalism. Adam Smith slipped into Paris just to sit at a table where Quesnay was conversing on the principles of a free market.

In 1789 Louis XVI's court was so lax that leading merchants no longer feared violating the strict mercantilist rules of trade that had been in force for centuries. The greatest crime of 1789 was the French merchants' export abroad of valuable grain because they could make higher profits abroad. The result was hunger and suffering in Paris. This dilemma -- free market profit versus overriding moral concern -- provoked an emotion-charged debate on both sides of the Atlantic.

Louis XVI was as inept as a head of state as was England's Charles II a century and a half earlier -- the difference in circumstances being that England was awash in foodstuffs, whereas the lower third of France's population was starving.

In June 1789, the Third Estate -- the common people of France -- did the radical American thing by defying their king and electing one of their own -- Jean-Sylvain Bailly -- as President of the Third Estate. The Third Estate represented over 95% of the French population. In July, Bailly became the first mayor of Paris, just in time for the riots at the flour mill, the riots at the veterans hospital, and the assault upon the Bastille armory and prison. Poor Bailly decried the violence but was powerless to stop it.

Jean-Sylvain Bailly did not live long enough to become the George Washington of France. The fury of the revolution engulfed him as Robespierre's deemed him to be an "enemy of the people." His head rolled on the guillotine during the Reign of Terror. Regrettably for France, the hunger and years of accumulated injustices combined to catapult their turmoil into uncontrollable chaos.

Dinner conversation in Charleston exactly 222 years ago was riveting. Talk revolved around Mr. Madison's bold amendments and the dramatic rise to prominence in France of an astronomer named Jean-Sylvain Bailly.

Finding a Sunken Steamboat Buried in a Cornfield in Kansas

Just when you're sure you've heard everything, there comes a story to top it all. There're few things that thrill us more than hearing about sunken treasure and the discovery of old shipwrecks long forgotten. Ever since Jacques Cousteau captivated us in the 1960s with his underwater archaeological expedition on the *Mahdia*, a Roman galley that sank off Tunesia in 1087. Closer to home, local diver Lee Spence publicized in the 1980s that he thought he'd located the site of the *Hunley* wreck off Breach Inlet. A decade later, the adventure novelist and marine archaeologist, Clive Cussler, did actually pinpoint the wreck of the *Hunley* in the shallow waters off our coast. We're no strangers here to shipwreck legends and the lure of sunken treasure. After all, the famed "ship of gold," the sidewheel steamer, *S.S. Central America* was located not far from here, as were a couple of old Spanish galleons and a pirate ship, or two. However, the granddaddy tale of sunken treasure comes to us -- not from the Mediterranean coast or some South Atlantic port, but rather, this "believe it, or not" sunken treasure yarn originated 23 years ago in a Kansas cornfield a half mile inland from the Missouri River.

In 1987 there was a lot of buzz among divers and sunken treasure hunters about the efforts to locate and salvage the wreck of the *S.S. Central America* off the coast of North Carolina. Newspapers began to carry exciting accounts of an underwater search team called Columbia-America Discovery Group. Lead investors Tommy Thompson and Bob Evans had to pioneer new techniques and equipment for a sustained dive in such deep water. Eleven hundred miles west of Thompson and Evans' dive location in 1987 there was a refrigerator dealer from Independence, Missouri, Bob Hawley, who was searching for a sunken treasure ship -- the *Arabia*. It was 170-foot-long paddle wheeler that sank suddenly from a collision with a log on September 5, 1856, just past the stockyards of Kansas City.

There's a curious parallel between the sinking of the steamships Arabia and the *S.S. Central America*. The *Arabia* sank in September 1856, whereas the *Central America* went down a year later in September 1857. Both ships were loaded with expensive cargo -- the *Central America* had 30,000 pounds of gold aboard when she sank, while the *Arabia* carried 200 tons of general merchandise. The wrecks of both were discovered within a few weeks of each other and newspapers had a field day in that pre-internet era. Today, weblogs sap the vitality from newspaper reporting on events such as the *Arabia* and the *Central America*.

Pringle Boatworks on Pennsylvania's Monongahela River was the place where the *Arabia's* keel was laid back in 1853. The sleek paddlewheel riverboat had a length of 171 feet and a breadth of 29, and she could carry 220 tons of cargo plus crew and passengers. Pringle craftsmen built many of the boats and barges that ferried the "manifest destiny" crowd west. Oak timbers and oak deck planks were thick and sturdy enough to herd mules aboard. It would take a mighty snag to gouge a hole in the *Arabia's* hull. Yet, the swift moving torrent of silt and debris that is the "Mighty Missouri" has been a riverboat captain's nightmare to navigate since the days of Mark Twain.

Those hardy folks who went west by wagon train or by flatboat roughed it in the wild, but they didn't go without for long. Entrepreneurs from back east saw profits in those prairies of Kansas and Nebraska. Before the first oxen team was set loose to graze at its destination at Fort Laramie, New England speculators had figured a way to bring them luxuries from back home. It's been said that when Hawley and his friends uncovered the 45 feet of silt from the wreck of the *Arabia* that one of them exclaimed, "this thing was a floating Wal-Mart."

In the 3 years that the *Arabia* was afloat she plied the waters of the Ohio, the Mississippi, and the Missouri hauling people, livestock, and supplies into the western territories. Investors from the big cities made fortunes on the mercantile companies providing wares for the westward migration.

On Friday afternoon, September 5, 1856, the passengers of the *Arabia* were just sitting down to supper when the flat-bottomed riverboat lurched and angled sideways in the water. It was obvious from the moment that she was going down and that no one had time to retrieve a thing before entering the life boats.

Unlike the *S.S. Central America* which went down with over 400 souls in a hurricane off Hatteras, the steamship *Arabia* had just one casualty -- a mule that was tethered to the deck. A published account of the last voyage of the ill-fated ship states, "the *Arabia* departed from St. Louis on August 30, 1856, at 4:00 p.m., en route to Kansas, Weston, St. Joseph, Council Bluffs and Sioux City, with stops at intermediate ports. Seven days later, on September 5, 1856, she left Westport Landing in the afternoon, carrying 150 passengers, and more than 200 tons of freight, bound for her next stop which was Parkville, Missouri." Parkville was just downriver from Kansas City. Cargo aboard the *Arabia* included cases of Belgian-made rifles and great quantities of ammunition. This discovery in 1988 was significant because the steamship sank in waters just 35 miles away from Lawrence, Kansas. Three months earlier a band of pro-slavery raiders sacked Lawrence and drove away a number of the town's abolitionist settlers recently arrived from New England. The mob violence has been viewed as the first sign of the coming of disunion -- five years almost to the day. Was the *Arabia* taking arms to abolitionists, to pro-slavery factions, or merely selling fine, breech-loading weapons on a first-come, first served basis?

Arabia sank to the bottom of the river in minutes leaving just its smoke stacks visible. A day later the smokestacks were washed away and the *Arabia* sank deep into the silt. Soon the Missouri River formed a sand embankment around the wreck site. Over the next 130 years the river shifted westward a half mile, leaving the wreck 45 feet deep in alluvial soil -- soil that made the corn grow tall on Judge Norman Sortor's farm in 1988.

In 1877 rumors that 400 casks of Kentucky bourbon were part of the *Arabia*'s lading induced Kansas City locals to probe the river bottom, but to no avail. In the 1970s another more sophisticated effort was made in the very same cornfield that Bob Hawley eventually made his find. Hawley used sensitive metal detecting equipment and within a few days the *Arabia*'s big boilers gave off signals loud and clear.

Less than three weeks after George H.W. Bush defeated Michael Dukakis in the 1988 presidential election, there was wild celebration of another sort going on amidst bulldozed corn stubble in a muddy field in Kansas. After sinking his life savings and going to the bank a couple of times, Hawley and his family members had enough pumps and generators to draw 20,000 gallons of water a minute from the excavated wreck site.

What they found was a treasure perfectly preserved at a depth of 45 feet of river silt washed down from as far as Montana. Soon Hawley and crew were pulling up "coffee beans from Brazil; bolts of silk from China; dishes, locks, keys, pocketknives and almonds from England; perfume; porcelain buttons, pins, needles and writing pens from France; gin from Holland; glass Indian trade beads from Italy; tobacco boxes, cigars and coffee beans from South America; pencils from Switzerland, and nutmeg from the West Indies." It is maintained that this find is the largest wet organic collection of artifacts of any archaeological site in the world. The *Arabi*a is one of the world's best preserved time capsules. It shows that the folks who went west didn't rough it for very long before they demanded the luxuries that money could buy.

The sheer amount of well-preserved 130-year-old merchandise is staggering -- 4000 pairs of boots, hundreds of sets of china, bolts of fine silk cloth, and thousands of odds and ends used around a prairie home. Unlike Tommy Thompson and his cache of gold from the *S.S. Central America*, Bob Hawes decided not to sell off his treasure bit by bit. The entire collection is on display in a special museum in downtown Kansas City.

July 13 Marks 148th Anniversary of Worst Riot in American History

Anyone who thinks that the Battle of Gettysburg is all that Abe Lincoln had on his mind in July of 1863 needs to think again. Lincoln was so concerned in the last week of June that he ordered more Federal troops posted around Washington, D.C. Old Abe had a fright on Sunday, June 28 as J.E.B. Stuart's cavalry rode within two miles of the District of Columbia. The Confederate cavalry's feint toward the capital caused Union generals Howard, Reynolds, Sickles, and Sedgwick temporarily to march east and away from the Union army of Meade which was then moving toward Gettysburg.

Secretary of War Edwin M. Stanton called in the 7th New York Volunteers (7th NYV) to move from Frederick, Maryland, to a position closer to Washington in case Lee chose to seize the city. A plan was drawn up for Lincoln and his cabinet to flee much the way President Madison had fled the British capture of Washington in 1814.

The 7th NYV was made up mostly of German immigrants who'd recently arrived in this country eager for work. Unscrupulous army recruiters promised them citizenship, financial bounties, and free land in the West if they'd enlist for a brief tour of patriotic military service. J.E.B. Stuart's cavalry dash toward Washington proved to be Lady Luck's way of not spewing them forth upon the gory field of Gettysburg as these were the forces recalled to protect the federal government from rebel capture.

Lincoln and his Cabinet sat by the telegraph machine for hours on Friday, July 3 and Saturday, July 4 awaiting the tap-tap-tap of Morse code messages from Meade's army just 64 miles westward. The news was ominous. Meade appeared overly cautious even though he outnumbered Lee. By the evening of July 4, it became apparent that Lee was defeated in his objective at Gettysburg but that his army was not crushed. Twenty-eight thousand Confederates lay dead as opposed to twenty-three thousand Federals. The townspeople of Gettysburg were sickened for days by the stench of burning horse carcasses. Shallow graves hastily dug for the human dead began to expose their ghastly contents with the thunderstorm downpours of July 4.

Lee learned sometime after Lincoln did on July 4 of the surrender of Vicksburg in the West to Ulysses S. Grant. The slow retreat of Lee back to the Potomac was not actively pressed by Meade.

The hot, sultry week of July 5 through 11, Lee's decimated army retreated slowly southward as Confederate engineers rebuilt the Potomac bridge that the Union had destroyed in an attempt to trap Lee. Confederate generals Imboden, Fitzhugh Lee, and J.E.B. Stuart served as the rearguard.

A much perturbed Abe Lincoln sent a message to General Meade, "My dear general, I do not believe you appreciate the magnitude of the misfortune involved in Lee's escape. He was within your easy grasp, and to have closed upon him would, in connection with our other late successes, have ended the war. As it is, the war will be prolonged indefinitely. If you could not safely attack Lee last Monday, how can you possibly do so South of the river, when you can take with you very few more than two-thirds of the force you then had in hand? It would be unreasonable to expect, and I do not expect you can now effect much. Your golden opportunity is gone, and I am distressed immeasurably because of it."

As the cautious Meade allowed the southern forces to escape annihilation, intelligence reports began to arrive at the White House that New York City was seething in rebellion against the war and the March 3 conscription law. Desertion was the Union Army's number one problem in 1863 as many northern soldiers and civilians alike interpreted Lincoln's emancipation address of January 1, 1863, as changing the war's original purpose from preserving the union to that of liberating the slaves.

The March 3 Conscription Act called for a draft lottery drawing to take place on Monday, July 13. A similar draft drawing had taken place that morning amidst jeers and protests. Over the weekend of July 10, 11, and 12, thousands of working class men drank their beer in New York saloons as was their custom. On this particular weekend the bar talk concerned the grisly accounts of Gettysburg then being reported in such daily papers as the New York World, the Tribune, and the Times.

The saloon gatherings soon turned malicious with rancorous talk of blacks taking all the manual day labor and the likelihood of hundreds of thousands of liberated blacks pouring into New York City soon. Amidst the alcohol and the vitriol of the saloon district on Saturday night, July 11, a plot was hatched to form a mob on Monday for purposes of ransacking the Draft Lottery building.

For years historians believed that the New York City Riots were a spontaneous outpouring of working class discontent over the war and the ease with which the middle class and the wealthy could dodge military service. The Lincoln government wanted the public to believe that the week of rioting, the bloodiest and deadliest in American history, was just a venting of wartime frustrations. However, evidence now appears to lead to well-organized groups of working class men carrying out sabotage, arson, and mayhem in a systematic fashion that threatened the future of the Union war effort.

Lincoln was fearful that the New York riots would jeopardize the recent successes in the field. According to Roy Basler's The Collected Works of Abraham Lincoln (1953), he remarks: "On Saturday, July 11, President Lincoln telegraphed his son Robert at the New-York Fifth Avenue hotel in Manhattan: 'Come to Washington.'" Lincoln had early warning of the impending riot, feared the worst.

Sunday, July 12, the city of New York dawned quiet and shops of all kinds opened for business -- few observing the Sabbath. William O. Stoddard, an aide to Lincoln, happened to be in the city on a leave of absence from the White House. He and his brother Henry were having breakfast in City Hall Park when a great commotion caught their attention. A mob of armed white men was chasing after an ambulance carrying a wounded black man. Soon the sound of cursing, shouting, and the shattering of glass was heard. It didn't take them long to see that a retaliatory attack was being made upon the black population of the city. The Stoddard brothers returned to their hotel to retrieve a weapon and then proceeded downtown to purchase a larger caliber handgun.

New York City officials deputized hundreds of citizens and opened the armories to arm them. Wall Street was the first area posted with armed citizens. Someone dragged a howitzer in front of the Treasury building. Young J.P. Morgan watched from a street corner. He'd just returned to the city from one of his most successful business ventures yet. Morgan had purchased a supply of cheaply made rifles for $3 apiece and sold them in the field to a Union general for $22 each. Fortunately for Morgan, he was already far away when the weapons proved too defective to use.

By Monday morning Irish rioters fearing unwanted competition from increasing numbers of blacks caroused around the streets rolling barrels of kerosene. They attacked the first of two lottery offices and set it ablaze. The lottery system was so fraught with corrupt loopholes that a mere 7% of those drafted actually ended up in uniform. Only the most destitute men who could not bribe or buy their way out of the obligation were netted by the system.

The mob searched out black businesses and looted them. Black merchants were beaten and strung up on lamp posts. The Colored Orphanage was torched and the commander of a state militia unit, Colonel H.F. O'Brien was beaten to death as he tried to stop the violence.

Federal troops were called in and the 7th New York Volunteers were among the first on the scene, fresh from their non-combat posting just west of the nation's capital during the Battle of Gettysburg. Other army units called to New York City included the 152nd New York, the 26th Michigan, the 27th Indiana and the 7th Regiment New York State Militia. By Wednesday, July 15 some semblance of order had returned. Estimates of dead and wounded tallied around 2,500. Actual dead ranged from 100 to 1000 depending upon whose sensational newspaper report one chose to believe. The riot was the ugliest incident of its kind in American history.

President Lincoln barely had time to digest the implications of the Gettysburg and Vicksburg news before the New York riots made him fear that similar violent outbreaks might occur in other cities. Lincoln learned not long after that the *U.S.S. Wyoming*, an American warship in the Pacific searching for Raphael Semmes and the *C.S.S. Alabama*, had wandered into Japanese waters and opened fire on the navy of Japanese lord, Mori Takachika, in what became known as the Battle of Shimonoseki Straits. America joined with Britain in trying to force Japan to open trade with the West.

"What next?" Lincoln must have thought during this week of July 12 through 18 in 1863. When Secretary of the Treasury, Salmon P. Chase, entered the President's office to announce yet another record increase of the Federal debt, it must have sounded almost cheery to have some nonviolent news for a change!

Honoring Duportail and L'Enfant for Their Dogged Defense of Charleston, 1780

When civilians talk of the art of war, the menial business involving the pick and the shovel pale in public interest to that of the cannon, the musket, and the sword. How many monuments have been dedicated to brilliant military engineers? Ask a career soldier, however, and he'll tell you in a snap that if you don't have engineers with you, then you'd better have a plan to skedaddle. The Army of Northern Virginia didn't call Robert E. Lee the "King of Spades" for nothing.

Two-hundred and thirty-one years ago this summer two of France's finest military engineers languished in an intolerably hot imprisonment here because Charleston was forced to capitulate to the British. General Louis Lebègue Duportail and his assistant, Captain Pierre Charles L'Enfant, known as Peter, advised patriot General Benjamin Lincoln and the City Fathers that our city was indefensible and that they'd better make the best deal with British General Clinton that they could before the siege began in earnest. This affair occurred in April 1780. By May 12, 1780, the American colonies suffered the greatest loss of the War -- the loss of Charleston. In this defeat for the Patriots, it appeared that the Southern colonies were cut off entirely from Washington's force in New England. Duportail and L'Enfant might have worked a miracle had they been dispatched by Congress earlier; however, their plight as prisoners of war in steamy Charleston was almost as much a blow to the cause of liberty as was the loss of our city and Lincoln's army.

The history of military engineering is not quite as ancient as first records of warfare, but it is ancient. The Old Testament book of Jeremiah, 52nd chapter, tells of King Zedediah of Jerusalem being besieged by special forts built by Nebuchadnezzar, King of Babylon. Roman military engineers such as Vitruvius designed and built everything from forts and siege weapons to roads, canals, and viaducts. The ruins of these great works can be seen all over Europe 2000 years later. Colonial America possessed artisans skilled in constructing two and three story masonry buildings; however, we did not have men trained in the grand and terrible art of fortifying strategic points or of waging war against a powerful foe. No small wonder that Ben Franklin sought divine providence when the Continental Congress met at Philadelphia. We needed professionals and we needed them by the dozen. There was just one hope of securing such highly trained men, and that was through the aid of Britain's arch enemy France -- a nation that had a score to settle with her enemy over her loss of Canada in the French and Indian War. Our fortunes began to change for the better the month that Louis Lebègue Duportail, Jean Baptiste Joseph, Chevalier de Laumoy, Hays de la Radière, and Gouvion Saint Cyr, a cousin to the great field marshal, arrived on American soil. The conspiracy that brought them here is a story in itself.

French historian Daniel Jouve published in the journal les Amis de la Grive (on-line): "In September 1775, Foreign Minister Vergennes gave the young secret agent, Julien Achard de Bonvouloir, the mission to sound out the newly formed government of the insurgent American colonies. De Bonvouloir met secretly with Benjamin Franklin in Philadelphia and advised Vergennes that Congress would like to have two skilled and well-recommended military engineers. That request would increase to four engineers in 1776 when Franklin arrived in Paris to represent the insurgent colonies."

Duportail and his colleagues were academic disciples of the legendary Marquis de Vauban and Jean Errard, the early modern masters of military engineering science. Errard's Calais - Citadelle and the massive walled fortification of Boulogne are masterpieces of defense still studied today by architects and engineers. Vauban's intricate coastal canal system and corresponding forts at Gravelines intrigued George Patton two centuries later, as did his fort at Le Quesnoy. Duportail's training was accomplished at the Royal School of Engineering in Mézières, capital of the Ardennes. The government of Louis XVI had Duportail moved up in rank several grades to Lieutenant-Colonel. This was done to impress the American revolutionary leaders.

Moving stealthily through their own country to avoid detection by British spies, the cadre of engineers departed Nantes in disguise bound for Cap Français in Saint-Domingue. Espionage was at an all time high during the era of the American revolution. So much was at stake for European powers contesting over new world colonies. Ben Franklin's personal secretary, Dr. Edward Bancroft, appears to have been a double-agent, spying for the colonies while at the same time providing information to the British.

Upon reaching Cap Français, our allied engineers contacted a mysterious fellow named Pierre-Augustin Caron de Beaumarchais, a watchmaker, merchant, playwright, gun-runner, and spy. Beaumarchais, a pen name, was the publisher of Voltaire's banned works as well as the author of numerous plays -- including some that won acclaim from Marie-Antoinette. More important to the American cause, however, Beaumarchais was the head of a dummy corporation, Roderigue Hortalez and Company, set up in France to funnel arms and money to America in support of our revolution. Roderigue Hortalez and Company was, on paper at least, a respectable trading company carrying on the sugar trade in the Caribbean for France. In reality, guns and money came into Charleston and other accessible ports.

It was Beaumarchais who arranged for Duportail and his colleagues to have a fast schooner to run the Frenchmen into the New River headwaters where an agent provided the Frenchmen with horses to go overland for Philadelphia. One of the gentlemen who interceded with Beaumarchais to aid the French engineering experts was the Virginian, Arthur Lee, brother to famed cavalry leader, Lighthorse Harry Lee. Once in Philadelphia, George Washington arranged for the Congress to cover the salaries and expenditures of these gallant soldiers whose expertise we so desperately needed. Franklin arranged a generous stipend for each of them, but the arrangement fell through and Duportail ended up paying over 17,000 pounds sterling of his own money to cover his expenses over here.

Duportail and his French associates assisted in the fortification of Valley Forge and of our forts on the Hudson. This versatile French officer was brought into Washington's innermost circle, often sitting in on the critical war councils. The Commander-in-Chief's councils were much influenced by the European commanders of whom Washington thought so highly: Duportail, the Marquis de La Fayette, Baron de Kalb, and Baron von Steuben.

When the British army and navy moved from Savannah to lay siege to Charleston, it was imperative that Congress send engineering expertise immediately. Men such as William Moultrie and Charles Lee could erect fortifications, but they had an imperfect understanding of escarpments, batterie de bombardes, revetments, traverses, and the like.

Getting in to Charleston in the spring of 1780 proved to be a difficult matter. Duportail and L'Enfant used water and overland routes to reach us. Some suspect that slaves employed a pirogue to slip the French duo into the city during the night. Duportail and L'Enfant arrived on Tuesday night, April 25, 1780. General Lincoln showed the men the defenses, much of which ran from where Chapel Street intersects East Bay Street in modern times to where the parking garage for Roper Hospital is near Calhoun Street. Duportail shook his head in despair.

The Charleston defenses were totally inadequate against the overwhelming power of the British artillery. Duportail counseled Lincoln to make a deal with Britain's General Clinton. Lincoln was hamstrung because Charleston merchants demanded that the city be defended at all costs.

When the British lobbed hotshot into the city setting a number of wooden buildings on fire, the residents and the recalcitrant merchants then demanded surrender rather than see the city destroyed. For his part, Duportail insisted upon completing the hornwork into a complete walled citadel with guns on three sides. Sixty years later City Fathers resurrected the term, Citadel, for the State's new military college. And today, there is a remnant of the tabby hornwork still standing in Marion Square.

The Patriot forces had 5200 men captured, the entire division of Benjamin Lincoln. For Clinton and Cornwallis, it was a magnificent victory that played well in Parliament for Lord North's faction. Duportail developed a low-opinion of Charlestonians who he felt had no appreciation for the grand scheme of warfare. He and Laumoy, Cambray, and L'Enfant were made prisoners and whiled away some exceptionally hot days and nights here in the summer of 1780. For Laumoy, Cambray, and L'Enfant, the war was over. They were not paroled, but Duportail was able to manage an exchange and returned to Washington's side where he developed the grand battle plan for the siege at Yorktown. Duportail became the "father" of the U.S. Army Corps of Engineers as well as one of the originators of the idea for a United States Military Academy at West Point. Had he been able to arrive here more than two weeks prior to the surrender of Charleston, there might have been a different chapter written in our history. Pierre L'Enfant later on had the honor of laying out the streets of our new capital in Washington, D.C.

Headmaster Jaycocks Recalls Life on the Savannah and Cape Romain Refuges

For southern boys growing up in the 1950s and early '60s, the only television that interested us was Fess Parker's *Daniel Boone*, the goofy Maynard B. Kreps of *Gilligan's Island*, and Marlin Perkins' amazing *Wild Kingdom*. Episodes from those TV shows fed our imagination with adventure beyond what was possible then -- even in the rural South. One Lowcountry native, however, lived the boyhood dreams that all the rest of us yearned for. Ned Jaycocks, the retired headmaster of Charleston Day School and longtime math teacher at Porter-Gaud, grew up as son of a federal refuge manager on the Savannah Wildlife Refuge until age ten and then on the Cape Romain Refuge until he went off to the College of Charleston. Ned is a native son of the Carolina Lowcountry from his accent to his crisp khakis and button-down oxford shirt. This affable Lowcountry gentleman and outdoor enthusiast was grandson of the youngest member of Butler's Cavalry.

Those who are native to Charleston need no introduction to Ned Jaycocks, or to his family, for they've been a part of the coastal plantation culture for generations. In Duncan Clinch Heyward's 1937 classic book on the Carolina rice culture, *Seed From Madagascar*, there's a tribute to the Jaycocks family who served as plantation overseers for Heyward holdings along the Combahee River in the late 1800s and early1900s. There's even a picture of Ned's grandfather standing near a rice field.

Of course, the hurricane of 1912 ended forever much of the cultivation of rice in South Carolina. Preservationists and sportsmen have kept tracts as part of a precious and historic nature conservancy known these days as the ACE Basin. The letters refer to the wetlands encompassed by the Ashepoo, Combahee, and Edisto Rivers. In his youth, Ned Jaycocks lived the life of Tom Sawyer and Huckleberry Finn as he accompanied his father through the entanglement of estuaries that make up the ecosystem of the Carolina coast.

Plantation overseers along the Carolina coast were a tight-knit fraternity. Those unique men were masters of many trades relating to agriculture. From getting the crops to grow, to tending the livestock, to engineering of rice trunks or constructing barns, the overseer possessed the requisite skills. His essential skill, however, was the effective management of people. Ned's father worked for a number of years for the Heywards before going to work in wildlife conservation.

Just a month prior to Ned's birth in the 1940s his parents were living on a federal wildlife refuge so remote in the Mississippi Delta that medical help was a day away. Fearing that childbirth in the primitive Delta was too risky, Ned's father brought his wife to Savannah to deliver. Soon thereafter the family took up quarters in the manager's cottage deep inside the Savannah Wildlife Refuge. The nearest town was Hardeeville, and that rural community was reachable only by a series of rural roads leading ultimately to U.S. Highway 17.

Don't rat on him to the Wildlife folks, but Ned learned to drive using their vehicles when he was age 9. He remembers well the day his father sent him to bring the car around and he bent the driver's door backward. So excited was he to be behind the wheel that he forgot to shut the door as he wheeled the big Buick out of the garage.

When the rest of us were going off to summer camp to canoe and learn archery, Ned was acquiring the basics of farm tractors and how to cut a fire line through the woods. What boy wouldn't trade pottery and tossing horseshoes for some real-life experience in the wild woods?

The wetlands surrounded the manager's cottage so the family dog had to be gator savvy in order to see the next sunrise. Ned recalls something about those days that he doesn't recommend anyone try, but when you have few playmates and television is a fuzzy two-channel thing with rabbit ears, you have to create your own fun. He winces when he tells about putting fried chicken bits on a four-foot stick and holding it for alligators to snap it off. Before long, gators lined up in the yard with their ugly jaws gaping open awaiting their chicken treats.

When the rest of us pedaled our bikes to the country club pools to splash around in the summer heat, we thought we were young princes of the realm. Not so for Ned. His backyard was thousands of acres of marsh and coastal plain. He had a hundred options for a summer's day of play. Jaycocks' father built him an eight - foot diving platform on a riverbank where the water was well over the boy's head at high tide.

Porpoises, turtles, sharks, and pelicans vied to amuse Ned as his imagination conjured Indians and pirates maneuvering through the creeks.

Pirates such as Blackbeard, Calico Jack, Anne Bonny, and Stede Bonnet really did comb this part of the Carolina coast -- so did Confederate blockade runners and prohibition era rumrunners. Ned's closest neighbor was the son of the African-American shop foreman on the vast property. Segregation meant very little on the Savannah Wildlife Refuge. A friend was a friend, no matter what color the skin. Ned's other best friend was his pinto pony named Nightwind and his gator-savvy dog, Bingo.

While the rest of us were watching the adventures of Lloyd Bridges and his famed *Sea Hunt* television series, Ned experienced the real thing by growing up as the son of a wildlife manager. One day when he was about age ten, he and his father were out cruising the waters and marshes when they noticed a suspicious watercraft. Moonshiners were known to inhabit the coastal swamps, and one of the Wildlife Department's duties was to break up stills and make arrests. Ned's father swung the bow around and gave chase, but the powerful engines of the moonshiners outran them. Soon a shot was fired in their direction and Ned's dad reached for his sidearm and returned fire as the moonshiners roared out of sight. Few city boys can match that one.

Another great TV program that captivated red-blooded males growing up in the '60s was *Sky King*, a sort of aerial highway patrolman over the vast Arizona deserts. *Sky King* flew a twin-engined Cessna 310 Songbird, and he always bagged his quarry by derring-do in the air. Ned didn't have to watch *Sky King* for his aviation fixes. Every now and then a sea plane owned by the Fish and Wildlife Service would circle the family compound, swoop in and land on the pond. Ned would run out and greet the pilot and climb up on the pontoons. Being aboard a seaplane while it taxies to a dock is a thrilling moment in a boy's life. Taking off from the water and climbing into the summer sky is an adventure not to be found even in the best summer camps.

Occasionally Ned's family would load the motor launch and navigate the labyrinthine-like network of creeks and inlets that led to the city of Savannah. Going by water was more of a diversion than a necessity in the 1950s, but this outdoor boy soon learned the art of maneuvering an inboard motor launch through tidal waters. Along the way his father pointed out ring-necks, teals, pintails, red tail hawks, and ospreys.

By age 12 young Jaycocks was adept at throwing a cast net and setting crab trotlines. He could fillet a sea bass and find enough wild rice for dinner. Mark Twain's fictional characters had nothing on this most fortunate of Carolina lads.

Ned spent the first decade of his youth on the Savannah Refuge, and the second he spent on the Cape Romain Refuge with his family living in

McClellanville. As he got older, the adventures of being the son of a refuge manager just got grander. He recalls that at Cape Romain his father's job required, among other things, driving a small patrol boat. Of course, Ned hopped aboard and learned to maneuver that powerful seahorse. Then there was the 65-foot Army landing craft that the agency used to haul vehicles over to Bull's Island and other remote locations. He knew many of the watermen who fished the local waters, and he learned from the masters how to set a gill net and pull a seine.

Not far down the street was Archibald Rutledge, the State's poet laureate and owner of Hampton Plantation. Rutledge preferred to live in his small McClellanville cottage and Ned remembers the old gentleman well. The fire tower with its old-time vector device for reckoning the direction of forest fires was another dimension to Ned's father's Cape Romain work. He laughs when he recalls that the wildlife officials sometimes used the tower to look for smoke indicating moonshine stills along the Santee delta.

The happy days of living on a wildlife refuge ended when Ned went away to the College of Charleston in the early 1960s. In his 40-plus years as an educator -- much of it as a headmaster, Ned has had many occasions to share his love of nature with his students. Today, a retired Ned Jaycocks remains an avid outdoorsman and bides his time with his wife Lucia between McClellanville, Mount Pleasant's Old Village, and the mountains of North Carolina.

Kershaw Folks Believe There's Gold Beneath Snowy Owl Road

Did you miss the headline on Monday, July 25 -- the one touting gold at an all time high? "(Reuters) - Gold rose to fresh record high on Monday as talks over lifting the debt ceiling appeared to be stalling just days before the August 2 deadline, raising the prospect of a debt default." So, as of a week ago, an ounce of gold fetched $1,622.49 on the spot market. Gold has more than tripled in value since 2005. There's never been a time in our nation's history when the price of gold has been so high, even when an adjustment has been made for inflation.

For most of us, the cost of an ounce of gold comes up twice -- the college ring and the wedding ring. Yet, the sinister truth is that gold has for years been a barometer of impending doom. Back in 1934 President Roosevelt affixed the value of an ounce of gold to be $59.06. In today's valuation that amount comes to $979.66. The modern history of the gold standard embraces the period between the Bretton Woods Conference 67 years ago this month to the 1971 abandonment of the gold standard in the Nixon administration. So what gives with the wild rise of gold prices today?

One group of people in South Carolina with an expert understanding is Romarco Minerals, Inc., a Toronto based corporation currently doing intense exploration in Lancaster and Kershaw counties of the upstate. Those familiar with the geological history of the State will know that gold has been mined in the Kershaw area since 1827. The Haile Gold Mine was the biggest producing gold mine east of the Mississippi River in the 19th century. Recently the Haile Mine site was reopened by Romarco, and mine officials have been quietly buying up tracts of land that appear promising. New drill sites with names such as Horseshoe, Snake Pit, and South Site are causing quite a stir among the town folk in Kershaw, and the residents of Snowy Owl Road on the outskirts of town have recently witnessed their whole neighborhood bought up and their homes jacked up by house movers and carted away. Some homeowners appear quite happy with the deal they received for their tiny parcel and house trailer site. Others wonder how much wealth their half acre really sat on.

On Monday, July 25, the day that gold hit another all time high, Diane R. Garrett, Ph.D., President and CEO of Romarco Minerals, put out a news release announcing that "it has drilled the fourth best hole ever completed on the Haile property." The test hole, denoted as RCT-29 is significant. Garrett goes on to state: "We typically do not release single drill holes at this stage of our company's development, however, the grade and width of RCT-29 at 23.0 meters of 45.8 g/t gold make this one of the very best holes ever drilled at Haile since its discovery in 1827."

What the casual observer notes when driving around Kershaw, especially the Northeast quadrant, is that there're quite a few white pickup trucks riding about with the HGM logo for Haile Gold Mine. These trucks usually have crews wearing hardhats and carrying survey maps and drilling equipment. The town and its environs are abuzz with talk of new gold strikes. Folks living on the farm roads near the original Haile Mine are wondering if they're going to be bought out by Romarco, Strong Bow, Resolution, or any of the other mining prospect companies that are flocking to this rural section of the upstate.

If you've ever laughed at the old expression, "They're sitting on a gold mine with that piece of property," then you ought to take a ride 130 miles upstate and marvel at the good fortune of the folks dwelling within the seven-mile circle encompassing so much of the speculation. However, getting there may be half the fun.

For the seriously history - minded, Kershaw township is 22 miles due north of Camden, one of our state's most interesting places. When you're near to the Springdale Steeplechase course, you're also near U.S. Highway 521 / 601 which leads to Kershaw, just 22 miles up the road. Head north and cross over Granny's Quarter Creek -- the spot where legend has it that Revolutionary General Horatio Gates put the spurs to his horse to outrun capture in the patriot defeat at Camden.

If the truth be known, that stretch of asphalt between Camden and Kershaw holds about as much history as any of the old roads running along the coast. Near where Granny's Quarter Creek crosses U.S. 521 / 601 there's a side road, S-28-58, known to locals as Flat Rock Road, and just a short distance up that route is the overgrown site of Rugeley's Mill where some fleeing Patriots had a nasty encounter with the British Dragoon, Banastre Tarleton. You'll also pass the site where brave Baron de Kalb died fighting the British as our revolutionary ancestors beat a hasty retreat.

Not everything on the 22-mile stretch between Camden and Kershaw is connected with the Revolution, though. Carolina Motor Sports is a reduced version of the Sebring Sports car race track and it is known far and wide to Ferrari, Lotus, Porsche, and Corvette enthusiasts who want to "race for a day" with their expensive, high-speed machines. A tragic incident occurred there a year ago when a Charlotte sports car enthusiast lost control of his Lotus and died in a high-speed accident. The whine of the fast cars can be heard miles away -- even at the Haile Gold Mine which is more than ten miles as the crow flies.

Don't blink or you'll miss Westville, named for the West family prominent in Camden since the earliest times. Westville was the home of Richard Hobson Hinson, one of eight Medal of Honor winners in World War I from South Carolina.

Sergeant Hinson, U.S. Army, Company M, 118th Infantry, 30th Division, "was advancing through the village of Brancourt when [his unit] was held up by intense enfilading fire from a machinegun. Discovering that this fire came from a machine gun nest among shell holes at the edge of the town, Sgt. Hilton, accompanied by a few other soldiers, but well in advance of them, pressed on toward this position, firing with his rifle until his ammunition was exhausted, and then with his pistol, killing 6 of the enemy and capturing 10. In the course of this daring exploit he received a wound from a bursting shell, which resulted in the loss of his arm."

War heroes abound along this old road. The old house is gone now, but the site remains where Captain S.M. Boykin of the 20th S.C.V., Keitt's Regiment, Kershaw's Brigade, lived and farmed after the War Between the States. He and his boys were at most of the bloody battles fought by the Army of Northern Virginia.

Slow down as you enter the town limits of Kershaw. That was once John T. Stevens' town. "Cap'n Johnny," as he was known by locals, was a millionaire before anyone used the word. Stevens was the man responsible for U.S. 601 taking its route through Orangeburg, the town where he purchased cotton seed for his Kershaw Cotton - seed Oil Mill. Stevens was a partner in Heath, Springs Corporation, reputedly one of the largest mercantile businesses in the South at the turn of the last century. Capt'n Johnny built a mansion in the town that had a garage step measured to fit his Packard automobile. According to an essay on Stevens by Louise Pettus, Stevens, as Highway Commissioner, developed the novel idea of putting "shoulders" on our thoroughfares. He also kept this state's credit rating at "A" during the height of the Great Depression. Cap'n Johnny was a big man in these parts -- so big that when he died in 1949, U.S. Supreme Court Justice James F. Byrnes came down to Kershaw for his funeral.

While in town don't miss out on the chance to have lunch at Mrs. Cromer's diner. If you've been sampling Charleston's 4-star cuisine, then you need to experience honest upcountry workingman's fare. It's a meat and three that will see you through any exertions you may encounter before nightfall.

The route U.S. 601 branches off from U.S. 501 in Kershaw and the curious traveler follows 601 which just coincidentily becomes known as "Gold Mine Highway." You may not realize it, but the land used to be King's Grant land to the tidewater Virginians who rolled into this backcountry in the 1740s. These hardy fellows were recruited by the silk, satin, and lace Charleston crowd to tame the frontier and keep the Cherokee and the Creek nations from rampaging in the Lowcountry. These straight-backed, square-jawed, steely-eyed fellows in buckskin did their job -- but they demanded that our capital be moved to the center of the state. They were populist politician Pitchfork Ben Tillman's "one-gallus brigade" in the 1890s.

A few miles out of Kershaw you'll spot Snowy Owl Road. It's a ghost town of a residential area now, for Romarco has purchased most of the houses and house-trailers that once occupied that mile and half lane. Even the church has been jacked up and rolled away. Rumor has it that there's gold under the ground like you've never seen before. Hang a right on Ernest Scott Road and then another right on Gene Lewellen and merge into Haile Gold Mine Road. Don't wander off the road; however, for the land is posted "no trespassing." You're very near places that may be worth millions or billions -- who knows. Places named "Snakepit, Horseshoe, South Pit may mean nothing now, but in the annals of Carolina mining lore and to gold bugs who think the metal may go as high as $4000 an ounce, these names are now key players in the industry.

Most of the mining companies doing business in the area, Romarco, Strong Bow, and Resolution to cite a few, are publicly traded as penny stocks on the over-the counter markets. Romarco stock has gone from 16 cents a share to over $2, but who knows where the future lies in this economy? As you head back home, contemplate what wealth, if any, might be found 200 feet beneath your home!

Oldest Continuing School Board In Country Taps Former Moultrie News Editor

A few weeks ago an honor was bestowed upon Sullivan's Island resident and Summerville native, William (Bill) Lawrence Walker. Readers will recall that Bill Walker was formerly editor of this newspaper before retiring to take up the full-time hobby of pursuing pompano through the coastal waters. In case you missed the proclamation, Bill Walker's name was added to the list of commissioners for the Dorchester Free School Board. Ordinarily, this kind of story would be a back pager; however, there's not another story quite like this in the country.

For clarification, the Dorchester Free School Board is no longer associated with the operation of public schools in Dorchester County, though it has much to do with the establishment of the original free schools there in the 18th and 19th centuries. The essential fact is that the Dorchester Free School Board is the oldest school board in America still operating under its original charter. This year marks the 287th anniversary of the Carolina Privy Council's chartering of an Anglican Free School in the parish of St. George, and, by tradition, the board members are descendants of the original appointees!

Living in the South, we grow up respecting tradition. Our people are keepers of lost causes, shattered dreams, and faded glory. Outsiders are fond of describing the romantic nature of the Old South, and some observers describe us as hopelessly mired in the past. How else would one explain the string of fraternal and charitable organizations around here that have survived war, wind, plague, and high water to reach the three-century mark?

The Dorchester Free School Board was set up to operate in the most productive and promising region outside of Charles Town. From the earliest days of the Colony's location at White Point in 1680, English and Scottish immigrants, men with sterling to spare, rowed to the headwaters of the Ashley River as far as the tidal surge reached. Here they found alluvial soil with oaks and pines -- all a few feet above flood level. Here, too, arose the earliest known religious squabble in Old Carolina. Much of the land on the upper reaches of the Ashley had been acquired in 1680 by gentleman-adventurer, Daniel Axtell, son of the regicide, Daniel Axtell, Esquire. The elder Axtell had been hanged, drawn, and quartered in 1661 for being one of the Parliament leaders to authorize the beheading of Charles I. Daniel Axtell, the immigrant, did not live long on these shores, but his spouse, Lady Rebecca Axtell, did, and she constructed a "castle" at the headwaters of the Ashley River that she named Newington. It was not a castle in the grand European sense, but more like the large brick homes in the Sugar Islands of the Caribbean -- the thick-walled mansions that could serve as a fortification if necessary.

The Axtells were well-connected, and Charles Town grandees looked upon them as part of the Colony's aristocracy. Children of the Axtells married or befriended other great land holding families -- Middleton, Blake, Boone, Alexander, and Waring. By 1697, the village of Dorchester was evidence that the Carolina colony was prospering and earning the approval of the Lords Proprietors.

Another gentleman, John Smith, came out from England in 1676 with the well-wishes of Proprietor, the Earl of Shaftsbury, Lord Anthony Ashley Cooper, himself. With some encouragement from Lady Axtell, Smith settled a large tract of land on the upper Ashley that he named Boo Shoo Plantation, a name that had Indian origins. When John Smith died, his widow married nearby landowner, Arthur Middleton, a local stalwart for the Stuarts and the Church of England. Trouble brewed when Massachusetts Puritans descended upon Charles Town and curried favor with the dowager Axtell. In the late 1600s these puritans, known here as "Dissenters," laid out the town of Dorchester on 1600 acres of land purchased from Axtell. It was as fine a little English village as ever flew the cross of St. George, yet "low-church" clashed with "High Church," and planter families with newcomers. After 20 years the Dissenters pulled out and moved to Georgia.

In 1719, twenty-two years after the founding of Dorchester by the Massachusetts Dissenters, the local gentry along with some assistance from the London-based Society For the Propagation of the Gospel, erected a fine Anglican Church and bell tower. The bell tower, by 1751, had the first set of change ring bells anywhere south of Philadelphia. Not only did Dorchester look like an English village, complete with a market square and a river, it also sounded like one. The next logical step was the organization of an Anglican Free School. And so we come back to our story of a Lowcountry education tradition that is nearing its third century.

By decree of the Royal Privy Council in 1734, the first Dorchester Free School Board commissioners were appointed from the landowners -- Joseph Blake, William Catell, Ralph Izard, Walter Izard, Paul Jenys, Arthur Middleton, Alexander Skene, Francis Varnod, Benjamin Waring, Thomas Waring, John Williams and Robert Wright. The oldest surviving meeting minutes date to June 1757. Anglican Reverend John Allison served as headmaster of the school as well as rector of St. George's Church. If you're wondering why you haven't heard of the Dorchester Free School, its alumni, and its legacy of academic excellence in the Lowcountry, the reason is simple. The school no longer exists. It had a good run from 1758 until 1781 when British soldiers burned the buildings and much of the town. Francis Marion had turned the church and nearby buildings into a fort early on in the Revolutionary War, and when Charleston fell to British forces in May 1781, the great families who had supported the patriots were financially ruined.

Dorchester Free School was rebuilt in 1797 and remained in the tiny town of Dorchester near the intersection of Bacon's Bridge Road and Dorchester Road for 20 years until the commissioners deemed it wise to close the doors and start anew in the thriving new community of Summerville just a few miles away. The heyday of Dorchester Free School was the forty years during these antebellum days when cotton was king and Summerville was the popular resort for coastal planters escaping the heat and malaria of summer. Of course, war once again caused the school to close. The school commissioners invested the school funds in Confederate Bonds.

In 1906 the school reopened in a fine brick facility, this time on Laurel Street. Six years later Dorchester Free School was incorporated into the new public school system of Dorchester County. Descendants of the original commissioners function as an eleemosynary organization to award scholarships for university and graduate study. One scholarship awarded annually is the Daisy Richardson Doar Scholarship given in memory of a devoted teacher who was also instrumental in establishing the well-known Timrod Library and Literary Association back in 1897. Another scholarship the organization awards is the Tommy Cuthbert Memorial Scholarship named in honor of the legendary local golfer who served as Director of Golf at Kiawah Island and hosted the Ryder Cup in 1991. The scholarships are valued at $8000 payable over four years.

On Thursday, July 7, 2011, the Post and Courier noted that Alicia Brooke Davol had been selected to receive the Daisy Richardson Doar scholarship. "Davol, a 2009 graduate of Summerville High School and rising junior at Presbyterian College, is a daughter of Thomas and Lisa Davol of Summerville.

She is majoring in biology and minoring in chemistry and psychology, and plans to enter pharmacy school after she completes her undergraduate studies."

Carrying on in the tradition of their ancestors for ten generations, the current board members include Stephen F. Hutchinson, president of the board, and Col. Thomas R. Dion as clerk-treasurer. The remaining trustees are James R.B. Bailey, Walter M. Bailey, James T. Boyle, Grange S. Cuthbert, III, Dr. Thomas M. Leland, Edward H. Miler, John Hamilton Smith, William L. Walker, Jr., James B. Waring, Jr. and Jan Waring-Woods. Few communities in America can boast such a legacy of community devotion as is represented by the Dorchester Free School Board.

French Botanist Andrae Michaux Was 241 Yesterday

To set the record straight, French botanist -- Charleston native -- Andre Michaux did not willingly conspire against the government of the United States with regard to the Louisiana Territory in 1786. Michaux was, however, the unwitting dupe of that sly French envoy, Edmund Genet. Charlestonians choose to remember Andre Michaux for his botanical research farm across the Ashley River from Middleton Place and for his discovery of the Rhododendron, the Big Leaf Magnolia, and the Carolina Lily.

In 1785 - 1786, our city underwent a name change from Charles Town to Charleston, and a long-shelved plan to establish an institution of higher learning finally took form in the College of Charleston. The British had evacuated Charleston in mid-December 1782 and within a year international ships lined up at our wharves to load indigo, naval stores, and rice. Charleston recovered from the effects of the Revolutionary War more quickly than any other seaport in North America. Obviously, our area possessed the resources the world desired, and that led to dozens of foreign experts coming over here to study the flora and fauna, as well as the geological make-up of this budding new country.

In 1786, a decade after William Bartram, the English botanist, passed through these parts and a half-century before noted ornithologist John James Audubon dwelt among us, Andre Michaux, the man noted as Louis XVI's personal botanist, disembarked at Adger's Wharf and commenced a life-long love affair with the French Botanist Andrae Michaux Was 241 Yesterday Carolinas. This Frenchman's birthplace was within sight of the splendidly landscaped gardens of Versailles Palace. The elder Michaux was employed as a gardener there and thus the path was paved for a servant's son to receive a comprehensive agricultural education. In fact, upon his death in 1802, Andre Michaux was recognized as one of the world's premier botanical authorities. The next time that you're rushing along Aviation Avenue toward International Boulevard and the Charleston International Airport, look for the historical marker that notes the location of Michaux's experimental botanical gardens, circa 1788-1800. From that location, Michaux exported to France numerous plants unknown there that he had discovered in the Carolinas and Georgia. His discoveries excited the great naturalists on the Continent from Versailles to the Court of the Romanovs. Unfortunately, Andre Michaux's reputation was marred by his association with fellow French diplomat Edmund Genet and the conspiracy to thwart George Rogers Clark's expedition to wrest the Louisiana Territory from Spain.

The Frenchman who for twenty years was the toast of Charleston was a wizened little man bronzed by the sun and sinewy from years of rugged pursuits. From the time of his youth until his departure for America, Andre Michaux witnessed up close daily the splendor of the court of Louis XIV. The grand balls, the great hunts, and the continual festive existence of the Second Estate in that extravagant decade prior to the Revolution unfolded in a panoply of dazzling brilliance before Louis XVI's chief horticulturist. Charlestonians who'd just severed the relationship with one imposing monarchy -- Britain -- found themselves mesmerized by Michaux's eyewitness to the royal splendor. The idea that this internationally acclaimed tree and plant expert was over here to identify new species of plant life that might rival indigo and tobacco was an added blessing accruing from the meek foreigner who moved so well in any class of society.

Michaux had been born in Satory, in Versailles -- a part of Yvelines, Ile-de-France. Ile-de-France is and has traditionally been for generations, the wealthiest of the twenty-six administrative districts of France. Michaux's father had become notable for scientific agriculture a generation prior to such a movement occuring in Britain. Though royal stipends made it possible for Michaux to tour and study all over Europe, historians credit much of the great botanist's scientific method to the tutelage he received from his innovative father.

When Louis XVI offered the Versailles gardener 10,000 livres to tour America, a sum measuring approximately a quarter million dollars in today's purchasing power, Michaux rousted his son from a local school, and together the two set off for the port of New York with the intention of working their way (collecting plant specimens) to Florida. Some historians think that it was the Middleton family who persuaded the wandering scholar to establish his famous plant nursery here.

Andre's son managed the nursery -- much of which today is the property of the Charleston International Airport. Shortly upon the establishment of the experimental botanical plantation, the son, also named Andre, had an eye shot out by a Charlestonian shooting birds in a nearby field. The end result of the tragedy was that the elder Michaux traveled alone through long stretches of the North and South Carolina backwoods. Though he dressed as a rustic frontiersman and carried a weapon, Michaux was often in danger from the outlaws who waylaid travelers in the narrow mountain passes. However, the lure of new cures and new species of plants was too enticing to linger in the safety of the coast.

Botany in the 18th century enveloped the spectrum of herbal medical cures, the development of potentially lucrative colonial exports -- such as yellow pine, walnut wood, white oak, and previously unknown edibles such as pumpkins and butternut squash. Andre Michaux had established himself here with a base of operation and exploraton for nearly a decade prior to the arrival of his fellow countryman, Edmund Jacques Genet, or "Citizen" Genet, as this darling of the moderate revolutionary Girondist party preferred to be introduced in the newly republican France of the 1790s.

Perhaps the bonhomie of swashbuckling French military men such as Duportail, L'Enfant, De Kalb, and Lafayette had predisposed Charlestonians to embrace these sons of Gaul as deliverers and never as deceivers. Genet was sent here by Count Mirabeau, president of the new National Assembly, to pry America out of its neutral position in the great war taking shape between Britain and her allies and the revolutionary state of France. All up and down Charleston's French Quarter -- the streets parallel to Queen Street -- prominent Carolinians toasted Citizen Genet as the beau ideal of Europe's new breed, the "republican man." Our people opened their wallets and gave generously to support the revolution that had been thus far a peaceful transition away from absolute monarchy. That they were being used as pawns in an attempt to sway President Washington into a pro-France stance was a thought that never crossed our own citizens' minds until years later.

How did a man such as Andre Michaux who was so consumed with his botanical interests become ensnared in a web of intrigue that could have gotten him the hangman's noose? Michaux and Genet most likely had met prior to the latter's arrival here on the warship *Embuscade* in April of 1793 since they both hailed from the royal town of Versailles. Charlestonians approved of Genet's furtive mission of privately arming local privateers to raid British shipping in the Atlantic. Our forebears raised enough hard cash to outfit three sleek raiders -- Republicaine, the Anti-George, and the Sapoopnêt.

Charlestonians raised so much money for Genet's quasi-American interests that militia units were armed for the purpose of attacking Spanish-Florida. Hostile activities of this nature were illegal for Americans to engage in, yet

President Washington's proclamation of neutrality coincided with Genet's arrival in Charleston and news traveled slowly in those days.

Genet departed Charleston enroute for Philadelphia aboard the great French warship. He felt energized from the overwhelming reception that he'd gotten from the Francophile element at his first American stop. The reception in Philadelphia, however, was a different story. That city served as our nation's capital in 1793, and President George Washington's meeting with Citizen Genet was diplomatically icy, to say the least. Our first president saw Genet's mission here as being completely contrary to our young nation's best interests.

Ironically, as Genet made his way up the seaboard, so did Michaux, each with different objectives and destinations. Michaux was intent upon establishing another botanical nursery on the New Jersey side of New York harbor. Within the same time frame that Genet met Washington in Philadelphia, Michaux met Secretary of State Thomas Jefferson, a fellow naturalist. Jefferson had devised a grand scheme for charting the Midwest, the land owned then by Spain that one day would be called by France the "Louisiana Territory." Jefferson clearly had designs on this huge area in the center of the continent, and he asked Michaux to chart the territory and catalog the plant life and wildlife. Eighteen-year-old William Clark, of what would become the famed Lewis and Clark expedition of 1805, was turned down by Jefferson on account of age.

During the negotiations between Jefferson and Michaux over exploring Spain's land holdings in America, Edmund Genet connived with Michaux to pass strategic information intended for Jefferson on to him [Genet]. Jefferson got word of the foreign intrigue and warned Michaux that anything covert could earn him and Genet imprisonment -- or the hangman's noose. Who knows today what information ever passed between Michaux and Genet, but the moderate revolutionary party known as the Girondists lost power to the more radical Jacobins. Genet feared execution by guillotine if he returned to France; Michaux lost all of his French royal funding.

Andre Michaux returned to France and rode out the French Revolution on the island of Madagascar. Michaux's friend and financial backer, Pierre Samuel Du Pont de Nemours, sent an envoy to Charleston to sell the experimental nursery that now has the marker in Michaux's honor. However, the du Pont representative decided to acquire the New Jersey nursery for the du Pont family to use as a base of American commercial operations. Du Pont was Michaux's confidante and he was the patron of Francois Quesnay, the French economist who influenced Adam Smith. It's probably that Michaux would have known Quesnay, too. Andre Michaux's legacy as naturalist and cartographer survive today 241 years after his death in 1802.

Lincoln - McClellan 1864 Presidential Campaign Secured the Union

Not to worry if you're a southerner who has no knowledge whatever of the 1864 Presidential election. For our ancestors then, the U.S.A. was a militant rival and its politics were contemptible. After all, the South had elected Jeff Davis to a six year term with no provision for re-election, so 1864 had no political relevance down here -- except for the forlorn hope that former Union general George Brinton McClellan might defeat Old Abe in his wartime re-election bid.

Spring and summer of 1864 had been a slugfest between Union and Confederate armies from Tennessee across to Northern Virginia. Battle names that are now bloody legends in our country's history constitute much of the campaign rhetoric of the great Presidential campaign of '64 -- the Wilderness, Petersburg, Chattanooga, Atlanta. Grant was earning his nicknames -- "the Hammer," the "Butcher." "Marse Robert," as the southerners referred to Lee, was dazzling European military observers sent by Paris and London to note the tactics and strategies of both armies. Lincoln's popularity among Northerners ebbed and flowed in public opinion as did the blood of his soldiers in southern cornfields. The New York draft riots in July of 1863 showed Lincoln and the world just how unpopular the war had become. Timing could not have been better for a disgruntled Union general to take on the commander-in-chief in a winner-take-all Presidential campaign. Handsome, dashing, charismatic George "Little Mac," McClellan had been stung one too many times by Lincoln's sarcasm. Historians maintain that the election of 1864 preserved the original integrity of the Union and set the course for 20th century politics in the United States.

No Presidential decision is more onerous and fraught with angst than the daily war map -- not the economy, not even the prospect of a desperate reelection battle. Lincoln was vulnerable in 1864, and he knew it. "No more shilly-shallying," cried his opponents. Simon Cameron, allegedly one of the most corrupt politicians in Washington, D.C., was dispatched to Pennsylvania, his home state, to sew up the state legislature which controlled 26 electoral votes. When Cameron had been a U.S. Senator from Pennsylvania, it was said that he'd been the "King of Patronage." Fellow Pennsylvanian, Thad Stevens, an archenemy of the South, did the essential arm-twisting to ensure that Pennsylvania did not bolt the Republican fold. Political cartoonists savagely mocked Lincoln's awkward physique and long, sad face.

Contrast the sorrowful image of Abe Lincoln in 1864 with that of the heroic and short, but powerfully built West Point general who resigned with the intention of unseating Old Abe. George McClellan appeared to be a man born to lead. The way he spoke, the way he sat a horse, the way he looked men in the eye, McClellan was a man devoid of political ambition until his military prowess was disdained by the backwoods Illinois lawyer who'd lucked into the White House.

When Lincoln sent Simon Cameron to "lock up" Pennsylvania early for the Republicans, he had cause for concern. George McClellan was a native son of that state and the McClellans carried considerable influence. Philadelphia physician, Dr. George McClellan, father of the general, was looked upon as one of the pioneers in opthalmology. Doctor McClellan also had founded the Jefferson Medical College, one of the most renown schools of medicine in the country. Young George took after his mother, Elizabeth Brinton, daughter of one of Philadelphia's most well-to-do families. Her interests in the humanities that led precocious 13-year-old George to enroll in the University of Pennsylvania's law curriculum. However, a few years later his father secured through President John Tyler an appointment for 15-year-old George to enter the United States Military Academy at West Point.

Graduating number 2 in a class of 59, George Brinton McClellan counted Thomas J. "Stonewall" Jackson, Ambrose Powell Hill, George Pickett, George Stoneman, Cadmus Wilcox, and David R. Jones as his classmates. There was no part of the Academy's complex curriculum in which "Little Mac" did not excel. In year two the mathematically inclined McClellan was selected for the rigorous civil engineering program. In the next two years the ambitious cadet read the works of military strategists Dennis Mahan and Antoine-Henri Jomini. Jomini, one of Napoleon's generals, had a great impact upon the developing officer.

This number two graduate of the Academy's Class of 1846 made it out just in time to see hot action in the Mexican War. The lieutenant was cited several times for bravery by commanding general Winfield Scott. After the war, McClellan was selected as one of the American officers to go abroad to observe the Crimean War and report back to the War Department. Somewhere in this time period he also redesigned the U.S. Army's cavalry saddle, thus making it the most advanced piece of equine military equipment in use by any nation.

What led to his discomfiture and downgrading by President Lincoln? To Lincoln's credit, he gave George McClellan every opportunity to be the decisive factor in the terrible War Between the States. The young general who had had early successes in western Virginia in 1861 was promoted and given command of the huge "Army of the Peninsula," a massive army of 100,000 men and 360 pieces of artillery, not to mention thousands of horses, mules, ordnance wagons, and naval ships to seal off the York and James Rivers. By now, McClellan's nickname had been changed to "Little Napoleon." This hope of the Union was expected to destroy his Confederate opposition whom he outnumbered three to one. Yet week after week passed with no dramatic strategy taking shape. In fact, the Southern army was on the offensive everywhere while McClellan fretted over logistics and the continual juggling of his commanders. The President made a trip out to the field to have a conference with his top general. While waiting for a posed picture, Lincoln wrote his wife, "Mary dear, we are waiting to be seated for a photo. McClellan does not have any trouble with being seated. He likes to sit." Finally, an exasperated Lincoln quipped to a newspaper reporter in 1862, "If General McClellan isn't going to use his army, I'd like to borrow it for a time." This public statement by the Commander-in-Chief cut McClellan deeper than a saber wound. Unfortunately, the general made some unkind remarks about his commander-in-chief. "The good of my country requires me to submit to all this from men whom I know to be greatly my inferior socially, intellectually and morally! There never was a truer epithet applied to a certain individual than that of the "Gorilla." Even though McClellan defeated Lee at Antietam, he was soon sacked by Lincoln for failure to follow and destroy the southern army. The 35-year old general confided his intentions in letters to his beautiful young wife, Ellen Marcy of Orange, New Jersey. George McClellan left the army in an attempt to unseat the man that had, in his opinion, used him and the Union army so poorly.

George Brinton McClellan was nominated by the Democratic Party in convention in Chicago in the Spring of 1864. His running mate was the Democratic senator from Ohio, George Pendleton. The Democrats pledged to end the unpopular war by negotiating peace with the Confederacy. Back east the New York Times was not so sure. "We do not say that Gen. MCClellan may not have, for a time at least, views of his own . . . . But the trouble with him is that he lacks steadfastness of conviction. His opinions are shaped mainly by circumstances."

By August even Lincoln believed that re-election was hopeless as the stalemated war had become an albatross around his neck. Lincoln ran on the National Unity Party with Tennessee Senator Andrew Johnson. Unfortunately for the Democrats, their man McClellan came across as pompous and inflexible. His speeches, once wildly popular with soldiers, fell flat on the ears of potential voters. Even a pretty and pregnant wife did not help his candidacy, for expectant mothers were supposed to remain out of the public eye.

The coffin nail in George McClellan's bid to defeat his old commander-in-chief was the telegraph wire General Sherman sent from Atlanta on September 6, 1864, saying, "The city is ours." Suddenly the war looked winnable as Sherman pressed to the sea and Grant hammered Lee in Virginia. Old Abe handily defeated the upstart rival with 212 electoral votes to 21. The Union was preserved as much by Lincoln's re-election as it was by Grant's battlefield victories. McClellan became the first West Point man to run for president, and Lincoln became the first President in 32 years to win re-election.

War Brings Out Best and Worst of Character Traits

War is one of life's crucibles -- a dangerous time of testing where opponents contest for blood and treasure. National interests and strategic objectives often get forgotten in the fog of battle. These desperate struggles of kill or be killed, winner take all, summon every human quality -- especially those that expose strength or frailty. These days, even Harvard Business School uses the lessons gleaned from men in battle as case studies for their scholars bound for corporate boards.

The grizzled Marines of Merritt Edson's 1st Raider Battalion who endured the horrors of Hill 123, Edson's (Bloody) Ridge, Guadalcanal, in September, 1942, would guffaw at the idea of a business school teaching future CEOs decision-making strategy from the killing fields of war. Not even a dramatic Dow Jones sell-off induces the renown thousand-yard stare that the Marines of the 2nd and 3rd Battalions of the 3rd Marines had after withstanding 77 days of siege by the North Vietnamese. Even so, the crucible of battle forces leaders to react under pressure and to adjust to rapidly changing situations. The decision process of commanders, not to mention their ability to disseminate their strategy quickly and clearly to subordinates, is of inestimable value to everyone who deals with lesser things than life, death, or conquest.

Having clear objectives and developing viable options for achieving them is a common-shared charge of commanders, CEOs, and anyone else who manages an organization. The dynamics of effective decision-making are transferable regardless of whether the consequences are dire or not.

Michael Hyatt, chairman of Thomas Nelson Publishing House, gives leadership seminars in addition to running the country's largest Christian press. One of Hyatt's leadership initiatives used Union General George B. McClellan and the failed 1862 Peninsula Campaign as the basis for a fascinating lecture he entitled, "Five Flaws of Weak Leaders." You may recall that Lincoln placed McClellan in command of a superbly equipped army of a hundred-thousand men and he ordered that any war materiel that McClellan requested be supplied to him. Yet, the overly-cautious McClellan was continuously outmaneuvered by Robert E. Lee, his opponent. The fact that McClellan outnumbered Lee by more than two to one disappointed Lincoln and served as one of several reasons for McClellan being relieved of his command. Hyatt dissects McClellan's dilemma and makes a clever five point presentation that any manager can gain clarity and confidence from reviewing.

Since General McClellan can't defend himself from the grave, and since Michael Hyatt comes to "bury Caesar and not to praise him," it's only proper to clarify that George B. McClellan bore the promise of a fine commanding general in the early days of the war. During the hot summer of 1861, the general they called "Little Mac" defeated the Rebs under Porterfield at the Battle of Philippi and those under Pegram at Rich Mountain -- both in western Virginia. And since McClellan was a decorated veteran of the Mexican War and had seen service in the Indian campaigns, Lincoln had reason to be optimistic. McClellan's command papers reveal a methodical, calculating strategist who sought to strike one decisive knock-out blow that'd end the war quickly. And he wished too do so with a minimum of casualties. In many ways, he was the complete opposite of Ulysses S. Grant, the general who eventually brought the war to a conclusion.

For his part, Michael Hyatt utilizes Doris Kearns Goodwin's Pulitzer prize-winning book Team of Rivals (Simon and Schuster, 2005) as a source for his insight into the psyche of both Lincoln and McClellan. Hyatt just as easily could have drawn a character study of Lincoln's strategy process as he did of General McClellan's; however, it is the latter who bungles a fabulous opportunity to save the Union with one deft and fatal blow. It is Lincoln's lot to salvage the campaign in the wake of the overly cautious McClellan.

McClellan was relieved of command after being outmaneuvered by Confederate generals Johnston and G.W. Smith around Richmond in the Battle of Seven Pines. Though technically the Union won the battle, it was a pyrrhic victory as the Southern forces achieved most of their objectives. In Michael Hyatt's leadership assessment, point number one to take to heart from this wartime situation is "hesitating to take definitive action." Remember the ancient proverb, "He who hesitates is lost?" McClellan had prepared his finely equipped army for many weeks to seize this moment and to make the most of it militarily. Ultimately, the battle came down to which side blundered the fewer times. From Lincoln's point of view, McClellan had numerical superiority plus he had a flotilla of gun boats on the James and York Rivers to seal off the area.

Leadership flaws numbers two and three that Hyatt gleans from Doris Goodwin's book have to do with complaining about a lack of resources and then refusing to accept responsibility. These traits are odious in a subordinate and inexcusable for a general -- or executive. Lincoln provided McClellan with the most powerful military force ever mustered on these shores. McClellan's lack of confidence was reflected in his continual shuffling of brigade commanders. When objectives were unmet, McClellan placed the blame on everyone but himself. Everyone from generals to politicians to coaches and CEOs needs to heed harry Truman's maxim, "The buck stops here." It's a given that the public will quickly know who dropped the ball, and by taking responsibility, the commander gains statue -- even in defeat. Yet, McClellan was a proud man, and he had contempt for Lincoln's corn pone ways. Six weeks before First Manassas, in June 1861, a bold George McClellan caught Confederate Colonel George A. Porterfield and his regiment sleeping near Philippi crossroads in western Virginia. The rout of the southern boys was so complete that the Northern press dubbed the engagement the "Philippi Races," and hopeful Unionists began calling McClellan "Little Napoleon." It's likely that George McClellan, a student of Napoleonic tactics, saw his Virginia peninsula campaign as a stage where he might recreate Napoleon's grand Battle of Austerlitz (1805), or "Battle of the Nations." At Austerlitz Napoleon, the man admirers called "the Little Corporal," defeated the combined armies of Russia, Austria, Britain, and Portugal. His opponents had almost double the number of soldiers; however, the brilliant little Frenchman dazzled his foes. McClellan was no Napoleon, and more significantly, McClellan's subalterns -- Sykes, Sumner, Heintzelman, Reynolds, and Keyes were nowhere near the equal to Napoleon's field marshals -- Murat, Ney, Vandamme, Bernadotte, and Lannes. The message here is clear: the quality of the subalterns is every bit as essential as the quality of the commander.

Michael Hyatt labels McClellan as one who abused the privileges of leadership. Even though his men adored him, "Little Mac" lived in grand mansions while his soldiers roughed it on the hard, cold ground. That privilege worked for Europeans for centuries of war on the Continent, but Americans saw things differently in the 1860s. Hyatt writes that, "His extravagant lifestyle stood in stark contrast to his successor General Ulysses S. Grant, who often traveled with only a toothbrush."

The most damning criticism that Hyatt lifts from Goodwin's book deals with McClellan's acts of insubordination. The general often kept the President waiting, even for hours. He also referred to Lincoln in terms of Darwin's missing link, a gorilla -- a cruel reference to Lincoln's ungainly gait. It goes without saying that if one agrees to take the pay and the assignment, he should also take the directives that come with it. When an order is deemed unethical or immoral, or simply idiotic, then the responsible thing to do is to resign. McClellan was fortunate that Lincoln did not cashier him or have him incarcerated in the basement of the Capitol. Instead, Lincoln gained statue as a long-suffering and patient leader.

What Michael Hyatt has done is to seek character building lessons from the superabundance of American history books now in print. Hyatt's astute use of the Goodwin work illustrates best the words of Spanish philosopher, George Santayana, "Those who cannot remember the past are condemned to fulfill it."

Why Southerners Had Affection For Lehman Brothers

Not since the fall of the House of Usher has there been a wail raised on the street as was heard three years ago, when, on Monday, September 15, 2008, the world heard of the collapse of the investment banking house of Lehman Brothers. Edgar A. Poe's "Fall of the House of Usher" is a carefully contrived work of fiction. Bankrupt Lehman Brothers was the specter of economic apocalypse in the offing. New Yorkers, a particularly resilient breed, had seen it all before -- the names that commanded everyone's attention -- Loeb, Rhodes; Bear Stearns; E.F. Hutton; Hornblower and Company -- where are they now? But, for us southerners, Lehman Brothers was a bird of a different feather, or a bull of a different hue.

Henry Lehman had been one of us 150 years ago. Sure he immigrated from Bavaria, and his southern drawl was overwhelmed by his German brogue. He was a Montgomery, Alabama hardware merchant and cotton broker who made a fortune by the time he was 40. Henry Lehman, along with brothers Emanuel and Mayer, worked his way up from peddlers pushing carts through Montgomery's streets to tycoons wielding fortunes on Wall Street. Along the way they clandestinely helped to finance the Confederacy's failed attempt at southern independence. In the height of the 20th century, the House of Lehman were underwriters for mega-stock offerings for F.W. Woolworth, B.F. Goodrich, Gimbel Brothers, Studebaker, R. H. Macy, Endicott Johnson and a raft of lesser names.

Some of us had the feeling that things at Lehman were different after 1969 -- that was the year that Bobbie Lehman died -- the last year that a Lehman headed the firm. Bobbie's 44 years as head of one of investment banking's biggest names made him the "dean of the running bulls of Wall Street." Pete Peterson was brought over from Bell and Howell where he'd been CEO, but, Friedman conservative that he was, he was just a hired gun, and the House of Lehman began to drift. If Peterson was a hired gun, then Peterson's successor, Richard

Fuld, was the gun-slinger, a Wall Street cowboy who committed the aristocratic old firm to financial paper that the brothers Lehman of Montgomery, Alabama, would have swept out the back door with the day's cigar stubs. What went wrong at Lehman? For those of us who'd admired the storied old firm, there was too much New York and too little Montgomery at the end. The grand oak had lost all contact with its roots.

No place on this earth has seen poor boys go from rags to riches more than has this United States. Henry Lehman was no miserable immigrant fleeing persecution, however, when he disembarked the trans-Atlantic steamship from Le Harve on 9-11-1844. He and his younger brother, Mayer, and their mutual friend, Arnold Goldschmidt were dapper in attire and had pocket money to put themselves up in a proper hotel until they sorted their options in the New World where anything was possible for young men who hustled.

In a decade New York would be overflowing with the "poor, huddled masses yearning to be free." There was no Ellis Island immigration office to hassle Henry Lehman in 1844. He merely walked off the ship and the captain gave the NYC officials the ship's list of passengers complete with addresses back home. In those antebellum days New York's waterfront crawled with agents seeking eager immigrants as recruits for western settlements. One of the best-selling books across Germany in the 1840s was Gottfried Duden's *Report on a Journey to the Western States of North America*. Duden was a medical doctor who'd immigrated to Missouri in the early 1840s. His glowing account tells of the bounteous American west where a man was free to make his fortune and government intrusion was minimal. In Rimpar, Bavaria, a Jewish family was allowed to have just one adult son living in town. Henry Lehman was the sixth child and second son of his middle-class parents. That was the town's way of ensuring that the low-percentage of Jews did not rise to a controlling level in the commercial and professional sector. Then, too, every major town between the Main and Rhine Rivers had agents who hawked passage deals to America. This was two decades prior to the time when thousands of Germans fled because of Prussia's rising militarism.

Whereas later immigrants came to our shore with little to offer other than their back, Henry Lehman had been educated at Hebrew School in the mornings and Catholic School in the afternoons for the requisite six years. He'd been his father's apprentice and had pushed a peddler's cart for ten miles in every direction of Rimpar. America would be just another set of hills for an ambitious young man to conquer, and already the textile mills in Bavaria were switching to cotton fiber imported from the America South.

On a buying trip to New Orleans in the late 1840s, Lehman saw the paddlewheel steamers loaded with cotton bales. He factored in the new railroad just opened between Atlanta and Montgomery, and the idea of brokering cotton first entered this immigrant's head. He returned to the small store on Commerce Street in Montgomery, the one with the sign that read H. Lehman, and he prepared to add a new line of business -- that of a cotton factor. He would buy cotton from the local farmers and locate the best market with the best price and ship it by wagon, rail, or boat to market.

According to Peter Chapman, author of Lehman Brothers, *The Last of the Imperious Rich* (Penguin Group, 2010), Lehman and his brothers might have remained cotton brokers for the rest of their lives had not the local bank gone belly up from making wildcat loans during the land speculation fever of the 1840s. Montgomery citizens were wiped out as their savings disappeared in a pile of uncollectible bank loans. Henry Lehman went to a cash only policy and he loaned money to those who were nearly ruined by the bank's collapse. The people of Montgomery were indebted to Lehman as he added merchant banking as another of his occupations.

Seventy-five years in the future, the grandson of Henry Lehman, then a Wall Street financier, would help Woodrow Wilson set up the Federal Reserve Bank as the first central bank idea since the Jackson administration killed the idea. In Montgomery the name Lehman stood for fair dealing with people who were part of the community. Their toil was the toil of other southerners. When the planter had a bad year, Lehman Brothers had a bad year. And when the War of Disunion broke in 1861, the New York based Lehman Brothers found that there were about as many southern sympathizers on Wall Street as there were in Montgomery. Jefferson Davis had met Henry Lehman in the years that he, Jefferson, was a United States senator from Mississippi.

Henry's brother, Emanuel, traveled from New York to London and then to Hamburg. Emanuel was able to dicker with European banks to purchase Confederate bonds in return for favorable rates on cotton exports. Otto von Bismarck was then buying war materiel to equip a grand army of conquest.

The number of schemes attributed to the House of Lehman in New York to aide the southern cause reached fantastic proportions after the War, and no one is certain how much to believe. Yet, Lehman Brothers was able to walk the fine line of patriotism in a civil war and the firm's reputation remained untarnished.

With the rise of industrialism and railroad building following the war, Lehman was positioned well to become a part of numerous successful underwriting syndicates. Republican and Democrat alike sought advice from the astute financiers at the House of Lehman. One generation of Lehmans succeeded another, yet, the conservative investment philosophy that had been the trademark of the Alabama peddler-turned-Wall Street-tycoon still ruled the company's decisions.

In 1969, when Bobbie Lehman, grandson of the founder, died, the new fellows, the ones without sweat-equity, began to make deals that the old Lehman crowd would have shunned. And so it went. Thursday, September 15, 2011, will mark the third anniversary since the shock waves hit Wall Street and the rest of the financial world. Lehman was filing Chapter 11. Timothy Geitner, Governor of the New York Federal Reserve, pleaded for a bailout. Hank Paulson, Secretary of the Treasury, wavered. George Herbert Walker, IV, a cousin of the President and a senior executive with Lehman, placed a personal call to the White House. The President refused the call. There would be no bailout for Lehman Brothers. Since that day, however, there have been numerous bailouts for companies whose balance sheets were as toxic as Lehman's in its last days. Corporate reputations, like humans, take years to establish and only moments to ruin.

Reliving The Early Days of the Brokers Who Started Goldman-Sachs

Charles Ellis tells amazing stories about those immigrant mavericks who put together the Wall Street investment house Goldman-Sachs. Ellis admits that if he'd gotten his dream job right out of Harvard, that of an investment analyst with Goldman, then he would not have been able to divulge now what he knows. One thing is certain, Charles [Charley] Ellis knows the roller-coaster world of Wall Street finance, and he knows how to write corporate history. Ellis' book *The Partnership: The Making of Goldman Sachs* (Penguin Press, 2008) is a riveting read, not only for the insider tidbits associated with known titans of stock trading, but also, Ellis subtly drives home the message that even stock market success is the result of rising early and staying a step ahead of the other fellow.

For over thirty years Ellis served as managing partner of Greenwich Securities, a global equity strategy firm that has been providing economic decision makers -- be they private sector or public -- with precise and reliable financial data for accomplishing their stated objectives. The Yale and Harvard-trained businessman moves in the highest circles of the global financial reach, and he has a passion for sharing behind-the-scenes anecdotes and drama that puts the sizzle into corporate history.

The story of the colossus Goldman-Sachs, the world's mightiest investment banking house -- the successor to the Rothchilds -- is essentially what its founder, Marcus Goldman and his sons-in-law, Samuel Sachs and Ludwig Dreyfuss, did between the 1869 corporate startup on Wall Street and the 1880s when their descendants began to emerge as the "Young Bulls on the Street." However, Charley Ellis can't resist whetting his reader's appetite early on by fast-forwarding to 1915 when the brash 14-year-old school dropout, Sidney Weinberg, went to work for the firm emptying cuspidors -- the brass spittoons that were on every wall of American businesses in the 19th century. Years later, when Weinberg was a senior partner at Goldman-Sachs, he kept a highly polished spittoon in a glass case to remind him daily of his origins. The Sidney Weinberg story is just one of hundreds of Jewish immigrant success stories, and it gives citizens that "God Bless America" feeling just by hearing it repeated.

The czars of political correctness will have to forgive Ellis for telling Sidney Weinberg's story straight up. He was a bratty Jewish kid from Brooklyn, one of eleven children, and he was indecorously told by his detested stepmother to "hit the road" at age 13. Sidney was loud, brash, obnoxious, and small. This combination of traits and attributes had gotten him into numerous scrapes. Sidney had been a truant from school, a member of a street gang, and a very vocal opponent of his father's second marriage. All that the young Weinberg kid had going for him back then was a three sentence "To Whom It May Concern" recommendation from a teacher that he barely knew -- and she damned him with faint praise.

Suddenly, at the height of puberty when most boys' hormones propel them in any direction other than work, Sidney Weinberg found himself a hobo of sorts desperate for a job that'd pay for room and board. He was desperate for a wage-paying job and he had no time to be choosy. In a burst of adolescent intellectualism, he rationalized that if he wanted to make some money, then he ought to go where everyone else went to make it--the financial district--Wall Street and its intersecting avenues -- the four blocks between Broadway and Pearl. That was where men in Edwardian suits and expensive derby hats puffed cigars and scribbled cryptic orders on paper slips for runners to deliver to the floor of the Exchange. Why couldn't he be one of those boy runners, he reasoned to himself.

Only if life could be that easy -- for even in 1904 a runner on Wall Street had to be "somebody." He had scant work experience, but he had been a delivery boy for a retail ready to-war firm and a runner for an odd-lot trading company on the Curb Exchange. Even then Sidney Weinberg had a sharp eye for a deal. When he spotted a long line at a bank, or a store, he ran and got in it. When he had worked his way to the front, he'd offer to sell his spot. Thus nabbing a quarter, he'd dash back to the end of the line and work a trade over again. He saw that people were willing to pay for convenience.

On the auspicious morning that Sidney began his illustrious career at Goldman-Sachs, he arrived promptly at 8 o'clock in the morning in the cavern of skyscrapers that make up New York's financial district. He wore his best hand-me-down suit, the one he wore faithfully every week to Congregation Baith Israel Anshei Emes Synagogue in Brooklyn. With a smile and polished shoe leather Sidney Weinberg rode an Otis elevator to the top floor of the first building he came to, and he knocked on every door enunciating as politely as he could muster, "Need a boy?" A hundred times that day in a score of tall buildings all that Weinberg received for his efforts was a scowl and a "Beat it, kid," from one pompous clerk to another.

Toward evening and closing time -- the Exchange's bell had gonged hours earlier -- the forlorn boy was at wit's end. He stood in front of an office door at #43 Exchange Street that had the names "Goldman and Sachs" hand lettered on smoked glass. Summoning his last bit of gumption, the kid shouted, "Need a boy?" A somewhat taken-aback clerk stared at him and then said offhandedly to an unseen fellow, "Jarvis, you need an assistant?" Mumbles were heard and the clerk said those golden words, "Come back in the morning and we will see." In no more auspicious way than that, one of Wall Street's greatest tycoons was launched in the business of investments.

The next morning, Weinberg recalled he was there when the first clerk opened the door. "I have an appointment," he said brazenly, and that day the school-dropout from Brooklyn started at the bottom of the proverbial pyramid. He empted trash, he emptied spittoons, he polished spittoons, and he polished the shoes of Mister Goldman and Mister Sachs, as well. Soon, the hustling boy was asked to run confidential messages to nearby offices -- something his overlords referred to as the "underwriting syndicate." After hours when all had left for the night, Weinberg would sit in one of the partner's chair puffing on a fine cigar and contemplating what it'd be like to run a company.

The first errand that Weinberg was sent on in his career spanning a half century with Goldman-Sachs was to take a heavy metal office-sized flag pole "uptown on the trolley -- 'ever try to carry a flag pole on a trolley car? It's one hell of a job!,'" nasalized Weinberg as he related this seminal moment to an interviewer. When Weinberg arrived at the destination, he was met, not by Paul Sachs' butler, but by the financial grandee himself. The three minutes of conversation were memorable for both men. Sachs sent a note asking the office manager to place Weinberg in the mail room. The rest, as they say, is history. Of course, Sidney made the bulging mail room the smoothest operating one of its kind in the City. After this interlude, Weinberg always referred to Paul Sachs as his "rabbi."

Weinberg's mentor paid for him to take a couple of college courses at NYU and a one or two bookkeeping courses at a business school. Sidney never bothered to sit for the exams, something that would have given him a transcript. He just kept moving, always angling toward the top.

Goldman-Sachs was a firm divided in 1918 as America entered the Great War on the side of the Allies. Marcus Goldman was a loyal son of Bavaria, and he preferred neutrality above all, but he could not abide Wilson's decision to enter the war as an enemy of his homeland. Goldman-Sachs was primarily a commercial paper underwriter, so they had the ability to play a powerful role in sponsoring the sale of war bonds. Both Dreyfus and Sachs were pro-Wilson and pro-war. The unpleasantness that ensued led to an earlier-than-planned-for departure for founding partner Marcus Goldman. However, young Weinberg, the up and coming office boy of Wall Street, made a daring move. He resigned his position and enlisted in the navy. Following boot camp he was sent off to be trained as a cook, and Weinberg told the story for the rest of his life that he was a navy cook, but the truth is that after a short period Weinberg was made an enlisted rank appointment as an intelligence analyst. The story so fascinated J.P. Morgan after the war that Morgan intervened to get Weinberg his old job back.

It took less than a decade following the Great War before Weinberg became a broker for commercial paper, the financial instrument that tides great businesses over their times of monetary irregularity. Weinberg was also on the fringes of some of the big stock offerings in the 1920s. When Goldman-Sachs went out on a limb to "take public" the national mail-order house, Sears, Roebuck, Sidney Weinberg played a key role as go-between for Mister Roebuck and Mister Sachs. Soon, Weinberg was a partner at Goldman-Sachs and a director at Sears, Roebuck. In his life of high finance, Sidney Weinberg became a friend and confidante of Presidents, entertainers, and sports stars. He never forgot his humble roots and he managed to give away a fortune to the numerous charities, symphonies, hospitals, and universities that he supported.

With the odds stacked against him from the start, this Brooklyn Jewish kid -- son of immigrant parents who faced all sorts of discrimination and insult -- used some native ingenuity and a lot of hustle to achieve "the American Dream." Charley Ellis fills 500 pages with the rest of the story of the legendary firm that calls the shots on Wall Street.

Citadel Alum James Lide Coker's Business Empire Began With Rural Store

How seldom anymore it is that we hear the once familiar adage, "Character is forged upon the anvil of adversity." Prevalent among the masses is the labeling of successful people as "gifted," and less successful ones as "disadvantaged." It wasn't that many years ago that school children memorized the adages of Benjamin Franklin. Sayings such as, "Employ thy time well, if thou meanest to get leisure. Energy and persistence conquer all things," were required knowledge for school children. James Lide Coker of Hartsville probably read Franklin's proverbs as well as Mark Twain's 1901 business quotation: "The primary rule of business success is loyalty to your employer. That's all right--as a theory. What is the matter with loyalty to yourself?" The words of the riverboat sage imply that if you must work, then you may as well be your own boss. By 1901 James Coker was well on his way to being the master of his fate. The historical marker on Home Avenue in Hartsville ticks off the notable achievements of Major Coker in his life that spanned 81 years -- from the presidency of Andrew Jackson to Woodrow Wilson. Owing to the devastation of the Peedee region by General Sherman's pillaging, looting, and burning, Major Coker's accomplishments in the war's aftermath appear even more significant.

The Cokers were prominent in upstate South Carolina prior to the Americn Revolution. They were gentleman farmers and merchants in the Society Hill community not far from Hartsville. The family had come down the Great Wagon Road from Virginia in 1742. While the coast of Carolina was becoming fabulously wealthy from the harvest of rice, the area along the PeeDee River that's known as the Welsh Neck was becoming prosperous from timber and cotton. The Cokers were leaders in the antebellum era, and the wood frame mercantile business of Coker and Rogers still stands today in the center of Society Hill where it did business for 150 years.

Sons of wealthy upstate farmers had two choices for higher education in the 1850s -- South Carolina College and The South Carolina Military Academy, better known today as The Citadel. Though the students' scholarship was never disputed, the rowdiness and hard liquor at South Carolina College was off-putting to the Baptists in the Welsh Neck. Young James Coker was sent away to the S.C. Military Academy; however, his first two years were at The Arsenal in Columbia. The names of his classmates read like a Who's Who of the State during the Confederate Era -- Asbury Coward, C. T. Haskell, D.R. Jamison, Micah Jenkins, and J.M. Steedman. Coker did not stay to graduate but rather returned to take up a position in the family agricultural enterprise that included lumber, mercantile, cotton, and grain. Little did anyone know in the 1850s that the boys who counted cadence on the parade ground at The Citadel would soon become officers together in the terrible sectional struggle.

Lieutenant J.L. Coker, soon to be Captain Coker, marched off to Virginia with Company E of the 6th Regiment of the South Carolina Volunteers, a regiment commanded by his Citadel classmate, Colonel John M. Steedman of Batesburg, South Carolina. The 6th SCV was packed with Coker kin and neighbors, and they were baptized in battle by the bullets' angry hiss at First Manassas. Frazier's Farm, Malvern Hill, and Seven Pines. Agnew, Aiken, Alston, Bratton, Durant . . . the names of the 6th SCV are the names of the PeeDee region to this day. Captain James Coker was shot at the head of his company at Chickamauga in September of 1863 -- exactly 148 years ago this week. Coker was promoted to battalion executive officer of the 6th Regiment, serving under General John Bratton, but his wound was so severe that he was invalided out of service. When Coker returned to Society Hill from carrying a wagon load of food to the Confederates in Virginia, he was dismayed to find the desolation brought on by Sherman in his absence. The Coker plantation had been especially hard hit. Few places in the South were as vandalized as the PeeDee area even though no major battles had been fought there. Financially ruined and still in a state of limited exertion due to his wounds, the 28-year-old young Confederate veteran set about to bring order and economic recovery to his blighted area.

The radical republicans who seized control of Congress following the assassination of Lincoln were aghast that ex-Confederates were being elected to state legislatures in the defeated South. James Lide Coker was sent to Columbia as a House delegate from his county for the years 1866-1867. Fearing that there would be a return of old Southern ways, the radical Republicans, led by Thaddeus Stevens, Salmon Chase, James Garfield, and Benjamin Wade, imposed a draconian rule upon the vanquished South. The resentment brought about by this punitive measure has not healed in all quarters down to this day. The sectionalism wrought by slavery, division, and hateful reconstruction collectively constitutes the greatest challenge our country has ever had to weather. This era of ill feelings was the economic climate in which James Lide Coker founded a business empire that helped to lift his state from the doldrums of defeat. It's hard to envision how a few mules and a wood frame mercantile store could become the cornerstone of today's multimillion dollar international operation known as Sonoco Products, Inc. Financial integrity, perseverance, and old-fashioned business acumen on behalf of Coker and his associates brought an economic miracle to the PeeDee.

In 1865 James Coker started a mercantile business in Hartsville based upon the Coker and Rogers store that his family had operated in Society Hill since 1828. Working the fields himself and with a few hired hands, he put in a crop of cotton. He traveled north on the train to Boston to study scientific agriculture for a year at Harvard. Certainly, Coker had to put sectional feelings aside to go into the heart of the abolitionist northeast, but Coker was already a pioneer of the New South. Within a year or two of returning from Boston, the industrious young Coker went into the factor business with George Norwood in Charleston. By 1881 Coker had formed the Bank of Darlington. The Bank of Darlington, with Coker as the largest stockholder, capitalized the Darlington Manufacturing Company which had textiles and cotton mills as its primary focus. This dynamo of a man built a railroad connecting his business interests in Darlington with major rail lines that ran north and south. In all of his business endeavors, however, James Coker did not overlook philanthropy in reconstructing the infrastructure of his part of the State. His newly-earned wealth was instrumental in starting the Welsh Neck High School, and in a few years this institution was transformed into Coker College.

Major Coker noted that a niche manufacturer was desperately needed for the cones used by textile industries from New England to the Southern piedmont. Thus was born the Southern Novelty Company, hence the name Sonoco Products.

Major Coker died just five months prior to Armistice Day, 1918, and he missed the meteoric rise of American industry. However, Coker's grandson, Charles Westfield Coker, the Princeton and Harvard-educated heir, took the firm to its listing on the New York Stock Exchange. Today, Sonoco is a global corporation with offices in Hartsville, New York, and around the world.

Major James Lide Coker would have loved the press release put out by his company, Sonoco, a week ago Tuesday. "HARTSVILLE, S.C., Sep 13, 2011 (BUSINESS WIRE) -- Sonoco (NYSE: SON) announced that it has been selected to the Dow Jones Sustainability World Index (DJSI World) for the third consecutive year. DJSI World is comprised of the leading global companies in terms of economic performance, environmental stewardship and social responsibility."

Father of Southern Textile Industry Was Carolinian William Gregg

If historians can teach us anything about the current economic situation, then the lesson is that depressions and financial panics have been for entrepreneurs what cocoons are for butterflies. Scarcity, self-sacrifice, and the necessity of rethinking old ways have been the making of many of South Carolina's best known business barons. William Gregg, the founder of the Graniteville Manufacturing Company, knew hardship. Virginia born Gregg was orphaned at age 4, reared by a neighbor, and apprenticed at age 10 to his uncle, a watchmaker and inventor in Alexandria, Virginia. Fast forward twenty-five years to the 1830s. William Gregg was age 35 and one of the wealthiest merchants in Columbia and on the cusp of his second career -- the one that'd earn him the sobriquet, "Father of the Southern Textile Industry." Was it the Scots-Irish blood coursing through his veins that predisposed William Gregg to greatness, or was it his powerful drive to overcome adversity? There are just a handful of companies that are listed on the New York Stock Exchange that were started in South Carolina, and Gregg's Graniteville manufacturing concern is one of them. By the 1850s Gregg's textile mills were already the industry leader in the South. Then the war came and Gregg was dealt a grave blow by secession. Starting up a couple of new textile mills in Aiken in the aftermath of the Confederacy was a herculean effort in itself; however, William Gregg set out to revolutionize the way management treated labor, as well.

By the time of secession, William Gregg owned textile operations designed to produced coarse cotton material, a staple of the slave-holding South. When South Carolina's politicians called her citizens to arms, the uniforms that the rank and file wore as they marched off to war were produced by Gregg's factories -- a half score of factories stretching from the Vaucluse Mills in Edgefield to the Graniteville factories near Aiken. The peculiar pale color of those uniforms, a color known as "butternut," was produced locally from natural ingredients, and thus, it faded rapidly to an off-yellow, or khaki, appearance.

Confederate historian, Adam Pantaze of Virginia, writes, "Extracts from the Butternut (*Juglans cinerea*) tree can be used to produce either grey or brown dye."

The defining period in this uprooted child's life appears to have been in the time of the War of 1812. William Gregg's watchmaking uncle, Jacob Gregg, had turned his mechanical mind to improving upon the elaborate machinery then being used in the manufacturing of cotton cloth. Thanks to clever New Englanders who conducted industrial espionage missions in Bristol and Liverpool, American industry was fast gaining know-how in the art of manufacturing. Jacob Gregg of Virginia was determined to build a cotton mill in Georgia. This early attempt at manufacturing failed, due in part to the severe business slump caused by the War of 1812.

How often it is in life that we hear the adage, "When hard times close one door, opportunity opens another one somewhere else." Jacob Gregg was nearly ruined financially by his failed speculative venture into textiles. The best he could do for his 15-year-old nephew was to pack the boy off to a watchmaking apprenticeship in Lexington, Kentucky. Ambition met determination in the persona of William Gregg. What induced the young man to choose Columbia, South Carolina, as his new home is a matter lost to time. Gregg set up a jewelry and watch business not far from the state capitol, and he made business junkets to all of the neighboring states. Passing through Edgefield where he had a favorite tavern, inn, and stable, Gregg met the captivating Marina Jones, daughter of local planter. Thus, a kinship with this Savannah River Valley domain that would be central to the Gregg fortune.

Marina Jones's brother was General James Jones of the S.C. Militia. A grave marker located at the Jones cemetery near Saluda records: "Gen. James Jones (1805-1865), the son of Mathias & Clara Jones, is buried here. A partner in textile mills at Graniteville and Vaucluse, he was chairman of commissioners to build the State House 1855-61. Jones also served as adjutant & inspector general 1836-41, chairman of the board of visitors of the Citadel and the Arsenal Academy 1842-65, and state quartermaster general 1863-65." James Jones and brother-in-law, William Gregg, became a dynamic investment partnership in the antebellum and postbellum history of our state.

One of the best sources for the development of the cotton textile industry in the Carolinas is the unpublished doctoral dissertation of A.M. Holland. Holland lists himself as a, "Sometime Fellow in Political Economy, Columbia University, Instructor in History at the City College of New York around the turn of the last century" on the cover page of his dissertation entitled *From the Cotton*

Field to the Cotton Mill: A Study of the Industrial Transition in North Carolina. Holland speaks of the 200-plus cotton mills that sprang up in the piedmont of the Carolinas between 1830 and 1850 and how approximately 200,000 white southerners transitioned from the life of poor farm laborers in rural areas to poor mill workers living in huts on the outskirts of towns. The social change among poor whites on the eve of the War Between the States was profound.

Recognizing that textiles were the immediate economic future of South Carolina, William Gregg, the eminently successful jewelry operator in Columbia, retired from that career and invested with Jones, his bother-in-law, in the start-up of the Vaucluse Cotton Mill in Edgefield. The year was 1837, Martin Van Buren's first year as president and the year Texas was admitted to the Union. It was said that Texas could produce more cotton than all the rest of the South and that this productivity would overwhelm even the British and French demand for the fiber. Cotton growers in the Old South were frantic to come on line with their own cotton mills prior to Texas becoming economically developed. Speculation fever was rife, in both the South and New England. Investors speculated in land, factories, canals, turnpikes, riverboat companies, and anything that aided the manifest destiny spirit of the new nation. The bubble burst in 1837 and the heaviest investors were ruined.

The next year, 1838, William Gregg moved to Charleston and erected a mansion in a newly fashionable part of the city. He penned numerous articles in *The Courier* newspaper describing the role of manufacturing in the South. Gregg's wealth and his keen interest in manufacturing gave him entree into the elite Charleston planter society, and quite a few gentlemen wished to invest in his textile schemes.

In the mid-1840s Gregg moved from Charleston to Aiken, a thriving little town nestled on the edge of the Savannah River Valley. The town was not far from the South Carolina Railroad that ran from Charleston to Hamburg, near Augusta. The railroad's founder, Charleston native, William Aiken, was a friend of Gregg's. He likely was one of the early investors in Gregg's textile venture in the crossroads community along Horse Creek known as Graniteville -- for the quarry located nearby.

The Vaucluse Mill that William Gregg and James Jones had started in 1837 went under in the Panic of 1837; and Gregg always had a feeling that if the workers had been better cared for that, perhaps the mills might have ridden out the downturn. There were several utopian-styled communities taking root in America in the 1820s and '30s, most notably Robert Owens' New Harmony, Indiana, that were supposed to be ideal communities--worker paradises where good living conditions and fair wages made life pleasant for the working class. New Harmony failed, as did most of these well-intentioned, poorly thought-out schemes, but William Gregg set out to make a lasting change in the way workers were treated. He built his Graniteville Community as a showplace for labor -- spacious factories, a school, an infirmary, a church, and well-laid out cottages. For a while, the new concept worked well, but his home state elected to leave the Union and engage in a new confederation -- one that would suffer the ravages of war and conquest by a jealous and imperious foe. Once again, Gregg watched in despair as his dreams plummeted to earth. William Gregg was one of the few men in South Carolina who possessed any wealth in 1865, and he used a hundred-thousand dollars to start up his Graniteville textile operation anew after the war. Once again, thanks to Gregg's insight and business acumen, the textile mills prospered and Gregg again reconstructed the "ideal mill town."

Not all was perfection in Graniteville's little textile haven, however. William Gregg retired from his company to his grand mansion in Aiken and left the day-to- day operations to his son, James. William Gregg, a devotee of gardening, planted thousands of peaches and almost single-handedly started the peach industry in the state.

James Gregg had a different type of management style from his father, however, and one day, James was murdered by a former Graniteville employee -- Gregg was found shot dead in his office. Townspeople suspected that the matter was a work- related issue until prominent playwright Cormac McCarthy produced a two-act play for PBS entitled "The Gardener's Son" in 1977 that depicts James Gregg as a womanizer who would not leave the sister of the accused murderer alone. William Gregg's story has all the makings of a Hollywood screenplay, yet so far his fame has remained local.

Carolina Tycoons of Industry and Commerce Noted in Hall of Fame

"After all, the chief business of the American people is business. Of course the accumulation of wealth cannot be justified as the chief end of existence." Credit Calvin "Silent Cal" Coolidge with the phrase that pretty much sums up investment attitudes in 1925. In South Carolina, things are a bit different from the rest of the country. The business of this state is agribusiness, but that is changing fast as the small farmer cannot compete in the economy of scale it takes to be profitable. For a small state whose largest city, Columbia, is just under 130,000 according to the 2010 census, it comes as a shock to most of us that it's our bankers who have made the biggest splash in the business headlines -- in the fat years prior to the 2008 crash.

South Carolina owes much of its success to the integrity of its bankers, and in the harsh economic climate where greed and excess has claimed more corporate casualties than any time since the Great Depression, we need to commend the Carolina champions of capitalism who maintained both profits and corporate decency. The South Carolina Business Hall of Fame, a function of the Junior Achievement Organization, published a hardcover volume in 1999 (R.L. Bryan) celebrating the 300 years of Carolina's excellence in commerce. From Liza Lucas Pinckney's agricultural innovation, indigo, that led to our first export bonanza to Roger Milliken, the Spartanburg industrialist, our business innovators are chronicled. Few of the great business leaders could have achieved their goals without the timely capitalization made possible by a banker, and, fortunately, South Carolina has had a handful of bold banking visionaries in the last quarter century. A quintet comes readily to mind -- three Hughs, a Hootie, and a Bob -- five Carolina bankers who share honors in the S.C. Business Hall of Fame. Hugh Lane, Hugh Chapman, Hugh McColl, Hootie Johnson, and Robert "Bob" Royall deserve much credit for the boom times we enjoyed for two generations here in the palmetto state.

Who around here can forget the "Lion of Broad Street," Hugh C. Lane, Sr., who passed away in 2004. Hugh Lane, Senior, came up from Savannah in the midst of the Great Depression to work in the Citizens and Southern Bank of South Carolina (C & S of S.C.), an institution inspired by Lane's father's connection with the Citizens and Southern Bank of Georgia. For the next forty years Lane pioneered innovative banking strategies in South Carolina. Under his leadership C & S emerged as one of the state's greatest financial institutions, one capable of meeting the needs of emerging industry, commercial and residential development, and community enhancement. The endorsement by Hugh Lane, Sr., of a business venture or a political campaign virtually assured its success. Hugh Lane, Sr., was known throughout the South as a banker's banker; indeed, he was known to many as the "Dean of the Banking Industry." He was the "mover and shaker" for initiating the A.C.E. (Ashepoo, Combahee, Edisto) Basin conservation district. Without Lane's steady hand on the tiller, there no doubt would have been less vigorous economic growth in the Lowcountry and the state.

Hugh Lane, Sr., was succeeded in the post of Chairman of the Board by Hugh Chapman, a gentleman-banker if ever there was one. Chapman was a Spartanburg native and a UNC graduate, as was his predecessor, Hugh Lane. Lane had served a stint in the Navy, whereas Chapman had served in the Air Force. Both Lane and Chapman descended from prominent grandfathers -- Lane's was a banker and Chapman's founded Inman Mills, an upstate textile concern. Both Lane and Chapman married prominent young ladies who would ease their husbands through the barrage of social obligations that clog the CEO's appointment calendar. Bert Lunan, author of *Legacy of Leadership, the South Carolina Business Hall of Fame* (1999), states that it was "John A. Wallace, senior vice-president of C & S bank in Spartanburg who approached Chapman about a job with the bank." Chapman's rise through the ranks was meteoric. In 1974 when both Hugh Lane, Sr., Chairman, and Albert R. Simonds, Vice-Chairman, stepped down from decades of leadership, Hugh Chapman was promoted to chairman. By the 1980s the Reagan administration touted the deregulation of the banking industry, and C & S of South Carolina was able to unite with its "sister bank," C & S of Georgia to become C &S Corporation. Chapman was made president and he moved to the Atlanta headquarters. The multiple steps that led to the merger with NCNB can be gleaned in the *Legacy of Leadership* book authored by Lunan with foreword by Robert Pierce. Tragically, Hugh Chapman's beloved wife, Anne, was killed in a traffic accident in 1993 as merger mania was just beginning to consume bankers' focus for a decade or more.

Folks around here remember William H. "Hootie" Johnson as a hard-charging runningback on Rex Enright's Carolina Gamecock teams of the early '50s. Harry Blauvelt, of USA TODAY speaks in an article a decade ago on Hootie Johnson that Hootie holds a lot of records, one of them is the player with the most ejections (2) in one season for fighting in a game. Make no mistake, Hootie Johnson worked his way up the ranks of banking the way he worked his way up the field at Carolina Stadium -- renamed Williams-Brice in 1972. Johnson was born into a C & S family, so to speak -- his father was employed by C & S Bank in North Augusta before being tapped to lead the Bank of Greenwood in the mid-1940s. The athletically talented Hootie received a football scholarship to attend U.S.C., and, thus, Carolina reeled in one of its most faithful and generous alums. Years later the Bank of Greenwood morphed into State Bank and Trust and then into Bankers Trust, the builder of the 20-story glass and steel building that always mirrored the sky as one drove along Main, Gervais, and Sumter Streets in Columbia. Big banking had hit South Carolina and steadily the banks in our state were entwining with the mega-banks of the Southeast. Hootie headed Bankers Trust at age 35, thus making him one of the youngest titans in the banking industry. The State Ports Authority made him its board chairman, and like Lane and Chapman, Johnson was an integral part of the who's who and what's what of this state. By 1986 Bankers Trust merged with NCNB and the rest of us began making PacMan jokes about the banking industry. Even we "sidewalk superintendents" saw something unwholesome beginning to happen around us when the men we had known and trusted were gobbled up by financial leviathans larger than the blue sky their stocks traded under. Hootie retired to the chairmanship of the Augusta National and is battling with goliaths of a different sort these days.

Charleston native, Robert "Bob" Royall, a standout athlete at Moultrie High in the 1950s graduated from U.S.C. shortly after Hootie Johnson ended his ball playing days there. Royall did a stint as an officer in the United States Marine Corps, and upon returning to his hometown, he asked family friend Willington Edmundston "Wing" Freeman what he should do, and "Wing," an officer of C & S Bank advised Royall that he should go into banking. He married his childhood sweetheard, Edith Gregorie "Greg" Frampton, and commenced a 40-year career of banking where one success was soon crowned by another. At age 38 he was bank president, and as the merger mania began in earnest, Royall retired at age 56, only to reenter the banking industry with NBSC in time to take it to new heights and a merger with Synovus Financial of Georgia. In his blazing carrer, Royall headed many organizations and boards, among them the State Ports Authority Board and the boards of numerous colleges and universities. He served as S.C. Secretary of Commerce and as Ambassador to Tanzania. Few states can equal South Carolina in the number of "Blue-Chip" bankers that we have produced in the last 75 years.

Hugh McColl of Bennettsville is as far removed from a Hollywood studio as a man can possible get, but central casting in Tinsel Town could not have found a better character to play the role he played in taking old-fashioned Southern Banking on a roller-coaster ride to the pinnacle of financial success. McCall may be to banking what Ted Turner was to yacht racing and broadcasting, a slow-drawling, steel-nerved maverick who exudes more Rhett Butler than Milton Friedman in the board room.

The rest of us in the state swear that there's something in the water up there in Bennettsville that makes those fellows charge up the corporate ladder so fast. That town has produced a double handful of millionaires, Rick Hendrix and McColl, among others. Hugh McColl may be small, but he is every inch the Marine that he was in the late 1950s, and that hard-charging attitude that Hootie Johnson got on the playing field, McColl imbibed at Quantico. The UNC alum keeps a slogan on his desk that reads, so says author Lunan, "Do what you say you're going to do. Get the job done. Get it done right." You know already about the rise of NCNB and its leap into the number one slot in American banking with its takeover of Nations Bank. You know that McColl became the heart and rhythm of downtown Charlotte's revitalization and of its cultural life. He, like Calvin Coolidge, had the wisdom or the good fortune to retire before the bottom fell out of the bag with the banking industry. On any given weekday as you drive past your bank, you get that twinge of wishful thinking that wouldn't it be comforting if a Hugh Lane, a Hugh Chapman, a Hootie Johnson, a Robert "Bob" Royall, or a Hugh McColl had his steady hand on the financial tiller again.

Uncovering History At Hughes Lumber On Mary Street

The first export to the Lords Proprietors from the colony of Carolina was four large logs, one each of yellow pine, red cedar, white oak, and black cypress. That event happened almost 340 years ago, and Charlestonians still value lumber as the area's oldest commercial product. Through the years those who've cut timber and planed boards have done well for themselves and their communities. Around South Carolina there are old lumber yards and saw mills, but there are few that have been operating since 1888. Hughes Lumber located on 82 Mary Street near upper King, the establishment of H. Cameron (Cam) Burn, Jr., and his sons, is close to celebrating its 25th anniversary. Recently I asked Mount Pleasant resident Cam Burn to show me around the business that his father bought in 1910 and that he has owned since 1947.

To prepare me for my tour, Cam loaned me a thick folder containing documents and old news clippings concerning this historic downtown establishment. Hughes Lumber dates to 1888, a time when exports through the harbor exceeded their pre - Civil War level. A handful of old families here became very wealthy around that time by mining phosphate from river bottoms and low lying areas. However, most families planted cotton and cut timber as the generations before them had done. Instead of slaves doing the manual labor there were day laborers who eeked out a living on wages less than a dollar a day.

Charlestonians in 1888 had time for frivolity such as horse racing, drinking, and baseball. We were a wide-open city as far as toleration of the vices was concerned. Athletic leagues for baseball were common and and we even had one pro team, the Charleston Sea Gulls, who regularly hosted northern teams such as the Baltimore Orioles. Travel to and from Charleston was made easy by the Southern Railway and its station on John Street and the Clyde Shipping Line with its office on East Bay. There was even a martial air about the city again as The Citadel reopened in 1882, and city merchants, soda fountains, hotels, and bars catered to cadets and local customers.

The only discouraging word heard around town in the 1880s was Governor Benjamin T. "Pitchfork Ben" Tillman's tirade against liquor and the establishments that sold it. Charleston had always been a wide-open city as far as vice was concerned. Citizens saw no need for Tillman's new State Dispensary System and its draconian laws regulating production and sale of alcohol. Around this time, 1891, a local Tillmanite supporter, John Frederick Ficken became the mayor of Charleston. Ficken had been an officer in the Confederacy, having served gallantly in the locally organized German Artillery. He also had earned a law degree from the University of Berlin. Governor Tillman teamed up with Mayor Ficken and Tillman's hand-picked candidate for sheriff, Elmore Martin. Together, Ficken and Martin made war on the Chicco family's control of the local liquor trade. Tillman's words, "Raise Hell on Chicco Lane," rubbed a lot of Charlestonians the wrong way, as did Tillman's crazy dispensary system for producing and regulating alcoholic beverages. The high-principled Ficken and Martin collided head-on with centuries of governmental laissez-faire where morality was concerned, and Mayor Ficken soon lost out to J. Adger Smythe.

Into this bustle of commerce with steamships and rail locomotives vying to haul cotton and lumber north and west of here, an Irishman named Thomas Hughes settled on the upper end of King Street. Within a few months he entered the lumber trade. Hughes made an advantageous marriage in 1880 to a lady named Mary Ann Cassidy, daughter of Charles R. Cassidy. Mary Ann Cassidy Hughes received upon her father's death, an estate including the northeast corner of King and Mary Streets. Within a few years the newcomer Hughes was the city's lumber baron, and he built for his family a fine mansion at 502 King Street. The mansion survives today as office rentals and is in the possession of the H. Cameron Burn, Jr. family. Thomas Hughes purchased 82 Mary Street from H.C. Schirmer in 1901. Elmore Martin had used the site as a brickyard prior to his becoming sheriff. Hughes converted the wooden building at 82 Mary Street into an office for his extensive lumber yard. For a few years prior to Martin's occupation of the property, the two-story frame structure had housed Job Dawson's freight brokerage. However, as long as anyone could remember, the wooden structure had been a saloon owned by the Tillinghast family who lived upstairs over the bar. The Cooper River used to reach right up Mary Street past where it intersects King, and a dock made it convenient for the long boats of cargo vessels to tie up. Tillinghast's Saloon was the first watering hole that sailors met when they came ashore. There was a marsh surrounding the site and Cameron Burn has on display numerous old whiskey bottles that have been recovered during construction on the premises. Barges used to haul coal right up to the rail station across the street from Hughes Lumber and the boatmen slaked their thirst at the saloon. Tillinghast's saloon did a brisk trade during the era of the Confederacy.

As a young man working for his father who owned Hughes Lumber, Cameron recounts that an old fellow walked in and asked if he could look around. The man said that he'd been born upstairs in the apartment above the saloon. The old fellow remembered his uncle running upstairs in the winter of 1865 shouting that the Yankees had left a rail boxcar of potatoes unguarded and for them to grab a sack and come quick!

Thomas Hughes made a fortune by buying timber from Tuxberry's lumber yard in Moncks Corner and having the logs floated down the Cooper River to his lumber mill. The letterhead of Hughes's stationery notes that he deals in lumber, shingles, brick, lime, and gravel. Being located beside the Southern railway track made off-loading very convenient. Hughes made so much money that he built a county home in Summerville and lived the life of a squire in that well-known resort area.

In 1904 Cam Burn's father, H. Cameron Burn, Sr., went to work for Hughes as a general employee. Burn had been working for Kracke Livery Stable over on Line Street -- a job that required being at the stable at 4 a.m., and then at Peekson's Hardware on Meeting Street. From day one Hughes and Burn got along in a capital fashion. Burn anticipated what needed doing and Hughes saw that Burn was promoted in the business. By 1910, Thomas Hughes was considered the largest property holder in Charleston County, and he chose to sell his lucrative lumber business to Cameron Burn, Sr., and his brother, Ernest P. Burn, for the then modest sum of $3000 -- an amount that would be about $70,000 today. Hughes also gave Burn a lot on Sullivan's Island during that time. The bill of sale notes that it transfers, as well as buildings and lumber, brick, etc., two mules, three carts, and a harness. Cameron Burn, Sr., was Thomas Hughes's executor.

Hughes continued to live part-time at his 502 King mansion and part time in Summerville. He and his wife had one child, Charles, who was disabled from polio. The conveyance of the lumber yard to the Burn brothers for a modest sum denotes Hughes's affection for them. That explains why Burn never changed the name of the business. Cameron says that his father told him about Hughes coming into the business and directing things just as he had when he had owned it. Hughes died in 1924.

Cam Burn recalled visiting Charles Hughes at his waterfront home in Mount Pleasant many years ago. That home, until recently, was the home owned by

Congressman Arthur Ravenel on the corner of Middle and Center Streets. When Charles passed away, a scholarship for students to study science and the arts was established in his name. For years the scholarship was managed by former mayor J. Palmer Gaillard. Now local attorney Charlton de Saussure handles the fund. There was little interaction between Charles Hughes and his father's former business. The bulk of the Hughes fortune passed to the Catholic Church.

In 1914, a difference of opinion over how to proceed in repairing the warehouse caused Cameron Burn, Sr., and his brother, Ernest, to have a falling out. Cameron wanted to anchor the joists and sills to steel iron rails. Ernest considered that to be extravagant, so the two parted ways. Cam's father took out a loan to buy his brother's half interest, and then he expanded the business to include gravel and terra cotta piping. He also bought a truck, an oddity on King Street at the time.

Cam Burn remembers working at the family business in the 1930s and early '40s before he went off to study mechanical engineering in 1944 at Georgia Tech. While he was away pursuing his degree and enjoying life in the big city, Cam received news that his father had had a stroke. Without hesitation, Cam withdrew after 5 semesters and returned to Charleston. It was not the path that he had chosen, but, rather, the path that was thrust upon him. Cam smiles and says that he suspects that he'd have come back to the lumber business even if he had completed his degree.

The transition from university student to lumber and building supply manager was not a smooth one, however. With his father incapacitated, the younger Burn had to make some tough personnel decisions over store policies -- including the letting go of his aunt. He knew a fair amount of advanced mathematics but he knew little of bookkeeping and accounting, so Burn attended Murray Vocational School at night to take Bookkeeping 101. A local C.P.A. named McKnight was persuaded to set up a better accounting technique as Cam did a complete cost inventory of every item.

Cam's best decision was in marrying Elizabeth "Betty" Coker Wall in 1948. After that, his smartest move was in hiring longtime friend, C.L. "Buddy" Smith to be a salesman. Wadmalaw native, Fred White, ran the lumber yard, and Fred was Cam's righthand man. When Fred passed away, Cam was the only white mourner in the church, and Cam says that the loss of Fred was a tremendous blow.

Though Hughes Lumber continued through the 1960s to do a great business in longleaf "unbled" pine as they had always done, there was no more black cypress. When Cox Wood Preserving Company in Orangeburg began using the

Wolmanizing Process, Hughes Lumber was the first dealer in the region selected to offer the new product. Wolmanizing replaced creosoting as a preserving method. Burn added exterior and interior paints to his business, and he took on cement coating, then known as Thoro Seal. The Citadel was one of his first clients for Thoro Seal as they used the rock hard cement sealer on the barracks in the early 1960s. After that several hotels in Myrtle Beach wanted the same thing. Today, sealers, paints, and building supplies account for a high percentage of company sales. Cam Burn expanded into the rental business, too, and his son, John, runs both the downtown and the Mount Pleasant rental businesses. Cam's son, Edward, has taken over the lumber and building supplies division on Mary Street and continues to expand the trade as the business nears its 125th anniversary. From his upstairs office at 82 Mary Street, Cam Burn reflects over his three-quarters of a century association with a living piece of Charleston's history.

Has Charleston Become a Playground for the Rich?

Archie Butt had company this week. The Archie Butt is the semi-submerged hull of an old troop ship that you see from the Ravenel Bridge as you near Mount Pleasant. *Archie Butt's* ferro cement hull has lain in the plough mud for 82 years and it's an icon for East Cooper. Anchored downriver a couple of hundred yards off was the yacht *SeaFair*, the pretentious, five-story, 228 foot one of a kind floating art gallery owned by the New York couple, David and Lee Ann Lester. For five days *SeaFair* lay in shallow water well away from the main shipping channel. Commuters descending the second span peered past scantily-clad joggers at the stately craft that showed no sign of activity for almost a week. Apparently the yacht *SeaFair* was between art exhibits and was just hanging out for awhile in the Holy City -- one of its occasional port-of-call cities.

When *SeaFair* entered Charleston harbor last week, the sailing yacht *Mirabella V* was tied up at the Mega Dock of the Charleston City Marina. *Mirabella V*, the 247 foot sailing yacht belonging to Avis Car Rental CEO Joe Vittoria, dwarfed litigator Ron Motley's yacht, *Themis*, taking up nearly a hundred more feet of dock space.

City Marina is home to a hundred yachts that cost more than the average Charlestonian will make in a lifetime, yet last week everything tied up there looked like matchbox toys compared to *Mirabella V*. These two yachts together, *Mirabella* and *SeaFair*, cost an estimated $80 million dollars to build. For the curious, $80 million is the amount the make-over of Johnnie Dodds Boulevard will cost the taxpayers when it's done. So, why were *SeaFair* and *Mirabella V* here -- no one seemed to know. The yacht owners were not thought to be aboard. It is a wonderful coincidence the week that these sleek water craft lay in our waters was the week that *CondeNast* chose to name Charleston the number one tourist city in the United States. It was left to the tourists to determine if these opulent international yachts made a spectacular backdrop for this historic old port city -- or the other way around.

Some here may recall that in April of 1985 rocker Billy Joel married the *Uptown Girl*, Christy Brinkley aboard the yacht R*iveranda* and for a week one of the world's most glamorous couples honeymooned here on that 147 foot luxury yacht. In the 1960s William F. Buckley's 60-foot trans-oceanic sailing yacht *Cyrano* used to slip into Charleston harbor and tie up at the City Marina. The conservative columnist, editor of *National Review*, and host of the long-running PBS show *Firing Line*, was spotted more than once reading newspapers on the deck of his beloved yacht and dining at local lunch spots such as the Ice House in The Market.

Jacqueline Kennedy Onassis passed through town aboard the grand yacht *Christina,* the flagship of shipping magnate Aristotle Onassis's personal fleet. Local wags claimed that the former first lady was traveling up the coast with longtime friend, Maurice Tempelsman, the New York jewelry millionaire. She was spotted by locals dining at the renowned Perdita's on Exchange Street.

In the late 1990s Charlestonians peered out over the Battery seawall at 151-foot yacht, *Highlander*, belonging to Steve Forbes, publisher of Forbes magazine. Rumored to be onboard with Forbes were former Prime Minister Margaret Thatcher and Sir Denis Thatcher, General and Mrs. Colin Powell, and Secretary of Defense and Mrs. Caspar Weinberger. Police boats hovering near the craft seemed to confirm the rumors. Just before sunset one evening the *Highlander's* dinghy, a large cabin cruiser in itself, was lowered to the water and the distinguished couples disembarked. A few minutes later they were spotted entering Magnolia's restaurant on East Bay Street. Chef John Varanese tells that the evening he prepared dinner for the Thatchers, Powells, Forbes, and Weinbergers is his most memorable moment in cooking. Besides being a very busy evening, the FBI was everywhere. He says that one restaurant employee could not come to work that evening because he was from Ireland and had suspected links to the IRA. Varanese owns an upmarket restaurant that goes by his name in Louisville.

Old timers recall that in the 1960s there was a chrome reduction company, Air Reduction Corporation (Airco Alloy), a division of its Pittsburgh parent, located in the North area along the Cooper River. A very patrician gentleman of Pittsburgh and Palm Beach named Charles Francis Colbert, Jr., was CEO of Airco during that time and he became fast friends with Citadel president, General Mark W. Clark. Upon Colbert's retirement from corporate life, he bestowed his own private yacht, the *Southwind,* to The Citadel in honor of General Clark. *Southwind* was a 51-foot motor yacht that boasted double staterooms, a grand lounge, galley, and crew quarters, not to mention twin 190-horsepower inboard engines. For years afterward this yacht with its crew of cadets dressed in all white trousers and shirts hosted VIPs on harbor cruises. Often around sunset strollers on the Battery would gaze out on the splendid vessel with its polished wooden cabin and its smart-looking deckhands as it sliced through the waves.

Who among us can recall when *Miss Budweiser*, the trophy yacht of Augie Busch, then CEO of Anheuser Busch, sailed into our harbor in the late 1960s with comedian and Budweiser adman, Ed McMahon, aboard? *Miss Budweiser* may be the sleekest sailing craft to wear sail in these waters in a hundred years. The Stephens Brothers Yacht Corporation in Stockton, California, custom built the magnificent 85-foot boat in 1962. A few fortunate Charlestonians, including the higher-ups at Pearlstine Distributors, got a tour and a local cruise. One recalled the gold-plated fixtures adorning the polished mahogany interior.

Perhaps the most intriguing yacht to be moored here in some time was the converted trawler *Caliban* of French registry. The Bernard Gallay Yacht Brokerage offered *Caliban* for sale at a reduced sum from its original offering. The yacht's sales brochure gave the following description: "A very well built trawler type classic motor yacht with heavy displacement and two internal keels. The boat served during WWII as an espionage boat for the English Navy in the Mediterranean. It was transformed into a gentleman's yacht just after the war. The boat has been classified as a "boat of historic interest." One would expect to see Humphrey Bogart and Ingrid Bergman having a smoke on the fantail.

Without a doubt, the most romantic yacht in Charleston harbor is the Mathis - Trumpy motor yacht, *Innisfail*, built for Chicago millionaire industrialist, Joseph Cudahy in the 1930s. Cudahy had to wait his turn for the elite ship builder to complete work for such names as Chrysler, Dodge, Guggenheim, Dupont, and Whitney. The 92-foot cruiser was commissioned by the U.S.Navy in 1942 as a shore patrol vessel and she was outfitted with deck guns and depth charges for anti-submarine warfare. After World War II, *Innisfail* hosted presidents and world leaders -- names such as Truman, Eisenhower, Kennedy, DeGaulle, Nixon, and Clinton. Charleston businessman, Frank Lynch, owns *Innisfail* now and makes it available for charter.

"Has Charleston become a yacht haven and a playground for the rich and famous?" The answer is "No." Charleston has been a lay-by for the powerful ones afloat since the days of gentlemen pirates such as Captain Morgan and Stede Bonnet. Even in the formation of the new republic, we are told that the Charleston delegates to the Constitutional convention in Philadelphia arrived on the Schuylkill River aboard their own private yachts, somewhat to the disdain of the less well-off delegates from New England.

Best Book For October Evenings Is Jackpot By Jason Ryan

Greed, lust, pride, arrogance, and envy are a sampling of character flaws on public display in Jack Ryan's *Jackpot: High Times, High Seas, and the Sting That Launched the War on Drugs* (Lyons Press, 2011). If you have not read this new work of nonfiction, put the newspaper down now and go find a copy. You'll have as many "Now I get it," and "You've got to be kidding," moments as I've had in the day or two it's taken me to devour this book. This is one hot read for cool October nights. Ryan spins his story of modern-day drug buccaneering in such a compelling way that it's hard to put the book down. Operation Jackpot, the code name for the special task force designed to cripple marijuana smuggling on the Carolina coast, was a story that dominated the headlines of the *News and Courier* in the 1980s. Stories of mega-yachts running marijuana into our inlets invoked images of our rum running days. Some compared these kids to pirates from our romantic past. Don't be surprised at the names you read in this narrative of the "Mother of All Drug Busts." The good guys are all there -- Judge Falcon Hawkins, U.S. Attorneys Henry D. McMaster, Bart Daniel, Lionel Lofton, to name a few, and the bad guys, too -- disgraced sons of some of South Carolina's prominent families -- all chronicled. For the lawmen Jackpot was the making of their careers. The innovative strategies in apprehending drug traffickers and running down their assets quickly became methods adopted around the country. Who says that the "good ol' boys can't get it right every now and again! For the bad apples in our midst, their stories are laid out by Ryan for us to shake our heads in disbelief that country club kids with every advantage in life could go so far out on the dark side of respectability. However, for a few years, make it a decade give or take, some South Carolina boys broke the record for smuggling contraband and they lived lavishly in tropical paradise settings right up until the day of their comeuppance.

Anyone familiar with former Philadelphia *Enquirer* investigative reporter turned best-selling author, Mark Bowden, author of inside accounts such as

Black Hawk Down, *Killing Pablo*, and *Guests of the Ayatollah*, will immediately note the similarity in the fast-moving prose style that Jack Ryan utilizes to tell this saga of thrill-seeking, risk-taking dope smugglers. Most of the Carolina smugglers reveled in the "kingpin" label that U.S. Attorney for South Carolina, Charles D. McMaster, used to differentiate between the little fish and the King Fish of the marijuana cartels. No one will ever know how much of the estimated $100 million in profit the convicted felons stashed in offshore banks and hitherto undiscovered lockboxes. What we do know is that hundreds of thousands of pounds of Colombian pot entered the country through tidal inlets from Daufuskie Island near Hilton Head to the tributaries of the ACE Basin to Cape Romain and Little River. The smugglers were youthful fellows, many from well-to-do families in our state, and they seldom bothered to pack a gun. Their strategy was to use fast boats, the cover of moonless nights, and local contacts to cover their highly illegal million dollar adventures. As we learn, the boys were as hooked on the thrill of the deal as they were on the material goods they acquired from their all-cash deals. Living on the lam in luxury yachts and million dollar condos that overlook the world's most scenic vistas sounds like the stuff of Hollywood's silver screen, not something concocted by U.S.C. frat-row dropouts. Make no mistake, Jack Ryan does not glorify the deeds of drug lords, nor does he mitigate the dangers associated with even the occasional usage of illegal substances such as marijuana or hashish. Most of these fellows had serious cocaine addictions when apprehended. Rather, he matter-of-factly pulls together all of the pieces of a very large and complex story that we all watched unfold on the front page of the newspaper 30 years ago. There were folks aplenty here who knew Barry Foy, Les Riley, and Tom Rhoad -- men who were prosecuted under the then Federal "kingpin" statue during the Reagan era "War on Drugs."

From Greenville to McClellanville, from Spartanburg to Hilton Head, the nefarious weed known on college campuses as Mary Jane, street slang for marijuana, made its way in bales and bundles, into the hands of middle and upper-class Carolinians. College campuses were the prime destination for much of the leafy product. The amazing and sometime wacky story of how that marijuana got here and was off-loaded and trucked by convoy to every corner of the state and beyond is the subject of Ryan's work. Sometimes you wonder if our state's so-called kingpins had not been inspired by watching too many Dukes of Hazzard reruns. Sometimes our own politicians and law-enforcement types seemed to be real life "Boss Hoggs." And a few of their girlfriends resembled Daisy Duke, except Daisy Duke never had a Ladies' Rolex on her dainty wrist, nor did she spin around in a Porsche 911 with a hundred thousand in cash stuffed under the passenger's seat. All would have been comical, of course, had not we been keenly aware that drug addiction was a Pandora's box of demons being unleashed upon society by these happy-go-lucky, daredevil boys. In reality, they were young, arrogant punks who were willing to risk 25 years in the Federal pen for a chance to make four or five million dollars on a clandestine drug run into some tidal creek.

From page one of *Jackpot* you'll laugh out loud, scratch your head in disbelief, nod knowingly, and bite your nails through the 250 page account. There's the story of a 90-year-old grandmother, heiress to a grand fortune in real estate, who peers out the window of her Edisto Island plantation home to discover her grandson being arrested by dozens of law enforcement officers as a helicopter and an airplane circle overhead in the night sky. Charlestonians are still reminiscing about that one.

Jason Ryan gives new details on the direct descendant of the Carolina signer of the Declaration whose private airplane crash landed at a remote Georgia airfield because it was overloaded with Colombian pot. Then, there's the sad saga of the Branchville son of a state legislator who used his influence as a lawyer to aid and assist drug kingpins. So keen was this young attorney to provide legal cover that the bosses brought him into their inner circle, and he became one of the most wanted men in America. When he was arrested in La Jolla, California, after a decade of being on the run and frequenting the world's ritziest places, this drug dandy's dad had former state speaker of the House Sol Blatt to make an impassioned plea for leniency saying that the boy had found religion while on the run. Judge Hawkins gave him 15 years in the Federal lockup and promised that he'd find him help for his cocaine problem.

There's the story of Carolinians running a tramp steamer into Lebanon in the midst of its civil war and obtaining a cease fire between combatants so that their ship could be loaded with hashish. Upon leaving the harbor, the smugglers learn that the cash they just handed over would be used to buy more guns and explosives.

Then the story you will get instant recall from is the time in 1984 when "kingpin" Bob "the Boss" Byers walked out the back door of the Charleston County jail unbeknownst to his security detail. He entered a conveniently parked white, unmarked police cruiser complete with keys in the ignition and had 10 hours grace time before he was reported as missing. Most of us never knew how that deal went down -- until now.

There's a lot that will amaze you in Ryan's fast-paced drama -- the care-free, hedonistic, life among drug runners -- the nonchalance of their women when the boys' attentions wander to many other women -- the extravagance of having a cool million in cash lying in odd places around the house -- and the constant fear and dread of knowing that one day everything will come crashing down in the worst possible way. One thing is certain after reading Jason Ryan's book, *Jackpot,* crime does often pay, but the long arm of the law always -- always makes the final deal.

Laying Bare the 150 Year-old Hammond-Hampton Feud

Sordid, salacious, and the ultimate betrayal of trust is how the Hamptons, Prestons, and the Mannings viewed the matter. Maligned, framed, and too gentlemanly to utter the truth is how James Hammond saw it -- "it" being the scandal of the century that involved the governor of South Carolina and his improper relationship with his teenage nieces. Could Shakespeare have known of this matter, it'd have made a much seamier tale of seduction than Richard III's attempted tryst with Lady Anne. Only in the last quarter of a century has the general public become aware of the circumstances of the rift between famous Carolina families united by marriage.

The tale of James Henry Hammond has broken into the mainstream and away from the restricting barriers set up by the Hammond family -- barriers to conceal the private matters of their famous kinsman -- 19th century governor, senator, states rights champion -- James Hammond. This is the same James Hammond who made the famous "mud sill" and "cotton is king" speeches in the United States Senate. A brooder and a loner by nature, James Hammond lacked a confidante with whom to vent his worries and frustrations, so he did what Samuel Pepys, John Evelyn, and numerous other gentlemen of the 18th and 19th centuries did -- he kept a private journal. A formerly private diary entitled *Secret and Sacred: The Diaries of James Henry Hammond, a Southern Slaveholder* (University of South Carolina Press, 2008) edited by Carol Bleser with a foreword by Charleston native Louis D. Rubin, Jr., presently of Chapel Hill, lays bare the most private thoughts of an esteemed antebellum statesman. What we discover by reading Hammond's brutally honest reflections is that Hammond, the most ardent states rights advocate in The South following the death of John C. Calhoun, was a man beset with self-doubts, fears of inadequacy. Most of all, Hammond is revealed to us as a man consumed with remorse for transgressions committed with his underage nieces while he served as governor in the early 1840s.

One must be careful to note when reading this private diary that Hammond depicts himself as a man set upon by precocious and adoring young women who, because they were motherless, lacked the proper upbringing that they would certainly have had in their lot as a Hampton of Millwood Plantation had their mother not died at an early age. Hammond admits to undue familiarity but vehemently denies the seduction charge hurled at him by his brother-in-law, Wade Hampton II. Hammond actually saw himself as showing enormous restraint in resisting the numerous advances of his nieces as they cuddled alone in his townhouse in Columbia.

The forbidden dalliances took place under the nose of Hammond's long-suffering wife, Catherine Fitzsimons Hammond, a Charleston heiress and the source of the Hammond family fortune. Her sister married Wade Hampton II, the son of the great Revolutionary War leader and the father of Wade Hampton III, the Confederate cavalry general. The Hamptons were spoken of as the wealthiest planters in the South. They cultivated land in three states and possessed more than 3000 slaves. Apparently after numerous illicit and amorous encounters with their uncle James, the eldest Hampton niece, Harriet, confided some of the sordid details to her father while they were attending race week in Nashville. The Hamptons owned a stable of fleet thoroughbreds that were raced for grand purses across the South.

Wade Hampton II returned abruptly to Columbia determined to kill James Hammond in a duel. Hampton's confidantes, the Prestons and Mannings, waylaid Hampton and persuaded him that such a rash deed would forever cast his daughters in an unladylike way and that he could better deal with the matter by working privately to destroy the reputation of Hammond by character assassination. Thus began the bitterest era of whispering campaigns in the State's history. Both men walked around the capitol armed with pocket pistols. Hammond abandoned his mansion in Columbia after his two-year gubernatorial term concluded and removed to his plantation on Beech Island near the Savannah River. He continued his political career through the publication of speeches and essays -- most dealing with the legitimacy of slavery as a sanctioned institution. Hammond also continued to confide his innermost thoughts concerning the leading personalities of his day, many of whom he knew personally. The diary, however, dwells but little upon the debauched nature of James Hammond's relation with his female kin. He also confides his lust for one of his slave women, a seamstress named Sally. Were these immoral lapses the only topics, *Secret and Sacred* would hardly be worth the time it takes to flip the pages. What lovers of antebellum history will find appealing is the "unvarnished truth" of the

State's leading men on the run up to secession as seen by a well-connected keen observer.

James Hammond was the son of Massachusetts-born Elisha Hammond. Elisha worked his way through Dartmouth after the Revolution and bought passage in 1802 on a schooner bound for Charleston. He taught for a while in a classical academy he founded in Newberry, and then Elisha became a professor of languages at the new South Carolina College in Columbia. He married Catherine Fox Spann of Edgefield, perhaps with an eye toward winning an inheritance from Catherine's rich uncle, John Fox. Acrimony ensued and Catherine was cut from the will and the Hammonds were poor as church mice for much of James Hammond's youth.

Envy of his wealthy Carolina classmates and their splendid country estates tormented James in his teen years as a college student and law apprentice. James Hammond bore the markings of a stern New England Puritan upbringing, yet his surroundings were those of the Cavalier South. Young James possessed the passion for intellectual pursuits while his associates gambled, smoked cigars, and sampled the forbidden pleasures that college life in Columbia afforded.

Wealth, then as well as now, could be had by earning it, inheriting it or by marrying it, and James Hammond exploited in all avenues. It wasn't uncommon in the 19th century for older men to pursue the hand of a teenager in marriage, especially if the young lady possessed a large dowry. Catherine Fitzsimons, age 15, was eight years the junior of her suitor, yet that was not the reason that her family protested the union. The Fitzsimons clan and their allied Hampton and Manning kin labeled Hammond a parvenu, a propertyless, low-society son of a New England schoolmaster. Stung to the bone, Hammond redoubled his amorous pursuit of plain looking Catherine, and she did her part by pitching a fit to have the man she chose over the men her parents would rather her have. A dutiful Paul Fitzsimons bestowed Redcliffe Plantation on Beech Island on his daughter and son-in-law. To James Hammond's credit he took to farming and improved the place and made a handsome go of plantation life -- even if he did father more children with slave women than he did with Catherine. Redcliffe gave Hammond entree into the realm of the landed aristocracy of Carolina. Politics was his ambition, and the issue he embraced more than any other was the preservation of slavery. To this end, James Hammond was second only to Calhoun in publicly defending the "peculiar institution." In his famed *Letter to a Glasgow Congregation*, leading men in the State rated him as the most eloquent apologist of Southern rights.

After the lapse of 150 years, the descendants of James Hammond together with the overseers of the manuscript repositories where the diaries are filed have allowed the "secret and sacred" thoughts of Hammond to be opened to public scrutiny. What is evident from the first few pages is that James Hammond is a towering intellect, a man so insightful that had he not succumbed to prurient desires, he might have walked boldly onto the national stage rather than be the one issue man in Washington that his U.S Senate role amounted to.

What else we learn about Hammond is that he had a profound love for the so-called "life of the mind," a trait not shared by many of his plantation-owning contemporaries. He was a lonely man, an introspective fellow haunted constantly by fears that others plotted his ruin or that others would gain something that by right should be his. However, rarely does one see such honesty in the self-admissions of another. Hammond is self-effacing in his journal at times, not giving himself the appropriate credit that he deserves in a political or literary triumph. He provided amply for his family and even managed to get the will of his uncle broken when he had been cut out of it.

History books will forever remember James Hammond as the author of the "Mud-sill theory." In a speech before the Senate in 1858 Hammond stated "All great civilizations require menials to perform the drudgery of life; such an inferior class constitutes the very mud-sill of society and of political government." South Carolinians of the planter class cheered the speech but privately whispered about the integrity of the quiet and withdrawn man who made it. Now they know the truth.

Did Your Grandmother Go To Memminger?

Since Memminger High School for girls graduated its last class decades ago, there are but a few around who can boast that their grandmother was a Memminger girl. Yet, just two decades ago many Charleston women proudly had that detail noted in their marriage announcement as well as in their obituary. This was most likely the first teacher training facility in the State as well as the South, and it gained the respect of prominent educators the nation over. Today, just the facade of that grand Lancastrian structure remains as tribute to the noble women's institution that thrived there for three generations. Three generations of children, Gentile and Jew, Caucasian and African, have matured under the tutelage of Memminger Normal School alumnae.

Coeducation, desegregation, curriculum changes and outdated facilities, as well as the overwhelming demand placed upon the Charleston County School Board to accomplish things that once were the province of the home -- all combined to close Memminger High School's doors a generation ago. Of late, Memminger Auditorium, located on 56 Beaufain Street, has been refurbished and utilized for concerts and political gatherings. Hundreds of young women from across our state competed for admission to this prestigious teacher training school, or Normal School, as it was called in bygone days. Sisters Louise and Carrie Pollitzer, longtime local educators and women's rights advocates are but two of the lengthy list of distinguished alumnae.

South Carolina lagged behind her sister states in developing a public education system. There was no education for former slaves until philanthropic organizations in the North established a few schools among the ruins here and in Columbia. It was deemed more important to have cheap child labor on the farms and in the textile mills than to have compulsory attendance at school. What public education system the state did develop was due to the exertions of forward-thinking men such as Governor James Hammond and local financier, later Confederate Secretary of the Treasury, Christopher Memminger.

Memminger Normal School was a vital part of antebellum South Carolina's public education system, and it served as a teaching center for the children of the freedmen during the Era of Reconstruction. The George Peabody Foundation made grants to the school in the 1870s as long as it remained in the hands of capable New Englanders who had opposed secession. By the 1880s Memminger Normal School was again under state sponsorship, and it resumed its original role of training young women, albeit white and middle class, in the art of pedagogy.

A "Normal" school is one patterned after the 17th century French model of teacher training academies that originated in Paris under Louis XIV and spread throughout the Sun King's realm. The use of the word "normal" implies that what is learned there, as well as the methods of pedagogy, and even the style of architecture and classroom layout will become the "norm" across the land. The graduates of Normal Schools are selected from many applicants, and their diploma is always distinguished above that of a general school diploma. Often, the tuition is free or greatly reduced if the student enters the teaching profession. Students of Normal Schools were usually female, and they were held to a higher standard of academic excellence as well as personal decorum. The status of being a part of a normal school was a bit akin to being accepted at one of the nation's military academies.

Curriculum in the Memminger Normal School in 1858 included numerous courses per term with two terms comprising a school year. Reading, Spelling, Writing, Grammar, Drawing, Arithmetic, Physical Geography, History, French, Music and Composition were the introductory courses in First Year, Term 1. By year 3 the girls added Spanish in addition to French and they studied Astronomy and Orthography among other courses. Year 3 saw the introduction of Intellectual and Moral Science. Matriculation required three years of successful study. Memminger was noted for its academic rigor and its strictness in behavior. Porter Military and Citadel cadets were not allowed to come calling after 5 p.m.

Christopher Memminger was the driving force for the school's creation. Himself an orphan, Memminger had received a wonderful classical education from the time of his adoption at age 9 by the Thomas Bennett family. It was Memminger who went about Charleston soliciting cash donations for the school, and it was he who made eloquent entreaties to the State Legislature for yearly financial support.

Land near a large meadow, now the corner of Pinckney and Beaufain Streets, was purchased from Henry L. Pinckney. The land was leased by Pinckney from the Glebe Land Trust of St. Michael's Church. Under the agreement, the School Commissioners had to pay off the lease agreement of $122.46 per year for the remaining 31 years of the lease. A magnificent garden, one of Charleston's finest, occupied about an acre of the original property and Daniel Meagher, an Irish immigrant, was hired to tend the carefully laid out shrubs, trees, flowers, and herbs. One nondescript building was pulled down, but a delightful Victorian-styled overseer's cottage was kept for Meagher and his family's use.Charlestonians were widely traveled and well-read, so it is no surprise that the Commissioners with Memminger as Chairman, selected the Lancastrian style of architecture for the school building. Joseph Lancaster (1778-1838) of Southwark, south of London, was one of the leading lights of progressive educational thinking in his day. He is credited with developing the so-called Monitorial System of teaching -- a technique where older students who are proficient assist the instructor in teaching the younger ones. Lancaster's Free School on Borough Road in Southwark became a pilgrimage destination for scholars interested in developing a model of how better to educate the youth. Dr. Andrew Bell, an Englishman who went out to Madras, India, with the British East India Company simultaneously developed the "Madras System," a method similar to Lancaster's. The Bell method has come down to us today as the "each one teach one" idea -- as one student masters a skill, he or she shares it with another student.

Lancaster was not the first philosopher of eduction to develop a systematic theory of education; however, his appeal to the Americans was elevated in the era of the French Revolution, partly because Jean Jacques Rousseau, another pedagogical thinker, was less a church man than his English peer, Joseph Lancaster. The Church of England expected to take a leading role in education, and the Americans, though averse to the union of Church and State, were accepting of religious oversight and tolerant of religious instruction in the curriculum. Lancaster emphasized a Georgian architectural plan with Palladian-styled domes, great halls, exterior columns, and large, arched windows five feet above floor level. The architecture was intelligently designed to foster the magnificent presence of academia in a community with the functionality of generous space for lecture hall instruction. Schools of this type had long been associated with quaint New England towns, and it was not uncommon that young divinity students spent a year or two teaching before taking on a congregational charge. In the South, wealthy planters sent their sons abroad or to New England schools while their daughters received instruction from polite and well-trained young scholars who did that sort of thing. For the rest of society, it was catch as catch can as far as the "Three R's" were concerned. Such was the legacy of education below the Mason-Dixon Line. The intelligentsia were among the nation's most elite thinkers. The masses, white and black, were often unlettered.

The Charleston Normal School, as it was referred to until the 1880s when it was redesignated "Memminger Normal School," solicited at least three young female candidates from each county in the State. The application process was demanding, and being selected to pack up and take a train to far off Charleston was the highlight of many an upstate girl's life.

Money was always a problem for the school, yet people and organizations stepped up and took on the challenge. Two local organizations not recognizable today that came through financially time and again were the Apprentices' Library Society and the Fellowship Society of St. Michael's Church. Various individuals, too, set examples of philanthropy when the State Legislature voted funds for everything from railroads to munitions in the 1850s, but precious little to the teacher training institute.

Leadership of the institution was entrusted to competent New Englanders, men and ladies from Boston and Philadelphia. Mister Frederick A. Sawyer, a teacher in the Primary School of Boston, was selected as Principal. The course of study was said to be one that "embraces the whole curriculum of a liberal education." Fifty-seven students from around the State, each girl dressed in white, stood for opening convocation on Friday morning of January 21, 1859. Unfortunately, the seeds of secession had been sown and North - South rivalry soon engulfed the faculty, students, and community. Teachers stood to their tasks despite the partisan political environment.

School continued through the chaotic five-way splintering of the Democratic Nominating Convention held here in 1860 and through the Secession Convention in December. Miss Anna C. Brackett, a Memminger teacher, presented a memoir to *Harper's Magazine,* May 1894, where she notes that she was working at her desk very early on Wednesday, January 9, 1861, when she heard the terrible rumble of big guns being fired from the sea islands. Of course, it was the firing upon the Federal steamer *Star of the West* that was sent clandestinely by Lincoln to resupply Fort Sumter. There was much excitement in the classroom that day. The teachers and Frederick Sawyer stayed at their posts until "Mister Sawyer indulged in activities which showed his Northern sympathies" in the Fall of 1863. Somewhere around the battles of Chickamauga and Chattanooga, Sawyer said something inflammatory, and the community decided that he and his host of northern women must go. A flag of truce got the faculty through the lines to a Federal steamer bound for New York. One teacher stayed another month, but she, too, left and went by train and coach through Cincinnati. School was suspended until the carpetbaggers reopened it after the War as a school for freed slaves.

The George Peabody Foundation led the way with funding for the reopening of the Normal School in 1866 as a free school for the sons and daughters of former slaves. Across town the Episcopalian rector of the Church of the Holy Communion recognized that sectional prejudices during Reconstruction would prevent white children, many of whom were now orphans, from getting an education, so he started the institute of the Church of the Holy Communion -- the forerunner of Porter Military School. Reverend Porter also founded a trade school for the Freedmen that eventually became the Jenkins Orphanage School. Northern men and women, and even President Hayes himself, wrote large checks to support Porter's endeavors.

The Normal School reopened under Charleston leadership during the Hampton Redshirt Campaign of 1876, the campaign that ended reconstruction in South Carolina. The name was changed to Memminger School in honor of Wade Hampton's good friend, Christopher Memminger, who had done so much for education. Soon, young ladies gathered from around the State and teachers went forth to every corner teaching male and female, young and old, black and white. One of the notable celebrations in the Spring of each year was the gathering to hear the Mitchell Essay winner read her paper at Memminger. The paper was named for another notable educator in Charleston's history.

The best book to date about Memminger School is the published Masters Thesis entitled "A History of The Memminger Normal School, Charleston, S.C., 1858-1932," by Mary Taylor, in partial fulfillment of her master's work at George Peabody College for Teachers in Nashville. The copy of the book in this writer's possession came from the library of the late Dr. Berkeley Grimball, former headmaster of The Gaud School, 1952-1964, and former headmaster of The Porter-Gaud School, 1965-1988. Grimball's mother, Anne Carson Strohecker Grimball, a Memminger graduate, founded The Watt's Elementary School on Broad Street in 1931 after she was widowed in 1929 and remarried. The Watt's School is the forerunner of the Porter-Gaud Lower School.

What We Don't Know About History Can Hurt Us -- Bretton Woods

"If you aren't in over your head, how do you know how tall you are?" T.S. Eliot wasn't speaking of the Bretton Woods Agreement when he penned those words to a friend, yet, the phraseology seems apropos as the world's economies are perched perilously close to the abyss of financial disaster. Why is it that in all things physical and metaphysical, the most obtuse element in the realm of understanding, is that which is in the jurisdiction of Mammon? The world's greatest minds -- from Solomon to Chaucer, from John Stuart Mill to Milton Friedman -- all have had a go at describing society's craving for wealth. In their own ways each of these sages made a point of prescribing time-tested strategies for avoiding the pit reserved for those whose sin is avarice. The finger pointers in our time are stepping up their denunciation of America's role in the global financial meltdown. Harsh critics, such as World Bank president Robert Zoellick, have recently (Friday, November 11) "called for a return to a gold anchor in the global financial system." On the other hand, staunch defenders of the present global market and banking system such as "Keynesian Brad DeLong [anoint] Zoellick the "Stupidest Man Alive." Robert P. Murphy, Ph.D., president of the Ludwig von Mises Institute, publishes an on-line blog where he champions the "Austrian School" of Economic Theory popularized by former Prime Minister Margaret Thatcher and the late President Ronald Reagan. Austrian School economists hold dear the theories of Ludwig von Mises and Nobel Prize winning economist, Friedrich Hayek. Most Austrian School disciples desire the abolition of the central bank concept and its fractional reserve system and recommend, instead, a return to the gold standard.

As confusing as all of this debate is to us, the citizens of an economically illiterate, consumption-oriented society, we can draw comfort in the fact that President Truman, himself, was confused. Harry Truman once remarked, "Give me a one-handed economist; all of my economists are always saying, 'On the other hand...."" What we do not know about economics can come back to hurt us.

After World War II it was clear that the Western World was locked in an ideological struggle between the lovers of the free market and the proponents of collectivist thought. Even with the collapse of the Soviet Union in 1989, the ideological struggle continues. As the world's population edged past 7 billion souls a couple of weeks ago, a less published statistic is the idea of "middle class" spreading to its highest ever level in world history. The middle class "mind set" drives consumerism, and consumerism drives the free world's great economic engines. Therefore, traditional banking systems operating along individualist and nationalistic assumptions are no longer viable. That leads us all to the debate about the viability of continuing to print paper money as a means of bailing out failed corporations and insolvent governments. Is a country that is admittedly untutored in competing economic ideas capable of solving this issue through assemblies of elected officials -- officials, who, themselves, are often poorly versed in the pros and cons of economic theories? Perhaps that reason explains the success of Robert P. Murphy's book entitled *Chaos Theory* (2002) and *The Politically Incorrect Guide To Capitalism* (2007).

As we Americans are about to commemorate the 70th anniversary of the attack on Pearl Harbor, few know, that before three weeks had passed after the devastating attack Assistant U.S. Treasurer, Harry Dexter White began work on a top-secret project in the United States Treasury Department. White's mission was to "internationalize" the economies of the Allies immediately following the successful conclusion of the World War. The word "Globalism" was not a common term then. White's secret project, undertaken as the United States frantically prepared for a two-front war, became the 28,000 word draft known as the 1944 Bretton Woods Agreement. That pact has critics these days claiming that it was what set the free world on a collision path with economic collapse.

Harry Dexter White wrote the broad outline of the Bretton Woods Agreement; however, he worked under the close supervision of his superior, Henry Morgenthau, Jr., the Secretary of the Treasury for Franklin Roosevelt's administration. That Dexter White wrote the entire economic draft that created the International Monetary Fund and the World Bank is not a consideration any longer. He had collaboration from John Maynard Keynes of Britain, who styled himself John Maynard, Lord Keynes in the 1940s. An economist from Australia named Sir Leslie Melville crafted a portion of the remake of the western world's finance and trade policies, as did India's Sir Chintāman Dwārakānāth Deshmukh and China's H.H. Kung. Mexico sent Victor Urquidi. These men were the leading central bank proponents in the free world. Opponents to central banking were missing at the elite gathering at Bretton Woods, New Hampshire. With these men were large delegations of number crunchers and fact finders, and for three weeks in July of 1944 intellectuals worked night and day inside the posh Mount Washington Hotel in the quaint New Hampshire ski resort of Bretton Woods.

The grand architect of the Agreement is thought to have been Secretary of the Treasury, Henry Morgenthau, Jr., White's superior in Washington, yet some scholars are not so certain. Some of the papers relating to the world-changing agreement have only recently been made public. What is certain is that the American people were told little except that sweeping changes were being worked out for the postwar era. Details were highly classified, and who would have understood? How much Congress was told is debatable. During wartime it was necessary to work quickly with committee chairmen and to beg tacit consent of the rank and file for security reasons. South Carolina was represented in the Senate by Burnett Rhett Maybank and Ellison D. "Cotton Ed" Smith. At that time we had Mendel Rivers, Hamp Fulmer, Butler Hare, Joe Bryson, James Richards, and John McMillan in the House. What these men actually knew about the vast changes being brought to our nation's economy and that of the world is uncertain. Fellow South Carolinian Jimmy Byrnes was the Director of the all-powerful War Mobilization Board. He was the most astute of the S.C. men in Washington, and he had daily contact with Roosevelt, yet Byrnes' autobiography *Speaking Frankly* (1947) makes just passing reference to the whole affair.

A question that scholars have posed in recent years deals with whether the complete reorganization of international finances was the logical outgrowth of lessons learned from the Great Depression and the five financial panics of the 19th century or whether the dramatic agreement constituted a radical departure from tradition due to the outcome of Russia's Bolshevik Revolution in 1917. Economists argue in one direction and diplomats in the other. Academics straddle the fence and the American public flips to the sports page. The general public has been confused for nearly 70 years following the Bretton Woods Agreement.

To throw more confusion upon the already puzzling history of the Agreement that thrust us into financial globalism is the postwar discovery that Harry Dexter White was secretly feeding Joseph Stalin's spies details on American postwar plans. A top secret network of counter espionage agents known as "code Verona" watched the movements and monitored the communication of key American government employees during World War II. The extent of White's breach of trust is not fully known today, but it adds fuel to the anti-central bank argument -- even though we do know that Stalin viewed the World Bank and the IMF as agencies whose clandestine purpose was to advance capitalism and frustrate communism in war-torn and developing areas.

The debate of more central banking versus gold as a standard continues, and, to date, our schools do as little to educate the citizenry in the great economic dilemmas as they did in the 1930s. Maybe the ones who have wrestled with that bear of a problem should be given the benefit of the doubt. Theodore Roosevelt once shot back at a critic, "It is not the critic who counts; not the man who points out how the strong man stumbles, or where the doer of deeds could have done them better. The credit belongs to the man who is actually in the arena, whose face is marred by dust and sweat and blood; who strives valiantly; who errs, who comes short again and again, because there is no effort without error and shortcoming; but who does actually strive to do the deeds . . . etc."

Charlestonian Was Acquaintance of Edgar Degas in New Orleans

Call us what you may, but we southerners are a romantic lot. Perhaps it is because so many of us hailed from the hinterlands -- Scotland, Wales, Cornwall, or Ireland -- that we're drawn to the turf and the sound of thundering hooves and the sight of thoroughbreds pounding around a track. Last Saturday was the 18th running of the Charleston Cup, a steeplechase race hosted by the South Carolina Jockey Club at Stono Ferry. As this column is being written, the Colonial Cup is being run on the famed Springdale course in Camden, and preparations are already being made for the Aiken and Elloree Trials in March 2012. Though horseracing is still popular throughout the South, it's Kentucky's Keeneland and Churchill Downs that attract national interest today. However, in the 19th century it was the Crescent City, New Orleans, that captivated French Impressionist and noted equine artist, Edgar Degas. The canvasses painted by Degas during his Louisiana sojourn will forever be trademarks of Southern culture.

The horse has been a theme of artists since classical times, and Degas, along with fellow Frenchman, Eugène Delacroix, featured Europe's finest bloodlines in scenes that celebrated their fleet-footed dominance of the turf. *Race Horses* is a famous canvas that has been reproduced numerous times for jockey clubs around the Western world, and so has his *At the Races* and so has his *Jockey in Blue on a Chestnut Horse*. Southerners who to this day believe the old adage that, "A horse without a rider is still a horse, but that a man without a horse is only a man," have almost spiritual reverence for Degas' depiction of the noble creatures so cherished by warriors and sportsmen alike.

Artists argue among themselves about which school influenced Degas more -- the Impressionists, the Realists, or the Romantics. When we view his painting (1873) entitled "Portraits in a New Orleans Cotton Office," we are drawn to gentlemen factors grading cotton on long tables in the New Orleans Cotton Exchange -- a scene common to southern cities from Nashville to Mobile to

Charleston. Top hat, cigar, fine horses, and bourbon completed the Southern gentleman's equipage as he speculated on the futures market. No one could foresee the demise of the *"Cotton Republic"* after its rebirth in the wake of the failed Confederacy -- nothing seemed able to dethrone "*King Cotton*" except that insidious insect known as the boll weevil. Degas captured the essence of post-Civil War New Orleans 50 years before the boll weevil plague cast a pall across the Old South.

Degas was one of us, for his mother and grandmother were New Orleans ladies -- Creoles born a half mile from the Mississippi River. When Degas arrived in New Orleans in 1872, the 38-year-old artist embraced the sultry, sinful city as if it were his native Paris. There was a similarity if one used some imagination -- the dampness of New Orleans and its occasional floods bore resemblance to Paris where workmen occasionally built levees to contain the Seine at Quai d' Orsay just as New Orleans citizens did near Canal Street. Then, too, New Orleans bore marks of the recent war, and it was a city under occupation by Federal Troops while Degas was in residence. Ironically, the artist's beloved Paris was occupied by Prussian soldiers following the defeat of his country in the Franco-Prussian War. An air of "bowed, but unbeaten" prevailed then in both cities.

Edgar Degas had been a rifleman in Patrice de Mac-Mahon, Duke of Magenta's I Corps, in the four-month siege of Paris in 1870, a mere two years prior to his arrival in New Orleans. He'd just experienced the turbulent period known as the Paris Commune where unemployed workers called themselves Communards and followed the leadership of socialist Louis Auguste Blanqui. Blanqui a popular leader who advocated that government endorse a more equitable distribution of wealth. The commerce that Degas witnessed from Chartres Street to Peters Street in New Orleans made him optimistic that his uncle, Rene de Gas (the old aristocratic spelling shunned used by the artist) would regain his prewar prominence in the city.

In the celebrated painting that Degas did of his uncle's cotton exchange, Rene de Gas is portrayed in the upper left leaning nonchalantly against the window frame. In the foreground is New Orleans cotton merchant Michel Musson as he is depicted sitting in a chair pulling a boll of cotton fiber apart with his fingers. At the time that Degas painted this canvas, Michel Musson was the head of the "Council of One-Hundred," a society similar to Wade Hampton's Red Shirts in Reconstruction Era South Carolina. Musson was engaged in open negotiations with the Federal government over the removal of occupation forces from New Orleans and the reopening of the port to international commerce.

Clandestinely, Musson was organizing a vigilante force similar to Hampton's for the purpose of confronting the carpetbagger regime.

Opposing Musson's overt acts of reconciliation and deal making with the Federal authorities was a much more radical White League that advocated, among other things, a renewal of hostilities between the citizens of Louisiana and the Federal government. A medical doctor, John Dickson Bruns, who had just moved to New Orleans from Charleston, became a member of the Musson inner-circle of conspirators.

John Dickson Bruns, M.D., became acquainted with Edgar Degas through Michel Musson's connection with the de Gas brother's Cotton Exchange in the French Quarter. Both Degas and Bruns were about the same age, and both shared an interest in fine cuisine, beautiful Creole women, and Cuban cigars. Like Degas, Bruns had served in the Army as a surgeon for the Confederacy. And, like Degas, Bruns had had an aristocratic upbringing in a time of opulence and political stability. Now both men faced uncertainty in their own futures. Both were cast adrift in a new place and each doubted, in the wake of catastrophic defeat, the restoration of his native country to its former glory. Bruns had been educated at the College of Charleston and at the Medical College here. Among Bruns wide circle of acquaintances was the poet, Henry Timrod. Bruns's classical education at The College induced him to write verse in the spare time that he had when he was not seeing patients, conducting research, and editing the *Charleston Medical Journal*. When Fort Sumter shattered the Union, Bruns enlisted in the service of his state and served as a surgeon throughout the war in Virginia and the Carolinas.

Musson collaborated with New Orleans native and fellow carpetbag opponent, P.G.T. Beauregard, the famed Confederate general and victor at Fort Sumter in 1861. Degas would have moved in a circle of Creole elites, including Beauregard, in 1872, and Doctor Bruns was part of that clique. Beauregard had been hired by the city of New Orleans as City Engineer in charge of levees and dikes. Edgar Degas appears not to have been anymore than passively engaged in anti-Federal activities while he lived two years in the Crescent City. He spent much time amusing himself at the horse races and socializing in the French Quarter with the vast circle of his uncle's customers and friends.

New Orleans was America's most sensual city in the 19th century, far surpassing New York, Baltimore, and Charleston for that dubious distinction. After dusk fell upon the gas lit streets, there was "casual commingling of a all races in the most shocking manner," wrote Fanny Wright, an English woman traveling through America. The postwar literary circle of this delta city included poets, novelists, artists, and illustrators, and Doctor John Bruns gained immediate entree because of his friendship with the widely acclaimed South Carolina poet Henry Timrod. Bruns penned 40 lines entitled "The Foe At The Gates" as the Confederacy prepared in January of 1865 for the bitter end. His poem closes with the line:

> *So, dying, ye shall win a high renown,*
> *If not in life, at least by death, set free;*
> *And send her fame through endless ages down--*
> *The last grand holocaust of Liberty.*

In those heady times when New Orleans resonated with disunionists, conspirtors, and Cuban filibusterers, the Medoc wine flowed freely from the Bordeaux region and the Creole girls danced seductively in the shadows as their lovers puffed away on Havana cigars -- or segars, as they spelled it. George Washington Cable was a young, aspiring poet and novelist who was in Bruns's medical practice at the time of Degas' sojourn in New Orleans. Through the five surviving letters from New Orleans that Edgar Degas mailed home, it is clear that the young artist's life revolved around hours spent at the De Gas Cotton Exchange where he interacted with his kinsmen and dangerous political men such as Michel Musson and the new Fair Grounds Race Track that was 11 blocks away. However, Degas also notes a close-knit circle of writers and artists with whom he associates, and that would be the coterie of poets, writers, and painters known to John Dickson Bruns, formerly of Charleston.

Why Southern Men Approve of the Poetry of William Butler Yeats

In the protracted debate over slavery, Northern intellectuals were surprised that Southern Congressmen rarely resorted to Aristotle's well-known defense of slavery found in that sage's Book 1 of Politics. Time and again defenders of the "slavocracy" tossed out passages from The Bible or passages from the Cleveland Presbyterian Reverend F. A. Ross's 1857 sermon entitled "Slavery Ordained By God." Abolitionists accused the rank and file of southern men of being unrefined.

We Southrons are a bardic lot and our ancestors hunted, fought, distilled malt liquor, and celebrated their heroic deeds with ballads and dancing. Highbrow literature such as critical essays and poetry doesn't come to us naturally. Southern men prefer horse racing to *Hamlet* and duck blinds to Diderot, but even the most rustic of us appreciates the pounding rhythm and haunting themes of William Butler Yeats's Irish poems.

To date not a single Charlestonian has been identified as having met or corresponded with the Irish poet and nationalist, William Butler Yeats. Well, Josephine Pinckney did entertain Padraic Colum, another Irish poet and playwright at her family's home on 21 King Street in 1922. Colum regaled Pinckney, along with Hervey Allen and Dubose Heyward, with tales of how Yeats and others of the Celtic Movement had founded the Abbey Theater in Dublin.

There were quite a few Charlestonians of the Hibernian connection, however, who boasted of friendship with Irish nationalist Eamon de Valera when he came here in 1920. Charles Stuart Parnell, another Irish apostle of secession, who visited here before de Valera, also had backers here. William Butler Yeats may not have been the charismatic commander as was the big fellow, Michael Collins, and he may not have had the rawboned courage of his convictions as did the Irish martyr, Patrick "Padraig" Pearse. Yet, in spite of his protestant roots and abhorrence of violence, W.B. Yeats remains for many the pure essence of Irish nationalism. The lack of personal identification with the Old South doesn't limit the appeal of Yeats and his poetry among Southern gentlemen, however. From Oxford, Mississippi, to Charlottesville, Virginia, to the Horseshoe in Columbia, well-read Southern men reserve a prominent spot on the bookshelf for *The Collected Poems of William Butler Yeats*. There's something about Yeats that just fits in with the volumes of Douglas Southall Freeman, Dumas Malone, and Robert Penn Warren. There's something, too, about Yeats's poems that resonates with that unvanquished mood in the Old South. Scholars have pored over recurring themes in this iconic Irishman's works looking for those haunting refrains of dashed hope and disillusionment -- themes akin to Faulkner's tales of Yoknapatawpha in the aftermath of the Confederacy -- or Thomas Wolfe's "Oh, Lost" illusions in *Look Homeward Angel*.

Yeats was an ardent Irish nationalist even when the odds of independence from Britain were long. Yeats was a womanizer even when the charge for churchmen was adultery. He was obsessed with spiritualism and the occult when damnation of the soul was the risk. His near fatal attraction to the beautiful Maude Gonne -- and even to her alluring young daughter -- bespeaks the unrequited passion for illicit amours that so many southern men seem prey to. Any man who could pen the lines of "The Second Coming, or Slouching Towards Bethlehem," containing the immortal refrain "Things fall apart; the centre cannot hold; / Mere anarchy is loosed, and everywhere / The ceremony of innocence is drowned; / The best all lack conviction, while the worst / Are full of passionate intensity" is a kindred soul with all true sons of the American South.

The idea of independence in our south land was not the long-burning ember known by clandestine Sinn-Fein and the Irish Republican Brotherhood. Old Eire's sufferings at the hands of England began centuries ago with its conquest by William of Orange. Even so, many southerners found themselves sympathetic with the cause of Old Eire. Ireland's angst embraced the conquerer's disdain for its language, its religion--the entire Celtic culture was anathema. Ireland's conquerers even found its wearing of green to be offensive as if it expressed some symbolic rebellion to British authority. Yeats longed for Irish independence, but he thought that the 1916 Easter Rising was foolhardy and poorly planned. The seven-day uprising resulted in much destruction to Dublin's center-city as the British navy was able to get a gunboat in close. Many here in the South thought that the attack on Fort Sumter was foolhardy. Brash acts motivated by lofty, often unattainable ideals go right along with both the American South and the Irish cultures. One of the Irish rebels who was executed by Britain for his part in the rebellion was John MacBride, William Butler Yeats's rival for the affections of the beautiful, willowy Maude

Gonne. MacBride seduced Gonne -- or it may have been the other way around -- and a son, Sean, was the product of their unhappy union. Yet, in the spirit of chivalry, Yeats composed a stanza to commemorate his tragic rival's heroic demise: "This other man I had dreamed/A drunken, vain-glorious lout. He had done most bitter wrong/To some who are near to my heart,/Yet I number him in the song; He, too, has resigned his part/In the casual comedy;/He, too, has been changed in his turn,/Transformed utterly:/A terrible beauty is born." Maude Gonne, the object of Yeats's adoration, belittled him for casting MacBride, a hero of both the Boer War and the latest failed Irish Rising, as lager lout.

Just as the Virginia ex-Confederate, John Esten Cooke, gave us *Wearing of the Gray*, a collection of Southern tales of the southern lost cause, Yeats created the phrase "wearing of the green" in his "Easter Rising"--"I write it out in a verse: 'MacDonagh and Mac-Bride And Connolly and Pearse/ Now and in time to be, Wherever green is worn,/Are changed, changed utterly;/ A terrible beauty is born.'" We understand the loss of promising young men cut down in their prime -- dying for a cause they felt was noble. Yeats brings his reader into the midst of great human tragedy. Through rhyme and cadence we feel the fight is joined, the foe well met. Southerners have Timrod and Lanier, yet, there's room on our shelf for Yeats, as well.

The fact that he was a horse lover and a frequenter of the race track endears the Irishman even more to his admirers in this part of the country. His poem "At Galway Races" closes with the refrain,

> *Sing on: somewhere at some new moon,*
> *We'll learn that sleeping is not death,*
> *Hearing the whole earth change its tune,*
> *Its flesh being wild, and it again*
> *Crying aloud as the racecourse is, And we find hearteners among*
> *Men that ride upon horses.*

William Butler Yeats was elected senator in the new Irish Republic, and in those stormy times he packed a pistol in his coat pocket as he watched the proceedings of the drafting of the Irish Constitution in Dublin in 1922. The masonry outside the Shelbourne Hotel on St. Stephen's Green is pockmocked with bullet holes from the gun battles that raged there in the struggle for independence.

The epithet on Yeats's grave comes from the last lines of his poem, "Under Ben Bulben": "Cast a cold eye/On life, on death./Horseman, pass by." If those words don't sound like something that Confederate raider Turner Ashby or Nathan Bedford Forrest might have said, then Ireland doesn't have 40 shades of green and southerners don't like football.

The Citadel Paradigm Appreciated

"It is what it is," has become an oft repeated but meaningless idiom in our ineloquent culture. When words fail us or when matters become too complex to explain, we fall back on our idioms. With The Citadel being in the news lately and much of its press being unfavorable, it's an opportune time to examine that institution's purpose and practices as stated in its own words -- to pick apart its paradigm and to determine what makes it unique.

A look at the school's statement of purpose in 1969 reveals that, "While the college is justly proud of the war records of its sons and will always expect them to respond in national emergencies, its chief purpose is to prepare men for civil pursuits by giving them a sound education reinforced by the best features of military training." Up front the school implies that it is not a recruit depot like Fort Jackson or Parris Island. By implication it can be gathered that the school does not proclaim that it's in the league with Harvard academically.

Forty-two years later, the 2011 mission statement says the school's "mission is to educate and develop our students to become principled leaders in all walks of life by instilling the core values [Honor, Duty, Respect] of The Citadel in a disciplined and intellectually challenging environment. A unique feature of this environment for the South Carolina Corps of Cadets is the sense of camaraderie produced through teamwork and service to others while following a military lifestyle."

From the outside, The Citadel is an imposing mass of Moorish gray architecture peopled by gray-clad cadets traversing a green lawn called a parade ground. Unlike other college campuses the shrill sound of a bugle amplified over a loud speaker pierces the calm, and cadets stride quickly to meet one of the numerous required formations of the day. Personal appearance is noted by a cadet squad sergeant whose job it is to maintain standards. A cadet officer takes charge and marches the unit smartly to some nonacademic cadet function such as close-order drill, intramural sports, a meal in the mess hall, or P.T., physical training. How amazing it is that this college can recruit young people who're willing to forego the usual college freedoms, fraternities, and tailgating at great football games. Instead, The Citadel replaces these adolescent rites of passage with harsh military rigor supplemented by a full load of classes -- where oversleeping or cutting is not an option. What makes these people tick -- what rationale do they find there that rewards them greater than the pleasure and opportunities they forego at a traditional college or university? What is it that bonds Citadel graduates as closely as brothers? There should be no mystery about the transformation in human behavior that takes place inside those barracks over the 36 months that cadets wear the gray uniform of The South Carolina Corps of Cadets.

On the inside of those walls something is going on that the outside world never sees -- something cadets and alums refer to simply as "the system." "The system" is the term they use to describe the unique mix of academic, athletic, and military activities and the tremendous amount of information that must be processed and dealt with every single day of one's Citadel career. "The system" has turned boys into men and cadets into useful citizens for more than 160 years. In the 1990s the institution became coeducational after a much publicized campaign to remain as a state-sponsored, single-gender school. Some things had to change, i.e., locks on doors, separate latrines, and modification of some training routines. Today, the emphasis is on personal development in all areas with the inculcation of values such as duty, honor, and respect being paramount. Much of the language in The Citadel's 2011 Mission Statement reads like the training directives produced by the Armed Services in the 1970s on race and gender relations. It goes without saying that there is an accentuation upon "expanded cultural awareness" that was not attendant to the school's agenda even during the transformation from a segregated to an integrated establishment. Some of the graduates from the "Old Corps" have questioned what they perceive as a more relaxed corps "system." Be that as it may, the Corps today is strong and it is tough, and furthermore, the academic standards have improved. The rigid cadet-run honor code of not lying, cheating, or tolerating these things is still an almost sacred part of the school tradition -- just as it was a hundred or more years ago. Older graduates are not as aware of how the dynamics of society have changed over the decades as are recent alumni. Title 20 of the United States Code was not a concern when many of our grads matriculated. Neither had there been a bruising U.S. Supreme Court case that would break the 150 year all-male tradition. Perhaps the greatest change in society over the past 50 years is that most households require two income earners, something that was unthinkable then. Women are in every type of job slot the country offers. The word "pluralism" is bandied about today to an extent that was undreamed of by the old timers. In the 1960s the words emblazoned on plaques around the old school read "Duty, Honor, Country." Quotes such as "Duty is the sublimest word in the English language" adorned the inside of the barracks' sallyport. Even the winding stairwells ascending the four divisions -- floors -- of the barracks contained rugged proverbs on how life is to be lived. One saying stenciled on a wall said "Pain is the feeling of weakness leaving the body." It's not hard to acquire a bit of a rugged attitude about life when one is immersed in a 24 / 7 environment that calls for self-discipline and ever increasing levels of stamina. Just the daily grind that "knobs" go through of trying to keep all smudges off of a highly polished brass buckle and walking as if one's shoes were made of glass in order to keep from blemishing the spit shine -- is enough to drive part of the class "over the wall" -- literally. One memorable slogan from 40 years ago that was seen a dozen times a day said, "That which does not kill you makes you stronger." As was the case 40 years ago, now many of the upperclassmen who hold cadet rank are already on contract or scholarship to one of the branches of the military, and they infuse things into the regimen that they have picked up in special courses they've participated in at Fort Bragg or Quantico. Something that used to be known as "Jody calls" were chants sung in a sing-song rhythm for cadence while running lap after lap around the parade ground. They were quite clever and sometimes ribald, but these chants reinforced in one's mind forever that you were a breed apart from all the others who had chosen the road "most traveled." Somehow you felt that more was expected from you. Who are the youth who willingly trade away the opportunity of the so-called "Greek life" on the university campus for 8 a.m. S.M.I. -- Saturday Morning Inspection, Friday afternoon dress parade, the daily 7:15 a.m. room inspection, and endless drill with an M-16 rifle? Plebes, a polite name for close-cropped cadets who resemble door knobs, have been known to stay up all Friday night shining shoes, folding laundry in a precise manner, cleaning rifles, and putting hospital corners on bedsheets so tightly that a quarter flips as if the bed were a hardwood table. There's quite a lot of wistful thinking about the student bars at Five Points in Columbia and College Avenue in Clemson. Pardon the Citadel grad if he (or she) is over-trained in the trait of self-denial, or if he prides himself in a king-sized abundance of stamina.

    What makes daily life at The Citadel so much different from any other college is not the uniform, the required formations, or even the daily regimen of academics and military instruction. The difference lies in the aspects of the institution that do not change over time -- the fact that every young person entering Lesesne Gate will be tested to his or her limits -- academically and physically as well as put through a rigorous military system that forces one to budget time and energy for numerous things -- all of which must be done well -- and there's accountability at every step of the process. Citadel cadets are taught about accountability from the moment they don the uniform. Citadel graduates expect to be held accountable to the demanding standards and values that are detailed in the school's mission statement. When a graduate falls short on an objective, the paradigm remains in tact, and the rest carry on. The standards and the system that forged so many prepared and determined graduates endure.

However, even The Citadel cannot work miracles, though most who graduate admit that "the system" worked a miracle in them individually. Somewhere in those 36 months between the knob -- freshman year -- and the ring ceremony there has to be a "buy in" on the part of each of the cadets who attend. That some merely give lip service to the ideals taught there and tough it while hating the place is a recognized, but unspoken aspect of daily life there. Even within the so-called "band of brothers," there is knowledge that some are not holding dear the values learned there even if they do "wear the ring" and tap into the powerful network of contacts,

Speaking of the ring, I don't think that it'd be far-fetched to say that the Citadel ring is one of the most coveted pieces of jewelry that can be had anywhere. It cannot be purchased, though it does cost quite a lot of money. The prominent gold nugget has to be earned through months of upholding standards that slowly but surely become a permanent way of living and thinking. Most Citadel men would not consider leaving the house without a neat, well-groomed appearance and shined shoes. If for no other reason -- what would another Citadel grad think?

Though some graduates may cast its values aside, the paradigm is what it is, and it certainly has stood the test of time. Furthermore, the ring is never a paperweight or a trinket to cast aside when things go awry -- the ring is a gold seal and a constant reminder of the values all Citadel graduates aspire to live up to.

What Happened to Puritan John Winthrop's "City Upon a Hill" Idea?"

Wherever you turn for news these days, you are confronted with the most polarized political views we've had in this country in four generations. It's as if no one -- no one reads the early documents associated with our nation's founding. In times past school children memorized and wrote essays that included such pertinent phrases as "We the people etc. . . ." and "We hold these truths to be self-evident, that all men are created equal, that they are endowed by their Creator with certain unalienable Rights," etc. Actual examples of essay topics in some schools include interesting, but trendy titles such as "Nice planet. Don't blow it," "Government Serves People - Corporations Serve Profits," and everyone's favorite theme for reflection, "Live locally, think globally." It's time to recall that old 1630s Puritan preacher John Winthrop and renew our acquaintance with the cluster of conclusions he made about establishing a new and enduring country. The chasm between the opinions of the left and the right these days is not necessarily a bad thing for a democracy. It makes for lively debates and it heightens attendance at the polls if nothing else. However, there's something disturbing about the tone of the debates we're hearing these days. Two hundred and twenty years ago the issue that divided us and nearly derailed the fragile republic was whether the federal government would assume the war debts incurred by the various states. That struggle nearly derailed our country before we were a decade old. Then nullification, sectionalism, and slavery became insurmountable obstacles for the Union.

Even the collapse of the economy in 1929 did not shake our determination as much as has the convergence of global financial panic and the rising belief that the United States is less capable than anytime since the 1940s of shaping world affairs. To this end, media pundits of the left invoke 19th century Alexis de Tocqueville's phrase of "American exceptionalism" to justify their argument explaining the cause of our demise. Pundits of "the right" use the phrase as a mandate for American assertiveness in global matters.

"American Exceptionalism" is a term coined by Tocqueville, the French jurist and political theorist, who traveled through America in the 1830s making observations about the new-style republic and the "new man" that inhabited it. What's amazing about Tocqueville is that he was educated as a lawyer and was sent here on official business to investigate the unique prisons we were building in New York where criminal offenders would be rehabilitated rather than locked away for life. Tocqueville was so intrigued by what he saw in our republic that he extended his time to visit different parts of the country. He made numerous observations about the new classless social order where "no one cared who your grandfather was," or whether you made your fortune from selling hogs, importing tea from China, or planting hundreds of acres of cotton. The stirring words "We the people . . ." writ large by Jefferson across the Declaration of Independence intrigued Tocqueville; the Frenchman's ancestors had to straddle both sides of the French Revolution to survive. He appreciated the fact that our revolution had been nothing like theirs. Today, "American exceptionalism" is code for conservatives such as Palin, Bachmann, Santorum, Perry, and Ron Paul who believe that America has received a special dispensation from God to be what Puritan preacher John Winthrop called "a city upon a hill" -- a shining beacon of hope to the world -- a place where liberty and justice would produce an everlasting republic of virtue. Politicians ranging from Kennedy to Reagan to Gary Bauer have echoed Winthrop's phrase. Winthrop got the phrase from scripture -- Matthew 5:14: Christ says, "You are the light of the world. A city that is set on a hill cannot be hidden." Psalm 48 contains the phrase, too, so we do not know the identity of the earliest user since King David did not write that particular one. The implication by Winthrop is that our country is a land chosen by Providence for the purpose of upholding all that is good and just. American Exceptionalism is an idea that polarizes a room instantly. Fundamentalists adhere to its God and country refrains just as John Winthrop espoused in 1630. Liberals and most world leaders are infuriated that people in this country see themselves as God's chosen ones to shape world culture. Republican primary debates have excited everyone to get into the heated discussion. Some proponents believe that "American Exceptionalism" is a modern extension of the 19th century idea of Manifest Destiny. That popular slogan served as a cover for numerous politically inspired acts that increased the geographical size of the country.

Recently Stanley Fish of the *New York Times* devoted a column to the idea, and Rick Amato, the conservative radio talk show host, avowed that he -- Amato -- was an American Exceptionalist. Professor Erik Jones of the London

School of Economics (LSE) published an article in a British journal accusing America of possessing an "Exceptionalist" attitude in its dealings with Europe. He specifically criticized recently retired Secretary of Defense, Robert Gates, for possessing the disdainful "American Exceptionalist" idealogy when Gates lectured Europe on its need to shoulder more of its own defense and anti-terror responsibility. Perhaps LSE Professor Jones has modified his opinion in light of America's role in resolving Europe's colossal bank and currency crisis.

Professor Jones, in his rush to judgment, obviously did little research on the origins of "American Exceptionalism" as originally extolled by John Winthrop, an English ex-patriot. Winthrop was of the gentry class in the 17th century. His family were the perennial lords of the manor in Groton, a village in County Suffolk. Compelled by the religious tyranny of absolutist-minded Charles I, the Puritan John Winthrop and his family helped finance a fleet of like-minded Puritans known as the Winthrop Fleet to flee England for the New World in 1630. Winthrop was superbly educated in both law and theology, and he penned the famed "City Upon A Hill" proclamation while still aboard the ship Arabella somewhere off Narragansett Bay.

John Winthrop lived just 60 miles from the home of another prominent Puritan, Oliver Cromwell. At the time that Winthrop and his followers departed England for America, Cromwell was in the throes of his decision about whether to join the Winthrop Fleet, or not. Imagine the consequences for both sides of the Atlantic if Cromwell had not chosen to remain in Parliament and see his ideals through.

Winthrop's contribution to our nation's great collection of documents is just 563 words in length -- 40 words fewer than Jefferson and Madison's Bill of Rights document. Being the ardent Calvinist, Winthrop begins his proclamation with a quote from the Old Testament book of Micah, Chapter 6, verse 8: "to doe Justly, to love mercy, to walke humbly with our God." Winthrop's entire opening sentence "Now the onely way to avoyde this shipwracke and to provide for our posterity is to followe the Counsell of Micah, to doe Justly, to love mercy, to walke humbly with our God," has probably not enjoyed the attention of secondary students in more than a hundred years. That they were passengers escaping religious persecution in England and were miserable from their storm-tossed voyage -- not to mention apprehensive about their undertaking of founding a new city in a far-flung wilderness -- is an understatement.

John Winthrop was one of the guiding lights of the Massachusetts Bay Colony and a founding father of the city of Boston -- named for the quaint village of the the same name on the English Channel which served as a departure point for the Puritans of Suffolk.

What would Congress -- or even the Massachusetts legislature -- have to say about the ideals referenced as paramount by Winthrop and his cohorts aboard the *Arabella* in those early days? Paraphrased in modern English the refrains of Winthrop are: "To do justly - to love mercy -- to walk humbly with God -- to knit together as one and have brotherly affection. To use our surplus to help others in need -- to conduct trade in all fairness and to joy in one another. To be our brother's keeper -- to share each other's burdens -- to always hold true to these convictions we establish here. To be united in peaceableness -- asking the Lord to dwell among us and make us his people -- to seek God's wisdom and by so doing we will be faithful servants of God, and therefore, unbeatable by evil forces. We shall pray and praise the Lord. People from afar shall say, 'Make us like New England.' We shall be like a City Upon A Hill -- the eyes of all people will be upon us. And if we deal falsely with our God and cause Him to withdraw His presence from us, we shall be made a byword, an example, throughout the world. We shall see the mouths of our enemies speak evil of our God -- we shall lose the manifold blessings that God has bestowed upon us."

Winthrop closes with this final call to action as the settlers prepare to disembark for shore: "Therefore lett us choose life, that wee, and our Seede, may live; by obeyeing his voyce, and cleaveing to him, for hee is our life, and our prosperity." Our duty compels us to ponder why we have outgrown the need to discuss such things openly in our much troubled society today.

Carolina Should Boast of its Connection With Locke

Locating a marker honoring John Locke, the English philosopher who wrote the first constitution for Carolina, is a frustrating assignment. It stands to reason that Charleston's connection with the preeminent political philosopher of the 18th century would be reckoned with in divers ways. Yet, there was no Lockeville built upon a tidal basin, no Locke River, not even Locke Swamp. The best we could do for the brilliant man who counseled Lord Anthony Ashley Cooper was Locke Lane over in the Windemere subdivision. It's high time that we Carolinians do something on a grander scale to pay homage to the author of the Fundamental Orders [Constitutions] of Carolina, the author of religious toleration, the *tabula rasa* idea, the father of classical liberalism, and, among numerous other things, the philosopher most admired by Thomas Jefferson.

John Locke was educated as a physician at Oxford's Christ Church College, the foremost academic institution in England. As an undergraduate there he'd been the top scholar and was made a lecturer in Greek and Rhetoric for a year prior to commencing his medical studies under the mentorship of Robert Boyle and Robert Hooke, two of the leading scientists of the era. Thomas Willis, one of the fathers of neurology as well as a founder of the Royal Society, was another of Locke's medical professors, as was Thomas Sydenham. Christ Church College attracted the creme de la creme of the academic talent in England, and it was noted that only Latin and Greek were heard voiced about the campus. Even the college dining hall staff responded to Latin commands from the students and tutors.

Not to demean the Lords Proprietors in any way or to take away their claim to the many grand things over here that bear testimony to their namesakes -- Albemarle, Berkeley, Colleton, Carteret, Monck, *et al*, but they were men who by and large inherited their position and their wealth. Then little prudence on their behalf in the aftermath of Cromwell's death brought about the restoration of Charles II. A grateful Charles bestowed an enormous land grant upon the proprietors and, since few of them were as well read in political philosophy, they wisely deferred to the well-read Locke to draft the governmental charter for the colony. John Locke was serving as personal physician to Anthony Ashley Cooper, the Earl of Shaftsbury, who was the most powerful man in England after the King. Earl Shaftsbury, better known to us as Lord Ashley Cooper, was one of the founders in 1679 of the Whig political movement -- the believers in constitutional monarchy. John Locke, on the other hand, was a commoner, a self-made man from Belluton in Somerset. Belluton, a village in Somerset, was just down the road from such thriving metropolises as Chew Magna and Wokey Hole. As the son of a modest village lawyer, John Locke was one of the few scholars at Christ Church who did not arrive with servants in tow. His hardworking father did manage to send the boy to Westminster School, however, the most prestigious preparatory school in the land. While at Westminster Locke befriended Richard Lower, a fellow student. Lower, who later pioneered pulmonary medicine, persuaded Locke to go to Oxford and pursue medicine rather than law or theology. Thus, by his wits and his disciplined mind, Locke carved a place for himself in the history of two great nations -- England and the United States. However, it would be in politics and not medicine that John Locke would make his mark.

While at Oxford young Locke became enamored with the study of political philosophy as an adjunct to his scientific studies. During his Oxford years Locke spoke as enthusiastically about his philosophical readings as he did of his medical studies. In the routine course of his medical training, Locke was asked to accompany a university physician to assist in the treatment of a sick aristocrat who was visiting in the area of Oxford. That happenstance of a medical student assisting in a rural house call changed the course of history, for the ailing aristocrat was none other than Anthony Ashley Cooper. Sir Ashley, Baron Cooper took a liking to the politically savvy young doctor and offered him an invitation to join his household as his personal physician and philosophical consultant. Thirty years later Sir Ashley became the 1st Earl of Shaftsbury, a title bestowed by King Charles II on the man known as the "king maker" in the English realm.

The Charleston County Library web site has the most concise explanation of the Carolina land grant to Lords Proprietors, of whom Lord Ashley was the chief: "On March 24, 1663, Charles II granted to the Lords Proprietors a slice of North America running from the Atlantic to the Pacific, lying between 36 degrees latitude on the north and 31 degrees on the south. This huge section of continent was granted absolutely to the following men, to be financed by them, and for them to profit by, and to rule, with the help or interference of such a local government as they might permit. Above them was only the King. In the order named in Charles' charter they were: the Earl of Clarendon, the Duke of Albemarle, Lord Craven, Lord Berkeley, Lord Ashley, Sir George Carteret, Sir William Berkeley, and Sir John Colleton. The most important of these was Lord Ashley (Anthony Ashley Cooper), who specified the street plan for the new city and whose secretary, the philosopher John Locke, wrote the Fundamental Constitution of Carolina."

In 1669 when John Locke was asked to develop a constitution for the colony Carolina, Exeter House in the center of London was the official residence of Lord Ashley Cooper. It was a mansion with a considerable library and several large drawing rooms where Locke could spread out charts, books, and papers. It was at Exeter House that the Fundamental Orders [or Constitutions] of Carolina was written. Exeter House was a center of hubbub in 1669 for a number of reasons. The Great Fire of 1666 which had destroyed much of the city of London was still the topic of discussion as debris was being removed, and Sir Christopher Wren was being commissioned to rebuild many of the landmark Anglican churches. In 1669 when Locke was working on the first Carolina constitution, King Charles II was downright giddy about the prospects of the new Hudson Bay Company charter that was being worked up at Whitehall. The King's cousin, Prince Rupert of the Palatine, was being honored as the first director of the promising Hudson Bay Company in what is now the Hudson Bay area of Canada. In that time the area was named Prince Rupert Land. Then too, the Crown had commissioned Captain Henry Morgan of the British Navy to raid the Spanish port of Panama City on the Isthmus of Panama. In the midst of all of these doings, the royal family was dealing with the death of Henrietta Maria, mother of the King and widow of Charles I. Locke is to be forgiven if he erred a bit on the side of romanticism with his rather feudalistic political model for Carolina, for all around him were indications that Britain was developing into a great empire.

Turning to the archives in Whitehall, Locke pulled a copy of the palatinate that was in use for Durham, England -- then a frontier area with minimal oversight from London. In the Durham model, a "palatine," or frontier outpost, owed religious allegiance to the Bishop of London, owed taxes -- both ecclesiastical and civil--to the Exchequer in London, and swore allegiance to the Crown. In all other matters the palatinate was independent and able to settle its own affairs. That was Locke's template, and in all fairness, the template had already been used by Lord Baltimore for Maryland's governance.

Locke devised a complex scheme of feudalistic aristocracy based upon royal land grants to English commoners on good terms with church and state. As a way of preserving order and regularity in affairs, a small number of Landgraves owning 48,000 acres, Cassiques owning 24,000 acres, and Barons owning 12,000 acres were to preside over commoners known as leetmen. The commoners (male and Church of England communicants) possessing land of 150 acres were to be electors of a Commons Assembly. The hereditary nobility sat in the upper chamber and retained most of the power. Locke notably allowed a wide toleration for religious beliefs outside of the Church of England, and for that reason he is credited with being one of the fathers of the idea of religious toleration.

The Carolina colonists did not respect the Locke Constitution, nor did they buckle to the idea of an hereditary aristocracy. The Lords Proprietors lost control of their vast domain largely by entrusting the day-to-day management to appointed agents rather than assuming direct control. John Locke was one of the original Landgraves, as were the Proprietors and high-born men such as Edmund Bellinger, Thomas Ash, Edmund Andros, Daniel Axtell, Sr., and Joseph Blake. By 1700, however, the Fundamental Orders had been cast aside for a more practical and modern arrangement that anticipated America's growing distrust of oligarchy.

Today, John Locke is relegated to the study of our Declaration of Independence and the influence that his political writings, especially the 1690 Second Treatise on Government, had upon our founding fathers. Our local history would have been even richer had we incorporated something around here as a namesake for the great English philosopher and physician.

How a Group Called "The Inquiry" Shaped American History

"I always tried to turn every disaster into an opportunity," so said John D. Rockefeller, the Chairman of Standard Oil. Old man John D. Rockefeller, age 78, was not invited by President Woodrow Wilson to be a part of a secret committee in the winter of 1917-'18 to plan for the aftermath of World War I. Events might have turned out better if he had been included, for old "John D.," as the multimillionaire was called, was the "master of disaster" -- had dealt successfully with everything from huge oil derrick fires to the Ludlow Mining strike to the stock market panic of 1907. Wilson didn't call in the millionaire Rockefeller with his international connections because of Rockefeller's lifelong Republican party affiliation. Would the Paris Peace of 1919 have turned out differently if the crusty oil man had sat at that long table is a conjecture open only to dreamers? What is known is that Wilson's select group of intellectuals dubbed "The Inquiry" used the global disaster known as "The Great War" as their opportunity to redefine American economic and foreign policy.

Woodrow Wilson was no pacifist; however, he did campaign for re-election in 1916 as "the president who'd kept us out of war." Confusion still reigns over the two events that ultimately drew us into the War -- the sinking of the *R.M.S. Lusitania* and the Zimmerman Telegram. To date, those unprovoked catastrophes rank with the attack on Pearl Harbor and the Gulf of Tonkin incident in the list of unadulterated provocations. When the *Lusitania* went down, there were initial reports that the sinking was deliberate because of Albert L. Hopkins being aboard. Hopkins was president of the Newport News Shipbuilding facility that had laid the keels for so many of America's great battleships. Arthur Adams, president of U.S. Rubber Corporation, and Ogden Hammond, U.S. Ambassador to Spain, were mentioned as potential assassination targets; however, the international sportsman and philanthropist, Alfred Gwynne Vanderbilt, was not considered a target. Today there are dark conspiracy theorists at work who claim that Wilson advisor Edward M. House, a believer in one world government, actually coordinated the disaster to provoke an American response. No proof of House's culpability has been forthcoming, but Edward M. House was one of the members of Wilson's covert group, The Inquiry.

Aside from House, who were the members of Woodrow Wilson's brain trust for reshaping America's and the world's economy following the Great War? Now we know the men who composed The Inquiry were Paul Warburg, Herbert Hoover, Harold Temperley, Lionel Curtis, Lord Eustace Percy, Christian Herter, James Thomson Shotwell of Columbia University, Archibald Cary Coolidge of Harvard, and Charles Seymour of Yale. Herbert Hoover's republican credentials were not well honed in the winter of 1917.

Like all clandestine activities, The Inquiry needed an out-of-the-way place to meet and plan. It just so happened that way up on 155th Street in New York City, out near the Polo Grounds where in the future the New York Giants and the New York Mets would play, there's a collection of Beaux Arts buildings known as Audubon Terrace. The architecturally significant buildings dating from the turn of the century include the American Numismatic Society, the Museum of the American Indian-Heye Foundation, the Hispanic Society of America, the American Academy of Arts and Letters, and a Greek Orthodox Church. Tucked away on a corner is the headquarters of the American Geographical Society (A.G.S.). Isaiah Bowman, Ph.D., a Director of the A.G.S. and perhaps the leading geopolitical thinker in America, was a confidante of Woodrow Wilson. Bowman arranged for the members of The Inquiry to meet in one of the secluded board rooms of the A.G.S. building in Audubon Terrace. No one at all would be suspicious of the important-looking men with attache cases who came and went daily from December 1917, through the Spring of 1919. After all, the A.G.S. headquarters building was one of the most international sites in all of New York.

Paul Warburg was an immigrant to the United States coming from Hamburg, Germany, where his family owned the House of Warburg, one of the largest merchant banks in Germany. Warburg was a frequenter to New York where his family did business on Wall Street and sometimes allied with the firm of Kuhn, Loeb on the underwriting of railroads. Warburg married a daughter of Kuhn, Loeb investment firm's managing partner, Solomon Loeb. Within two years Paul Warburg entered Kuhn, Loeb in New York as a liaison with the family bank, M.M. Warburg of Hamburg. Paul Warburg was one of Woodrow Wilson's first picks for the group, and in many ways, Warburg was the key economic intellectual -- rivaling even John Maynard Keynes in England. Members came and went over twenty-four months; however, Warburg, Hoover, Percy, and Christian Herter stayed the course.

Warburg had been on the famous so-called "duck-hunt" on Jekyl Island in the winter of 1910 -- the clandestine gathering of financial elites who met under the guise of a sportsman's retreat, but in reality their purpose was to draw up the plans for a grand central bank for the U.S. that would be similar to the Bank of England. They used the name "Federal Reserve bank" as a less-threatening moniker to allay the suspicions of an already dubious and mistrusting American public. The Financial Panic of 1907 was, until 2008, the most perplexing of all the financial debacles. No one, not even John D. Rockefeller, saw it coming. Warburg was one of the few men alive who understood completely the notion of fractional banking theory then in play in Europe's central banks. The grand idea was seen as a panacea for smoothing banking operations in times of uncertainty.

Lionel Curtis was an Oxford-educated Brit who lectured widely in America on a theme of British Empire Federalism -- a continuation of the old Cecil Rhodes Cairo to Cape Town Axis idea that was rudely interrupted by the Boer War. Where did Wilson collect these zany characters that he allowed free rein to plan the grand scheme for the 20th century? Many of the Wilson intimates were acquaintances of Edward M. House, a wealthy, but mysterious man who hailed from Houston. Some said that House's money came from his father who had been a Confederate blockade runner. One bold rumor alleged that the elder House had been entrusted in 1865 with the gold from the Texas treasury -- that House was to take the gold to deposit in a London bank so that it could not be captured by the Federal army. The legend has it that the gold never made it to London. Whatever the case is, House never worked a day in his life, and he hobnobbed with the Rothchilds and the Astors and the Mellons. House became Wilson's most trusted advisor outside the cabinet, and it was House who had much input on the famed 14-point peace plan that Wilson took to Paris in 1919.

On the voyage over to France, Wilson's Secretary of State Robert Lansing had serious mistrust of the twenty-three idealists that Wilson's advisor Edward M. House insisted upon bringing along. Lansing had The Inquiry group on one of the lower decks of the *U.S.S. George Washington* while the State Department officials vied for Wilson's attention on the upper level. Once at Paris, House and unofficial advisors moved behind the scenes to manipulate the peace talks. Within a week both Lloyd-George of Britain and Clemenceau of France had seen enough of American idealism. Woodrow Wilson caught the influenza virus in Paris, and House began to run the American end of things. Meanwhile, American millionaires Andrew Carnegie and Henry Ford each launched their own international peace initiatives. The world began to think of Americans as too idealistic to enter the arena of international diplomacy.

Back home the old man, John D. Rockefeller, the millionaire who carried his lunch to work in a paper bag, sat idly by unheard. What difference he may have made if he'd been included in the legendary small group. Rockefeller had a different appreciation for Europe than did some of the other thinkers -- and "John D." drove a hard bargain on every board that he sat on. "The Inquiry" continued to meet off and on after the War and eventually grew into an elaborate think tank that today is known as the Council On Foreign Relations.

Did Wilson's White House Physician Exceed His Authority?

In the realm of confidentiality, hardly anything exceeds the patient / physician relationship. The physician's code of ethics is one of the most sacred trusts in our society. Yet, even that almost inviolable trust has its limits. When the doctor's patient is the President of the United States, there can be times when confidentiality and national security collide head-on. Such a situation existed in 1919 when President Woodrow Wilson collapsed with a stroke in Pueblo, Colorado, on September 25, 1919. He'd been campaigning for ratification of the controversial 1919 Peace Treaty. During the period of his convalescence presidential physician, Dr. Cary T. Grayson, withheld all details of the President's illness from Congress, cabinet, and the Vice-President. Together with the First Lady and presidential aide, Joe Tumulty, Grayson made political decisions for the stricken head of state. Wilson friend, Herbert Hoover, was also in on the secret.

Thomas Woodrow Wilson, known to his Princeton classmates as Tommy, earned a law degree and a Ph.D. in American Government before he was 30 years old -- so he knew by heart Section II, Article 1 of the Constitution. Among other things, Article I of Section II deals with what happens upon the incapacitation of a President. "In Case of the Removal of the President from Office, or of his Death, Resignation, or Inability to discharge the Powers and Duties of the said Office, the same shall devolve on the Vice President." As a former American Government professor at Bryn Mawr, Johns Hopkins, and Princeton, Wilson had quoted lengthy sections of the Constitution verbatim. Therefore, it was not a befuddled mind of Wilson, but rather, a desperate effort on the part of Wilson's wife and doctor to preserve the Wilson Peace Initiative-- the peace for the "war to end all wars." Dr. Cary Grayson displayed extraordinary resourcefulness in second-guessing the Commander-in-Chief's mind, but he was afoul of The Constitution and could have been subject to court-martialed if the truth had leaked to the press. Even 93 years later it is difficult to piece together what the President knowingly approved and what he did not approve in the period between October 1919 and February 1920. By all accounts, the President was incoherent, paralyzed on the left side of his body, and unable to recall much at all of what had been going on prior to his series of strokes.

Wilson may have been one of our smartest presidents, but he was never a crafty politician. His was an embattled presidency as he was a Democrat and both Houses of Congress were in the hands of Republicans. The leading Republican was Senator Henry Cabot Lodge, and he and Wilson were barely on speaking terms. At the behest of Colonel Edward M. House, a close advisor to Wilson on international affairs, no republican senator was invited to attend the 1919 Peace Conference in Paris. No Democrat senators were invited either, and that is very odd, because the Constitution mandates that the Senate ratify or reject all treaty proposals. Wilson's Peace Initiative was the most radical departure ever from traditional diplomacy. In Wilson's mind he was establishing a Monroe Doctrine type of arrangement for Europe. It was as if the old schoolmaster was the only one to comprehend the "grand fix" that'd insure world peace, and that was his 14 Point Peace Plan that brought into being the arbitration body known as the League of Nations. And he was desperate to see his plan through. Wife Edith Bolling Galt Wilson and Cary Grayson, M.D., carried out the sick man's commands and interpreted his wishes when he was not in touch with reality. Fortunately, neither Edith Wilson nor Dr. Grayson was a sinister character bent upon carrying on his own agenda. The pair of furtive operatives kept the President secluded and incommunicado with the rest of the government -- much to the consternation of Congress. Even more amazing is the fact that the two protectors denied access to Colonel Edward House -- the architect of the 14 Point Peace Plan -- the man who had maneuvered Woodrow Wilson into complete acceptance of both the League of Nations idea and the Federal Reserve central bank concept. The anti-Wilson faction rejoiced at the decline of House's influence.

What the First Lady and the President's physician did over the months of October, November, and December of 1919, and January and February of 1920, became a part of the rationale for the 25th Amendment (1967) that says in part that if two-thirds of Congress deems that the President is incapacitated and unfit to serve, then Congress may appoint the Vice-President to assume the duties of the Chief Executive until such time as the President may be able to resume his duties. Why it took Congress 47 years to amend the Constitution on this issue remains a mystery. This Amendment was in place by 1981 for the attempted Reagan assassination and it quickly clarified the confusing statement made by

Secretary of State Haig of "I'm in charge." Reagan's physician, Dr. Daniel Ruge did not occupy himself with any other matters than his patient's recovery.

Cary Grayson's career thus far had been a physician's dream. He had grown up on the old family plantation outside Culpepper, Virginia, just 60 miles from where Woodrow Wilson had been born two decades earlier in Staunton. The Graysons were direct descendants of Founding Father George Mason, one of the leading theorists of the U.S. Constitution. Grayson's father was a country doctor who tended to the needs of the rural folk and even some of the livestock within a 10-mile radius of Culpepper in the latter part of the 19th century. Grayson graduated Phi Beta Kappa from William and Mary and pursued the study of medicine and pharmacy simultaneously at the Medical College of Richmond and then at the University of the South at Sewanee. He was awarded both degrees and after what we would call a residency at Columbia Women's Hospital in Washington, Grayson did a second medical degree at the Medical College of Richmond, thus making him one of the most learned physicians of his time.

Eager to serve his country, Grayson volunteered for active duty in the Navy and served as surgeon aboard the heavy cruiser *U.S.S. Maryland*. Following that tour he applied for and received the appointment of crew physician for the presidential yacht *Mayflower* moored on the Potomac. The young doctor had occasion to treat Presidents Theodore Roosevelt and Howard Taft for minor illnesses. Being a dapper fellow and cutting a fine image in his naval uniform, the popular doctor was a frequent guest at White House parties, and it was in that capacity that he had the opportunity to do a medical favor for the sister of newly elected Woodrow Wilson in 1913 following a fall the lady had had at the White House.

Wilson took an instant liking to Grayson. Both men were Virginians of old stock, and both were Phi Beta Kappa scholars and shared common political ideals. The President bestowed rank on the young Grayson, advancing the 36-year-old Lieutenant to the rank of Rear Admiral--by-passing the usual progression. Grayson had spent time at the Bureau of Naval Medicine and had had a good rapport with his seniors, but "feathers were ruffled" at the abrupt, unprecedented jump in rank. Again, this promotion reflected poorly on Wilson's political judgment among insiders in both the Navy and the politicians in the Capital.

When the Great War was won and Germany signed the Wilson Armistice, Dr. Grayson was at Wilson's side, and sometimes this annoyed Colonel House, the foreign affairs advisor -- and it certainly annoyed Secretary of State, Robert Lansing, who was all but shut out of the serious negotiations in Paris. Wilson's refusal to bring Senate Majority Leader Henry Cabot Lodge into the loop of the deliberations has been ranked as one of the greatest political blunders ever committed by a sitting President. Scholars today still wonder at how a President could have been so learned in matters of government and history and, yet, so inept in the art of governing. Wilson's learning and his idealism have made him a byword for the faction that distrusts academicians in politics.

Cary Grayson did a serious surgical procedure on Wilson in early 1920 when he removed several polyps from inside the President's nose. No other attending physician was called in. The press was told that Wilson needed seclusion and quiet. Edith Wilson despised Wilson's Vice-President, Thomas R. Marshall, and forbade him access to any part of the White House. Marshall had opposed both our entry into the War and the 14 Point Peace Plan. Twice Marshall made inroads to have Congress install him as acting president, but Henry Cabot Lodge blocked these moves. It was to the Republican Party's advantage to have a stricken president as they organized the Senate's rejection of Wilson's grand Paris Peace scheme. They wanted no part of entangling alliances.

Grayson placed President Wilson in the back seat of his (Grayson's) personal automobile and sneaked him out of the White House to see an eye surgeon in Philadelphia. For a year and a half this bizarre episode dragged on, and Wilson's second term came to an end. Grayson eventually became the head of the American Red Cross. Wilson died in 1924, less than three years after leaving office. Dr. Grayson's personal papers have just recently been made available to historians.

Tragic Upstate School Fire Gave Us Fire Codes and Fire Drills in 1923

How quickly our heritage is slipping away. Each day the obituaries toll the passing of more souls of the "greatest generation." With each passing of these grand dames and gentlemen goes a pocket load of Carolina cultural lore that will never be known again. We in the Lowcountry almost missed this one -- the obituary notice [January 3, 2012] in *The State* newspaper of Pearl Godwin Tiller of McBee. One sentence in the brief death notice leaps from the small print and into the headlines -- "She was the last survivor of the Cleveland School Fire in Camden, SC."

If you've ever been annoyed by the shrill sound of a fire alarm and if you've ever been interrupted with one of those non-announced fire drills at school where everyone follows an orderly, prearranged exit from the building, then you can reflect upon the origin of all of that protocol now. Much of the school fire drill regimen we're used to came about because of a tragic school fire in Kershaw County on Thursday evening of May 17, 1923.

Cleveland School was located approximately 8 miles east of Camden, S.C., in what was known as the Sandy Mill community. The rural area was home to Davises, Dixons, Godwins Hendrixes, McCleods, McCaskills, Phillips, Sowells, Truesdales, and Wests. Many were of Scots-Irish descent and had roots in the region dating to pre-Revolutionary days when Camden was known simply as Pine Top. The father of former Governor John Carl West was one of the ones to perish in the awful fire that occurred when a lantern fell off a wall in the school auditorium and caught the stage curtain on fire.

For a number of years, a commencement play had been held at the Cleveland School, an institution named in honor of the first Democratic president since the War Between the States. In 1923 the upstairs auditorium was packed with an overflow crowd of nearly 300 people because this was the last event before the old building was to be torn down. The play that Thursday evening was

Topsy-Turvy, a comedy and there were expected to be lots of laughs before the curtain fell for the final time.

Sixteen-year-old Bertie Hendrix, daughter of William and Johanna Irene Hendrix, had the lead role, and tradition has it that she was to be the class valedictorian, as well. As the playgoers were becoming entranced in the unfolding comedy, a spotlight that was, in fact, a gas lantern suspended on a nail by the stage, suddenly dropped to the stage floor with a loud crash and flames spread across the floor to some bales of straw that were serving as a backdrop. Everyone, even the actors, remained calm as men from the front rows leaped to the stage to beat out the quickly spreading flames.

In the minute or so that it took to comprehend the seriousness of the event many theater-goers in the back started down the narrow, 30-inch-wide, stairwell which bottlenecked at a small landing before descending at right angles down another flight. Panic swept through the auditorium when the theater curtain burst into flames and wood from the heart pine flooring began to burn. Meanwhile, at the stair landing someone tripped and a pile up of bodies occurred with no way of warning the stampeders that there was a crush of bodies ahead of them. Someone flung open a window and leaped two floors to the hard earth below. Some opened a few more windows for others to jump, but the open windows fed oxygen into the already raging combustion and the result was a fireball that developed inside the heart pine second floor auditorium.

The year 1923 was not the "dark ages," and rural South Carolinians were especially alert to the dangers of fire. A 1915 school fire in Peabody, Massachusetts, a few miles west of Salem and Marblehead, killed 21 girls as fire swept through the multi-story building. The building had no fire escape; however, the Sisters who ran the Catholic school for girls routinely conducted fire drills. St. John School had made news in *The State* newspaper and on the radio, yet, no efforts were made nationwide to standardize firefighting or fire safety procedures.

A similar incident, though much deadlier, had occurred in 1908 in Collinwood, Ohio, when a school building caught fire and 172 students and teachers died. School superintendents around the land knew of these things, yet establishing a nationwide set of standards seemed beyond the scope of the times.

Fifty years had passed since Mrs. O'Leary's cow supposedly knocked over a lantern and set all of Chicago ablaze in 1871. Banjo pickers and pianists plucked out the tune of "It'll Be A Hot Time In The Old Town Tonight," at every political rally, and the newest line of business in nearby Camden was the property and casualty insurance agency. San Francisco erupted into flames in 1909 as gas lines broke during the 7.9 magnitude earthquake and 450 people died as a result of the flames and smoke inhalation -- almost double the number that had died in the Chicago fire. Various fires in commercial districts throughout the northeast dramatized the need to standardize fire hose and fire hydrant couplings so that various fire fighting units could use hydrants with universal fittings, and sprinklers were coming into use in high rise buildings in New York after the terrible 1911 fire at the Triangle Shirtwaist Company where so many young female seamstresses leapt to their death. Henry Parmalee of New Haven had developed a sprinkler system for commercial buildings, but it did not become a part of very many fire prevention plans until the Triangle fire.

News of the Cleveland School fire spread across America almost as quickly as the flames had caught fire to the stage curtains. The Detroit *Free Press* used the story as its lead on the front page for Saturday, May 19, 1923. "Toll of Death in School Fire Mounts to 76: Victims of South Carolina tragedy are buried in one huge grave," says the bold print. A country music singer recorded a song about the Cleveland School fire, and it made the rounds on radio stations. More importantly, legislators, city council members, and school boards across the land were motivated to make improvements in fire safety. Nothing came overnight; however, within a decade all schools mandated fire drills, safe occupancy number limitations, marked and lighted exits, and routine fire marshal inspections. Firefighters swapped information and learned from each other across the region. Fire escape plans and fire escape ladders became standard fixtures in schools.

A website entitled "Walking with Ghosts -- a website for the descendants of Angus and Nancy McCutchen MacLeod," has lovingly preserved the memory of so many of the victims as well as quite a few of the survivors. It has been said that this school fire is, to date, our state's single worst tragedy as far as death toll is concerned. To compare, the crash of Eastern Airlines Flight 212 in Charlotte in 1974 claimed 74 lives, most of whom were South Carolinians.

As the fire swept across the stage, Charlie Hendrix, age 52, the father of Bertie Hendrix, the 16-year-old star of the show, guided others to safety and returned to the blaze to search for his daughter. The second floor was buckling and appeared ready to plunge into the ground floor as Hendrix started back up. A man tried to hold Charlie Hendrix back, but he said, "I must find Bertie." Bertie Hendrix was an only child and the pride of the entire community. "You'll never make it back!" shouted the bystander. "Then watch me die with her," came Hendrix' reply. Father's and daughter's remains were indeed found close together in the smoldering ashes. The fire had been so hot that even the nails and metal fixtures had melted. Many of the dead were unidentifiable, and all were buried in a common grave at Beulah United Methodist Church just a mile away.

The passing of 93-year-year-old Pearl Godwin Tiller of McBee is the end of the era where eyewitnesses kept the memory alive. She was a 5-year-old child and lost a relative, probably a sister, named Mary Lyne Godwin, in the fire. Think on these things the next time a fire drill interrupts your day or the red glare of an exit light distracts you at a theater.

Ex-Slave Harriet Tubman Led Union Raid on the Combahee in 1863

Driving south on U.S.-17 is pure excitement for history lovers. Well, one does have to be "in the know," for very little of the history is marked. However, for those who care to read the treasured lore of the Lowcountry -- or even tap a few keys on the compuber keyboard -- a whole new world opens up in front of you -- a world of "what once was" replaces battered buildings and abandoned gas stations. So rich in history is this stretch of road leading through Jacksonboro, Poco Sabo, Green Pond, Ashepoo, Pocotaligo, and eventually on to Savannah, that one can revel in a half-dozen historical periods along the route. There's colonial history aplenty. In 1739 runaway slaves from the Stono Rebellion fled through swamps and woodland paralleling this road. Four decades later, Francis Marion's brilliant ambush of the British at Parker's Ferry occurred just off this road on State Road S-1038. South Carolina's Patriot assembly re-established the state government in 1782 in Jacksonboro as the British evacuated Charleston. Eighty years later, Confederate and Union military operations were so numerous through this area that there's probably not enough bronze in the country to make highway markers. There is one story, however, so unusual that it deserves retelling. One of the most unusual historical episodes to take place on Highway 17-South features Harriet Tubman, an ex-slave woman, who guided Union forces on a daring raid up the Combahee River on June 2, 1863. When the time comes to sound off on the theme of American heroines, Harriet Tubman's name will resound, for she, more than any other female in the War between the States, faced danger and changed the course of history. Like Wolfe Tone of Ireland or Joan of Arc to the people of Lorraine, the ex-slave Harriet Tubman emboldened her people. Tubman was the "Mistress of the Underground Railroad" before the War broke out, and she was the "Moses" who liberated hundreds of slaves during the War.

Slaves seldom knew the particulars of their birth or even the whereabouts of their siblings. Slave families were separated, sold, traded, or sent off as collateral. The most famous liberated slave woman in our history figured that she was born sometime between 1819 and 1825. Araminta (Minty) Harriet Ross was the name that appeared on the official slave records, but in freedom she was known as Harriet Tubman. Her youth was spent on the middling-sized Brodess farm in Dorchester County, Maryland, a protrusion of land that is bounded on three sides by the Chesapeake Bay. One of Tubman's earliest memories was of her mama threatening to kill a slave trader who approached young Harriet one day on the farm. When excessive cruelty in the form of lashings and a life-threatening concussion led her to concoct an elaborate escape plan, Harriet's one regret in 1849 was that she had to act alone in order to be successful.

Moving stealthily by night and lying still in the woods during the day; Harriet soon reached the Mason-Dixon Line and entered the free state of Pennsylvania. Eventually, she made her way to Philadelphia. Tubman's insolence from her injustices resulted in her being assigned heavy work with the men. She hauled logs and worked mule teams rather than tending pots and ovens. The endurance and brute strength came in handy when she decided to return to Maryland to sneak some of her relatives out of bondage.

It was the Fugitive Slave Law that became the catalyst for Tubman's inspiration to liberate slaves through what was already being called "the underground railroad," a network of paths, swamp trails, safe houses, and out-of-the-way river crossings that facilitated black fugitives who were bold enough to undertake the extremely risky venture of "slipping away" from the overseer's notice. Harriet Tubman claims to have had visions where God told her to lead her people from bondage. She was deeply religious and had been brought up Christian through the devotions and fervent prayers of her mama.

Of rough features and possessing a head of coarse, unruly hair that had never known a brush or comb, this simple black woman moved about with an ambling gait when it suited her purpose to blend in -- and she could be swift as a deer when she had to elude pursuers. Those that knew her said that Tubman had an uncanny sense of danger and that she could maneuver in the forests and swamps as stealthily as an Indian. That she was cunning and bold is not doubted. However, no one really knows how much education she possessed. Her admirers and acquaintances, the elites of the New England abolition movement, bear testimony to her intellect.

The extreme unpopularity in the North of the Fugitive Slave Law catapulted Harriet Tubman into near celebrity status. With her homespun wear and ways she resonated well with the Old Puritan ideals of New England. The cadence and rhythm of her speech was straight from the cotton field, yet she conversed on equal terms with Cabots and Lodges, Beechers and Stowes, and Goulds and Shaws. Long, fervent public prayers convinced devout Congregationalists that this woman was a prophetess such as the ancient Hebrews had when they labored in bondage under the Pharaohs. Frederick Douglass admired Tubman and gained much of his insight into the evils of slavery from her direct experience. What few people knew about Harriet Tubman, however, was the extent of her covert activities. Most would have been amazed if they'd known that she packed a pistol beneath her flowing skirt and navigated dangerous swamps at night by using the North Star.

The passing of fifteen decades has allowed myth and legend to cloud the facts of Tubman's exploits. Federal authorities purposely omitted all references of her name from official records -- probably to protect her in the event of her capture by irate Confederates. It is a proven fact that Tubman picked some of John Brown's Harper's Ferry raiders. One story still in need of verification has Harriet making a bold foray almost to the Carolina coast to lead a file of runaways to safety. That particular story has the wily insurgent fording the Ashley River just below Bacon's Bridge. She was like a phantom. She left no trail for her pursuers, and she boasted of never losing a soul on "their night flight to the Promised Land."

When the Union Army under General David Hunter reached 50,000 men in the Fall of 1862 and the Union blockade had closed Savannah and Charleston to the Confederates, then, and only then, did they begin to make forays north and west from their Hilton Head and Beaufort encampments. Lincoln was plagued by the timidity of McClellan on the Peninsula and Hunter on the Carolina coast. Only Grant in the West appeared to be decisive in his tactics. Even so, Grant paid dearly for his victories as steel met steel and blood flowed freely from Southern defenders such as Beauregard, Hood, Bragg, Forrest, and the two Johnstons -- Joseph and Albert Sidney.

On orders from Washington, General Hunter cautiously began to feel his way up the estuaries that flow southeast toward Beaufort. One of the purposes of the river raids of Spring and Summer of 1863 was to deny the South the rice, cotton, grain, and hams of the region. Another purpose was to cut the rail links between Charleston and Georgia. Yet another purpose was to give newly recruited Black Union regiments some experience in the field and under fire. Liberation of slaves was considered a purpose of the raid, but, in actuality, liberation was a necessary evil in the eyes of many of the Union commanders. It brought them more problems than it solved.

Just who came up with the idea that Harriet Tubman would be the military scout operating independently, but coordinating with Union Colonels Higgenson and Montgomery, is unknown due to scant records. The Black 54th Massachusetts Regiment recruited in the Boston area was one of the units that Tubman scouted for. She had met the dashing, young Colonel Robert Gould Shaw a few years earlier in Boston. Tubman had stood with Governor Andrews of Massachusetts when the 54th was presented its regimental colors prior to departing for duty in South Carolina.

Tubman knew the objectives of the Union army on the Combahee expedition, and she led troops to unguarded crossings of the rivers and through shortcuts that by-passed well-patrolled rice fields. Little Confederate opposition was met with, and to Harriet's delight, over 700 fugitive slaves met her along the Combahee at various crossings to flee with the army to safety. A special tent city called Mitchellville was set up to tend to the newly liberated families. Harriet Tubman stayed a while with these grateful men and women and helped to organize them into domestic units where literacy, hygiene, and citizenship could be taught by the northern missionaries that were coming in by the boatload to Beaufort.

In later years Harriet Tubman was active in women's suffrage and in the development of retirement homes for elderly blacks and for sanitariums for the mentally ill. A bridge over the Combahee River has been named in her honor. Even *Liberty* ship was named for her in 1944. Her people were brought here from Ghana; therefore, she was most likely descended from the Ashanti people of that region. The Ashanti are matriarchal to this day and are known for their strong and capable women. Booker T. Washington eulogized Harriet Tubman when she died, and Dr. Martin Luther King often made reference to her great moral courage.

Saluting the Palatines' 300 Years in South Carolina

One of the more sensible minds to come out of the early 20th century was Gustav Stresemann, the Chancellor of the Weimar Republic. "Just as the British subject loves England despite her faults, so we must insist that all Germans who were part of the old Germany and helped shape her, recognize the greatness and worthiness of present-day Germany," declared Stresemann in his acceptance speech for the 1926 Nobel Peace Prize. On that stately occasion the world needed reassuring that Germans were safe bets for citizenship after the Kaiser's bloody romp across Belgium and France.

South Carolinians, on the other hand, have never needed reassuring that the Deutschlanders are handy folks to have as neighbors. It's been 300 years since the arrival here of the first wave of "Palatines," as German-speaking people were referred to in colonial times. The Palitinate was the 18th century designation for the West-Franconian dialect of the Rhine Valley, especially Baden-Wurttemberg near the Swiss border. Many of the colonials here with German surnames stole away from the bonds of serfdom in the Wurttemburg area or one of the German-speaking cantons of Switzerland such as Lucerne, Thurgau, or Zurich. Seeking political and economic freedom, these fugitives paddled down the Rhine to Rotterdam. From there they made it to London. However, soon after arrival the Catholics -- Papists -- as Londoners disdainfully labelled them -- were identified and shipped back to their irate overlords.

East London's Spittalfields in 1710 became a maze of hovels from whence throngs of once-proud men sought alms from the Anglican Church or performed menial of tasks for a few pence. They were safe, for the moment, from conscription into some German Duke's army to be used as cannon fodder in the War of Spanish Succession. Free, too, they were from the dozen or more taxes imposed upon serfs. Yet, in Britain, a debate simmered in Parliament between Whigs and Tories as to the future of the German settlement on the outskirts of London. Within four years Britain would have a German-born king, George

I of Hanover, and Germans would be viewed in a different light, but in 1710, the Tories were for shutting off immigration and expelling the ones that were already there. On the other hand, the Whigs argued for leniency for German immigrants. Whigs saw them as cheap and useful labor for the emerging tide of industrialism. From thence, the immigrants embraced Whig middle-class values -- land ownership, commerce, and protestantism. They had a healthy disdain for royalty and aristocracy.

When the Provincial Assembly in Charleston appealed to the Crown for more settlers to serve as a buffer between the Cherokee and the coast, the convenient solution was to make passage over here affordable to the "Palatines." In a clever political stroke, King George I's government solved two problems -- it cleared out Spittalfields, and it secured the Carolina frontier from savage Indian raids. An unexpected dividend of bringing in hundreds of German-speaking families from Wurttemburg and the nearby Swiss cantons was that these people were industrious, and many possessed skills such as wine making or carpentry. Already, the backcountry of Carolina was teeming with some of the lower elements of Irish and Scottish society. It was felt that German influence would quickly establish orderliness.

The first great wave of German-speaking people came in through the port of Charleston, and the ones who were not indentured servants received land grants between the Edisto and the Saluda Rivers in the central part of the colony. New names began showing up on land deeds - Wannamaker, Geiger, Dantzler, Whetstone, Rumph, Miller, and Zimmerman, to name a few. The Edisto was not the Rhine, for sure, but the fertile soil, mild climate, and the relaxed government of the Colonial Assembly in Charleston made up for their desertion of the Fatherland.

Soon new roads were cut through the backwoods, grist mills sprang up around mill ponds, and the Reverend John Gissendanner rode a 500-mile circuit to take the Lutheran gospel to these German and Swiss-German settlers. By 1740 the word had spread throughout the old country that Saxe Gotha at the fork of the Congaree and the Broad Rivers was a new Germany in a New World.

Arriving here in 1747 as an indentured servant was Former Wurttemburg native Michael Kalteisen. Prominent men from the coast to the piedmont were seeking new sources of wealth. In *South Carolina, A History* by Walter Edgar (c.1998), we learn that 300,000 oranges had been shipped the year before, but a hard freeze had killed most of the crop in '47. Alexander Garden, William Bull, Henry Laurens, and Hector Berringer de Beaufain experimented with everything from olives to iron ore mining to mahogany as a potential export for Carolina. Into this hotbed of entrepreneurism came 18-year-old Kalteisen.

Kalteisen's American years, which spanned 60 of his 78 total, are exemplary of the German immigrant to this country. That these people were industrious, efficient, and frugal was an understatement. The correspondence of Governor William Bull to George II's colonial minister, Lord Hillsdale, reveals concerns that recent English immigrants to the Carolina backcountry descended quickly into a depraved condition -- an opinion concurred by Anglican itinerant clergyman, Charles Woodmason who rode the religious circuit between the PeeDee and the Congaree Rivers.

Upon completion of his indenture in the mid-1750s, Michael Kalteisen applied for and received 50 acres on Indian Creek between the Saluda and Congaree Rivers -- a site thought to be in the Irmo area today. Within ten years Kalteisen had amassed over 2000 acres in the colony, a spacious home that he and his wife turned into a wayfarer's inn, and he operated a mule train between Charleston and the settlements of the upstate. Whig politics continued to appeal to the German-speaking interests in Carolina -- wealth accumulation, the people's control of the Assembly and tax matters, and a healthy contempt for royalty. Michael Kalteisen was an early proponent of independence, and he was a key man in the Quartermaster Corps of the Patriot cause here.

In the 1760s Kalteisen's prominence in both Charleston and the Upcountry made him an important link in subverting loyalist tendencies north of Charleston and west of the Santee. He was elected to both Provincial Assemblies in the mid-1770s and was awarded a captain's commission so that he could coordinate the logistics of war materiel from the fork of the Saluda and the Congaree down to the Coast. Kalteisen was an intermediary for German Whigs in their struggle against the Tories in the center of the State. Jacob Rumph of Orangeburg was one of those German-speaking immigrants who was also in the mule-team trade. Rumph raised a Whig Militia to dampen the ardor of the Loyalists in the Edisto area -- many of whom were of Scot, Irish, or English descent. The 120-mile stretch between the Edisto and the Pacolet Rivers became one of the bloodiest bushwacking feuds in American history, especially in the 1780-1782 period of the Revolution. In some respects the mini-war in this vast backwoods area was a German versus Scots-Irish affair with the Germans aligned on the Patriot side and the Scots-Irish remaining loyal to the Crown.

Bloodletting on both sides of the partisan divide left ugly scars in the center of the State with some hard feelings descending to the present. Jacob Rumph operated as a "Swampfox" type of guerilla warfare leader, boasting that he took no prisoners. In fact, he did take prisoners, but they soon swung from an oak tree on his farm five miles above Orangeburg. Rumph's nemesis who often impeded the Whig wagon trains of supplies going to Quartermaster Kalteisen in Chaleston was "Bloody Bill" Cunningham and his lieutenant, William Parker. The tales of violence and gore that these men brought to the Upcountry are equalled only in the ferocity of heartless revenge sought by Rumph's militia. Assassinations, house and barn arson, livestock slaughtering, and the violation of women and the elderly were common depredations inflicted upon each side in the 24-months from 1781 - 1782 that finally culminated in the Patriot victory and independence from Britain.

Rumph's men killed William Parker. Cunningham's men killed Rumph's lieutenant, Henry Felder. Legend has it that Bill Cunningham escaped with the departing British fleet and that he was awarded land on a Caribbean island as payback for his loyalist support. Jacob Rumph became a general of militia while Michael Kalteisen gained lasting statue in the Charleston area as a founder of St. John's Lutheran Church and the German Friendly Society. He was serving as colonel and commanding officer of Fort Johnson when he died in 1807. There is no denying that the War of Independence in the Carolina Upcountry would have gone much differently had not the German-speaking element stood with the Whigs for independence. We celebrate 300 years of German heritage in South Carolina.

The Luces of Mepkin Were No Ordinary Couple

Simple, but elegant was the way that Clare Boothe Luce ordered her surroundings. The second wife of *Time-Life* publisher Henry R. Luce was mistress of a 59-acre estate in Stamford, Connecticut, and a 7,000 acre plantation in South Carolina. Her personal stationery was embossed with only "The House" for the Connecticut property and "Mepkin" for the Carolina place. Enough said -- for the receipt of a billet-doux from Mme. Luce incited scenes of cozy gatherings of well-heeled New Yorkers mixing with up-and-coming authors and Broadway stars.

The Luces never used Mepkin Plantation for anything more than an occasional getaway; however, the Cooper River, framed by moss-draped oaks at sunset, made such a powerful impression upon both Clare Boothe and Henry that they arranged for Mepkin to be their final resting place. In her heyday, 1935 to 1955, Clare Boothe's Buick Roadmaster could be spotted raising a cloud of dust and running flat out on the dirt roads from Mepkin to Cordesville to Huger and Awendaw on up US-17-N toward Georgetown. Of course, her only reason for going up there was that Hobcaw Barony on Cat Island was the Lowcountry retreat of her confidante, Bernard Baruch. FDR once quipped to a friend after overhearing an anti-New Deal remark from Mrs. Luce that pretty Clare Booth was "Bernie's girl." Whether true, or not, both Clare Boothe and Henry Luce had "a past" prior to their 1935 nuptials.

Rockaway Beach, 1903, was the site of infant Clare's nativity. Her mother was an unmarried chorus girl saddled with a baby from a tryst gone wrong. Hell's Kitchen, or Midtown West near the Hudson, was the shabby childhood neighborhood of this little girl who'd grown up to charm powerful men and antagonize the dames of "Mrs. Astor's 400" -- New York's WASP-ish elites. The who's who list skips any mention of Luce -- going from Mrs Maturin Livingston [jr] to Miss Lusk. The man who made the difference and paved the way for the budding beauty's social climbing was Clare's stepfather, Albert E. Austin, M.D., of Connecticut. He provided money for boarding school in Tarrytown and an understudy arrangement with Mary Pickford for her on Broadway. By then Clare

Boothe was one of the prettiest and most flirtatious girls in New York City. She'd attracted the notice of the Wall Street tycoon, Bernard Baruch, as well as several leading actors on Broadway. It was, however, attorney George Tuttle Brokaw, a millionaire, who resided at 1 East 79th Street in Manhattan, who first won pretty Clare's hand in marriage. From age 16, the "drenchingly beautiful" blue-eyed blonde Clare Boothe, had been elevated to the life of a princess destined to rule men and kingdoms.

George Tuttle Brokaw's father had been the wealthiest man in New York City a generation earlier. He'd presided over the cloth importing firm of Wilson G. Hunt & Company. It had been the elder Brokaw who'd built the elegant mansion on the corner of 5th Avenue and East 79th Street just across from Central Park. The grand house was built in the French chateau style popular among the nouveau riche at the turn of the century in the northeast. Chateau de Chenonceau near village of Chenonceaux in the Loire Valley, was the inspiration for this magnificent New York mansion that 20-year-old Clare Boothe presided over as the bride of George Tuttle Brokaw. Regrettably, the marriage was not a happy one. Claire spent his money and he spent his time elsewhere. One child, Ann, was born to this ill-fated union, and, on the eve of the Great Stock Market Crash in 1929, the couple was granted a divorce. George Brokaw soon married Francis Ford Seymour, who, upon George's death in 1935, married Henry Fonda. She became the mother of Henry Fonda, Jr. and Jane. These details are pertinent to show that absolutely nothing about Clare Boothe Luce's life was mundane.

Claire Boothe Brokaw was talented in her own right, and she was tapped to be managing editor of Conde-Nast's *Vanity Fair* magazine when she was 29 years old.

She staked out a cocktail party where she knew Henry Luce, the founder of *Time- Life*, would be attending and she made her move. As Henry was returning to his table with two glasses of champagne, one for himself and one for his wife, the pretty and demure Clare looked up from where she sat alone and said, "Oh, Mr. Luce, did you bring me a glass of champagne?" Two hours later Henry Luce left her table to return to his chagrinned wife. The next night Henry Luce had dinner in Clare Boothe's apartment.

Like Clare, Henry was no stranger to the upper rungs of the social ladder. Like Clare, he had known the more humble side as he'd been the son of Presbyterian missionaries in China. His stern, Calvinistic father had scraped to send him to Hotchkiss boarding school and, from there, to Yale. While at Hotchkiss, Henry palled around with Briton Hadden. Hadden was somewhat of a child genius when it came to writing -- he edited the Hotchkiss campus newspaper as well as the Yale daily paper, and he'd co-founded *Time* magazine with Luce. While the two young men were on ROTC training at Camp (later Fort) Jackson near Columbia, S.C., in 1918, Hadden envisioned a weekly magazine that'd explain complex world affairs in a way that everyday folks could comprehend. It was Hadden who developed the new "Timestyle" literary form of writing that came to dominate journalism in the 20th century. Hadden developed strep throat and died in 1929, just about the time that Clare Boothe was getting a divorce from Brokaw. The stars were aligning for Henry Luce. Though Hadden left his mother his 49% share of the fledgling Time-Life Corporate stock, Henry Luce managed to gain control of it, and from that time on, Luce seldom mentioned Hadden's role in the magazine venture. When Henry Luce finally got his divorce from wife number one and married young Clare Boothe, the creative sparks began to fly. He boasted that the idea of *Sports Illustrated* came to him while honeymooning in Havana. Clare claimed it was her idea! She turned her hand to being a playwright and her first effort, *The Women* (1936), debuted on Broadway and ran for 625 nights before becoming a film. The plot arose from an overheard conversation among society women in the ladies' room of the Waldorf-Astoria. Tart and acid-tongued, the cast had 44 women and no males. *Time* magazine labeled the theatrical debut as Clare Boothe Luce's "Little Kettle of Venom."

Shortly after Luce married Clare Boothe, their bookkeeper questioned a bill from one of Mrs. Luce's shopping sprees. A ticket for $7000 in lingerie ($109,000 in today's currency) seemed outrageous. A nonchalant Clare responded petulantly, "Well, are we wealthy, or are we not?" Henry instructed that the bill be paid. Likewise, it was Clare who wanted to purchase a plantation near Bernard Baruch's Belle Isle near Georgetown. Mepkin was for sale and the Luces paid $150,000, an amount equal to $2.3 million today. The plantation was purchased simultaneously with a box at the Metropolitan Opera House in New York. With these purchases, the social life of the Luces improved dramatically.

Retreating from the city to the rural splendor offered at Mepkin was not only a respite from producing issue after issue of *Time, Life, Fortune*, and the other magazines under the Time, Life banner, but it also gave the Luces an opportunity to hobnob with other grandees on an historic southern shooting plantation. Secretary of the Navy, James Forrestal, came down in the mid-1930s to shoot duck and talk about the publishing industry. Forrestal had been editor of the *Daily Princetonian* while in college.

There was a constant turnover of "the help" at Mepkin while the Luces owned the place. Henry said that they never could acquire good help at either of their estates, and he blamed FDR's New Deal "giveaways." Guests that accompanied them noted that Henry was often abrupt with the staff and, worse yet, that Clare was sarcastic. Then, too, there were arguments that sometimes punctuated the dinner hour. At one such dispute between the two Luces seated at opposite ends on a long table, Henry challenged a statement that Clare had made and questioned her sharply in front of the guests. He concluded by telling her to bet him one-million dollars. The stunned guests watched as Clare gave Henry the interminably long, icy stare.

In 1949 a vacationing Henry Luce read in the *News and Courier* that evangelist Billy Graham was going to be in Columbia speaking at a crusade. Luce, who was usually chauffeured, insisted upon driving to Columbia. The couple managed to get Governor Strom Thurmond and his young bride, Jean, to accompany them. Luce finagled Graham to come back to the Governor's mansion for a long discussion on the declining morals of the country. The story in *Time* started a lengthy debate on moral decay in the post-war era. This national dialogue was exactly what Luce had envisioned when he started the magazine more than a decade earlier. Publicity from the article helped spread Billy Graham's fame across the nation. The fact that a highway patrolman nearly arrested Henry Luce for reckless driving in Calhoun County on the couple's way back to Mepkin was not mentioned in the epic piece on Billy Graham. Clare Boothe Luce, the retired editor, playwright, Congress woman, socialite and philanthropist, willed a central portion of Mepkin to the Catholic Church, and today the magnificent estate belongs to the Trappist Monks. Henry and Clare Boothe Luce are interred there, as are other members of their family.

South Carolina Native Was *Life* Magazine's Founding Editor

When Henry Luce formed Time, Life, Inc. in 1936, a wiseacre said, *Life* magazine is for those who can read, but can't think. *Life* magazine is for those who can't read or think." Nothing could have been further from the truth, for *Time* was the first to broach the philosophies of existentialism and Keynesianism to the general public, and *Life* produced a photographic record so complete that it could be subtitled, "The American Century." Illustrators such as Charles Dana Gibson and Norman Rockwell left indelible impressions upon the 13 million weekly subscribers that *Life* enjoyed during its heyday from 1936 to 1976. By the 1980s television had catapulted video journalism beyond the reach of the print media. Gone are the iconic Gibson Girls of the golden age of print advertising and gone are the heartwarming Rockwell scenes of Americana. Few folks remember that *Time* magazine was under the able leadership of a native South Carolinian, John Shaw Billings -- the great grandson of secessionist, James Hammond.

Time, Life, Inc. would have had a field day if it had existed in March of 1858 when James Hammond, the South Carolinian successor to John C. Calhoun's secessionist rhetoric, made his inflammatory "Mudsill" speech. "In all social systems there must be a class to do the menial duties, to perform the drudgery of life. That is, a class requiring but a low order of intellect and but little skill. Its requisites are vigor, docility, fidelity. Such a class you must have, or you would not have that other class which leads progress, civilization, and refinement." Hammond referred to slavery as essential to the Southern economy. The Northern press went on a tirade as southerners galvanized around Hammond's theory.

Irony of ironies is that arch secessionist James Hammond's granddaughter, Katherine Fitzsimmons Hammond, daughter of James Henry (Harry) Hammond fell in love with and married a Yankee -- John S. Billings. That granddaughter -- Katherine -- was born nearly 4 years after her famous grandfather had gone to his eternal reward, but the old Hammond plantation, Redcliffe on Beech Island near Augusta, played a central role in her life and in that of her famous son, John Shaw Billings, the long time managing editor of *Life* magazine.

When Katherine Hammond married Doctor J.S. Billings at her ancestral home, Redcliffe, she well knew the life that she was getting herself into. Her father, Harry Hammond, had gone away to school prior to the War Between the States, first at Harvard and then at the University of Pennsylvania, and he pushed Katherine into pursuing a nursing degree at Johns Hopkins in Baltimore. It was at Johns Hopkins that the beautiful southern belle met her beau -- she a homesick student and he a handsome medical student. John S. Billings, M.D., became renown in medical circles over the next three decades. He taught at Harvard and Johns Hopkins' medical schools, and upon retirement, the doctor became the head librarian of the famed New York Public Library. Doctor Billings and Katherine Hammond Billings produced three male offspring, the most remembered was John Shaw Billings, born May 11, 1898, at the Hammond family plantation, Redcliffe.

Katherine Hammond Billings consented to rearing her three sons in New York, but she demanded that the family vacations center around Redcliffe, the 2,700 acre plantation located near the Savannah River. At Redcliffe, John Billings, the boy who'd grow up to be managing editor of *Time* and founding editor of *Life* magazine, learned to catch bream and eat southern delicacies such as grits and okra soup. The young Billings, despite his southern birth, was a true product of the "up east" boarding schools -- Repton and St. Paul's. It was in these hallowed halls of privilege that John Billings drew his inspiration from the grammarians rather than the dissection lab. Like his future boss, Henry Luce, John Billings wrote prose and verse for his school newspaper. At St. Paul's School in Concord, New Hampshire, Billings associated with Anthony Joseph Drexel Biddle, Jr., the future diplomat who served as ambassador to eight different countries. Getting accepted at Harvard was not a problem for boys coming out of St. Paul's School.

For the man who'd aid Henry Luce in establishing the TimeStyle form of journalism, John Billings was not an enthusiastic student at Harvard. As did Henry Adams before him, Billings complained that Harvard lacked imagination and creativity in its curriculum. Even before the Great War lured America into aiding France, John Billings and a number of his classmates left their classwork to volunteer. For Billings it was the Ambulance Corps that appealed to him. A number of Harvard boys, including Alan Seeger, Victor Chapman, Harvey Cushing, George Benet, Richard Norton, and Waldo Pierce, went over to France prior to America's involvement. Their stories in letters home played a role in the Wilson propaganda campaign to get America into the War.

With no wounds and no medals, Army Private Billings returned to his college studies, but for a chap who'd seen some of the world, Harvard no longer held any allure. John Billings quit the University one semester shy of his classics diploma and embarked on a newspaper career with the Brooklyn *Daily Eagle.* Thirty dollars a week was a lot of money in 1920. *Time* magazine editor John Martin met Billings at a Washington, D.C. restaurant and invited him to come work at the foreign news desk of *Time*. In New York John Billings met Time cofounder, Henry Luce, and the two hit it off immediately with their staunch Republican Party politics. Luce and Billings, approximately the same age, admired each other's work ethic, and they shared the vision that a bold, new journalistic form could arise from America's postwar thirst for national and international news. Luce admired the low-key nature of Billings for he, Luce, had a tendency to be overbearing and even rude to co-workers.

During the Republican administrations of Coolidge and Hoover, John Shaw Billings honed his writing and editing skills. When Hoover' s presidency collapsed under the weight of the Great Depression, John Shaw Billings was not kind to Franklin Roosevelt's New Deal ideas, and soon, Henry Luce and Billings were on the Democrat's "watch list." In 1934, Henry Luce made the tall, handsome South Carolina native managing editor of *Time* magazine while he, Luce, devoted all of his attention to developing *Time magazine*. In 1936 the *Life* project was floundering, in part because of Henry Luce's heavy-handed manner with the staff. Partly out of desperation Luce called Billings and asked him to take over as managing editor of *Life,* and the rest is the stuff of journalistic legend. Of course, John Billings protested, and of course, Luce dangled a huge salary of $25,000 a year.

The terrible dust bowl in the Midwest and the Tennessee Valley Authority mammoth hydroelectric project beckoned a bevy of young *Life* photographers and journalists. The latest film developing techniques made black and white photographic a stark and very realistic means for capturing the bleakness of the Great Depression. The old adage that a "picture is worth a thousand words," was never more true than when one flipped the pages of *Life* Magazine. The story of the twentieth century is literally punctuated with the iconic photos that appeared on the cover of *Life*. From the soup lines of the unemployed to the sailor kissing the girl on the New York street when the news of V-E day was announced, from the inauguration of John Kennedy to the lunar space landing, *Life* magazine held Americans in awe of the power of the print media. At its height, John Shaw Billings saw *Life* subscriptions top 13 million a week.

Billings and his wife, Fredericka Wade, daughter of the chief justice of the Georgia Supreme Court, were wealthy enough to buy Redcliffe Plantation from the estate of his aunt Julia. In his papers that he donated to the Thomas Cooper Library of the University of South Carolina, we learn that John Shaw Billings, one of America's great journalists, liked trains and railroads, the actress Shirley Temple, and pretty girls. He disliked Native Americans, South Americans, New Dealers, and refugees. Upon his death in 1975, Redcliffe Plantation, ancestral home of the Hammonds, became a state park and historical site.

Urban Graffiti: Criminal Act or Pop Art?

"Bozo Texino bumped Sumo's slap-tag off the bridge ramp. Wallbangin' Spatz jacked Mongo's tribe stamp with a Bad Seedz patch. Radz is gonna get up tonight if the whoadies keep po-po occupotty." If you understand any part of this hip street talk, then you're deep enough in hip-hop and gangland culture to get a bachelor's in epigraphology. While urban graffiti in Charleston has not reached the scale of L.A. or New York, it's definitely on the rise. A controversy brewing in cities around the globe is whether the bizarre, multicolored shadow fonts and zany wall paintings should continue to be prosecutable vandalism of private property or whether they should be respected as civilization's oldest known art form.

Drive along East Bay and glance over at the rail cars sitting on the sidings near the port terminal. You'll see an array of shadowbox graffiti "tags" clandestinely executed in rail yards from Lincoln to Trenton to Charleston's Columbus Street Terminal. Society's view that utilitarian, drab boxcars have been desecrated by street punks clashes with a chorus of libertarians and academics who maintain that "graf writers" are channeling amazing creativity in a sensible way on a shared-use space. You get to be the judge in a debate that is as old as time.

From World War II came reports that Marines landing on Pacific islands were startled to see hilarious, sometimes vulgar greetings scrawled across walls, invariably signed "Seabees," the U.S. Navy construction battalions who often went ashore ahead of the invasion. Then, G.I.s advancing through European towns in 1943 reported the strange cartoon fellow "Kilroy" peering at them with the words "Kilroy was here." Some old-timers have mused that Air Transport Command crew members scrawled the drawing and words on hangers across Europe wherever the allies liberated airfields. It was daunting for U.S. troops entering newly liberated areas to see the distinctly American cartoon image greeting them around every corner. Some captured Germans revealed that they believed that "Kilroy" was code for the pro-American German resistance movement.

Graffiti greeted the westward rolling wagon trains at Signature Rock, or Independence Rock as it's also known, 35 miles south of Casper, Wyoming. That grand old granite formation looks like a half-buried egg, reaching 135 feet high and more than a mile around at the base as it sits alone on the prairie. Thousands of names and slogans were etched into the rock or painted on in axle grease. Folks on the westward migration clambered all over that rock trying to find names of anyone they might know from back east. One dog-eared diary kept by west-bound pioneer, Lydia Allen Rudd records: "July 5,1852 Came to independence rock about ten o'clock this morning I presume there are a million of names wrote [sic] on this rock...." In the rolling plains surrounding this landmark are the unmarked graves of hundreds who died of cholera and never got to inscribe the rock. Ironically, the Wyoming Park commission sign states "No defacing or writing on the rock." Natural Bridge, the curious land bridge formation in Virginia, has had graffiti writers defacing, or decorating, it since colonial days. And Daniel Boone even carved the words, "D. Boon Cilled a. Bar [killed a bear] on [this] tree in the year 1760" in Washington County, Tennessee.

Even literary giants have had a go at graffiti. Lord Byron's public defacings survive on one of the columns of the Temple of Poseidon at Cape Sounion in Attica, Greece. Jack London revealed his inclinations during his hobo years. And Jack Kerouac was not above the deed, himself, in the heady days when he accumulated firsthand knowledge for *On the Road, Mexico City Blues,* and *Big Sur.*

Legendary graffiti artists with aliases such as Skeme, Zephyr, and Bozo Texino have gained widespread acclaim in avant garde cliques for their clever, oftentimes, raw interpretation of social injustice. They've chosen to cloak themselves in anonymity with tag-names, yet they're widely known in the art underworld. The so-called "graffiti art form" rises in cult significance because it is an illegal activity -- an "in your face" gesture to "The Man." Scholars such as Susan A. Phillips, an anthropologist from U.C.L.A., have confirmed what we've suspected for years to be true -- that "graf-writers" are deftly conveying the ultimate expletive in ever more cunning and colorful ways.

Susan A. Phillips, Ph.D., a young, attractive white woman in L.A. with a penchant for understanding the mysteries of urban gang life, has published her dissertation for her doctoral work at U.C.L.A. -- *Wallbangin': Graffiti and Gangs in L.A.* (c.1999: Univ. of Chicago Press). "This masterful, scholarly work humanizes gang members without glorifying their violence," says the *Library Journal*. Whether Phillips is just another privileged, prep-school, white girl engaging in the thrill of "gangsta" life from the safety of the ivory tower, or whether she's cracked the code of what inspires humans to violate another's space is an open, on-going dialogue taking place in police departments, city council chambers, university classrooms, and public forums across the country.

A recent (Feb. 4, 2012) *New York Times* article entitled "The Upside of Dyslexia," by Annie Murphy Paul, reveals that new studies show that dyslexia [is] "not just an impediment, but an advantage, especially in certain artistic and scientific fields." Murphy goes on to state "people with dyslexia, who have a bias in favor of the visual periphery, can rapidly take in a scene as a whole — what researchers call absorbing the 'visual gist.'" Some sociologists have thought that the higher caliber graffiti artist was just a frustrated, and perhaps, dyslexic, Michelangelo from the housing project.

There's a darker side to the so-called "street art" phenomenon. The same sociologists imagine that some of the higher caliber "graf-writers" are budding Michelangelos from the housing projects. Perhaps they are dyslexic youths unable to afford medication and the advantages offered to the social elites. The same sociologists use terms such as "alienated" and "disaffected" to describe the inner city youths who engage in defacing public property. The academics use terminology that describes Marxist behavior, yet they fall short of labeling the graffiti artist as a Marxist. There could be an association with the rising anarchist movement.

A website entitled "How Does Graffiti Hurt?" posts this statement for those wavering as to the artistic value and the freedom of expression associated with the so-called art form. "Graffiti vandals believe their actions harm no one. The reality is graffiti hurts everyone. And, those who practice it risk personal injury, violence, and arrest. Graffiti contributes to lost revenue associated with reduced ridership on transit systems, reduced retail sales and declines in property value. In addition, graffiti generates the perception of blight and heightens fear of gang activity. The appearance of graffiti is often perceived by residents and passersby as a sign that a downward spiral has begun, even though this may not be true."

Charleston remains relatively untouched by the growing graffiti craze. The rail yards and a few warehouses near the docks exhibit some clever designs. As Susan A. Phillips discusses in her book, *Wallbangin'*, there's a lot more to this phenomenon than meets the eye.

South Carolina Scalawags -- Scoundrels or Political Progressives?

Remember back when everyone had a Great Aunt Mae to reveal to them all those little hush-hush things that southerners know -- things such as when to wear seersucker and when not and the best item to take to the home of the bereaved is a gallon of sweet iced tea with cups, ice, and lemon? Those little conversations that took place in rockers on the side porch or evenings shelling butter beans were when you learned the family lore -- who'd eloped, who had been an alcoholic, and who had lost everything in a poker game. Of course, when the youngsters weren't around, Great Aunt would lower her voice and reveal who in the county was descended from "scalawags," those vile, detested scoundrels who toadied up to the Carpetbaggers and Federals during Reconstruction in the South. Given the way your trusted kin revealed through pursed lips and whispers these "truths," you imagined these miserable souls had a scarlet letter S for "Scalawag" or "Scum" embroidered across their Sunday white shirt or blouse.

Many of those grand dames who fulfilled this role of "keeper of the lore" have gone to that roll call up yonder, and their sage advice and furtive revelations have disappeared like fog from morning. It was only a matter of time before some serious-minded scholar poked through our state's official records and revealed the identity of South Carolina's scalawags -- all 432 of them -- with details of their involvement with the so-called "Black Reconstructionists." And, wouldn't you know it -- there's a new twist to the "Scalawag" era. These fellows who were and still are derided as turncoats, conspirators, and plunderers may be re-labeled as progressives -- fathers of the state's Republican Party!

There can be no denying that resentment over the reversal of fortune motivated some white Carolinians to take out their frustrations upon the Freedmen and their carpetbagger, do-good friends from up north. Likewise, there's no enigma as to why a considerable number of middle-class whites would see the proverbial "handwriting upon the wall" and ally themselves with the victors. The social fabric of the South had been ripped asunder by Sherman's

Field Orders, Number 15, issued on Monday, January 16, 1865. Fresh from his conquest of Savannah, Sherman and his staff had just arrived in Beaufort by steamship and awaited the cumbersome crossing of the Savannah River by the two wings of his immense army. Field Orders, No. 15 directed Union forces to seize 400,000 acres of coastal land from Northern Florida through the Carolinas and to resettle Freedmen on plots of 40 acres per family. They Army also supplied a mule. Though President Andrew Johnson overturned Sherman's Field Orders, No. 15 when he became president, the die was cast as far as the sons of the Confederacy were concerned. Yankees and their cohorts were thought of as detestable predators bent upon doing to the South what Rome had done to Carthage.

However, Sherman's Field Orders, No. 15 never reached the counties beyond the immediate coast. The farther one traveled inland, the more likely he was to encounter ex-Confederates prone to heed Lee's advice at Appomattox to "go home and be good citizens." In their minds, "being good citizens" meant cooperating with the conquerers. One source maintains that South Carolina had as many as 10,000 white citizens who allied with the Republicans in South Carolina as early as 1868. Lifelong Democrats accused the cooperationists as "crossing Jordan," implying that a point of no reconciliation had been reached. The whites who "crossed over" saw themselves as the sensible ones trying to make the best of General Lee's postwar advice. Even General Grant said that, "The Rebels are our Countrymen now." The majority of South Carolina's all-white Democratic party saw themselves as "diehards," the incorrigibles. They viewed their fellow whites as the lowest of the low, the meanest of the mean, i.e., scalawags.

South Carolinians who "crossed over Jordan" took the "Ironclad Oath," a part of the detested Wade-Davis Bill of 1864 that was passed in anticipation of defeated ex-Confederates seeking to return to political office. The "Ironclad Oath" swore the taker to a statement that he had not voluntarily taken part in the Confederacy, i.e., that his military service was not of his own choosing. Non-takers called it the "Damnasty Oath." James Lawrence Orr of Anderson was the state's most well-known scalawag. Orr graduated from the University of Virginia at age 21 and was admitted to the South Carolina bar. He represented the state in Congress from 1849 until 1859 and served as Speaker of the House in the years that Oregon and Minnesota were admitted as states. After having dutifully supported states rights, he opposed secession as long as he prudently could. Orr remained popular in the state and served in the Confederate Congress. James Orr saw himself as the "sensible Democrat" and, as such, he felt honor-bound to alleviate the suffering in his state following the War. He took the "Ironclad Oath" and was elected governor of South Carolina from 1865 till 1868 whereupon President Grant appointed him Ambassador to Russia. James Orr's personal integrity preserved him from the tirade of abuse heaped upon others of his kind who "crossed Jordan" for less noble reasons.

General James Longstreet of Edgefield, often referred to as Lee's "War Horse," abandoned the all-white Democratic Party soon after the War. He settled in New Orleans and played an active role in the election of Ulysses S. Grant. The two men had known and respected each other at West Point where both had been less than model cadets. A grateful Grant showed his appreciation by making Longstreet the customs collector for the Port of New Orleans. Former Confederate generals were quick to show their disdain for their old comrade in arms. When Longstreet was made commander of the constabulary during the reconstruction riots, he commanded a mostly black battalion of troops. When assassination attempts blundered, Longstreet, his wife and ten children moved to Gainsville, Georgia, where he sought and was awarded Federal posts from Rutherford B. Hayes. The rest of his life Longstreet engaged in acrimony with his fellow Confederate generals.

The most odious of the state's scalawags was Franklin Israel Moses, Jr., son of the esteemed Judge Franklin Moses. The younger Moses was the son of a Jewish father; however, he himself was a communicant of the Episcopalian Church. With less than one year of education at South Carolina College, young Moses read law and attained the position of secretary to Governor Francis W. Pickens at the outset of the Fort Sumter crisis. He was given the rank of Colonel and made chief conscription officer for the state during the War; however, he was quick to jump ship when the tide turned. Moses was elected governor on the Republican ticket when just a few white South Carolinians were allowed to vote. The Moses years were some of the most corrupt in our state's history as carpetbaggers helped themselves to state's coffers and an obliging state legislature filled with carpetbaggers and black republicans acquiesced in Moses' lining his own pockets. When his wife divorced him for adultery, Moses abandoned the state for Massachusetts where he served several years of prison time for fraud and theft.

In a curious turn of events, the current popularity of the Republican party in South Carolina has led some researchers to consider whether the scalawags and carpetbaggers of the 1870s could be the true predecessors of the modern day Republican party in the state. The 1870s Republicans believed in social and racial equality and in moving on from the antebellum Southern existence. They also bear the iniquity of having presided over the systematic looting of state government. Quite a few South Carolina Republicans view Teddy Roosevelt or Howard Taft as the true inspiration of the Republican movement. Others see Eisenhower, and still others say the modern founder was Barry Goldwater. None of these fellows had any connection with the reconstruction era.

For the best account yet written chronicling the scalawags of South Carolina, including the list of the 432 known scalawags, check out Hyman Rubin III's new book, *South Carolina Scalawags* (c. 2006, USC Press). Dr. Rubin is professor of United States History at Columbia College, and he's the grandson of the late Senator Hyman Rubin (Dem., Richland County) in the South Carolina General Assembly.

The Road To Utopia Begins At Number 2 Meeting Street

Though we natives may think of Charleston and the surrounding Lowcountry as Utopia -- an ideal place of laws, government, and society-- newcomers tell us that traffic here is congested, that real estate is expensive, and the drainage is poor. The newcomers are right, Charleston is more of an Eden than it is a Utopia. We're a subtropical paradise until the noseeums come out in the Spring.

Though Charleston may never be that perfect ideal that philosophers and tourists alike search for, this is where the road to Utopia begins -- really. You can find the real Utopia by beginning your journey right here at Number 2 Meeting Street where Meeting intersects with South Battery. If the adventuresome idealist motors up Meeting Street and continues on as Meeting becomes U.S. Highway 52, then it's just 465 miles before you drive into the town limits of Utopia. Now this may come as a shock to some Charlestonians, but Utopia is located in Ohio, and the rural crossroads was once the model ideal community established in 1844 by French philosopher and communalist, Charles Fourier. When things around the office get tough, or the weather here turns unbearably hot, it's wonderful to know that for approximatley $65 in gasoline you can drive from here to Utopia and leave our worries behind!

That old English Whig pamphleteer John Oldmixon, who traveled the American colonies in 1708, wrote of this old path that we now call U.S. Highway 52: "[The route] is beautified with odoriferous and fragrant Woods, pleasantly green all the year; as the Pine, Cedar, and Cypress, insomuch, that out of Charles-Town for three or four Miles, called the Broadway, is so delightful a Road and Walk of a great breadth, so pleasantly Green, that I believe no Prince in Europe, by all their Art, can make so pleasant a Sight for the whole Year: in short, its natural Fertility and easy Manurement, is apt to make the People incline to Sloth; for should they be as Industrious as the Northern Colonies, Riches would flow in upon them . . . ." A better description of paradise has yet to be written, and if it falls just short of describing a Utopia. Another foreign traveler, Charles Fourier, of France went one step further. He seized upon the richness and beauty of the American countryside and devised the society and culture that he thought would bring about the complete perfection of human existence -- and he conducted his grand cultural experiment just 465 miles from here on U.S. Highway 52.

U.S. Highway 52 was authorized by Congress in 1926 as part of a federal highway package signed into law by Calvin Coolidge. The highway was begun in the Charleston area and continued along a northwest colonial-era road that had been an Indian trail long before the English settlers ever came here. Construction slowed as the Great Depression settled in, but by 1934 the Highway was extended through New Deal legislation from Cheraw through North Carolina and nine more states until it reached its completion near the town of Portal, North Dakota, at the Canadian border state of Saskatchewan. There are 2,072 miles of asphalt traversing eleven states, two-hundred communities, a dozen major rivers, and three mountain chains. U.S. 52 confirmed to the motorist what Irving Berlin put to music in 1918: "From the mountains, to the prairies, to the oceans, white with foam, God bless America, My home sweet home."

If you're inclined to be philosophical, you can explore this so-called Utopia of Charles Fourier and you can acquaint yourself with some old-fashioned Americana that hasn't been touted since the heyday of motoring and the tourist court.

Our journey begins at the corner of Meeting and South Battery near that wonderful Victorian Inn. Point your vehicle north, say a prayer for safe travel, and off you go in search of Utopia. Of course, you must stop at The Four Corners of Law at Meeting and Broad, and your senses tell you that that may be the last time in our long journey that you'll see such civility symbolized so prominently and elegantly. On you go through Oakley, Moncks Corner, Saint Stephens, and Kingstree. Cades, Lake City, and Florence roll by. Here you pause for a moment as you drive through tiny Scranton, population 1020. Scranton is home to nationally famous McKenzie Farms Nursery. Stan McKenzie ships all sorts of tropical fruit plants across the country -- everything from Pineapple Guava to Ogeechee Limes. From McKenzie's Farm you motor on through Darlington with its "Yankee Hill" where a hundred Yankees were buried and on through to Society Hill, the ancestral home of the Cokers. You exit the state after touring Cheraw, the capital of "The Olde English District." Besides being the steamboat capital of the state, this bluff town on the PeeDee was home to a dozen Revolutionary War heroes as well as the jazz legend, Dizzy Gillespie. As romantic as the place is with its antique stores and old homes, you press on as Candide, Cunegonde, and Dr. Pangloss did to El Dorado.

Pilgrims on their way to Utopia (Ohio) exit South Carolina near Cheraw and enter North Carolina near Albemarle, an ancient settlement known to the same mound-building natives who constructed Cahokia in the 1500s. The area became known as Albemarle when the first white settlers planted a trade outpost there in the 17th century. They named it after George Monck, Duke of Albemarle, one of the Lords Proprietors. You cross the famed Piedmont Triad and approach Mount Airy, the boyhood home of Andy Griffith and country music singer, Donna Fargo. Nearby is Pilot Mountain, one of the most curious geological sites east of the Mississippi River.

From Mount Airy the curious traveller rolls on through the foothills of the Appalachians to Cana, Virginia, and from there to neighboring Hillsville. No one here knows much about Hillsville; however it was the terrible Hillsville Carroll County Courthouse gunfight in 1913 that seized national headlines for days until the sinking of the *Titanic* knocked the story to page two.

For some reason the state of Kentucky reduces the speed limit to 55 M.P.H. whereas a mile or two back in Virginia the same highway allowed you to cruise at 65. From Rushtown to Morristown to Colfax you persevere knowing that you're in the midst of the Daniel Boone National Forest, and if he could make it through here with no roads, you can do it on U.S. 52. In Colfax you have to pull over to sample the local fare at Granny and Pappy's diner. Take comfort that Alexis de Tocqueville kept a journal as he crossed through this region. Tocqueville's published notes about that 1830s tour have become legendary. Your travel stories might improve, too, once you tell friends here that you hung out at a place called "Out in the Backwoods" and heard a Bluegrass band led by "Dirty Larry" McLaughlin singing "The Colfax County Blues." Get a good night's sleep in nearby Morehead, Kentucky, where in the 1880s the Craig Tolliver political faction seized control of the town in a gunfight that killed a dozen people. For nearly a decade the Tolliver gang ran the town to their liking until Kentucky governor, Simon Bolivar Buckner, brought a posse of a hundred men in and restored order and paved the way for a civil election. Buckner later became a Confederate general.

Finally, after several days and nights of the kind of sightseeing that you haven't done since childhood, you arrive in Utopia, Ohio. It's helpful to keep in mind Utopia is an unincorporated town located on the northern bank of the Ohio River. Charles Fourier, the French communalist, brought his idea of "phalanxes," or completely self-sustaining communes" to America in 1844. Fourier chose

Ohio as the most likely venue to establish his pacifistic, free-love, barter society. The idea lasted barely three years before the communalists quarreled and broke apart. In the next few years Utopia became home to religious spiritualists under the leadership of John Wattles who preached "the end is near." They were soon swept away in a powerful flood. By 1850 Utopia had been resettled by anarchists led by Josiah Warren. By the time you've read all the plaques in Utopia, you will rethink the whole notion and retrace your route to the corner of Meeting and South Battery. There, as Voltaire intimated in *Candide* with the immortal lines "we must tend our own garden," you'll rediscover the El Dorado, Utopia of your dreams.

The Tales They Tell About Horrell Hill

Just 93 miles northwest of us on the U.S. 378 highway connecting Sumter to Columbia there's a bulbous-shaped summit called Horrell Hill that rises 410 feet above sea level. Regrettably, the stories of Horrell Hill's romantic past are ebbing away as northeast Columbia's suburban sprawl envelopes its tangled woods and Carolina red clay.

Oldtimers used to say that a person could stand atop Horrell Hill and see ten miles in every direction. Within that circumference, so said the sages, one would encounter the homesteads of the men who would rise up twice to save this state -- once from the British after the fall of Charleston and again when Carpetbaggers overran the State during Reconstruction.

Horrell Hill seldom makes the news. About the last time the crossroads community got national attention was Wednesday, April 30, 1924, when *The State* newspaper carried the news that a powerful tornado had touched down there during the previous afternoon and that 12 people were dead and 1300 buildings heavily damaged or destroyed. Four of the dead were students at the Horrell Hill Consolidated School. Of course, there were no alarms or radio alerts to announce the oncoming threat as a storm system crossed Georgia and entered South Carolina around noon on Tuesday, April 29th. The tornado that struck Horrell Hill ripped a path of destruction 64 miles long, finally breaking apart near Darlington. Assessed damage in Horrell Hill amounted to $1,000,000 -- or, $12.6 million in today's currency. Other tornadoes spawned by the same system killed an additional 39 people before the system fizzled out over Virginia. Rural schools in the 1920s were usually small wooden structures that proved to be flimsy shelters in violent weather. By the 1940s elementary and secondary school buildings were being constructed of brick and stone. Meteorologists have calculated that this tornado was an F4 on the Tetsuya Theodore "Ted" Fujita scale of tornado storm assessment. The April 29, 1924 storms constitute the worst outbreak of tornadic activity in our state. The Fujita ("F") Scale assigns a wind value from 207 to 260 m.p.h. for an F-4. Though Ted Fujita designed his sophisticated wind damage scale in 1971 while doing research at The

University of Chicago, the National Weather Service did not officially adopt it for descriptive purposes until 2007. Fujita's scale was an outgrowth of his studies calculating the bomb blast effect of the atomic bomb at Hiroshima.

The Horrell name originates with Thomas Howell who owned the land containing the large hill as early as the 1770s. The Roster of South Carolina Patriots in the American Revolution by Lander College Professor Bobby Gilmer Moss lists Thomas Howell as serving in the Rangers commanded by Colonel Eli Kershaw during the dark days of the Revolution. Though not officially one of the so-called "High Hills of the Santee," Horrell Hill's proximity to the Wateree and Congaree Rivers makes it a unique geographical area in the midlands. The strategic hill was valued by the various Indian tribes who inhabited the area, and commanders in both sides of the Revolutionary War made it an outpost. Just south and east of the fall line, the great hill is nestled near the head of the navigable portions of the Wateree River, as well as where the Saluda and the Broad Rivers come together to form the Congaree. The alluvial soil is so fertile that the surrounding country was named "Richland" in 1787. Timber, both hardwood and softwood, abound in the dense forests, and landowners have always made large sums of money selling timber around here. Moonshiners also had lucrative operations in the nearby swamps from the time of Prohibition until the early 1970s. The base commanders at nearby Shaw A.F.B allowed some of their reconnaissance aircraft to perform low-level, infrared photographic flights over the area for law enforcement. Hillbilly bootlegging can't compete with the government's eyes in the sky.

Continental commander General Nathanael Greene had an outpost on Horrell Hill as he rested his army in the High Hills of the Santee, just 20 miles east of Horrell Hill. Opposing commanders Banastre Tarleton and Thomas Sumter knew the place as a rendezvous for Tories or Whigs, whichever was in the ascendancy. Colonel John Marshall, whose mill was located on nearby Cedar Creek, was one of General Sumter's subalterns. Marshall's command extended from Flat Rock, near present day Kershaw, to the present day town of Hopkins. Marshall was cashiered on orders of General Greene following 1781 operations around Georgetown for being overzealous in enacting "Sumter's Law." Sumter's policy was to exact tribute from Loyalists as a way to pay his soldiers. Just 8 miles west of Horrell Hill is the site of Woodlands Plantation, once the grand home of Wade Hampton I. Hampton had been a colonel and cohort of Francis Marion and Thomas Sumter in the Revolution and a brigadier general in the War of 1812 where he served as adjutant to General Andrew Jackson in New Orleans. Hampton owned extensive agricultural acreage throughout the South and was considered the South's wealthiest planter at the time of his death in 1835. Wade Hampton I and his son Wade II helped develop the the Columbia Race Course very near Woodlands. Wade II brought in a builder from Rhode Island to construct a grand Greek Revival mansion he called Millwood on land adjacent to Woodlands. These mansions were torched by Sherman's men during the War Between the States. Wade Hampton III, born at Millwood, became Lee's commander of cavalry upon the death of J.E.B. Stuart, and it was Hampton and his famed Red Shirts who rid the state of the detested Carpetbaggers in the Campaign of 1876.

Of interest to educators is the Minerva Academy located on Cabin Creek barely two miles from Horrell Hill. This early 19th century classical academy in the backwoods was one of the famed Bingham schools of Hillsboro, North Carolina fame. William James Bingham I, one of the early graduates of the University of North Carolina, founded Mount Repose Academy in Hillsboro in the late 1790s. Other Bingham schools were located in rural Alamance County, Asheville, and Mebane. During the schools' most prosperous times in the 1870s and 1880s there were students from 33 states and a dozen foreign countries enrolled. The South Carolina Bingham School was named Minerva Academy in honor of the Greek goddess of wisdom. The school's headmaster was William James Bingham II, and the dates of operation were approximately 1802 until 1834. Many prominent South Carolinians were educated there, including three grandsons of Revolutionary War soldier and S.C. legislator Joel Adams.

From atop Horrell Hill the summit of Cook's Mountain (370 feet above sea level) can be seen just a few miles east. A real estate brochure for the sale of the moutain property notes: "Seventeen miles east of Columbia on the Wateree River is a property known as Cook's Mountain. It is one of the most spectacular properties in South Carolina. Land types on the property range from an almost primeval hardwood forest along the river rising through uplands to the highest elevations in the central part of the state. The property has a wide variety of plant and animal life. The 'mountain' itself rises to an elevation of 372 feet above sea level, an anomaly in this area that offers scenic views for miles. The mountain was the home of Mr. James Cook, a famous cartographer, who produced the Cook Map of South Carolina in 1773." Many of the old-timers agreed that James Cook reserved the grandest view of all in South Carolina for himself.

When you are next on U.S. Highway 378 traveling to or from Sumter to Columbia, pull over by the road marker that celebrates Horrell Hill. Like so many crossroads communities in South Carolina, Horrell Hill holds many secrets.

Stateburg's Angelica Singleton Was America's First Lady, 1839 - 1841

As significant as the role of "First Lady" is to the American tradition you'd think that the Founding Fathers would have enshrined it in the Constitution. Presidential candidates are vetted on what kind of image their wives would give to the rest of the world. Our nation's first First Lady was regally referred to as Lady Washington, a form of address that did not carry into the Adams' administration. Receptions, soirees, teas, and even picnics were the province of the "Lady-in-Chief," and Martha Dandridge Custis Washington wore the title well and her Tidewater accent welcomed all comers to the Chief Executive's mansion at the corner of 6th and Market Street. The first lady with an opportunity to take part in decorating the White House was Dolley Madison, wife our fourth president, James Madison. Twenty years later, in 1837, Dolley Madison maneuvered behind the scenes to arrange for her cousin, the South Carolina born Angelica Singleton to wed Abram Van Buren, eldest son of President Martin Van Buren. Because Martin Van Buren had been a widower for a dozen years, the young and vivacious Angelica, formerly of Stateburg, served as hostess at all White House functions from 1838 through 1841.

Quite probably, a more elegant, refined, and gracious young lady could not have been found in the wide reaches of this continent to fulfill the duties as Martin Van Buren's official hostess at the White House. Angelica Singleton was born in Wedgefield, an adjunct to Stateburg in 1818, the second year of President James Monroe's administration. The infant's father was Colonel Richard Singleton, cotton planter, horse breeder, and owner of a half-dozen plantations ranging from the High Hills of the Santee to the rolling plains of the Congaree. Angelica's birthplace, Home Place Plantation, astride the Old Charleston Post Road was the former estate of Patriot General, later United States Senator, Thomas Sumter, more recognizeable by the sobriquet, "The Gamecock." The Sumter land eventually was sold to Colonel Richardson and then to Colonel Singleton. Sumter's tomb is a landmark of this serene plantation set amidst oaks and pines in the High Hills northeast of the Wateree River. The last will and testament of Richard Singleton dated 1852 details his ownership of a half-dozen plantations, more than 500 slaves, numerous thoroughbred horses, and gold and silver mounted double-barreled shotguns.

When it came time to enroll Angelica in a boarding school, her father overlooked the famed Madame Togno's school in Charleston where so many daughters of the Lowcountry rice and sea island cotton fortunes received their refinement. He chose instead the Philadelphia school of Madame Grelaud. Very likely it was Angelica's mother's cousin, Dolley Todd Madison, wife of James Monroe, who influenced them. The Singletons did not lack social contacts. Colonel Singleton's wife, Rebecca Coles had a sister, Sally, who was the wife of Andrew Stevenson, the Speaker of the House of Representatives. Stevenson later became President Van Buren's Minister to Great Britain, 1836-1841. Angelica's mother's brother, Virginia born Edward Coles, was the second governor of Illinois. Angelica's cousin, John White Stevenson, was governor of Kentucky. In South Carolina, the Singletons associated with the Hamptons, Mannings, Prestons, and McDuffies. Their social season revolved around thoroughbred horses and race week in Charleston, Columbia, and Saint Matthews -- known then as Lewisfield.

Madame Grelaud's School in Philadelphia was strict and academically rigorous. The well-heeled young ladies of both sides of the Mason-Dixon Line donned scuttle bonnets, long skirts, and blue frock coats to attend lectures on all aspects of the fine arts. Mississippi's Varina Howell, later Varina Howell Davis, wife of Jefferson Davis, overlapped with Angelica Singleton at Grelaud's School -- so, too, did the three granddaughters of Martha Custis Washington.

In the first half of the 19th century, Philadelphia was considered America's premier city for sophistication, culture, and intellectualism. The boutiques of Philadelphia rivaled those of New York. The City of Brotherly Love was also the sister of American fashion and good taste. Upon her completion of Madame Grelaud's institution, Angelica made the grand tour of European capitals. First stop was London where her uncle was Ambassador to the Court of St. James.

Meanwhile, the political scene at home was heating up in 1836. The presidential election was a three-way contest with Martin Van Buren, the sitting Vice-President running as the continuer of Andrew Jackson's Democratic policies. William Henry Harrison and Hugh Lawson White both ran as Whigs. Martin Van Buren was the odds on favorite, but the recent Nullification Crisis made South Carolinians fearful of him. Carolinians let John C. Calhoun dictate their electoral vote, and Calhoun chose to have our state senate throw her 11 electoral votes to Willie P. Magnum, a United States senator write-in candidate from North Carolina who was a protege of Calhoun. South Carolina's electoral decision in the election of 1836 was a harbinger of the Secession Convention in 1860. However, the vivacious teen Angelica Singleton was having the time of her life being courted by the aristocrats of London.

Upon her return from Europe, it was her father's wish that Angelica spend time in Washington, D.C., as the guest of family relative, William C. Preston, United States Senator from South Carolina. Preston was an 1812 graduate of South Carolina College (now U.S.C.) and a member of the college's famed literary society, Phi Alpha Epsilon, better known as the The Euphradian Society. The Euphradian membership reads like a "Who's Who" of the South Carolina secession movement -- Robert W. Barnwell, Preston "Bully" Brooks, Thomas Cooper, William Harper, James Henry Hammond, and Louis T. Wigfall, among other notables. Preston had studied law at the University of Edinburgh and was noted for his oratorical skills.

Angelica had not been in Washington, D.C., more than a couple of weeks before former First Lady, Dolley Madison sent an invitation for her to have tea. Mrs. Madison was a recent widow as her husband died in June of 1836. A first cousin of Angelica's mother, Dolley Madison quickly made her young kinsman an intimate of key Washington ladies. President Martin Van Buren, himself a widower, had intimated that he wanted Dolley Madison to serve as White House hostess, but she declined on account of her recent widowhood. However, Dolley lost no time in getting Angelica on the invitation list to grand Washington parties where eligible bachelors such as Abram Van Buren and others would be in attendance. Dolley's match-making skill was so finely honed that the lovely Angelica Singleton and Abram Van Buren never suspected a thing until they were well smitten with each other. Abram Van Buren was a dashing, sandy-haired Army captain of dragoons who had graduated from West Point as classmates with such future standouts as Jefferson Davis, Robert E. Lee, and Joseph E. Johnston. He had been in Indian fights on the frontier and had served in the Seminole War in Florida. Though he was 11 years older than Angelica, the two lovers appeared made for each other. Captain Van Buren had been granted leave of absence from the military in order to serve as his father's White House Secretary. He preferred a White House wedding, but Angelica deferred to her parents' wishes that the wedding be a grand scale affair at Home Place Plantation in Stateburg. The November 1838 wedding was one of the most sumptuous affairs ever held in South Carolina even though President Van Buren was unable to attend.

On January 1, 1838, Angelica Singleton Van Buren began her duties as First Lady in the White House. She was 20 years old and the center of national attention. The Jackson White House had been a rather dull place socially due to President Jackson's wife Rachel having died before he took office. All those years of watching her mother entertain Hamptons and Mannings and Prestons in Stateburg and all of the etiquette she learned at Madame Grelaud's School, not to mention the months she spent at the Court of St. James in London, came in handy as she began a round of dinners, teas, and picnics for Martin Van Buren. The state dinner where all cabinet members greet a foreign dignitary was originated during Van Buren's administration. Angelica planned and presided over these affairs patterned after those she had experienced in London. There where children's parties on the White House lawn and President Van Buren flapped his arms and strutted like a turkey to the amusement of the little ones and adults alike. The White House was lifted out of the sullenness that had enveloped it in the Jackson years.

Alas, not all was rosy in those years for Angelica. She bore a baby in the White House, but it did not live long. As she buried her first born, the country sank into its first great depression -- known then as the Panic of 1837. Martin Van Buren became tied down in a battle over banking regulations and his political enemies outnumbered his supporters. When he lost his re-election bid, Angelica and Abram followed him back to his home, Lindenwald, in Old Kinderhook, near Albany, New York. Angelica Singleton Van Buren lived out her days as a New Yorker, and in 1877, she sold her St. Matthews, S.C., plantations named "Singleton" and "True Blue" to Othniel H. Wienges, the grandfather of Othniel H. Wienges, III, the retired state legislator, cotton planter, horse breeder, and U.S.C. trustee.

The Charleston Side of the Landmark Hayne - Webster Debate

Page by page, decade by decade, our history is dropping from sight as today's urgent matters overtake us. Things that used to matter a lot are given short shrift in contemporary classrooms. Can it be that the famed Hayne - Webster debate has shriveled from two pages to two paragraphs in the U.S. History textbook in the past forty years? Not only has the landmark moment all but slipped from the text, but it's not even required knowledge on most state history achievement tests. How could this have happened to a bit of knowledge that our grandparents cherished knowing? Hayne - Webster has gone the way of such treasured Americana as the Seven Nations of the Iroquois and King Philip's War. For one reason, there are more "-isms" in the Hayne - Webster dispute than any other issue in American history. It's the ageless enigma -- ""What happens when an unstoppable force meets an immovable object?" Every nation comes upon a turning point, and the Hayne - Webster debate helped define ours. For the record, there's evidence in Robert Y. Hayne's papers alluding to sectionalism, nationalism, protectionism, agrarianism, and industrialism in his passionate exchange with Massachusetts' eloquent senator, Daniel Webster. To say that the issue was complex is an understatement. Not many people beyond the confines of the Capitol could comprehend the many facets of political and economic life that were then in play. From crossroads settlements to the burgeoning eastern cities, citizens grasped their two-bits' worth of the puzzle and left the big-picture to the politicians.

In layman's language, the catalyst for the verbal dustup occurred with a mundane address given to the Senate by Samuel A. Foot of Connecticut in December 1829 where he simply requested that Congress suspend the sale of public lands in what is called the Louisiana Purchase until proper record keeping and accounting procedures could be imposed upon the process. The pell mell rush to settle the interior had touched off a maelstrom of speculation and financial impropriety with many members of Congress deeply involved.

Thomas Hart Benton, senator from Missouri, rose to denounce the Foot measure as a not-too-thinly-disguised attempt by Northern manufacturing interests to check the prosperity of the West. To Benton it was obvious that the North was not eager to have another section to mollify in achieving favorable manufacturing and international trade policies. Seeing a chance to cement for the South a powerful ally, Robert Hayne sprang to his feet to support Benton.

Sitting less than thirty feet away was the staunch unionist, staunch federalist Massachusetts senator, Daniel Webster--Phillips Exeter and Dartmouth graduate -- and one of the finest extemporaneous speakers in the country. Webster was a staunch supporter of "The American Way," a big government idea involving support for a national bank to help regulate the economy and support for a host of government programs that would lead to internal communication and trade among the various states. Henry Clay was also a great supporter of this idea that originally belonged to Alexander Hamilton of Washington's administration.

The irritant in the otherwise routine bookkeeping speech and proposal by Foot was, as far as Hayne was concerned, the fear that rapid settling of the territories would have a deleterious effect upon the South's "peculiar institution." Peculiar it was, for that was the strange phrase that the South coined to connote the continuation of slavery as a part of southern culture while noting full well that it did not parallel the course of democracy with a people yearning to be free.

Hayne and Webster went at each other for a total of 16 hours spread over four days in front of a senate chamber and gallery that had standing room only. Hayne deplored the rise of grand government schemes as meddling into the rights intended for the states. Webster defended the need of government to take the lead in putting backbone and sinew into the rapidly emerging continental power. In retrospect, the thrilling polemic display was worthy of anything that Parliament could muster. Yet, it is ironic to note that Parliament had passed the Abolition of Slavery Act in 1807, a generation prior to the time when the topic would heat up the halls of Congress.

We can be certain that South Carolina and much of the South took pride in the rhetoric of Robert Young Hayne of Charleston. He stated unequivocally our state's strict constructionist interpretation of the Constitution as it related to the rights of the various states. Though Hayne's initial speech delivered on Tuesday, January 19, 1830, was not up to his usual oratorical standard, he, nonetheless, put the Senate and its northeastern trade faction on notice. South Carolina's interests would not be bullied into a timid submission to New England merchant wishes.

Most historians concur that Webster got the better of Hayne in the four-day debate that foreshadowed the coming of four decades of sectional friction and distrust. Some go even so far as to state that Webster boxed Hayne into a very narrow position with no room to maneuver without the state of South Carolina losing face before the nation and the world. The Nullification Crisis of 1832 was still twenty-two months in the future, and there was time for other great statesmen such as Henry Clay of Kentucky and Thomas Hart Benton of Missouri to defuse the tension. Meanwhile, fellow Carolinian John C. Calhoun, Vice President to Andrew Jackson, sat bolt upright paying rapt attention to every utterance of Hayne and his antagonist, Webster. The great debate was waged over four separate days in a nine - day stretch that began on Tuesday, January 19, 1830, and concluded the following Wednesday, January 27. In the two months since Hayne and Webster had sparred over the future course of the nation, Jackson and Calhoun had become enmeshed in a bitter quarrel regarding the new wife of Senator John Eaton of Tennessee and whether the woman in question was "a proper lady" worthy of dining in the White House. Peggy Timberlake Eaton was said woman's name and her questionable reputation stemmed from two concerns -- whether, or not her boarding house roots disqualified her from associating with proper company, and the unanswered questions arising from the nature of her relationship with Senator Eaton prior to her first husband's death. John C. Calhoun's wife, Floride, would have nothing to do with Mrs. Eaton, and that infuriated Calhoun who doted on the vivacious young woman. The Eaton affair was the backdrop to the emerging drama between the President and the Vice President as the two developed entirely opposing sides on the right of South Carolina to declare null and void the odious Tariff of 1828 and its successor, the Tariff of 1832.

Just 76 days elapsed before the sectional sparks flew again, this time in knife-edged remarks couched in the phraseology of President Jackson and Vice President Calhoun in presenting the customary toasts to the United States at the annual Jefferson Day banquet.

Sometimes historians talk about the "heavy hand of history" and it's clear from re-examining the Hayne - Webster Debate that South Carolina asked for and received the backhand of history from that rapid, but ill-timed exchange in Congress nearly 181 years ago. Robert Hayne was on the receiving end of one of Dan Webster's stemwinder speeches that served as a salvo of nationalism and patriotism in rebutting what many saw as Hayne's petty and parochial interpretation of the nation's founding fathers. Webster's reply to Hayne on January 26 is considered one of the greatest speeches ever made in the United

States Senate. To northerners and many midwesterners it was as if Hayne had walked into a trap, or as if he had verbalized a far-too-restricting political position for South Carolina and the South. One year later John C. Calhoun made his maiden speech on nullification and Calhoun rejected a portion of the Hayne logic. The die was cast and a Charlestonian was at the center of the greatest sectional dispute this nation has ever had.

Robert Y. Hayne was of the lineage of the St. Paul's Parish Haynes, and he proudly claimed kin to the Patriot martyr, Isaac Hayne. Robert Young Hayne read law under Langdon Cheves and he served as Intendant (mayor) of Charleston, as governor and militia general, and as United States Senator. He prospered as an attorney and as a business man, and his home at number 4 Ladson Street was one of the most magnificent in the City. Robert Y. Hayne is a colorful thread in the tapestry of America's history.

Mount Pleasant's Earliest Known Historic Site Is 203 King Street

How many times has the historian run into a brick wall and had to be rescued by the archaeologist? That's the case with the 17th century stockade fort once centered where the Old Village's King Street runs into the harbor. The folklore of 203 King Street has surfaced a half-dozen times this century, yet no one has confirmed what went on there over 300 years ago. Entombed beneath the brick and mortar of Cameron and Betty Burn's circa 1912 residence is a stockpile of archaeological evidence. And like a fox chased by hounds, the history of what's beneath 203 King has gone to ground.

Petrona Royall McIver's *History of Mount Pleasant, South Carolina* (c. 1960, Mount Pleasant Town Council) mentions an early east of the Cooper settler, the Irish soldier of fortune, Florentia (Florence) O'Sullivan, as having constructed a fort overlooking Hog Island Channel. McIver's research done in the 1950s reveals that the highest bluff in what is now the old part of Mount Pleasant was referred to as Hog Island Hill. Florence O'Sullivan, for better or worse, became the principal character in the earliest years of the English settlement on this side of the Cooper River.

Mentioned also in Petrona McIver's work is the "Moll Map of 1715" [1717?] that labels this area with the words "Silver Privet," a term we use for the indigenous Ligustrum plant which grows in great profusion along our coast. Herman Moll was a German immigrant to London during the reign of Charles II, arriving in 1678 just as the talk around the city was of the new Charles Town settlement in Carolina. Moll was a talented illustrator and cartographer who picked up commissions to make maps for Daniel DeFoe's *Robinson Crusoe* and Jonathan Swift's *Gulliver's Travels*. He was one of the earliest authoritative map makers to chart the southeastern coast of North America, and his 1717 map was the best representation of the Carolina coast until his 1746 map was published. Saturday, July 6, 1680, was the date that O'Sullivan brought settlers over to Oldwanus Point, the jutting prominence of land bounded by Charleston

Harbor, Shem Creek, and Cove Inlet. Unlike today, the hard-packed sand shore of Oldwanus Point was cut by small tidal marsh creeks and bogs. O'Sullivan quickly located a defensive position on a high sand dune commanding the harbor approaches. A bloody war that eradicated much of the Westoe Indian tribe had just been concluded, yet the earliest settlers here carried a musket in one hand as they fished or plowed a garden, for Westoes still lurked in the woods.

Tradition has it that Florence O'Sullivan chose the sandy bluff that is now the site of the Burn residence at 203 King Street. He was Surveyor General of the Colony for a few years, and he'd been a soldier of fortune fighting against the French in the Caribbean before being made an officer on board the ship Carolina. How far O' Sullivan's land grant extended is not known, but some authorities believe that he owned the land between Shem Creek and Cove Inlet as well as the island that bears his name. One thing is certain, and that is O'Sullivan set up a heavy artillery piece on the island we call Sullivan's, and he erected bonfire stacks like hayricks as an early warning system for the peninsula of Charles Town in the event of a seaborne invasion.

These stories passed from one generation to another and some facts were corroborated by written documents. When Cameron and Betty Burn bought 203 King in the early 1960s, they were aware that the 50-year-old house was straddling a significant archaeological site. Just what was underneath it was unknown to them until 1965 when Cameron Burn decided to excavate beneath the basement for the purpose of installing a new furnace. Upon removing a four by six foot section of basement flooring Burn encountered loose sandy soil so dense with the detritus of a former time that he stopped shoveling and recovered the hole.

Wishing to resolve once and for all what type of structure originally occupied this site, Burn called on local historian and writer, Elias Bull, to research 203 King Street, or Lot 6, as it was known on the oldest maps of the area. Bull conducted an exhaustive search of archives in the area and concluded that Captain O'Sullivan was granted a warrant for Lot 6 and considerable other land on September 7, 1672. Twenty-five successive owners secured title to the site prior to the Burns taking ownership on August 28, 1959. By April 1692, Lot 6 had been passed to Katherine O'Sullivan, daughter of Florence. In the intervening 270 years ownership bore surnames of Barksdale, Hancock, Villeponteaux, Scott, Bonneau, Hibben, Kerrison, Prioleau, and DuPre, among others. It is likely that Freedmen possessed an unrecorded deed to the property in the years immediately following the War Between the States and that the

United States government purchased the land from them in 1873 to be used in the maintenance of the lights marking the harbor.

Elias Bull's search examined over 40 sources and established provenance for the property, but it did not answer the all-important question of what purpose the site served in the critical years of the colony's earliest existence. If local legends and historians' theories are ever borne out, the 203 King Street site and surrounding lots may prove to be the European structures built upon soil east of the Cooper. Presently, Fort Moultrie is the area's number one historic location, and for good reason. However, if some day an archaeological dig confirms that O'Sullivan developed his hilltop fort here in the late 17th century, then a significant re-interpretation of written history must take place.

Intrigued by the bottles, musket balls, pottery shards, colored glass, and nails that he pulled up with just a few shovelfuls of dirt, Cameron Burn contacted the University of South Carolina Department of Anthropology. There was no Institute of Archaeology at the University then. Professor William D. Edwards was fascinated by the prospect of locating an undisturbed 17th century colonial site, and he commenced a preliminary investigation with a few of his students in the summer of 1966. When the rest of America was questioning Beatle John Lennon's statement that, "The Beatles are more popular than Jesus Christ," the Burns family was adjusting to a team of archaeology students and their rather absent-minded professor cutting shallow trenches beneath their home and into the front and side yards.

The southeast wall of 203 King contains a semicircular protrusion much like a well that extends beneath ground level. The structure is made of very old brick, perhaps of English origin due to the pinkish color and texture, and it may have been a well, or it may have been part of the masonry protecting a gun port. Nearly everyone who has formed an opinion on the site over the years has suspected that 203 King was the location of a fort built to protect the tiny English colony during what was known as the Queen Anne's War, 1702-1713. This set of engagements was part of a much larger struggle known as the War of Spanish Succession.

Edwards and crew unearthed a hearth in the rectangular dig beneath 203 King, and that, in itself, would not be very significant as every dwelling would require one or more hearths. However, forts located near the coast were equipped with the apparatus to produce hotshot -- red hot cannonballs that would ignite wooden ship hulls upon contact.

It is known that the present height of the foundation of 203 King is 16 feet lower than the sand dune that once towered over the harbor. Even today the angle of fire from the bluff is militarily significant in commanding all water approaches east of the Cooper. But, was there another purpose for the settlement here beyond that of defense?

The Westoe War of 1679 opened the way for colonials to trade with several small tribes in the region -- tribes which reached far inland. Wampun beads have been discovered in quantity, and some of the beads are purple and handsomely decorated. This site may have been part of a network of trading sites extending to Bull's Island and beyond.

Florence O'Sullivan may have represented a contentious faction of early settlers, for he helped lead a hunger riot against the royal authorities in 1673. There's no correlation so far between this area being called "Hungry Neck" and the rebellion of 1673; however one of the ringleaders abandoned his post and became an insurrectionary on the Charles Town peninsula. Were the other settlers here considered rebellious, too? There is much more to the story of 203 King than has been unearthed so far. Professor Edwards moved on after a few weeks and the artifacts of his dig are now in the hands of the Charleston Museum and archaeologist, Martha Zierdan. Reopening the site would be costly and somewhat disruptive to the owners of 203 King and to the neighborhood; however, should grant funds become available, the interpretation of Mount Pleasant's economic, military, and social past would, by necessity, have to be rewritten.

From St. Philip's Street to Schloss Cecilienhof

Potsdam, a suburb of Berlin, is a place to remember! Potsdam has much of the charm of old Charleston, yet it is 4,586 miles northeast of here and dates to the Bronze Age. The name "Potsdam" translates loosely from Slavic to "beneath the oaks." For years the town was the ancestral home of the Kaisers, but for two weeks in July 1945, it was home to President Harry Truman and his Charleston-born Secretary of State, James (Jimmy) F. Byrnes. Potsdam is a beautiful and clean town devoid of the graffiti and bland buildings. Potsdam is to Berlin as Summerville is to Charleston. It comes as a surprise to learn that we bombed Potsdam in May 1945, as it appears that virtually all of the old town remains intact. This old community is aristocratic, clean, quiet, and a wonderful place to stroll cobbled streets and admire 17th and 18th century Europe at its finest! And the best chocolate confections can be had with coffee at a dozen sidewalk cafes--with not a tourist in sight anywhere!

One main street winds its way through Potsdam, *Friedrich Ebert Strasse* -- remember him -- the Weimar Republic president? Five or six cobbled streets intersect this street. Two blocks north of Friedrich Ebert Strasse begins the great Hohenzollern compound. The Hohenzollerns, crown princes of Prussia, were war lords of Nuremberg brought in in the early 1600s to rid Prussia of rival robber barons. They did such a wonderful job that they were invited to stay awhile. Stay they did--and the rest of German history attaches to their aggressive rule. At Potsdam they built a series of little palaces -- nothing even close to being the size of one wing at Versailles. Of course, they had homes in Charlottenburg just up the road, and in Berlin city proper, as well. The Hohenzollerns have not the social cachet of the Hapsburgs or the Bourbons, or even of the rival German houses -- such as the Hanoverians, Brunswicks, or Liechtensteins. It's evident in their tastes. Duke Frederick II of Prussia -- the one they called "the Great" -- broke with the mold and excelled in cultural attainments -- composing with Bach and conversing with Voltaire and painting with Watteau -- while still beating up severely upon his kingdom's neighbors. Frederick's military aggression was expressed in an audacity that was emulated a few decades later by the Corsican roughneck turned-French emperor Napoleon Bonaparte. Just on the outskirts of Potsdam, one comes upon Sans Souci palace perched upon a hill that once was a grape vineyard. This diminutive palace is half the length of a football field and about half as wide. There are six or seven rooms on each side with an unseen service hallway running down the center. Since Frederick the Great was not much of a ladies' man (in fact, he was repelled by their company--estranged from his wife after two weeks of marriage), the palace is an accommodation to his personal interests--music, philosophy, the art of Watteau. Oddly, nothing at all martial appears in the home, and he is remembered as one of the greatest military minds of his time. The oversized green leather wingback chair in the drawing room is where Frederick died (1786). After Frederick II, the family relied upon outside counsel in all its future endeavors. Sans Souci sits upon a 50 to 70 foot prominence. Today, it is terraced, still a vineyard, with 40 steps and a plateau, 40 more steps and a plateau, and so on, for several levels until one mounts the hill. From a distance the appearance is of a house sitting on a rectangular pyramid.

Schloss Cecilienhof sits a mile away from Sans Souci in the great park of the Hohenzollerns. Duke Frederick William IV (Kaiser Wilhelm I) built the place to look like an English half timber Tudor house and garden. Duke Frederick got the idea from his many visits to see his relatives at Windsor and Balmoral. Cecilienhof backs up on a marsh and water as if it were a Carolina Lowcountry plantation. Schloss Cecilienhof intrigues us because this was where the "Big Three" -- the U.S.A., Britain, and the U.S.S.R. -- met in July 1945, for the Potsdam Conference. That conference settled the partitioning of Germany and made the infamous pact with Stalin concerning Japan. Churchill had already been defeated in his bid for prime minister by an ungrateful British nation, but he was representing Britain as his last official public act. Clement Attlee, Britain's socialist Prime Minister, was at Potsdam but very much in the background. Truman represented American interests; however, he had been President only three months. Our favorite person in Potsdam is former Charlestonian, Jimmy Byrnes, Secretary of State to Truman. Byrnes had been Secretary of State just a few weeks. Byrnes was a former South Carolina Legislator, Congressman, US Senator, Supreme Court Justice, and the Chairman of the War Mobilization Board for FDR prior to becoming Truman's Secretary of State and then Governor of S.C. FDR referred to Jimmy Byrnes as the "only indispensable man" in his administration. Roosevelt wanted Jimmy Byrnes to be his running mate in '44, but Democratic party officials nixed the idea as Jimmy represented segregation and was no friend to labor unions. Young Byrnes grew up on St. Philip's Street in Charleston and attended St. Patrick Catholic Church. His home site is unmarked but sat on the southeast corner where St. Philip's Street intersects Calhoun. Jimmy's father died while he, Jimmy, was a schoolboy, and he had to leave school and go to work to support his mother and little sister. His mother took in washing. Byrnes went to work as a runner in the law office of Hagood, Mordecai, Gadsden, and Rutledge at 35 Broad Street. He cleaned offices and ran errands. Ben Rutledge took out a library subscription in the Charleston Library Society -- then located on Broad Street -- in Jimmy's name. Rutledge set up reading assignments for Byrnes and quizzed him on his work. Later Byrnes learned shorthand so that he could upgrade to become a court reporter. He used these note taking skills to catch Stalin and Molotov in numerous lies at Potsdam. Young Byrnes read law at night in the law library of Hagood, Mordecai, Gadsden, and Rutledge and sat for the bar exam in Columbia after 5 years of private study. His law exam score was the highest in S.C.! The young attorney began his practice of law in Aiken, and he married a pretty Episcopalian girl, Maude Perkins Busch. The Irish Catholic Byrnes changed his religion to Episcopalian in order to avoid the stigma then associated with Catholicism in the South, but Governor Cole Blease smeared him with anti-Catholic rhetoric even so. Jimmy Byrnes became SC's most distinguished citizen of the 20th century, perhaps of all time. He resigned as Secretary of State for Truman to become Governor of S.C. Back home he worked to reduce the "Jim Crow" laws and to improve education.

The Byrnes family owned a beach house on Sullivan's Island, and each Friday afternoon South Carolinians would line U.S. Highway 176 to catch a view of the motorcade. While Governor, Byrnes maneuvered to get his former aide, Donald Russell, appointed as President of the University of South Carolina. Byrnes later became a trustee of USC, and he set up a trust fund from his modest estate to educate orphans. Byrnes, an influential man who was self-taught, educated his younger sister at the College of Charleston and sent his daughter to Converse. His son became a surgeon in Florence. James Francis Byrnes was a partner in what became the most powerful law firm in the state in the pre-WW II years -- Nichols, Wyche & Byrnes in Spartanburg. He and wife Maude built a beautiful but not ostentatious home on Otis Boulevard in that upstate city. A young attorney, Donald Russell, became associated with the firm and soon became Jimmy Byrnes's right-hand man, serving as a staff member while Byrnes was Secretary of State.

At Potsdam it was Byrnes who picked up on evidence that, despite what Stalin said publicly at the conference, his intentions were to subvert Rumania,

Bulgaria, and Hungary completely to Soviet control. In economic negotiations about German reparations, Byrnes got the better of Soviet negotiator Maisky over whether the West or the Soviets would supervise the heavily industrialized western German sector. Maisky was relieved of duty and never seen or heard of again.

Truman later relied upon Byrnes's advice to make the decision to drop the atomic bombs. Secretary of State Byrnes brought the key staff of the State Department to his Otis Boulevard home in Spartanburg to deliberate upon this awesome decision. Byrnes' death on April 9, 1972, led to the most publicized funeral in state history. Today, Schloss Cecilienhof is a pricey hotel that sits unmarked amidst an enormous manicured garden. While savoring weiner schnitzel and Reisling the diner overlooks the museum room where the conference took place. Being at Schloss Cecilienhof in Potsdam where Charlestonian Jimmy Byrnes helped to reconfigure Europe is an unforgettable experience.

Hamburg, Germany Has Played a Key Role in Charleston History

Just the other day the 706-foot container ship Cap Castillo of the Hamburg-Sud line was being worked at the Wando-Welch Terminal. Hamburg-Sud line operates 170 cargo vessels and several of them make regular calls in Charleston. A hundred and fifty years ago lumber man and shipbuilder Henry Buck of Bucksport on the Waccamaw River sent ships filled with lumber to Hamburg, Germany. During the era of the Confederacy, Charles Prioleau, the Liverpool manager of George Alfred Trenholm's Fraser and Trenholm Company, arranged for shipments of Austrian-made Lorenz rifles to be shipped from Hamburg to Charleston on blockade runners. From 1862 to 1865 Confederate sailors walked the streets of Hamburg and reveled in the culture of this old Baltic Port. Although World War II left Hamburg in ruins, several blocks of the old city by the Elbe River remain to give the modern traveler a sense of what an old Hanseatic League city was like. Few Charlestonians wander as far afield today, but for those who do, there is still adventure aplenty.

Traveling from Berlin to Hamburg takes one through Saxony (the heart of the old Saxon world where many migrated to Britain 1500 years ago), through Anhalt and Bremen-Lower Saxony. This is the region where Napoleon drafted many of his men for the invasion of Russia in 1812. You come close to Holstein of the old Schleiswig-Holstein province that was held by the Danish after the Thirty-Years War but taken by Prussia and Austria in the 1860s. The terrain traversed is so rich in history; it was bloody soil in the Thirty Years War (1618-48)--some of it burned as many as nine times by marauding armies. Through here King Gustavus Adolphus IV marched with his Protestant army from Denmark to ally with the Germanic confederation against the Holy Roman Empire. It was through here that Allied bombers dropped hundreds of tons of bombs each day between 1944 and 1945. Over 3,200 American air crew were lost over France and Germany in 26 months in '43-'45. Here is a quote from the historian of the 8th Air Force Museum:

During the spring, summer, and fall of the 1943 Eighth Air Force losses of planes and men sometimes reached 12% for a day's raid. One in four airmen was being lost. At one point it became statistically impossible for a bomber crewman to survive a 25-mission tour of duty.

It is hard to stare at the loamy brown soil that today produces huge rolls of hay without thinking of its bloodstained history. The train rolls into Madgeburg, Luther's hometown as a lad. He would recognize nothing but the fir trees. A few church spires reach up; however, few attend regularly.

The reason for going to Hamburg is to see firsthand one of the principal cities of the old Hanseatic League, the 12th and thirteenth century fringe of "free cities" (not ruled by princes, but rather governed by merchant bankers). Adam Smith figured out his free-market theory based upon what he'd studied about the Mediterranean trade between Genoa and Venice. He saw more clearly than anyone else that a free market, unrestricted by pompous, greedy kings was the unstoppable tide of trade that we know as capitalism. Money is like water. It flows where it wants to, and with water and money, restraints are eventually worn down. Hanseatic League towns range from Brugges on the North Sea to Riga on the Daugava River in Latvia. The major trade port was Lubeck and minor ports were Danzig on the Baltic, Bergen on the North Sea side of Norway, Hamburg on the Elbe, Cologne on the Rhine, London on the Thames, and Novgorod on the Volkov River in Russia. Most of these ports escaped domination by princes during the early middle ages, and most of this area escaped the ravages of the Thirty Years War (1618-48). So the wispy ghost of the modern free market economy rises from the murky tide of the Elbe flowing through Hamburg.

By rail the rural scenery is punctuated by the graffiti on every underpass or building. There is a symmetry and balance to the three dimensional letters and characters, but why is it everywhere?

Rolling into the *hauptbahnhof* in downtown Hamburg, one can see the Europaischer Hotel from the train window. One may want to see the cabaret "piano" bars that were so much a part of German culture in the 1930s -- remember Liza Minelli in *Caberet*? However, jazz clubs abound in Hamburg, and alternative rock and underground music clubs line the river front. It was in Hamburg in December 1959, that four scruffy lads known as "Johnny and the Moon Dogs" played an eight week gig (12 hours a day) at Club Grosse Freiheit on the Reeperbahn. They were the cheap cellar act not good enough to play upstairs. The Moon Dogs shared a one-room apartment in the rundown district--known even then for sleaze and drugs. John Lennon, Paul McCartney, George Harrison, and Stu Sutcliffe pounded out a Liverpool R&B sound that was five years away from bursting on the world rock music scene. Stu dropped out of the Moon Dogs and George Harrison moved over to bass. The band picked up Rick Starkey -- AKA Ringo Starr -- at some dive in Liverpool. The rest is music history. The way to become intimate with Hamburg is to stroll to the waterfront and take a harbor cruise all around the world's third largest port. This port city dwarfs Charleston in tonnage, containers, and in tall cranes -- as far as the eye can see, the Hamburg port stretches on. The wind whips up on this harbor which is just a few miles inland from the North Sea. An average of 55 cargo ships a day call at Hamburg. Charleston gets between five and eight a day. Hamburg-Sud, Cosco, P & O, Maersk Lines, P. & O. NedLloyd, and Hapag-Lloyd are huge container liners that call on Hamburg and Charleston. There is a weekly Hamburg-Charleston run. Several old three-masted sailing ships serve as colorful reminders of Hamburg before the age of steam. Hitler's *Graf Spree* pocket battleship was built in one of the many shipyards here. Upriver, a sleek, black U-Boat (#43) sits at a dock as a silent reminder that this was a major U - Boat base of operations in both world wars. The sight of that WW II submarine complete with swastika on the conning tower is startling, and no sign gives evidence that it is a museum display. From the Elbe one can see the city on a low ridge running a mile and a half along the river. Great homes -- none older than the 1950s -- grace the ridge, and an odd assortment of shipping industry structures jam the shore. Container ships dwarf the tour boats. Monster cranes deftly lift truck-sized containers and place them in neat stacks. These cranes never, ever stop roaring. The Hamburg port is six to eight times the size of ours in Charleston. It is the Euro hub for world trade, second only to Rotterdam.

The stately Atlantic Hotel sits on one of the great lakes in the city. This 19th century hotel was where the well-to-do Germans stayed prior to departing for transatlantic steamship voyages. Its elegance shines through to today's jet connected continent. The grand hotel still has elegant dining advertised. Sidewalk cafes abound in all Euro cities now, but the finest dining in Hamburg is along the city's canals. Around dusk, opera tenors and solo violinists perform on canal arcades sending haunting operatic aurias wafting over the water. Waiters pull corks on bottle after bottle of chilled Rhine wine!

The Reeperbahn is a sight to forget. You have been through the Bowery in New York and you have walked through Amsterdam's infamous waterfront, but the Reeperbahn takes it all for commercializing and marketing illicit behavior. Tourist bus tours market the Reeperbahn as unrivaled in Western Europe for a smorgasbord of red-light offerings. The street is about a half mile in length and four lanes separate the store fronts and cafes. The guide proudly announced that no prurient desires could be unsatisfied in the *Reeperbahn*.

The more innocent side of Hamburg lies near the Rathaus square and the few 18th century structures not leveled by the Brits in '44. On the canals there is a row of old warehouses dating back hundreds of years--warehouses still in use. The international shipping executives and the bankers are the "big boys" in town. Glass and steel structures abound, sometimes with a four-foot deep facade of a four-story 18th century building wedged in for old world flavor. Do not miss seeing the art museum containing German impressionism and the paintings of the Norwegian, Edvard Munch. They don't have "The Scream," Munch's most famous work. One doesn't see the Hamburg that the Confederacy's shipping agents of Fraser and Trenholm saw in 1862, but it is as exciting to us as it was to them!

Much of Charleston's German Population Hails From Berlin

It was Thomas Wolfe of Asheville who wrote a novel in the 1930s entitled *You Can't Go Home Again* (Scribner, Posthumously c.1940). In a prose style so real that you hear the Wolfe family's hall clock ticking in the background, Wolfe made certain he'd never be able to go home again -- not after what he revealed about the dysfunctional dynamics of his family! By way of contrast, Andrea Mehrländer of Berlin has written a revealing book, *The Germans of Charleston, Richmond and New Orleans During the Civil War* (De Gruyter, c. 2011). Berlin native Andrea Mehrländer's noteworthy work tells much about the experiences of Prussian Germans who immigrated to Charleston, the "Holy City" -- though they called it the "Black City" -- in antebellum times. Ohlandt, Wulbern, Stelling, Johanns, Lilenthal, *et al*, are names that resonate through the annals of Charleston history. The descendants of these grand old surnames can't go home again, either, for the Allied bombers of World War II removed any vestige of what would have been familiar to their ancestors.

Through Mehrländer we catch a glimpse of what the forebears of Charleston's German population experienced in their transition from European to American culture. For starters, we learn that the 1860 Census of Charleston reveals that 2,437 people of German birth dwelled in the city. A large proportion of these Deutschlanders hailed from Prussia -- many from the environs of Berlin. Captain Heinrich Wieting was master of the sailing bark Johann Friedrich, a ship built in Hamburg and designed especially for the Hamburg to Charleston maritime trade. Prussians preferred Wieting's ship for the crossing because the death rate on his ship was 25% that of other sea captains making the voyage. Wieting was a careful navigator, and he selected fruit and vegetable food stuffs that were wholesome and well-packed. So beloved was Wieting by the German population of Charleston that Saint Matthew's Lutheran Church held a special Thanksgiving service honoring him in 1850. He was given the title "Father of the Immigrants" by the locals. Wieting was like a family member to the

Germans here, for he kept them in touch with their connections back in the old country, and he even advanced his own money for his passengers to get started in their new life here. Mehrländer reveals that even though Charleston was 58% Caucasian on the eve of the War Between the States, German immigrants referred to this place as "that Black City."

Charleston's German-descended population today is fortunate to be able to travel uninhibited across the fatherland since the fall of the Berlin Wall in 1989. Checkpoint Charlie used to be as far as a tourist from the West could go in search of his roots during the 40-year Cold War. The Brandenburg Gate and the River Spree are assorted bits of the surviving culture and geography that would have been familiar to the immigrants.

Even though Berlin paid a terrible price for adhering to Adolf Hitler's Fascist regime, there's temptation aplenty to go and see what remains of the old and what passes for "New Berlin." Captain Wieting would know nothing of the scenes he'd see there today.

For Charlestonians the route to Berlin is a direct flight from Atlanta to Frankfurt with a connecting hop to Tegel Airport. Note the free coffee and hot chocolate bar as soon as you deplane. Ignore the skinheads who stroll menacingly about the luggage claim. A flight from Hamburg to Berlin takes barely 25 minutes. Tegel used to service East Berlin and the drabness is still apparent. A taxi ride into Hauptbahnhof (train station) winds through a shabby district that was Communist until 1989. Punks scrawl graffiti, some of it quite artistic, on every flat wall space available. This graffiti "art" represents a deep alienation in the youth culture. The main shopping district of Berlin is free of grafitti defacement, but the garish, modern architecture is not pleasing. One reason to go to Berlin is to explore the Bauhaus era of the 1920s -- or what's left of it. Bauhaus was a modern art, art deco architectural movement made popular by Walter Gropius during the time of the Weimar Republic, 1919 - 1931. The financial bleakness of the Great Depression stymied the movement, and Hitler's fascist architects killed it. Otte House and Sommerfeld House are the notable Bauhaus masterpieces in Berlin. The new Berlin, however, is the most unpleasant juxtaposition of the modern and the bizarre in architectural styles that most of us have ever seen. One might think that they designed it this way after the war just to punish us. It's as if the architects were saying, "Now look what you have made us do." Potsdamer Platz is the ritzy square where Herr Hitler had his underground bunker and command post in the Spring of '45. There's no resemblance to the 19th century Berlin that our Charleston immigrants would have known. The Hitlers committed suicide beneath the Platz, though nothing marks the site. An Imax theater occupies the spot. Posh arcades and pricey coffee shops are just across the street. Hitler stood in Potsdamer Square in 1935 and said, "In ten years I will change this city so that none will recognize it." Well, he did -- with a lot of help from U.S.A. 8th Air Force. Not even the survivors recognized Berlin in 1945. Of course, Herr Hitler meant that he would make it into a glass and steel city the way he was then transforming Munich. Apparently, the postwar Germans do not want to remember anything about the prewar Germany. "Berlin is content to be constantly under construction," is the comment one hears often from the locals. Tall construction cranes are everywhere. A blue hot air balloon tethered with a hundred yards of rope eases viewers up for a summit view of the city. It is a city of 3.4 million. East Berlin was separated from free Berlin by a street and a wall--the ugliest wall anyone has ever seen. It makes your skin crawl to ride down the streets of East Berlin -- though they have been free streets for 23 years. The drab sameness, the restraining walls behind the main wall, the concertina wire, the ugly council flats where the workers lived -- all reminders of daily life under Communist rule. It was supposed to be their workers' paradise. One hundred and one people died trying to get across that wall between 1961 and 1989. Going through Checkpoint Charlie is a lump in the throat experience. Talk about a tacky area, however! The Checkpoint Charlie intersection is the most historic landmark of the Cold War.

The River Spree makes a gentle curve by the Reichstag -- a reconstructed Reichstag with a curious glass dome that's open "so the great ideas within can pass out to the world." They say that the see-through dome represents reunification. Maybe it's a silent tribute to Point Number One of Wilson's Fourteen Points of 1919 -- the point about no future secret treaties. Ironically, the dome was designed by British architect, Norman Foster. The Yale - educated Foster grew up in war-torn Manchester, a city devastated by German bombers. The new Reichstag sits on the site of the old Reichstag that burned in 1933 -- probably sabotaged by Nazis. You may remember reading in William Shirer's *Berlin Diary* (1941) that Shirer took a midnight walk along the bank of the Spree near the Reichstag the night he learned he was expelled from Berlin (1940).

Our embassy is in the center of the city on Pariser Platz, yet it is behind bunkers and closed off streets with heavily armed German *polezei* toting submachine guns. We have a new embassy building, but, for the time being, we look very much under siege -- a glaring contrast to the sunny and open Russian embassy two streets over. The only church that you spot in downtown Berlin is the bombed out "Hollow Tooth," a ruin from the war glaringly out of place in the midst of the bustling city. The church spire has no pinnacle -- thus the name "hollow tooth" -- the *Kaiser - Wilhelm - Gedächtniskirche.* There is very little to remind one of spirituality in Berlin--or Hamburg and Cologne, for that matter. The churches and cathedrals are as cold and vacant as the ones in England. The spirit of Luther seems to have long departed Germany--at least in the cities. Unlike the British, however; the Germans do not use their cathedrals and churches as shrines to their empire and military. You will find more statues to Melancthon and Karlstadt than to Luther.

The Berliners love JFK! More than any other American, he captured their hearts. When he stood on Unter den Linden Strasse in 1962 and proclaimed, *"Ich bin Berliner,"* it was one of the best ever presidential goofs. *Berliner,* the way he pronounced it, meant "jelly doughnut," and the crowd cracked up at the result, "I am a Berliner jelly doughnut!" But they loved him, anyway. Suspended high over one thoroughfare is a McDonald-Douglas DC-3 aircraft with USAF markings on it to commemorate the Berlin Airlift in 1948. It is nicknamed "the raisin bomber" in honor of the pilots who dropped little parachutes filled with candy and fruit to the destitute children of Berlin during the Soviet blockade.

There are many reasons to visit Berlin even if it is nothing like the city that gave up a part of its population to Charleston a century and a half ago.

Vienna, St. Petersburg, Berlin, and Hamburg Once Were Thriving S.C. Towns

Once upon a time a fellow could hop a pole boat from Silver Bluff, James Henry Hammond's plantation high up the Savannah River, and glide past scenic river towns with whimsical names such as Vienna, St. Petersburg, Berlin, and Hamburg. That these townships once existed here is testimony to the active imagination as well as to the wanderlust of early Carolinians. Our nineteenth century citizens were far more mobile than we imagined when we studied about them in school. Sometimes our ancestors created place names to honor the old country, and sometimes they allowed their sense of humor to have its way. Assorted characters descended the ship's ladder and stepped off the planks of Adger's Wharf onto the cobbled streets of Charleston in the 1800s. There were peddlers, apothecaries, tinkers, and masons. There were itinerants, hustlers, and louts. No one epitomizes that devil-may-care, throw caution to the winds attitude more than does that flamboyant German land speculator, Henry Schultz -- the man who became the autocrat of his own "Hamburg on the Savannah." The Carolina upcountry that greeted Herr Schultz in the early 1800s was decidedly of a different era than what meets our eye today.

    The wide Savannah River meanders stogidly by the slight knoll on which was nestled the bustling village of Vienna. Across the way one could make out the houses, sheds, and docks of two other newly laid out towns, St. Petersburg near the confluence of the Savannah and Broad Rivers, and Lisbon on the west bank of the Broad. Not far up river was the little port of Southampton. A hint of Europe, if in name only, still flavored this frontier corner of America. The daylight hours in Vienna were rent by the sound of axes and cross-cut saws. The scent of fresh-hewn lumber stacked on wharves greeted the casual stroller just as nearby rafted river skiffs knocked and bumped monotonously in the gentle waves. Little Vienna was already known for its wealth and refinement, for much lumber was barged down-river to Augusta and Savannah. Cotton bales were piling up, too, for that crop was destined to bring great wealth to planters in the area. The town was characteristic of many "lumber" villages that sprang up upriver from larger towns, and as long as there was a building boom, these tiny metropolises prospered in the lumber trade.

From the scant background material available on Schultz, it seems likely that he was a self-taught mechanical whiz who exuded self-confidence and unbridled optimism for life in this new land. Schultz got out of his native Hamburg, Germany, just before Napoleon imposed the Convention of Artlenburg settlement upon Hanover. The French invader forced the surrender of surrounding Germanic kingdoms and conscripted German men into his occupying battalions. Quite a few men with ambition sought outbound ship passage from Bremen, Hamburg, and Kiel. According to Edwin J. Scott in his long out-of-print book *Random Recollections of A Long Life, 1806 to 1876*, Henry Schultz arrived in Charleston "with no capital but his head and his hands." Had Henry remained in Hamburg, Germany, beyond 1801, he may very well have been caught up in Napoleon's ill-fated invasion of Russia. Instead, Schultz had a meteoric rise to fame and fortune and a spectacular descent into financial ruin and ignominy on the western fringe of South Carolina in a town of his design that he named appropriately -- Hamburg.

Schultz entered Charleston just as the city began to quiet from the excitement of the Election of 1800 where Jefferson and Burr routed John Adams and Charles Cotesworth Pinckney with a whopping 61% of the vote. Though the state was solidly democratic, the coastal area possessed many Federalist backers of favorite son C. C. Pinckney. This was the first time in the United States that we had transferred leadership from one political party to another and no violence had erupted. And Jefferson captured the imagination of the common man so much more than the rigid Federalists. Schultz, who hailed from the free city of Hamburg, the old Hanseatic League port, relished this expectant air of opportunity.

The Old Hanse League dates to the 1300s when seaports on the Baltic, mostly of Teutonic origin, allied for trade purposes and managed to elude the rule of prince and bishop in their pursuit of free trade practices unheard since the time of the ancient Phoenicians. That bold spirit of the Hamburg free trader was the embodiment of Henry Schultz as he breathed the breezes of the salt marsh in this the South's most prosperous seaport. It can be assumed that he did not arrive here friendless because of the fraternal nature of the German people already inhabiting this area. It's likely that Schultz had connections here already.

Until the biographer brings the complete story of Henry Schultz to light, we must contend with what is readily known, and that is that Schultz arrived in

Charleston in 1801 and he made his way to Augusta in 1806. In the intervening years he very well may have been a peddler -- a traveling salesman of hardware. German immigrants to Charleston soon dominated the ironmonger trade.

Augusta, a small city inspired by the grandeur of Charleston, was a thriving commercial center. It was nestled against a bend in the broad Savannah River and was destined to become famous as a river port for tobacco and cotton. The area around Augusta had built up rapidly after the Revolution and served as the trading mart for the vast expanse of territory above it. Speculating in land and cock fighting were the two favorite pastimes. Fox's Tavern downtown was where men came together for spirits and for swapping stories. Warehouses for tobacco were springing up near the river. Gaff-rigged trading vessels tied up to numerous docks to off-load merchandise and to take on casks of pungent tobacco leaves. Cotton bales stacked higher than one's head would line those docks. The dusty, wide streets of Augusta were fringed with shops that had picturesque, swinging shop signs like "Johnson and Clark - Chair Makers," or "Francis Vallotton - Boots and Shoes."

In Augusta Henry Schultz found a true American frontier river town, and he was just one of many roughneck rivermen working a pole boat along the wharves. The Savannah River was not the Elbe or the Rhine, but it lured upland commerce to the coast where mighty sailing vessels made their way from the port of Savannah to all points. Just when it was that Henry Schultz dreamed of setting up a rival river port to Augusta is not known, but by 1814 Schultz had constructed a durable bridge across the Savannah River just a little north of where I-20 crosses today. In fact, the stone abutments are still visible. The Schultz bridge outlasted all of the others attempted in the early 19th century.

By 1821 this industrious immigrant had purchased significant land holdings on the South Carolina side of the river opposite Augusta. The swamp land was cheap and unsettled; however, that would soon change as Schultz drained and cleared his property. A few miles south of his location some nostalgic German newcomer had named a waterfront settlement Berlin. So, with a Vienna and a St. Petersburg across and upriver from him, Schultz called his fair knoll overlooking the river after his home town of Hamburg.

Hamburg had a half dozen streets, several hundred citizens, and connection to three roads leading inland and two roads leading westward. Schultz and business partner John McKinne started a major financial institution, the Bridge Bank of Augusta, which for years was the most solvent institution for miles around. Schultz became a wealthy man who engaged in commerce, toll-roads, waterborne freight, and agriculture. He was mayor, bank president, judge, and chief of police in his small town. However, Schultz had a temper and one day a suspected thief was ordered by him to undergo 40 lashes. The suspect died and Schultz was charged with the man's death. Thus began the unraveling of a mighty American success story. Schultz tried to commit suicide by shooting himself, but the bullet exited his head with no serious consequence. A run on his bank saw him unable to redeem notes into specie, and bankruptcy loomed on the horizon. The last anyone remembered of Henry Schultz before he died penniless was his pitiful attempts to harangue the South Carolina legislature for reimbursements for his failed toll-road venture. In later years Hamburg became the terminus of the Charleston to Hamburg Railroad venture, and the little town gained notoriety as the scene of a bloody riot in the Hampton Redshirt Campaign of 1876. Today, Hamburg is a bluff of 600 feet on the outskirts of North Augusta.

Retired Physician Receives Honor from SC Medical Association

For the folks who know retired physician Ira Horton, there's no need repeating the old phrase, "He's an original. The angels broke the mold when they made him." Those who've been associated with South Carolina medicine since the mid-1950s know Ira to be a strong advocate of family medicine and rural health care in this state. Some know him as the Orangeburg doctor who, in 1976, upon the urging of Floyd Spence, the ranking Republican on the House Armed Services Committee, left private practice after 17 years to start a family practice residency program for the U.S. Navy here in Charleston. All total, Ira Horton devoted 44 years to the medical profession, much of it here in South Carolina. The South Carolina Medical Association at its 150th annual meeting, held last Saturday at the Marriott Convention Center in Myrtle Beach, honored Ira Horton with the President's Award for his distinguished service to medicine. "This doctor has so much compassion that he'd stay up with you all night long if you were hurting," said outgoing SCMA president, Doctor Gary Delaney.

Growing up on a six-horse cotton farm in rural South Carolina might not seem to be the ideal preparation for medical school; however, Ira -- who was known by his initials "I.B." then -- disagrees. His elementary schooling was done in a one-room school where another of his schoolmates was the sister of Carlisle Floyd, the opera composer. Ira's father was overseer for a large family farm. Sharecropper families totaling 32 people also lived on the Horton place located northwest of Camden and equidistant to Hartsville and Kershaw. The nearest town is Bethune. Horton's earliest farm memory involves his helping farm hands take a wagon load of cotton overnight to be first in line the next morning at the Kershaw House cotton exchange 17 miles away. As a boy, Horton plowed a mule, hoed cotton, picked cotton, and knocked worms off of tobacco leaves just as the other farmers did; however, Ira "burned the midnight oil" to get top grades.

In 1943 standardized testing was in its infancy, but South Carolina high schools implemented a test for 11th graders that evaluated math and science aptitude. Despite the fact that his school did not offer such advanced courses, Ira's score prompted officials to recommend that he be allowed to skip his last year of school and enter a training program for jet propulsion at White Sands, New Mexico. His mother advised him to finish high school.

Disappointed, but not dissuaded from his ambition of obtaining a college education, Ira got a job as a soda jerk at the drugstore in Bethune. In that town the two most respected men were the town's lone physician and the pharmacist. Both were avid bird hunters. Horton's father was a keen sportsman, too, known for the quality of his short-haired pointers. Legend has it that Ira Sr. killed five quail with five shots, and his dogs deposited each bird deftly into his game pocket. "Doc" Braswell impressed the younger Ira with advice that a pharmacy degree would open doors.

On August 14, 1945, the six-foot, 17 year old drove to Columbia to see the Navy recruiter. With his high school diploma and Beta Club Award in hand, Ira was sworn in as a naval recruit as news was breaking that the ceasefire with Japan had been declared. He rushed back to Kershaw to see his girlfriend, Anne Jones, the younger sister of his high school English teacher. They celebrated with a burger and shake at Foster's Drive-in. He decided that day to marry Anne, but he didn't get up the nerve to ask her for another year. Ira's brother, Alva, was on destroyer duty in the North Atlantic and two cousins had survived Pearl Harbor. Soon after bootcamp this sandhills fella found himself attached to the 2nd Marine Division as a Hospital Corpsman. Postwar marines trained constantly and the lanky corpsman hunkered in a landing craft off Vieques Island as the battleship *Missouri* opened up with salvos of everything she had -- 16-inch guns and 5-inch guns. The *Mighty Mo*, site of the Japanese surrender in 1945, fired off all of her magazine rounds left over from the War. It was an awesome sight that the old sailor has never forgotten.

Hospital Corpsman Petty Officer First Class Horton served with Chief Pharmacist's Mate Wheeler B. Lipes, U.S.N. Lipes was the sailor who performed a successful appendectomy while submerged onboard a submarine in Tokyo harbor in 1942. There were no medical doctors, so Lipes had to do the procedure. The movie *Destination Tokyo* commemorates the event. When Admiral Chester Nimitz checked into the Philadelphia Naval Hospital for a checkup after World War II, Lipes and Horton processed a case of Scotch through the hospital pharmacy to stock the Admiral's bar. Lipes was another inspiration that led Horton to apply to pharmacy school.

When Horton was called back to duty in the Korean War, S.C. Medical College pharmacy professor Dr. Hoch (Hoke) finagled a way for him to do his military service at the naval hospital at night and attend classes during the day. There, a naval reserve psychiatrist, Lieutenant Neno, influenced Ira to push on beyond pharmacy school and to attend medical school, too. At the time, that seemed like a bridge too far, for Ira had married his sweetheart and the G.I. Bill paid only a little beyond tuition. To make ends meet, the ambitious young man worked the late shift at Gainey's Drug Store on the southwest corner of King and Calhoun Streets. In spite of the grueling schedule, Ira always ranked from number one to number three in his class. He studied after midnight and before dawn.

In 1957, Ira's mentor, Vince Mosely, M.D., was insistent upon Ira taking a residency in internal medicine. He relished every field that he rotated through -- especially obstetrics. Back in the 1950s, two well-known physicians were recruited to be on the faculty of the medical school here -- John Hawk and Robert Hagerty. Those two, plus Vince Mosely, held a regular Friday afternoon round table discussion on whatever medically remarkable topic struck their fancy. Sometimes the discussions went on into the night.

Back in the '50s Peter Gazes returned from his cardiology residency in Philadelphia and brought with him the technology of the EKG machine. Ira and his classmates were taught how to make their own EKG graph paper by using a candle to smoke the white paper in a way that would make the needle readings visible. There were legends teaching at the medical school -- Lynch, Knisely, Banov, Pratt-Thomas, Orvin, Cuttino to name a few. Despite working long hours at Gainey's, Ira still ranked with the top students in his class of 1957 and he earned scholastic honors from A.O.A. and Rho Chi.

The young doctor decided against a residency in internal medicine and chose family medicine in Orangeburg over Aiken and Spartanburg. Vince Mosely asked Ira to take on his aunt as a patient when he set up practice there, a request that Ira considers to be one of his greatest compliments.

Making house calls for thirty miles in every direction was a daily affair for this country doctor. He and Anne built their dream home, a replica of the Eisenhower cottage at the Augusta National, overlooking a lake. Occasionally, Ira drove a 1948 Bentley on his house calls much to the delight of his patients, including the legendary Bar-B-Que restauranteur, Earl Dukes. In July of 1966, Ira delivered 27 babies in between his daily office hours, hospital rounds, and house calls. He was on duty the night of the Orangeburg Massacre in 1968 and participated in the trauma unit that dealt with the numerous casualties.

Doctor Horton helped pioneer board certification for family medicine. In the 1970s family medicine was one of the first medical fields to pursue national certification. He served as Chief of Staff of the Orangeburg Regional Hospital for a term or two, and his peers elected him as president of the South Carolina Academy of Family Practice in 1972. In the early 1970s Horton broke the color barrier by bringing Dr. Spencer Disher of Orangeburg into that select group. For relaxation he bought a farm near Bowman, got his private pilot's license, and traveled to the Holy Land several times. However, studying and practicing medicine have been his vocation and avocation.

When Congressman Spence approached Ira about making military medicine more "people friendly" in 1974, Ira was already toying with an offer from Dr. Hiram B. Curry to come back as a teaching fellow at the Medical University. However, the idea of serving again in the Navy--this time as a Captain with a regular commission--was a great motivation. He helped start the family practice residency here at the Naval Hospital, and many doctors came through the program. Three of those doctors reached the rank of admiral. The Navy made Ira Chief of Medicine for the Naval Sealift Command and sent him all over the world. The Navy's family physicians elected him president of the Uniform Chapter of the Academy of Family Medicine. Horton's idea of retirement was to take the post of Medical Director of the Department of Health and Human Services in Columbia. In 2001 Governor Jim Hodges honored him for his service to South Carolina rural health care.

Retired and living at the Franke in Mt. Pleasant, Ira still makes house calls -- but now he brings boxes of Whitman's Sampler and encouragement instead of his black bag and stethoscope. He tells everyone to "practice the ministry of being." By the way, Ira Horton is my dad.

Lordy, Lordy, Travis Jervey Is 40

It's true! The Six-Million-Dollar Man, Number 32, Travis Jervey, quietly turned 40 this past Saturday, May 5, at his home in the Old Village surrounded by his adoring family and a yard full of exotic plants that signify his newest passion -- gardening! But don't think for a second that this two-time Super Bowl competitor is out to pasture. Take one look at his 6 foot, 220-pound frame and youthful face and you may mistake him for a 25-year-old. Though he's been retired from pro-football for a decade, he's still in tiptop shape physically, and he can be seen coaching others as a personal trainer at 101 Pitt Fitness Center. What other town this size offers a young athlete the chance to be trained daily by a former NFL great? Travis Jervey has earned the good life; however, the road to success in the National Football League is a route that very few of us will ever experience.

We all remember the lightning fast running back who starred for Coach Dickie Dingle's Wando Warriors back in the '90s. Those were glory days for Wando football, for they had as starters two stellar athletes who'd shine in the NFL -- Travis Jervey and Dexter Coakley. Coakley went on to star as a linebacker for Appalachian State and he played pro ball for the Dallas Cowboys. Travis Jervey was the record-breaking fullback for Charlie Taafe's Citadel Bulldogs, and he starred for the Green Bay Packers. Wando teammates Jervey and Coakley played opposite each other in the Southern Conference and in the NFL. They still keep up with each other today. Success in the NFL comes at a high price. Few will ever experience the tortuous training, the exhaustion, or the pain that these athletes put themselves through in order to play a few minutes on Sundays in the fall. Those few minutes may be worth millions to the players and mega-millions to their franchise, but the players must exhibit super-human strength and perform heroic feats of athleticism.

Everybody knows that Travis Jervey grew up here and attended Sullivan's Island Elementary. Shortly after Travis reached Wando, he became known as a bone-crunching ballcarrier who had rockets on his heels. The best season he had was the 1988 season when the Warriors went 9 and 4 -- losing to Middleton, Summerville, and Berkeley twice.

Though Travis is our local sports hero, he was actually born in Columbia. He has never known any other father except Ned Jervey -- who became Travis' dad when he, Ned, married Travis' mother in the early 1970s. However, recently Travis has come to terms with his biological father, Dyke Dolly, who passed away at age 59 two weeks ago in North Augusta. Dolly was among the football legends of North Augusta High School. He was a big man with speed. He starred on the 1971 Shrine Bowl team and parlayed that success into a football scholarship to the University of South Carolina. Gamecock faithful remember the fleet-footed Dolly with the number 10 on Coach Dietzel's roster. Dyke Dolly played pro-football in the Canadian League and was a walk on with several NFL teams. He spent most of his life as an iron worker around the country. Travis never really knew his biological father and has learned only recently that both Dyke Dolly and Dyke's father, Richard Dolly, played pro-football.

What Travis recently learned about his grandfather, Richard Dolly, is newsworthy in a big way. Richard Dolly, father to Dyke of 1970s Carolina fame and grandfather of NFL star Travis Jervey, won a football scholarship from Franklin High School near Augusta to attend West Virginia University in 1934. Dolly played defensive end and blocked the extra-point that gave the Mountaineers the victory in a 7-6 WVU win in the Sun Bowl. Prior to World War II, Travis' grandfather played both ways for the Steelers. He went in the military in WW II and returned to the Steelers and later had a career in the FBI.

Just two other players in professional football appear to have had a legacy of three generations in the sport -- George Pyne III, who is Travis' age, played for the Boston Patriots, and he is the third generation of his family to play. Clay Matthews III, currently of the Green Bay Packers, is a third generation pro-football family. Add Travis Jervey to that elite grouping.

What made fans love Travis Jervey from the first time he donned a Wando Warrior jersey through his Citadel days to his glory days at Green Bay was that he was absolutely fearless. Whether Travis was running with the football, or tackling someone, he'd charge like a runaway freight train. Violent midfield collisions with Travis sprinting away toward the goal are the memories most of us have of this incredible athlete. Anyone who was at Johnson-Hagood Stadium in 1994 when Citadel smashed VMI, witnessed one of Jervey's amazing trademark runs. He bolted through the defensive line and scampered 68 yards for a score. Every VMI player had a hand on him at some point. The next year in Norfolk Travis did it again against VMI -- this time taking the kickoff the length of the field to score. However, because Citadel played small teams the pro scouts didn't take the school's talent seriously. In fact, pro scouts were shocked at his 40-yard dash time. It was reported that Travis Jervey had the fastest 40-yard sprint of any of the NFL tryout in 1995. The Citadel standout paid his dues to get where he is. He spent many lonely hours sprinting up and down the steep hill at Battery Marshall on Sullivan's Island. He lifted weights and worked himself into such shape that *Muscle and Fitness* magazine named him "the best physique in pro-football." Travis was officially clocked as the 4th fastest player in the NFL. "Fast, but not elusive," was a quote that one sportswriter used.

The pro draft was a nail-biter for Jervey. "The Citadel doesn't have a tough enough schedule to impress the pros," said one writer. Well, Citadel's Number 32 went in the 5th round to the Green Bay Packers. The Packers were ready to draft Terrell Davis--the UGA running back who succeeded to Herschel Walker's slot -- when the recruiters suddenly dropped Davis and picked up Jervey instead. Terrell Davis had been injury prone in his senior year at Georgia, and Travis appeared indestructible.

Travis says that pro football is business -- for players and owners. Each week he got 1/17th of his yearly pay. "A lot of the young players can't handle that much money coming in all at once." During pre - season, all players received $1200 for what amounted to 14-hour days of gruelling practices and game film study. "You wouldn't do that kind of work for $1200 a week," he laughs. Our star stayed calm before games by reading Clive Cussler novels while immersed in a hot tub.

The playbook for Green Bay was complex for Travis coming from the Citadel's "wishbone" offense. Dorsey Levens was starting as tailback and Brett Farve was throwing the ball much more than C.J. Haynes had at The Citadel. The rookie made himself a place on the special teams squad. With his blinding speed and head-on-collision tackles, Travis had no trouble starting on the kickoff and punt-return teams. Green Bay's special teams soon became the best in the League.

Sports writer John Maxymuk wrote a book *Packers By the Numbers: Jersey Numbers and the Players Who Wore Them*, in which he humorously implies that Travis Jervey was "a few yards shy of the goal line" the years he played for Green Bay. Backing up his claim, Maxymuk claims that fumble-prone Jervey slept with a football and that he kept a lion cub as a pet.

"The lion story is true," says Travis. The Packers were on a bus to the Dallas airport to fly back to Green Bay after losing to the Dallas Cowboys, and Travis was reading the exotic pets section of the Dallas Sunday paper. "Look here, Shon [LeShon Johnson -- Green Bay special teams player]," he exclaimed,

"We can order a lion from this Dallas pet store!" LeShon already owned 19 pit bulls, but he was eager to go halves on the $900 lion cub. When the huge crate was delivered, the two pro-footballers hunkered down and gingerly unlocked the crate. The cat was huge! They named her Nala from the *Lion King,* and fed her mounds of frozen chicken wings. Even though she had been defanged and declawed, Nala was an awesome presence as she galumphed through the house and pounced upon their teammates and coaches who hung out there. Coach Mike Holmgren told Travis that the only Lions he cared about where in Detroit! Life was sweet in the NFL. Travis and his lioncub were the talk of the town in Green Bay, and he got to spend the off-season surfing in Costa Rica. Jervey even competed against some of the fastest men in the NFL and defeated them in the hundred meter dash. Herschel Walker lost to Travis. Yet, Coach Holmgren seldom called on his fleet-footed, but fumble-prone special teams star, to play offense.

Clearly one of the reasons the Packers went to Super Bowls XXXI and XXXII was play of the special teams. One of the most memorable plays that Travis recalls from his playing years was Desmond Howard's 98 yard kick-off return against the Patriots in Super Bowl XXXI. With textbook perfect execution, the Packers return team of Jervey, McKenzie, Thomason, Beebe, and Hollinquest body slammed would-be Patriot tacklers as 180-pound speedster, Desmond Howard, burned New England with the length-of-the-field run.

Before long the San Francisco 49ers came looking for a swift running back, and Travis signed a six-million dollar contract with the West coast team. However, his good fortune changed and his ankle was shattered. Even with the best surgeons and a lot of metal hardware, the ankle did not heal quickly. The 49ers traded him to the Falcons, but that never worked out for much playing time.

Today, you'll find hometown hero, Travis Jervey, living in the Old Village and exceedingly fit. He's enjoying life as much as ever and, even though he still surfs regularly, his most fun these days comes from being a family man and gardening!

The Powerful Intellect of James McBride Dabbs

Has a South Carolinian ever held his tongue -- or turned the other cheek when affronted? Were we called "Fire Eaters" and "Hotspurs" for chanting "Blessed are the meek?" Would that we Southrons possessed a pinch of reserve every now and then. Credit Scots-Irish heritage for our pugnacity. A glory of old Carolina is that when we're loud and cantankerous, there's another one of us who comes forth with an eloquent, passionate counterpoint. Take, for example, the case of Livingston Coleman "Cole" Blease and James McBride Dabbs, Jr., the "Jim Crow" governor and the socially progressive, agrarian intellectual from Dabbs Crossroads.

Cole Blease and "Pitchfork" Ben Tillman were the fruit of the so-called "wool hat" movement in early 20th century Carolina politics -- the triumph of the Upstate's two-horse farmers over the Bourbon Democrats of the Lowcountry. Though Blease and Tillman mutually distrusted each other, they were rivals for the same faction on election day. And that faction was staunchly for segregation and anti-labor union. Lynching, Black Codes, and voter intimidation were the modus operandi of South Carolina politics for the first four decades of the century. However, in the interval between the two world wars when some black men returned from army service abroad, there were a few southerners who realized that race relations were the South's Achilles heel as far as modernization and progress were concerned. To that extent, Howard Odum, an Emory and Columbia University-educated southern liberal, and James McBride Dabbs, a South Carolina college professor and plantation owner collaborated in forming the Southern Regional Council.

Cole Blease has a place in South Carolina political lore. So does "Pitchfork" Ben. Without Ben Tillman's bullying of the War Department, Charleston would never have wrested the naval base away from Port Royal -- the site deemed by Teddy Roosevelt's administration as the second best natural harbor on the East Coast. Yet, as far as moving the state along the course of racial harmony in the aftermath of war and reconstruction, Blease and Tillman were the troglodites of progressivism. Soft-spoken, pipe-smoking James McBride Dabbs, of Rip Raps

Plantation between Bishopville and Sumter, was the shining star of forward thinking in those days.

Professor Jim Dabbs would have been 116 years old last Tuesday, May 8, though the luminary has been gone from this earth for 40 years. Thanks to his descendants' putting up one of the finest family genealogy sites on the internet, the rest of us can peruse the life and times of this "upstream" thinking man who once dwelt amongst us. Just 99 miles northwest of here, for the traveler who motors up U.S. 52 to U.S. 527, there stands near the crossroads the old home of the 10,000 acre Rip Raps Plantation, an historic place that has been in McBride-Dabbs's possession for more than 180 years. Traversing the coastal plain, the traveler rides along the outermost reach of the forbidding Black River Swamp, once the lair of the Swamp Fox. North of Manning and east of Sumter, Rip Raps got its name from the first James McBride who was once encamped by the Rip Raps River in Virginia sometime in the 1820s. Since that long ago time, McBride and Dabbs families have become intertwined in marriage and land holdings with imposing antebellum home, crossroads, and even a small airport bearing their surnames.

Despite the imposing presence of large columned homes with land passed down in tact for generations, the McBride-Dabbs clan has never considered itself wealthy in any way other than in its heritage and character traits. In fact, "land poor" and "genteel straits" would more accurately describe the financial status of this old southern family that once possessed numerous slaves to till its soil and pick the cotton that was and still is so much a part of the rich acreage it owns. Down the road a mile is Old Salem Church, a classical revival red brick structure dating to 1759. On the axis from Rip Raps to Old Salem Church, a southern family has taken a leading role in every aspect of the country's history from the Revolution to Secession and Disunion, Reconstruction, Jim Crow, and Desegregation. Studying at Carolina, The Citadel, and Clemson -- not to mention Yale and Columbia -- soldiering in every war from Thomas Sumter's to William Westmoreland and Donald Rumsfeld's, Dabbses and McBrides have struck a blow for freedom.

The blow for freedom that CBS news man Mike Wallace found so intriguing in 1958 was that of James McBride Dabbs, gentleman farmer of Rip Raps Plantation and professor of English Literature at Coker College in nearby Hartsville. In what became known as the Ranson Center Interviews by CBS's Mike Wallace at the University of Texas, Austin, a young Mike Wallace interviewed the 62-year-old agrarian intellectual South Carolina plantation owner who was one of the early southern whites to champion desegregation.

The interview is available on the internet and is a valuable bit of American cultural history. The Ranson Center, U.T. interviews by Mike Wallace included discussions with Rod Serling, Mortimer Adler, John Maynard Hutchins, Salvador Dali, Kirk Douglas, and William O. Douglas around the same time that Dabbs was interviewed. None of the taped interviews, however, has the dramatic impact of Professor James McBride Dabbs gently advocating his beloved South to move on from its antebellum past and embrace the black race as fellow southerners bound to the soil.

Puffing on his pipe and looking decidedly professorial, James Dabbs dealt with the South's "lost cause" and tradition of Negro servitude in such a disarming manner that many whites came to realize that desegregation might not be the calamity that most had feared. Yet, there was an opposite reaction, too, and when Wallace asked Dabbs what many of his fellow southerners thought of him, he drawled, "They think I'm a d- - -ed fool." Fearful that the KKK might try to harm Dabbs upon his return from the taping of the Wallace interview, the African-American community nearby to Rip Raps lined the dismal dark road U.S. 527 that goes through Black River Swamp with their headlights to light the way for the returning Dabbs. And the Klan did pay a visit to Dabbs at Rip Raps back in the '50s.

Two years following the Mike Wallace interview, James McBride Dabbs published his autobiography entitled *The Road Home* (1960) about his "search for God and his personal growth to the understanding of racial justice." The book was widely read throughout the region, and it caught the notice of Hodding Carter II, a Pulitizer-prize-winning Louisiana journalist with degrees from Bowdoin and Columbia University. Carter's Pulitzer was for an editorial he wrote in the 1940s deploring the ill-treatment of the Japanese-Americans in internment camps in WW II. Some say that Hodding Carter was the James McBride Dabbs for Louisiana and Mississippi -- in other words, he was the state's moral conscience.

Dabbs publicly announced his support of fellow South Carolinian, Dr. Benjamin Elijah Mays, the president of Morehouse College in Atlanta, Georgia. Mays, the same age as Dabbs, had grown up in Epworth, S.C., a tiny community in Greenwood County. Despite his rural upbringing, Mays received his undergraduate degree from Bates College in Maine and his Ph.D. from the University of Chicago. An unabashed Christian and a hater of racial bigotry, Mays, Carter, and Dabbs frequently exchanged communication and became leaders in the Southern Regional Council, a group advocating desegregation in the 1950s and '60s. The North Carolina banker John Wheeler was another of these progressive thinkers. Through Mays, Dabbs became a friend of Dr. Martin Luther King, Jr., and Dr.King referenced James McBride Dabbs as an example of Southern reconciliation in his (King's) 1963 "Letter from Birmingham Jail."

Dabbs attended the University of South Carolina and Columbia University. He courted his first wife, Jesse Armstrong Dabbs, by reciting lengthy passages from the Romantic poets. When Jesse died early in life, James married one of his former students, Edith Mitchell. The Dabbs farm, Rip Raps, was never a model agricultural unit, but it provided adequately for the numerous families that lived on and around the old place. James McBride Dabbs, III, earned his Ph.D. in psychology at Yale and taught at Georgia State for years until he, too, came back to run the old plantation.

McBride published three other books -- *The Southern Heritage* (1958), *Who Speaks for the South* (1964) and *Haunted by God* (1972) -- all collector's items. According to the family historian, James McBride Dabbs "died the morning of May 30, 1970. He had just finished putting the last words on his manuscript, Haunted by God, signed his name and placed a period after it.....something he'd never done before. He was heard to say, 'I think that's all I can do.' He lay down on the couch to take a nap and never awoke."

Charleston Port of Call for Wallenius-Wilhelmsen M/V Turandot

An old friend breezed into town on business last week. She looked fabulous as always, wearing green and white to offset her windswept, slightly sun-baked features. She's sixteen, but in her native country, Sweden, that's quite mature in her line of work. She is quite popular down on the waterfront, I hear, but take your eyes off her for a minute and she's off again. With a catchy name, Wallenius-Wilhelmsen *Turandot*, she's bound to have admirers on both sides of the Atlantic. The fellows on the dock say that *Turandot* is a PCTC. In shipping terminology that stands for Pure Car Truck Carrier, and when *Turandot* sails into town, she's a majestic presence tied up at the Columbus Street Terminal. And since she and her associates do millions of dollars of business here, *Turandot* the PCTC is a V.I.P. when in the Port of Charleston.

Credit a stunning view from the Ravenel Bridge for Mount Pleasant commuters momentarily forgetting they are heading to the oblivion of another day at the office. The Walter Mitty in us takes hold as flight of fancy seizes our imagination. For a moment we are off on yonder ship churning toward the horizon's blue water. Reality sets in, however, as we shoot through the second diamond heading west. Oh, for the vagabond life of a maritime sailor and an adventure aboard a seagoing vessel such as Wallenius-Wilhelmsen *Turandot*.

What's an aristocratic name like *Turandot* doing around the Charleston waterfront, especially the Columbus Street terminal where scenes of labor unrest have occurred in years past? Maybe there's something in the origin of that romantic-sounding name -- *Turandot* (pronounced turan-do). We Americans would not expect a great cargo ship to be named after an Italian opera, but Europeans think differently. As it turns out, *Turandot* is a 1920s opera by Puccini and Giuseppe Adami. *Turandot* brought the house down on its debut in Milan on April 25, 1926. "*Encore!*" cried the audience as conductor Arturo Toscanini punctuated the last notes with his baton.

No one loves opera better than the Italians. Operas are really tragedies or sit-coms sung to classical music. Who knows why the art form never really caught on here. Turandot, says the interpreter's guide, means Turk's daughter. There has to be a pretty girl in distress. The Turk's daughter fell captive to Genghis Khan and his plundering hoardes. *Turandot* baffles her suitors through a series of riddles, each more elaborate that the previous one. In the end, the *femme fatale* has wagered with the best of the Mongols and won her freedom. What a name!

Wallenius-Wilhelmsen Turandot, like her Puccini namesake, is a beauty. Like any opera diva her dimensions are on the plus side. She's 105 feet across the middle and she stretches out to a stately length of 653 feet. From the Cooper River gazing upward, it's 108 feet to her deck. And her superstructure towers above the 13 decks of auto storage. *Stockholm* is emblazoned on her stern, and her flag of registry is that of Sweden, yet the stevedores of Southampton and Bremerhaven know her well.

Don't expect *Turandot* to rest long in your gaze, for she has one of the quickest turnaround times in the business. When her KHIC MAN BMW 8S60MC engine revs up to its 20,000 horsepower capacity, *Turandot* can skim the sea lanes at 23 knots. Someone asked how many cars can fit on a Rapid On / Rapid Off (RO/RO) ship. Though it's never nice to ask a lady what she's carrying, the answer is that she can hold over 2,900 automobiles.

Check the internet for the scuttlebutt on *Turandot's* activities. She's more popular than a teenager on Facebook. Here's a sample: "How can one determine the ship his car is on? I have a 335xi coupe in Bremerhaven now awaiting a ship and would appreciate it if someone could help me figure out when it will get on a ship, and if I can track that by VIN." Reply: Found my VIN on the *Turnadot*. Looks like it left port on the 8th of Feb., due in California March 2nd. Looks like it had a few stops after Bremerhaven . . . Kotka, Finland -- Gothenburg, Sweden -- Bremerhaven, Germany -- Zeebrugge, Belgium -- Southampton, U.K. -- Manzanillo, Panama -- Port Hueneme, California." Turandot gets around.

When *Turandot* blows into Charleston, she can be found at Columbus Street Terminal at the foot of the Ravenel Bridge. Columbus terminal boasts six berths and five cranes, not that *Turandot* needs a crane. She loads with a huge ramp that tucks neatly into the hull. Columbus Street possesses 14 exchange lanes to move cargo swiftly about, plus both the Norfolk Southern and CSX rail lines run right up to the staging area. Mount Pleasant hears train whistles in the night as freight moves away from Columbus Street. The sound of freight moving is something Charlestonians have relished for 300 years. Our terminal operates 232,000 square feet of transit shed, sprinkler protected, and 105,000 square feet of warehouse space. It's no coincidence at all that I-26 begins 1 1/2 miles away.

Now there was a time when the Columbus Terminal made the police blotter. An advertisement for the port lists the notice: "Vessel Labor - Union (ILA); Terminal Labor - Non-union." Problems arose in January 2000 when the Danish shipping line, Nordana, a non-union line, scheduled stops in Charleston where the International Longshoremen's Association has an agreement to work the cargo on the vessel. Nordana's plan was to use non-union labor to work the ship, and this led to a tense standoff in the predawn hours of Friday, January 19, 2000. Over 600 law enforcement personnel contended with hundreds of angry union workers. Brick bats and tear gas canisters crossed in the air. Ultimately five union members were arrested and indicted. "Free the Charleston Five" became a rallying cry among labor unions all over the country. Eventually the S.C. Attorney General withdrew most of the charges after consulting Mayor Riley. The ILA claimed a victory in this non-labor friendly state. For a week it looked as if Charleston's Columbus Street Terminal might become the scene for a remake of Marlon Brando's 1954 movie *On the Waterfront*. Nordana line has no connection with the Wallenius-Wilhelmsen shipping line. In the shipping industry there's never a dull minute.

From Port Said to the Suez Canal, from Colon to Barcelona, Wallenius ships call on ports experiencing political unrest. "Cargo such as a space shuttle to Australia, a 200 ton turbine to South Africa, a 25 - metre yacht to the USA is all in a day's work for us." Charleston's port is one of more than 2000 ocean-going vessel terminals in the world. Gone are the days when ship crews walked our the streets and their captains were guests of prominent local citizens. Ultra-fast turnaround times and national security issues eclipsed those times.

We miss the days of hearing Greek, Spanish, Chinese, and Italian spoken on East Bay and Market as weatherbeaten men took in the sights -- and the bars. Yet, Wallenius-Wilhelmsen takes care of its people even if they don't get a chance to sight-see. In 2011 the ICSW, known as The International Seafarers Welfare Organization, named Wallenius-Wilhelmsen "Shipping company of the year." Since the ICSW is at a vantage point to see the whole spectrum of international shipping, the rest of the awards may be of interest to our readers: "Port of the Year: The Port of Antwerp, Belgium Seafarer Centre of the Year: Duckdalben International Seamen's Club, Hamburg Welfare Personalities of the Year: Reverend Peter Ellis of Hong Kong and Mrs Paddy Percival of Durban. The Judge's Special Award for Outstanding Services to Seafarers' Welfare: Dr.

Suresh Idnani, India." That gives us something as a community to aim for in the future.

Headlines on May 17 read "U.S. Exports Reach Record High As Trade Deficit Widens -- March exports climb to $186.8 billion while rising imports increase the U.S. trade deficit to $51.8 billion. The latest trade figures appear to paint a "best of times, worst of times" picture for U.S. imports, exports and the economy in general."

The next time you head west over the Ravenel Bridge and you spot the Wallenius-Wilhelmsen M/V *Turandot*, longer than two football fields, being worked at the Columbus Street terminal, let your imagination take flight to where all she's been and where all she's likely to go before you see her again! And like Puccini's audience in Milan, you'll beg *Turandot* for an encore!

The H & R Sweet Shop on Royall Avenue Turns 65 This Month!

Without any celebration the H & R Sweetshop turned 65 this month. Three generations of customers have passed through its doors seeking friendship, good food, a haircut, or hats and suits.

H & R Sweet Shop located at 102 Royall Avenue in Mount Pleasant's Old Village may be the longest continually operating business east of the Cooper. It may be the oldest continually operating restaurant in the county! If you travel Royall Avenue, you're bound to notice the block and stucco building with "H & R Sweet Shop" stenciled on one pane glass window and "Major Hats and Suits" on the red awning to the right. If southern cuisine the way you remember it when a child is something that still haunts you, then you'll be in for a treat when you push open the door to Raliegh Johnson, Jr.'s world at 102 Royall.

Raliegh -- who prefers the "i" before the "e" spelling of his name -- wears a black turban and an ascot, no matter what the occasion or weather. The ensemble, together with his salt and pepper beard, makes him quite a memorable character. There's the spic-and-span tidiness one expects in a hometown diner, and soft jazz music wafts across the counter from an antique jukebox. Immediately, you like this place. It has a Lowcountry charm that refuses to be replicated. The aroma from the kitchen carries you back to the days of red rice cooked with sausage and ham hocks and collard greens flavored just right. If you're a one-armed fellow, there is no way that you'll be able to handle their hamburger. When you settle up the bill, you'll wonder if Raliegh undercharged you. Old fashioned courtesy, slow cooking to perfection, homemade sauces from 60-year-old-family recipes -- all are part of this little restaurant tucked amid the oaks of the Old Village.

The "H" stands for Harriet and the "R" is for Raliegh "Pat" Johnson, Sr. In 1947 Raliegh Johnson was discharged from the army and returned to Mount Pleasant where his father, Peter Johnson, owned a strip of land on the north side of Royall starting at Morrison and extending to the playground. Peter

Johnson, Sr., bought the property from the school district for $150 in 1903. The Inflation Calculator indicates that $150 in 1903 equates to $1,574 today. However, that amount of money was quite an investment in those days. In 109 years the property has not been out of family hands.

Years ago the Sweet Shop brought in jazz performers to entertain patrons in the club room in the rear. "Oscar and Fabian Rivers brought their Chicago-based band to Charleston," says Raliegh, and they performed here. Also performing were Nita Nelson with Donald Fields on drums, with Jack McDuff and Joy Pryor. All of this occurred when jazz was practically dead in this part of the country.

Raliegh Senior's brother Peter started the P.S. Johnson Funeral Home, now called Johnson and Hall, located on Venning Street. Together, the Johnson brothers were successful entrepreneurs in the area, and they were instrumental in the rebuilding of nearby Friendship A.M.E. Church. The Quaker Church of Philadelphia had operated a mission and a freedman's school on this land during Reconstruction. As years progressed, parcels of land were sold off to families who could afford it. The Johnsons have jealously guarded their inheritance and it appears that the H & R Sweet Shop and Major's Hats and Suit business is on track to see its 100th anniversary.

Raliegh, Sr., was both a cook and a barber in the U.S. Army. In 1947 he engaged a contractor to build the block and stucco building that you see today. On one side, Raliegh operated a barbershop and on the other, a full-service ice cream shop and diner. For a while Raliegh was the only licensed barber in Mount Pleasant. In the 1960s before desegregation, the Sweet Shop was a beehive of activity for the African-American community, and Raliegh was known to help a lot of people out when they got into a jam, financially.

Raliegh -- called Pat by his friends -- and his wife Harriet employed gentlemen named Edward "Poncho" Mazyck, Legrande Wilson, and Carney Smalls to work at the ice cream and custard counter. Raliegh made the special barbeque sauce for the ribs that became famous around town. By the mid 1970s, Raliegh, Jr., and Anthony joined in. Neighborhood folks of both races came in for ice cream, milk shakes, hot dogs, hamburgers, ribs, pork chops, fried chicken, friend shrimp and flounder, hush puppies, fries, and all the red rice, and collards. Raliegh made his own hogshead cheese and pickled eggs. Today, the ice cream and milk shakes are gone from the menu, but the soul food, hamburgers, and hot dogs are the same wonderful items that folks two generations ago bragged about. Locals still come in longing for the taste of southern cooking that is so hard to find.

The other side of the H & R Sweet Shop enterprise is called "Major Hats and Suits Shop." It's the six-year-old business of Anthony Major. Note the colorful hat sign that's part of his trademark. Anthony grew up in New York and Mount Pleasant. He finished Harren High School located near 59th Street and 10th Avenue in New York, not far from the Dakota Apartment Building where John Lennon was fatally shot. Though he was of draft age during the Vietnam War, Anthony says that demonstrators burned down the draft board building so no one he knew of from his neighborhood was called to active duty. He remembers the riot that broke out in New York after the Reverend Martin Luther King, Jr., was assassinated. Growing up in New York, Anthony learned to get along with numerous ethnic groups, especially Greek and Hispanic. Prior to returning to Mount Pleasant in the 1970s, Anthony worked with Synovox Productions in New York and got to know country music radio and television host, Ralph Emory. Anthony operated the reel-to-reel-tapes for many of Emory's productions. He also worked for Con-Edison for five or six years as a meter reader.

When his father became ill, Anthony returned to the Lowcountry to lend a hand at the Sweet Shop. He also took a job with the Charleston County School system and became supervisor of the furniture shop where he oversaw the repair of all school desks and furnishings for the county school system. His shop built and installed cabinets, counters, and bookshelves. Anthony retired from the school system after 28 years and opened the hat and suit shop in the space where his father's barbershop had been.

The hat and suit shop annex of the H & R Sweet Shop is a hit with the "hat ladies," and the establishment also is agent for Murphy church robes. The Johnson family has long had a connection with Friendship AME Church and the Johnson and Hall Funeral Home. Anthony makes purchasing trips to New York with his wife, Veronica, to keep his customers satisfied with the latest fashions. Veronica, or "Roni" to her friends, is a native of Mount Pleasant. Before working for Eastern Airlines she served as corporate sales manager for the Greater Miami Convention and Visitor's Bureau. She's also been station manager for Chalk's International Airlines.

Though H & R Sweetshop founders Harriet and Raliegh Johnson have passed on, their memory is preserved in numerous photographs in the restaurant. Folks still come by to reminisce about the times when "Pat," "Ponch," Legrande, and Carney kept the place lively with conversation, sweets, and good southern cooking.

Raliegh, Sr., hosted Christmas parties, Easter Egg hunts, and passed out school supplies. He sponsored Little League teams and bowling leagues. A faithful member of Friendship A.M.E. Church and Pisgah Lodge 169, Raliegh, Sr., was a pillar of the community. Harriet, the "H" in H & R Sweetshop, was a registered nurse and a member of the Order of the Eastern Star, Lodge 219. Whether one is stopping by to catch up on news in the Village, to check the latest in men's and women's fashions, or to visit Raliegh for some of his delicious fried shrimp and red rice, the H & R Sweet Shop is a treasured part of Old Mount Pleasant's heritage.

Anderson County Native Jack Swilling Founded Phoenix, Arizona

Don't look for the upstate town of Anderson to erect an historical marker to Jack Swilling anytime soon. Admittedly, it looks rather odd that one of that area's native sons migrated west, became influential, and founded a ditching and irrigation company whose name became synonymous with the great Arizona city of Phoenix. Why wouldn't any town boast of its connection with such a notable fellow? The answer lies in the roughhewn character of Jack Swilling -- a colorful, but completely unwholesome, fellow if ever there was one!

Piecing together what is known of Jack Swilling from what is oft repeated about him is an insurmountable task, looking back on 150 years of history. Swilling is a German name, and sometime prior to 1830 immigrant George Swilling came into South Carolina, probably through Charleston and made his way inland to Anderson where he became a cotton plantation overseer. We know that he married well because he was able to purchase a plantation from his father-in-law. That plantation became known in the area as Red House, and in 1830 a son named John William Swilling was born there on April 1. The upstate was alive with religious revivalism and what historians later would term "The Second Great Awakening." The growth of Baptist and Methodist congregations was notable during that time and soon the denominations would split with their northern brothers and sisters over the issue of abolition. In New England frustrated, land-hungry folks headed west over the Oregon Trail, but in South Carolina the opportunity lay much closer to home -- the opening of new lands in Georgia and Alabama. When the the price of cotton fell from eight cents a pound to five in the 1840s, the Swilling family moved a hundred west miles to the vicinity of Calhoun, Georgia.

Hard times befell the Swilling family, and records reflect that Red House Plantation was auctioned from the courthouse steps. The Swillings and their ten children migrated west about the same time that many South Carolinians did. Some were opportunists and some were one step ahead of the creditor. George

Swilling reportedly was able to purchase land from one of his sons-in-law who'd already settled in the area. President Andrew Jackson had just driven the Creek and the Cherokee out of Georgia in what became known as the "Trail of Tears" episode of American history. Word spread quickly that fertile soil could be had there for a song. Political leaders such as John C. Calhoun and Andrew Crawford encouraged migration into the area, and it didn't hurt the cause that gold nuggets had been discovered nearby in Dahlonega.

Rural northwest Georgia was a rugged frontier where men took the law into their own hands. At age 17 Jack Swilling killed a north Georgia man whose dog threatened him. Though Swilling acted in self-defense, he and his brother Berry left the area with a Forsythe County cavalry detachment destined for service in the Mexican War. Discharge papers in 1848 reflect that Jack Swilling made his mark, an "x," on the document. Brother Berry Swilling headed west to the new Bear Flag Republic founded by John C. Fremont in California. Jack returned to Georgia, packed up his meager belongings and moved to Yazoo Land of Alabama. Down in Tallapoosa County he met and married a young woman named Mary Jane Gray, the first of several women with whom Jack Swilling consorted and sired children. By 1852 Swilling's temperament changed and some believe that it had to do with a severe blow to the head that he received in a barroom brawl. He was shot twice in that fight and was lucky to alive. For the rest of his life, Jack Swilling was addicted to opium-based pain killers and liquor. Some people say that Swilling was "mean as a snake" and not nearly as trustworthy.

While he was staking out a small farm with Mary Jane Gray in south-central Alabama, Jack Swilling received word that his brother Berry had been murdered out in California. Convinced that he had to see justice done, Swilling left his family and headed west. Some records indicate that Jack Swilling was married to two women at one time -- Mary Jane and another woman whom he met while traveling through Missouri. Reports of him engaging in gunfights and even of him being wanted for a murder in El Paso surface in the sketchy account of his life.

Accounts of the time describe Jack Swilling as "a man of striking appearance, nearly six feet in height with broad shoulders and lengthy arms, and having the appearance of a man of great physical strength. He wore his black hair long, sweeping about his shoulders, while his carriage was erect and commanding. His clothing was always of ample size, which gave him the appearance of being even larger that he really was." He was good with a pistol, handy with a long knife, and he preferred to fight Indian style -- hand-to-hand.

What is known is that Jack Swilling abandoned Mary Jane Gray and his daughter, and he did the same with the Missouri relationship. For a while he was a teamster in a wagon train. Then he prospected for gold in Arizona. Legend has it that Jack Swilling discovered the bonanza strike in the late 1850s down on the Gila River in what was known then as the Gadsden Purchase. He was never one to be superstitious, but it surely appeared that the devil pursued Jack on occasion. His mine shaft that led him to nuggets galore soon flooded and no one in the region could devise a method to draw the water off. Then Swilling's lean-to hut caught fire and destroyed the baking soda can where he'd hidden the precious gold nuggets that he'd excavated. For making ends meet until he could purchase land, Jack Swilling rode for the Pony Express making mail deliveries throughout the southwestern territories. Rattlesnakes, prairie fires, flash floods, desperadoes, and Apaches all had a go at Jack at one time or another. The natives were not friendly in the Arizona territory because the white man kept insisting on redrawing boundaries when precious metals were discovered. Generals Stephen Kearny and John C. Fremont, along with Kit Carson, quelled insurrections along the Arizona-California border. Sometime after opening a gambling saloon he settled down and married again -- this time to a legendary raven-haired Spanish beauty, Trinidad Escalante. Reputedly, she was the first white woman in the Arizona territory.

The expert on Jack Swilling is Arizona historian Neal Du Shane. He has put together websites on Arizona's early days. His site records that Jack was drafted into Confederate service after Jefferson Davis declared Arizona a Confederate territory. The war in the West was one of bushwhacking, and Swilling was certainly adept at that, yet there was one pitched battle at El Picaho near Gila Bend.

Someone once asked Jack how many men he reckoned he'd killed. "Oh, somewhere between 2 and 14," he said. No one asked him how many women he married or how many children he'd fathered. Somehow between Indian skirmishes and brawling with desperadoes, Jack Swilling became a businessman. He owned a saloon and gambling parlor, a flower mill and a quartz mill. Perhaps his South Carolina and Georgia farming days convinced him that the arid desert would produce crops and fruit trees if only the folks could irrigate it. Swilling's big venture was the Phoenix Ditch and Irrigation Company which enjoyed some success in turning brown land green. Did Swilling see himself as the mythological Phoenix who rose from the ashes to do great works? When a nucleus of settlers incorporated a town near his holdings, the townsmen voted on the name of Phoenix. Jack Swilling wanted the town to be called Mill City in honor of his other operations. We wish we could say that Jack Swilling lived happily ever after; however, he was implicated in a stagecoach robbery and went to jail where he died on August 12, 1878, of unspecified cause. Unhappily for Jack and his wife Trinidad, much of the property he owned was liquidated in an attempt to clear his name. Trinidad remarried and lived until 1925.

When historians tell how the West was won, it's the stories such as South Carolinian Jack Swilling that bring the saga to life. Today, Phoenix is home to one and a half million people, many of whom know nothing of Jack Swilling and his S.C. roots.

Charleston Native Managed Kansas City's Famous Savoy For Nearly 50 Years

One hundred years ago the Omaha newspaper jibed, "If you want to see sin, go to Kansas City!" Back then the wide-open city on the wide Missouri was known as "the Paris of the Plains." They boasted their own version of the Moulin Rouge, and, though wine was not their forte, grain sufficed for distilling what could not be squeezed from the grape. Saloons near the river served patrons whiskey straight up, jokers were wild, and steaks were grilled rare. Back then, grifters, card sharks, cattle rustlers, and river boat captains rubbed elbows with bankers, brokers, preachers, and prostitutes. From West 3rd Street clear to the north end of Passeo Boulevard there was the meeting of the East and the West, the knave and the righteous -- all seeking something here at the confluence of the Kansas and Missouri Rivers. William Jennings Bryan was their Democratic hope as Midwest populism united the grain belt with the agricultural south.

Towering since 1888 over the bustle of Kansas City deep in America's heartland is the stately Savoy Hotel. Once the crown jewel of the Arbuckle Brothers business empire -- a conglomerate that controlled coffee markets, banks, grocers, and ironmongers -- the Savoy remains as one of the city's most enduring landmarks. It stood at the crossroads of what we'd once called Manifest Destiny and the city's merchants cheered those rawboned teamsters who rolled westward -- for Kansas City was the "jumping off place" for both the Oregon and the Santa Fe Trails.

Gone now are the cowboys, card sharks, and shady ladies in crinoline. Today's version of Kansas City is glass, steel, and wireless hi-speed connection. Folks come here for conventions and to dine on dry-aged steaks, the elaborate beef processing technique that's subscribed to by the finest steak houses. There are many steak houses in Kansas City; however, none can top the combination of delicious food served by the professional staff in a room steeped in American folklore.

Today, the five-story Savoy Hotel houses a bed and breakfast that harkens to the days of cable cars and gloved ladies in hats and men wearing spatterdashes. Few places have held on to their charm the way the Savoy has. Like the more famous Savoy in London there is that British regard for gentility. And, wouldn't you know it, a native Charlestonian has been the greeter and restaurant manager at the Kansas City Savoy for nearly 50 years!

Ron Garris, the 77-year-old singing troubadour and wait staff manager greets his regular customers by name and escorts them to their favorite table or booth in the historic wood-paneled, black and white Italian-tiled dining room. When the restaurant fills to capacity as it invariably does, Garris and waiter Mark Palmer entertain diners with their a cappella harmonizing of Everly Brothers and Beatles hits. Dining here brings together the best Kansas beef with the quiet, understated elegance of yesteryear -- all in a place where a never-ceasing parade of politicos, tycoons, ballplayers, and movie stars have indulged their appetites for the past 12 decades.

Ask Ron Garris and he'll happily tell you how he, a Charleston boy born at 114 Coming Street, chanced upon such a rewarding career. Irish, Roman Catholic to the core, Garris chuckles as he recounts his childhood in Depression-era Charleston. His father was a shipyard welder. St. Patrick's Church on St. Philip's Street was the focus of family spiritual and social life. Ron sang at St. Patrick's in the youth choir, and he sang live on WCSC radio every Saturday as the star performer on the "Uncle Russ" kiddie show in the early 1940s. Ron has been singing ever since, and he's a faithful chorister for the Kansas City St. Patrick's Catholic Church just a few blocks away from the Savoy.

Number 6 Judith Street, two blocks east, was the Charleston single house that Ron Garris remembers most. It was from there that he walked to Bishop England High School where Father Patat, Monsignor Doctor O'Brien and Sister Loyola ran a no-nonsense campus in the 1950s. He was friends with the Rileys and the McLaughlins while there. Upon graduation, Garris went across the street to the College of Charleston and "sang his way through," as he tells it.

After college Garris moved to St. Petersburg, Florida, where he worked as a regional manager for 7-Eleven, the hot franchise convenience chain that evolved from the 1920s era Southland Ice Company of Dallas. He would have stayed with 7-Eleven forever had not a manager of a store tipped him that a gang planned to waylay him on the road and seize the bag of store cash that he carried. Within a week of resigning someone informed him that a relative was retiring from the Savoy and that maybe Ron would like to apply. One interview with Don Lee, the owner, and Garris never looked back. He's the coat and tie front man for the Savoy and no one represents a beloved institution better than he. With pride Garris points out booth number 4 where Harry Truman always sat when he visited the Savoy. In a hallway is the framed job application that Truman filled out to work there when he was young. The Arbuckles realized his potential and took him on as a teller in one of their banks instead of having him wait tables.

Near the front, at table 11, was where Yogi Berra and his entourage always sat when the Yankees were in town to play the Royals. Berra had a following of diehard fans who followed him on every out-of-town game. There was much good-natured ribbing between Berra and the locals.

When asked for memories, Garris chuckles and replies: "When Lee Iacocca was sitting at table 10 and he was just having a blast of a time," Garris reminisces. "That was when he was chopping heads at Chrysler, and the people that were with him acted like they were pretty scared."

Pulitizer-prize winning author David McCullough researched his biography on Truman, and he reserved booth number 4 every day, Monday through Friday, for months. He spread his notes on the table and read while eating. Paul Newman liked that booth, too, when he and Joanne Woodward filmed "Mr. and Mrs. Bridge" there in 1990.

Bob Dole is a friend of Ron Garris and they reminisce every time the former Kansas Senator and presidential candidate drops in. Nancy Landon Kassebaum, daughter of Alf Landon and also formerly a Kansas Senator, dined there. Valerie Lee's history of the hotel mentions that the, "Hotel Savoy served such celebrities as Teddy Roosevelt, William Howard Taft, Marie Dressler, W.C. Fields, Will Rogers, Lillian Russell, Sara Bernhardt, and John D. Rockefeller." Famed "Booth No. 4, known as the presidents' booth, has been host to Warren Harding, Harry S. Truman, Gerald Ford and Ronald Reagan."

In less time than it takes to savor eight ounces of mouthwatering, tender Tournedos Rossini, you can hear about Bennie Goodman and Count Basie recording *Stompin' At the Savoy* in 1934. Since both musicians played in Kansas City, everyone naturally figured it was the Kansas City Savoy, but it was the Harlem Savoy that claims this fame. An original wax album and cover hangs in the hallway near the Harry Truman job application.

Was the Savoy a part of the Tom Pendergast political machine that controlled everything in Kansas City? Pendergast operated from the Fitzpatrick Saloon a block or two away -- now known as the Majestic Steak House, yet he probably frequented this place, too.

Grand murals by Edward J. Holsag that depict the pioneers heading west occupy eye level on the three walls facing the mirrored bar. Holsag had just completed murals for the Library of Congress when he took on Arbuckle's Savoy commission in 1922. The ladies room is next door in an adjoining ballroom because it was not until the flappers inundated the place in the 1920s that women entered the bar area.

"I'm a people person," says Ron Garris. "Dining at the Savoy in Kansas City is more than a meal," he says. It's a history lesson along with a new set of friends who'll remember your name and where you sat the last time you dined there. It's a wait staff that averages 25 years Savoy experience per person and they possess an extensive knowledge about how beef is aged, seasoned, and cooked. Every aspect of each meal is made from scratch the day it is served. When in Kansas City, take a pass on the trendy places that also offer high quality. Instead, go visit the Charleston fellow -- Ron Garris -- who has spent his life meeting the interesting clientele of the Savoy Grill in Kansas City.

Earthen Mound Was Holy Ground For Santee Tribe

Before our nation was formed with its institutions of economy, justice, religion, and foreign relations, there were other nations here long before us -- with their institutions of economy, justice, religion, and foreign relations. We believe that our culture is the culmination of all human existence with our sophisticated systems of banking, our courts and appellate courts, our freedom of religion and our global diplomacy. Could anything that existed before us have rivaled our ingenuity, our sophistication? Could there have been a man from this region who attained more recognition than did Rutledge, Calhoun, or Thurmond? Remember Percy Shelley's "Ozymandias"?: "'...My name is Ozymandias, king of kings: / Look on my works, ye Mighty, and despair!'/ Nothing beside remains. Round the decay / Of that colossal wreck, boundless and bare / The lone and level sands stretch far away."

Could the primitive Santee tribe of the Carolina coastal plains have possessed a civilization that equaled us in culture? There are more questions than answers to the meaning of a thousand-year-old, man-made earthen mound visible to boaters and motorists alike from the locale where I-95 crosses Lake Marion.

As Interstate-95 North crosses Lake Marion about 75 miles northwest of Mt. Pleasant, there's a 40-foot rise in elevation that's visible even to the speeding motorist. Locals around the town of Santee know the site as Fort Watson, the place where Francis Marion improvised a tower to shoot into and dislodge a British garrison during the Revolutionary War. That alone is reason enough to detour to this rather lonely state park located a mile off the Interstate. However, the events of the American Revolution hardly scratch the surface of what this man-made hill means for the members of the Santee tribe, a branch of the great Sioux nation of Native Americans.

You and I know Santee as a junction of state and federal highways connecting north and south. We know it as a place of outlets, restaurants, motels, and golf courses. Sportsmen know of the world-record land-locked bass that lie beneath the surface of Lake Marion, one of the state's premier recreational areas. Chief Randy Crummie of Holly Hill, S.C., knows this area for much more than its connection with Francis Marion or today's renown bass fishing tournaments.

Centuries before there were white man here there were powerful native American nations situated from the Great Lakes to what is now Florida. The Iroquois, Cherokee, and Sioux had outreaches in our region. Just as nations in the modern times speak different languages and live according to their own customs, so did these early Native American peoples. They formed alliances in time of war, and they sent traders, trappers, and hunters far inland to connect with other tribes and their religions. Their cultivation of corn, or maize, was more refined than in Europe, and their code of honor was as noble as anything found in the Arthurian legend.

The name "Santee" means "river people." Ironically, according to an article written by Paul R. Sarrett, Jr., the only known legacy of their lost language is "Hickerau," the name of a branch feeding into the Santee River. Then there is the great mound -- what did it signify to these people, the warriors of the Seven Council Fires? An article on the ways of the Sioux states that "The seven nations that comprise the Sioux are: Mdewakanton, Wahpeton, Sisseton, Yankton, and the Teton, or Lakota Sioux. The Seven Council Fires would assemble each summer to hold council, renew kinships, decide tribal matters, and participate in the Sun Dance. The seven divisions would select four leaders known as Wičháša Yatápika from among the leaders of each division. Being one of the four leaders was considered the highest honor for a leader." Since "Santee" is sometimes substituted for "Sioux," the mound on the north shore of Lake Marion may honor a mighty warrior who served as one of "the Four Chiefs."

Could it have been that a great chieftain from the Santee had been chosen far away on the Great Plains and sent to the Atlantic coast to govern a distant region just as the Pharaohs had their viziers? Whomever the great mound was built to honor, his likes were never known here again. Some accounts tell of mounds in the area that were destroyed for modern construction purposes in the 20th century. Carbon dating can be questionable in archaeological digs; however, a series of these tests determined that the Santee mound is at least 20,000 years old. Historians vary in their estimation of when activity was flourishing at this mound. For five-hundred to a thousand years, this mound may have been the center of human civilization for hundreds of miles in every direction.

The Santee Indian website maintains that 18th century explorer John Lawson engaged a Santee Indian to lead him deeper into the interior. Lawson tells of these people living in wood cabins, no doubt the bark-covered longhouses that have been depicted in early drawings. At the main settlement Lawson was introduced to the "King" and the medicine Man, both elaborately dressed. The Shaman, or Medicine Man, was robed in silk. The Santee tribe numbered about 90 when John Lawson was introduced to them in 1701. Their estimated number for a century earlier was put at approximately 1000 with the cause of their demise being smallpox. The "King" of the Santee made it known to Lawson that the great mound honored one of their great chieftains. Lawson's comment about the Santee was that they were hospitable and eager to be of service to the English settlers. Lawson was impressed with the pomp and ceremony associated with a tribe of such small numbers.

What is known is that the Santee became acquainted with the Spanish in the early 1600s when Captain Ferdinand de Ecija befriended tribesmen and asked to be escorted up the Santee River from its source on the great Santee Delta. Captain Ecija was based in Saint Augustine and commanded the warship *Asuncion de Christo*. He is known to have sailed into what is now Charleston harbor in 1605 and again in 1609. It's probable that some of Ecija's crew infected the Santee tribe with incurable smallpox at this time.

What else is known is that the top of the mound was the holy place where the great Medicine Man, clad in animal kins -- perhaps with a wolf's head, shook rattles, chanted, and danced to please the spirits. Contacting the spirit world meant going into a trance. The rank and file of the Santee tribe did not trespass on the sacred mound. Mounds were graded on all sides and level on top. In Missouri the great mounds had rectangular bark and pole huts situated along an avenue leading to the mound. It's probable that our Santee mound appeared the same as the Missouri mound. Long dugout canoes traversed the river, and corn fields and grain bins attested to the prosperity of the Santee. Whomever the great mound honored was a rare individual among the people, and the people were feared.

Santee tribe members believe that their people reached from the Santee delta to Awendaw (Avendaughbough in their time) all the way to Orangeburg County. Their website states that they were "attacked by coastal tribes in 1716, possibly the Cusabo, who attempted to remove them on behalf of the colonists. Many Santee warriors were captured and sent to the West Indies as slaves. Remaining Santee fled to Hickerau, the spiritual place of the Santee, located around present-day Elloree." At any rate, the Santee were here before we were, and the great earthen mound signifies that they were an extraordinary people.

The Eastern Cougar Does Inhabit South Carolina

I'm not Bill Bryson, and this column isn't entitled "A Walk In the Woods." Neither am I Rudy Mancke, Marlin Perkins, or Jim Fowler. Yet, something occurred yesterday on an upstate highway that has inspired me to postpone the column that I had planned for this week. I came face to face with the famed Carolina panther, and I don't mean the blue and black NFL variety. Long thought to be extinct, the Carolina version of the big Eastern cougar is alive and very well, thank you.

Driving along U. S. 341 an hour before sunset near the intersection of Winterhaven Road, one mile east of Kershaw, I saw what appeared to be a very large Tom cat crossing the road. In an instant my senses said, "Bobcat." The head was round and large, the color was mottled brown, the height exceeded that of a housecat -- that tail -- well, it was as long as the cat and very thick. He paused on the side of the road. I stopped the car thirty feet away, and we stared at each other for a few moments. Big Cat arched his back the way cats do when alarmed, and he bounded into the woods. That cat was gone in a flash. Driving on, I reflected that many of the Upstate servicemen called up for the Army in 1918 were placed in the 81st Wildcat Division. Those thoughts contented me for a few miles until some reflection revealed what should have been obvious when I first set eyes on the beast -- a Bobcat can't have a long, thick tail!

For two hours my mind replayed the details of my encounter with what has to be the Carolina panther. My fears were that folks would say that dusk had played tricks on my eyes, that somebody's big Tom was on the prowl. For years state biologists have treated sightings with suspicion. Two clicks on Google search brought up pictures exactly like what I had seen -- an Eastern cougar cub. Someone will ask why I didn't take a picture to confirm my sighting and the answer is that it all happened so fast -- thirty seconds and the cat vamoosed. It was not a matter of fight or flight with him; rather, he had no interest in being gawked at in daylight hours by a motorist.

The sighting of this cougar cub occurred about a mile west of the Little Lynches River and within a few hundred yards from one of its tributary streams. Coyotes, deer, boar, eagles, and every snake imaginable. Nothing there, however, is meaner than the redbugs which inhabit the pine straw. Old-timers there used to point out the bear pits where their ancestors trapped black bears for their pelts. In those streams where it's still possible to pan for tiny bits of gold, there can be heard the bone-chilling screech of the owl and the cry of the bobcat making a kill. Some say that the panther is a silent assassin and that he and his mate share their bounty.

From Mauldin to McClellanville, folks are coming forward to report their own sightings of the phantom panther. Some even claim to have spotted black panthers in the Lowcountry swamps. My father encountered one on U.S. Highway 172 north of Summerville 40 years ago. He recalls that the animal's tail was as long as its body and that the huge cat appeared to take up the whole lane as he crossed over. These days the internet has become a bulletin board of sorts for panther sightings here.

A sampling of panther blog entries includes "Seen [sic] a show on TV about black panthers in the Carolinas. Might have been Monster Quest. Anyway, 2 years ago in August I was driving down on the highway south of Ashboro & think I seen [sic] a dead one on the side of the road by mile marker 51 Long tail, all black but I couldn't see the head.Could not stop to look at it because I had traffic behind me.I just assumed they were common around the Carolinas.I did email the DNR when I got home 7 days later but never heard anything back."

A responder adds, "The DNR swears up and down there are no mountain lions left in SC. Even thought they're on the endangered species list. Still 3 coon hunters treed and killed one a few years ago. They went back to the truck for buckshot. Also have positively ID'ed a large cat tracks on a pond dam on the same property, and the owner saw one 5+ years ago and now carries a .44 Mag on his hip whenever he goes hunting. There's no question there are some. Something was making the d - - - edest noise at me early one morning before dawn. Never heard anything like it. I assumed it was a cat."

Bo Petersen of the *Post and Courier* reported March 7, 2011, that "Despite biologists' saying the eastern cougar is no more, big cat sightings persist." Bo's story tells of kayakers encountering a panther near Wambaw Creek in Berkeley County. Petersen quotes local nature guide Kathi Livingston, "I know they say the cougars we see are escaped or released. I'll tell you, these things are so fast I don't see any domestication at all."

Federal Fish and Wildlife experts studied the matter of the Eastern cougar and declared it to be extinct -- at least in this region it is gone, they say. Like the Carolina parakeet, the predator cat couldn't cope with spreading civilization encroaching upon its feeding fields. Or could it? Too many sightings, all reporting a big cat with a long tail, big head and paws -- can they all be explained away as poor visibility, overfed ferrel cats, or active imaginations?

Just as armadillo sightings and occasional crocodile visits are being noted around our coast, it's possible, that the Florida panther has made his way north, too. In olden days it was considered folly for a traveler to venture far without a firearm. A touring troupe of actors caravanned southward in the 18th century toward Savannah and were attacked by a pack of wolves near Jacksonboro. Foolishly, they threw a dried piece of beef to the hungry carnivores. The thespians were nearly the stars of a Greek tragedy that day. The wildness of our country and the inherent dangers in just taking a walk to the wood pile insured that we would have the 2nd amendment to the constitution.

Another panther blog carries a local comment, "My dad was born & raised in the Cainhoy area and used to tell me stories of the mountain lions that were around. He said there used to be a den behind the Bowles horse farm before the farm was there. Then about 8 years ago I was driving down Clements Ferry and one ran across the road in front of me just past the old Mikasa plant heading towards 526. Hubby's family lives in the Francis Marion forest and has seen a black panther along with black bears."

I'm sort of proud to be part of an elite little group that has made eye contact with the illusive Carolina panther. The few precious seconds that we locked eyes thirty feet from each other will remain one of my cherished memories.

Cowasee Basin Is Much More Than a Floodplain Forest in the Midlands

Cowasee is the name given to the 215,000 acres of floodplain associated with the Congaree, Wateree, and Santee Rivers that bisect our state on a northwest to southeast diagonal. To put things in perspective, the Cowasee Basin is 54 times greater in size than Daniel Island. For wilderness enthusiasts, and their numbers are increasing yearly, the Cowasee Basin is, in the words of John Cely, retired from the S.C. Department of Natural Resources (D.N.R.), "The Green Heart of South Carolina." For history lovers Cowasee is a well-preserved time capsule of Carolina.

Cely should know a bit about the Congaree as he has devoted much of his career as a natural resources biologist to helping preserve the beauty of this vast rural and wilderness domain. Cely has written numerous columns in the *Columbia Star* weekly newspaper detailing the history and legends of the swamps and woodlands that drain 45 counties in South and North Carolina. In March, Cely and the Congaree Land Trust collaborated in publishing a coffee-table-styled book of professional photographs and narratives of this basin and its environs. A foreward by Walter Edgar pays tribute to the human struggles that have taken place along the banks of these great rivers from the days of the native Catawba and Santee tribes to the industrialists who cooperate with the environmentalists here. Celebrated within is the camera work of some of the best photographers in the state.

A scant 24,000 acres of the great basin is marked as the Congaree National Park, and conservationists maintain that the preserve "is home to the largest old growth bottomland hardwood forest remaining in the eastern United States." Cypress trees that could easily produce an entire table top in one board and loblolly pines that reach a hundred feet in height are common sights here.

Pine trees are not the only things that soar in height on the Congaree. Though the coffee-colored river doesn't resemble the Rhine in many details, there are high bluffs, some surpassing 300 feet, that give the boater a feeling of traveling through Europe. In one of his many columns in the *Columbia Star*, John Cely wrote: "Commodore Alexander Gillon of the South Carolina Revolutionary War Navy had his plantation, "Gillon's Retreat" in the Congaree River Bluffs, as did Col. William Thomson and his Belleville Plantation. The famous battle of Fort Motte was fought on top of one of these bluffs." Commodore Gillon's primary residence was in Charleston.

Jacob and Rebecca Motte of Charleston owned a Congaree bluff plantation they named Mount Joseph, at the time of the American Revolution. The Motte plantation was at the confluence of the Wateree and the Congaree Rivers, a mile south of Colonel William Thomson's Belleville. Both homes were considered early American mansions in the grand style with magnificent furnishings and landscaping. Quite a number of wealthy Chalestonians purchased land on the Congaree in colonial days. Family names of Gadsden, Gillon, Huger, and Thomson survive on land parcels to this day. Colonel William "Danger" Thomson and his famed Congaree Raccoon Ranger Company defended Breach Inlet from General Clinton's army in June of 1776.

Perhaps most notable about the Congaree River are the steep ravines, or bluffs. The Congaree Bluffs Heritage Preserve in Calhoun County offers an unspoiled look at some of this state's grandest vistas. One can see what our ancestors marveled at when they ventured from the coast. The wilderness domain that was the last known haven of the Carolina parakeet resembles some forest primeval, and it's refreshing to be in an area so remote that not even mobile phones can penetrate.

Modern bridge construction makes it possible to cross the Congaree, Wateree, and Santee Rivers effortlessly in our time; however, in colonial days, the status of the upstate ferries was crucial for travelers and commerce. In our time, a delay at JFK, LaGuardia, or Hartsfield may mean hours in delay. Carolina travelers of olden times could be delayed for days if key ferries such as Ancrum's, Huger's, McCord's, or Friday's (Freidig's) were shut down due to a freshet. American and British commanders alike were often held captive by flooded upstate rivers. Even in the early 20th century, ferries were used in some rural areas to ford the Wateree and Congaree.

For the state's economic history, the Cowasee Basin which extends roughly from Columbia to Camden on the upper reaches and from Creston to Rimini on the lower, incorporates the rich land that gave rise to South Carolina's third wave of agricultural aristocrats. Ben Robertson's chronicle, *Red Hills and Cotton* (USC Press, 1960), speaks of these buckskin, frontier people, Scots-Irish and German, who first tamed the forests and then tilled the soil. Their cabins which bore marks of Indian assaults displayed the skins of bear, deer, panther, fox, and raccoon. Short staple cotton would make some of them as wealthy as English lords. The Congaree River floated their bales to the coast.

The boll weevil made his appearance here in the early 1920s. The soybean was introduced by Britain to the colonies in the 1760s; however, it was not a great cash crop here until after World War II. Cotton seed oil was ranked higher as a commodity from the Congaree Basin, and Kershaw agricultural tycoon John "Captain Johnny" Stevens prevailed upon the legislature to build Highway 601 so that he could obtain Orangeburg Mill cotton seed for his cotton seed oil mill in Kershaw. Captain Johnny's road bridged the wide Congaree near Fort Motte, thereby disenfranchising Bates' Ferry. Bates' Ferry was the successor to the famed old McCord's Ferry of Revolutionary days. Highway 601 from Orangeburg to Camden was once known as McCord's Ferry Road. There's a lot of history in those parts that Lowcountry folks never hear much about.

"The past that Southerners are forever talking about is not a dead past--it is a chapter from the legend that our kinfolks have told us, it is a living past, living for a reason. The past is a part of the present, it is a comfort, a guide, a lesson." The quote is from Ben Robertson's *Red Hills and Cotton*, a primer for southerners wishing to reach out and touch their roots. There's no better way to see what endures of "old Carolina" than taking a driving tour of the great Cowasse Basin.

Grandest Home Site in South Carolina Is Atop Cook's Mountain

Northeast of McCord's Ferry Road (Highway 601) near the Jumping Hill Gun Club, there's an unpaved turn off that leads toward Cook's Mountain. Few folks get into this wilderness because it's private property and posted "no trespassing." Before Union Camp Corporation reseeded their property north of the historic circa 1850 Wateree Country Store, motorists glimpsed that sugarloaf demi-mountain far in the distance where the Congaree and Wateree meet. Tucked into those sandhills and overlooking an oxbow on the Wateree is one of South Carolina's little-known treasures -- the homesite of the colonial English cartographer, James Cook.

An upstate legend maintains that the English cartographer traveled the Carolinas and knew the land better than any man before him and that he selected the area of Cook's Mountain as his personal fiefdom thinking it to be the choicest parcel in the colony.

No, our mountain is not named for "The" James Cook, explorer of the Pacific. The English cartographer who mapped colonial South Carolina in 1772 bears the same name as the Cook of Hawaii and New Zealand fame. Some Carolinians have mistakenly attributed Cook's Mountain to the man who charted the Pacific. Our "Carolina" Cook, however, held the regard of King George III for his highly accurate map and for completing the South Carolina / North Carolina boundary that had been an ongoing difficulty since 1736. James Cook used Cook's Mountain as his base of operations due to its central location in the state and its easy access to the Wateree, Congaree, and Santee Rivers, as well as to the nearby McCord's Ferry Road.

All land deeds in colonial South Carolina were required to be stamped and registered in Charleston, thereby frustrating and impeding the orderly development of the Carolina Upcountry. Yet, as onerous as the filing process was for backcountry settlers, James Cook's job of mapping was made much easier because he could examine numerous surveyor maps of land grants that saved him months, maybe years, of field work. Nowadays, having one's surname listed on the 1772 Cook Map of S.C. is one of those telltale marks of Carolina distinction.

As precise as most of it was, Cook's map was not without a few serious flaws. Our state's northern boundary shared with our sister, the old North State, does some fancy maneuvering around the old Waxhaws region. Cook was summoned from London to establish a proper boundary line 40 years after Carolina was divided into two colonies, North and South Carolina. James Cook surveyed the boundary to the Savannah River in 1771 through 1772 by slashing trees and dragging chains through some of the most impenetrable wilderness on the Eastern seaboard.

One of the most knowledgeable sources on the two-state boundary dispute is retired history professor, Louise Pettus, of Winthrop University in Rock Hill. According to Dr. Pettus, "There was no N.C. - S.C. boundary line at all before 1772. So both colonies claimed land east of the Catawba River and the northern most part of the Waxhaws. The exception is the northern part of Lancaster County, just above the Waxhaws, which was granted to the Catawba Indians who chose to be in SC rather than N.C. That line was drawn in 1764. Records of the land grants before 1772 are located in Anson County patent books (Mecklenburg was a part of Anson County until 1769.) All of the N.C. County records are in the North Carolina Archives in Raleigh, N.C. In 1772, British surveyors laid out the N.C. / S.C. boundary line west of the Catawba River in a straight line but they [James Cook and party] used the Camden (S.C.) road often called the Camden road or the Camden to Salisbury road, or the road was called the Salisbury road only; or, on some of the early Lancaster County plats, it is the "Great Road to Philadelphia," or just 'Great Road.'"

In another essay on the Cook survey confusion, Pettus states, "Surveyor, James Cook, finally drew a line eleven miles south of His Majesty's intention. Confused, fatigued, and suffering from the rains, the hot weather and the insects, the surveyor stopped on the Camden - Salisbury Road, south of the Catawba lands. Instead of latitude 35 degrees, the surveyors had run a course of 34 degrees and 49 minutes. The error cost South Carolina 660 square miles of land."

The highway known as the "Old Camden - Salisbury Road" has been replaced in more modern times by U.S. Highway 601 -- which is known as McCord's Ferry Road in Orangeburg and Calhoun Counties. James Cook probably had had enough of the heat and chiggers and headed for the more sublime environs of Cook's Mountain, elevation 372 feet above sea level. He submitted his map to London publishers, and in 1773 it became the most accurate scale drawing ever rendered of the colony. Certain challenges to river bends and tributaries caused Lowcountry native, Henry Mouzon, of Williamsburg County to undertake his own version of a South Carolina map, and in two years Mouzon corrected both the Catawba and the Upstate river errors of the Cook map. Mouzon, a descendant of Huguenots and a cousin and cohort of Francis Marion, was educated as an engineer at the Sorbonne.

A year ago a prominent property consultant, Plantation Services of Charleston and Albany, Georgia, circulated a prospectus offering the Cook's Mountain estate for sale. "1131 Acres near Columbia, South Carolina. A property on a mountain....on a river....less than two hours from the sea. $4,900,000. Seventeen miles east of Columbia on the Wateree River is a property known as Cook's Mountain. It is one of the most spectacular properties in South Carolina. Land types on the property range from an almost primeval hardwood forest along the river rising through uplands to the highest elevations in the central part of the state. The property has a wide variety of plant and animal life. The 'mountain' itself rises to an elevation of 372 feet above sea level, an anomaly in this area that offers scenic views for miles. The mountain was the home of Mr.James Cook, a famous cartographer, who produced the Cook Map of South Carolina in 1773."

Richland County Council desired to purchase the property to preserve it as a recreational site, but they were outbid by a national landfill company. A national garbage-disposal company now controls Cook's Mountain, a Richland County landmark that faces an uncertain future after years of public use.

A division of Republic Services bought the property last month from the mountain's longtime landowners for $5.1 million, according to Richland County property records. The March 1, 2012 transaction was expected and Republic is now actively marketing the property for resale. Will Flower, a spokesman for Republic, said the company is in no rush to sell the land, but also is "not in the property-holding business."

For the time being, the Cook's Mountain Hunt Club has an arrangement to lease a portion of the area for its members' use. Citizens of the Midlands hope that this beautiful historical site known as Cook's Mountain can someday be a county or state park where all may partake of the grand vistas and "salubrious clime" that so appealed to 18th century English cartographer James Cook.

Reverend Woodmason's 1762 Account of Upcountry Woes

Every Carolinian had grounds for shunning Anglican Reverend Charles Woodmason's 1760's era journal entitled *The Carolina Backcountry on the Eve of the Revolution,* published posthumously. The itinerant priest gave a bold and blunt denunciation of the backcountry's illiteracy and crudity, and he lambasted the Lowcountry's self-absorption and idleness. While traveling over 6,000 miles on foot and horseback through the settlements north and west of the Congaree, Woodmason baptized, preached, and catechized, all the while penning an eye-opening account of everyday life in South Carolina's earliest years.

Charles Woodmason, merchant and planter, was how Charlestonians of the 1750s knew him. He was a bachelor here who never spoke of his wife and family in England. Bookseller, indigo planter, and poet, Woodmason made his mark here among English, Irish, Scot, Dutch, and German immigrants. All anyone knew about him was that he hailed from the Portsmouth region of England and that he was quite learned. From time to time his poems appeared in *The Gentleman's Magazine,* a London publication prized in the Charleston taverns and coffeehouses.

There's one obscure entry in his lengthy journal that may give a clue why Woodmason abandoned his wife, Hannah Page, and their three children for a life in Carolina. The journal entry refers to sometime in his mature years that Woodmason was kicked by a horse and rendered impotent. Further details are left to the reader's imagination as the entrepreneur-turned-Anglican-evangelist endeavored to spend more than forty years unattached in Carolina. We know that a business reversal led him to seek employment here as a stamp tax collector in 1765, and his popularity ceased abruptly. Woodmason returned to England and was ordained as an Anglican deacon by the Bishop of Lincoln on Friday, April 25, 1767, and on Sunday, April 27, he was ordained a priest by the Bishop of Chester. This flurry of ecclesiastical activity was an attempt by the Anglican Bishops and a group of concerned London citizens who called themselves The

Society For The Propagation of the Gospel to proselytize the Southern Colonies for the Church of England. Church and State, Crown and the Bishop's Mitre were deemed as a righteous authority to be imposed upon rebellious colonials. Woodmason exhibited great courage by returning to Charleston in 1767 and volunteering for St. Mark's Parish, a jurisdiction that authorized him to preach the gospel from Pineville to the Cheraws. Woodmason was not a product of the Great Awakening which had brought George Whitefield and John Wesley here years earlier. The evangelical fervor of Calvin-styled Christianity with its emphasis upon self-denial and simplicity in worship did not encompass the fuller message of Charles Woodmason. The itinerant Anglican earnestly believed that the budding idea of liberty and republicanism bode ill for the colonies. Without the Monarch and the Archbishop of Canterbury to coordinate the temporal and the spiritual well-being of society, anarchy would undoubtedly follow. Woodmason saw himself as a man Heaven sent to bring Godly order to the Carolina backcountry where lawlessness and licentiousness appeared to be the norm. As scripture from the Old Testament Book of Judges revealed of Biblical times, "In those days there was no king in Israel: every man did that which was right in his own eyes."

Charles Woodmason must have had an emotional homecoming to Charleston in 1767. For 15 years he'd been a man of property and influence on Broad and Bay Streets. He'd corresponded with Benjamin Franklin about his electrical experiments, and he'd contributed to the local Gazette on a range of topics from the cultivation of indigo to the harnessing of electrical power in lightning. After falling from high esteem by seeking to become a stamp tax collector, Woodmason as an Anglican clergyman must have stirred many curious comments from his former associates upon his return. Tory to the bone, Woodmason was not without like companions in the Anglican clergy here as well as loyalist merchants and shippers on the waterfront. What caught Charlestonians by surprise was Reverend Woodmason's insistence to go into the wilderness parts of the colony, the fertile area between the Saluda and the Wateree Rivers where log-cabin pioneers cohabited in sin, cavorted in debauched revelry, and rarely heard God's Word preached on the Sabbath. One writer summarized the Reverend's intentions: "It is also apparent that Woodmason, a steadfast Anglican, had a genuine concern for the spiritual welfare of the frontier, where a number of enthusiastic religious sects, foremost among them the New Light Baptists, were threatening the scattered backcountry outposts of Anglicanism."

Woodmason had no use for Presbyterian and Baptist clergy in the Upcountry. Men of the cloth, regardless of denomination, were rare encounters for Upcountry settlers. Circuit-riding preachers came through once or twice a year to marry those who'd been cohabiting and to baptize their offspring. On those occasions, preaching was done outdoors since the largest structures were taverns.

Woodmason set out to live among the people in this vast and untamed wilderness. His purpose was to render the services that clergy traditionally do, but also to demonstrate that Church and State, Crown and Bishop, preserve that sacred order within which society thrives. He baptized hundreds, preached to thousands, married many, and dodged attempts upon his life and insults upon his person. In his defense of Anglicanism, Woodmason brought upon himself the wrath of the Calvinists. In his defense of the hapless backcountrymen in their dealings with colonial authority, he received the ridicule of the Charleston establishment.

After a few weeks in Pinetree, later renamed Camden, Woodmason wrote, "The people around, of abandon'd Morals, and profligate Principles -- Rude -- Ignorant -- Void of Manners, Education or Good Breeding -- No genteel or Polite Person among them -- save Mr. Kershaw an English Merchant settled here. The people are of all Sects and Denominations -- a mix'd medley from all Countries and the Off Scouring of America." These words were meant for his sponsors, the Bishop of London and the Society For the Propagation of the Gospel. Though American scholars knew of the journal's existence in the 19th century, the public did not get to read Woodmason's frank account until its publication in 1953. By the 1960s, people in Upstate South Carolina, especially those descended from the early settlers, were shocked at the Reverend's less-than-genteel appraisal of their ancestry. Lowcountry bluebloods fared little better as Woodmason portrayed them as haughty, frivolous, and domineering. Since he named people in his journal, it makes for interesting reading.

Charleston lawyers were on the receiving end of much of this Anglican Divine's wrath. All courts were centered in Charleston, and the expense to Upcountry folks of trying even the simplest case were enormous. Country people of the 18th century would rather take matters into their own hands than engage the Charleston bar. Though he was their severest critic, Charles Woodmason became sympathetic with the plight of his so-called parishioners up on the Congaree. He became an outspoken defender of the Regulator Movement, a high-handed, unauthorized attempt by Upstate colonials to impose their own law and order.

In a much-circulated letter begins, "We are free men, British subjects, not born slaves. We contribute our portion in all public taxations, and discharge our public duty equally with our fellow colonists. Yet we do not participate with them in the rights and benefits which they enjoy, though equally entitled to them." Charles Woodmason is believed to have authored the letter even if he did not initiate the idea. The missive further states the legal duress imposed upon the Upstate for effecting even the most routine business -- such as having to travel to Charleston to record a land deed. Legend has it that Woodmason traveled to Charleston to post a copy of the "South Carolina Protest" on the wall of the Exchange. Notice was served that the settlers beyond the Congaree and the Wateree were not going to suffer injustice indefinitely from Lowcountry officials.

Wearied by his horseback ministry and primitive existence, not to say his limited success at making good Anglicans out of the Scots-Irish and Welsh Upcountrymen, Woodmason moved on to more civilized posts in North Carolina and Virginia. He never knew the extent of his Christian ministry, nor did he realize the historical impact that his saddlebag journal would have upon scholars and the general public.

How Cully Cobb Helped Transform the South

There're folks around, mostly Atlantans, who'll tell you that it was newspaperman Henry Grady who did more than anyone else to lift the South from the "slough of despond" following the War. And Grady is a worthy candidate for honors. "There was a South of slavery and secession -- that South is dead. There is now a South of union and freedom -- that South, thank God, is living, breathing, and growing every hour," proclaimed *Atlanta Constitution* editor, Henry Grady, on Wednesday evening of December 22, 1886, at the annual banquet of The New England Society of the City of New York. J.P. Morgan and Henry Flagler were sitting nearby as reporters for James Gordon Bennett's *New York Herald* hurriedly scribbled the proclamation that'd be republished around the country in the ensuing weeks. The plantation South was gone with the winds of war, but there was a New South with timber barons, cotton and sugar cane planters, and railroad tycoons.

Historians tout the well-known apostles of new thinking such as Grady, Stephen Dill Lee, William Gregg, Richard Edmunds -- and the list of modern-thinking Southerners goes on and on. However, Cully Cobb of Prospect, Tennessee, did more to usher in a new, forward-thinking South through his influential self-help magazine -- *Progressive Farmer*. Every month farmers of small tracts and planters of great estates pulled from their mailbox a fifty-page illustrated journal containing insight and innovation in all things agricultural. Next to the King James Bible and the *News and World Report*, the *Progressive Farmer* was the rural southerner's most sought-after publication.

For all his fame as an apostle of a changing South, Henry Grady accomplished little more than heralding to the outside world that a new day had come below the Mason-Dixon Line. From Richmond to Atlanta, a legion of visionaries rose from the embers of the Confederacy to chart a new course. Charleston-born Stephen Dill Lee, a West Point graduate and Lieutenant-General in the War, exhorted his old comrades in arms to look to agriculture, manufacturing, and railroads to lift them into the new century. Richard Edmunds, a Baltimore newspaperman, also touted a smokestack economy. Wade

Hampton was another forward-thinking postwar politician whose ideas were not part of the diehard mentality. William Gregg of Graniteville brought "big industry" to South Carolina. However, without Cully Cobb and his monthly inspiration in the *Progressive Farmer*, the eloquent words of Grady, the business acumen of Edmunds and Gregg, and the heroic examples of Lee and Hampton, would have been wisps of smoke. Cobb's *Progressive Farmer* reshaped the rural South and shepherded its youth into the newly created Land Grant colleges that dotted the Old Confederacy. Cully Cobb of Prospect, Tennessee, ushered in a new, forward-thinking South that sought new solutions and new ventures.

If growing up in an antiquated log cabin in the most rural part of south-central Tennessee can be a recommendation for anything associated with academics, it'd have to be in the discipline of agricultural science. Napoleon Bonaparte Cobb, father of Cully, had had no part in the antebellum plantation culture, yet he cherished three ideals dear to the heart of the landed slave-owning elites -- books, land, and the bounty of the soil, and he was willing to sacrifice to see that his offspring had the advantage of all three. When Cully Cobb was born in 1884, Grover Cleveland was president and Mark Twain was publishing *Huckleberry Finn*. The country boy from Prospect, Tennessee by-passed the University of Alabama just a hundred miles south to study at Mississippi A. & M. (later Mississippi State) in Starkville -- a place twice as far from Prospect and accessible only by horse or rail.

Mississippi State was one of the second wave of Land Grant colleges created by the Morrill Act of 1862. Iowa State and Kansas State were established during the 1860s; Mississippi State in 1878. Charlestonian Stephen Dill Lee became the first president of Mississippi State. Lee had gone west to Mississippi following the War because his wife's family had land there and because he'd commanded Mississippians during the terrible Union siege of Vicksburg. With Stephen D. Lee's enlightened postwar attitude, young men such as Cully Cobb became devotees to forging a new southern outlook.

Upon graduation young Cobb accepted a position as Agricultural Science instructor at a rural crossroads community known as Buena Vista, one of several places in Mississippi named for battles in the Mexican War. Within a couple of years Cobb was superintendent of education for all public schools in the Chickasaw County. Cobb helped instill a passion for learning and a willingness to try new approaches to old problems. In the early 1900s a young man in the South with a university education could expect to move ahead in a hurry, and Cobb was a leading citizen in the county before he was age 30. Cobb was also considered a "catch" by the local girls, and he married Ora May Ball. Their legacy and namesakes are prominent Nashville surgeon, Cully Cobb, Jr., and Sacramento neurosurgeon Cully Cobb, III.

The career path that led Cobb to be the founder of the legendary periodical he's known for began with his being tapped for an "ag ed" teaching job and culminated with him heading up the most influential agricultural press in the country. He paid his dues to get where he got. Cobb introduced 4-H competition to Chickasaw County, Mississippi, and he became instrumental in every form of agricultural improvement from erosion control to the introduction of ground covers, from drainage solutions to weed suppression. His work was always associated with the daily "nuts and bolts" types of things that made sense to the rural people who made up 70 percent of the country's population 75 years ago. Cobb's reputation spread through the South as a new light in agricultural science. *The Ruralist Press* in Atlanta reached out to Cully Cobb during World War I with an offer to take over the publication of the *Hastings Seed Catalog*, a publication that went to more Southern mailboxes than any other. From that platform Cully Cobb was the driving force for bringing together a series of magazine mergers that resulted in the modern-day *Progressive Farmer* magazine.

Lafayette Polk of Winston, now Winston-Salem, originated the *Progressive Farmer* magazine name for a small publication that circulated in central North Carolina's tobacco belt in the 1890s. Clarence Poe of Raleigh took over the struggling periodical and tried to keep it afloat during the financial panic of 1893. Poe heard of a similar farm magazine in Starkville, Mississippi, called the *Southern Farm Gazette* and that it, too, was about to go under financially. In one of the great publishing coups of the last century, those two publishers agreed to sell out to Cully Cobb in Atlanta. This entrepreneur borrowed to start his own publishing business which he called the Ruralist Press. Cobb then branched out from just editing the *Hasting's Seed Catalog* to doing his own monthly regional farm magazine called the *Southern Ruralist* which reached out to farmers and dairymen in Georgia, north Florida, and southern Tennessee.

The *Southern Ruralist* was merged with the *Southern Farm Gazette* and the *Progressive Farmer* -- all consolidated under the Progressive Farmer name. Since agriculture was the South's greatest industry, this meant that Cully Cobb's monthly editorial was one of the most important economic and political viewpoints in the region. Cobb was sought out by governors and congressmen. Even Franklin Roosevelt tapped Cobb to become director of the Cotton Division of the controversial Agricultural Adjustment Commission. Cobb was disappointed that he did not get appointed as Secretary of Agriculture in FDR's second administration, but the poor boy from Prospect, Tennessee, had risen to the pinnacle of success and he'd raised the standard of living of tens of thousands across the South. How Cully Cobb and the *Progressive Farmer* magazine corporation met Emory Cunningham and launched *Southern Living* Magazine is the subject of yet another lost moment in history.

Why The Progressive Farmer Launched Southern Living Magazine

As late as the 1960s, there were thousands of rural homes across the South whose front porches were framed by shade trees and fresh-plowed fields. Turnpikes connected northern cities, but farm-to-market roads linked southern towns. Well water tasted different from county to county, and local accents were easily identifiable. Knock on a southern front door in those days and you were ushered into the front hall where the family telephone occupied a prominent table. Near the telephone were usually three magazines, *The Baptist Chronicle*, *U.S. News and World Report*, and *The Progressive Farmer*. Visitors were celebrated with a glass of sweet iced tea, and "y'all" was the only personal pronoun heard.

So, what's changed in fifty years? Well, the children who grew up in those rural homes attended state-supported universities and became a part of urban sprawl. They, too, have front porches, but it's a diminutive, decorative thing designed to balance the gaping three-car garage on one side with the gabled roofed master suite on the other. Front halls have given way to grand, marble entrances, and the central phone has morphed into a smart phone for guys and girls on the go. Oh yeah, that smart phone in M'lady's pocket has an "app" for *Southern Living* magazine, the number one "must read" for Southern Moms.

As the Virginia Slims ad said, "You've come a long way, baby." Just a fraction of those farm-raised kids of the '60s came back to their rural roots. Instead, they became brokers, bankers, attorneys, sales reps, or soccer moms in places like Mobile, or Tallahassee, or Charleston. You can bet one thing, though -- visit any one of them and you'll be offered sweet iced tea and "y'all" is still the only pronoun heard!

The South has undergone a transformation in our lifetime, and even the old-timers admit that much of that change is very good indeed. Television has subtly neutralized our accents the way a river stone loses its edges over time. Now some of our teens sound more like "Valley Girls" than the Carolina Girls we knew growing up. But give much of the credit for change to the print media -- especially Cully Cobb's Ruralist Press in Atlanta, the publishers of *The Progressive Farmer* and *Southern Living* magazines. As for *Southern Living*, its origin lies with that one-of-a kind Southern periodical -- *The Progressive Farmer*, and its course was charted by that visionary of the New South, the late journalist and publisher Cully Cobb. Back when our grandfathers were deliberating over whether the new tractor should be a John Deere, Ford, or Allis-Chalmers, Cobb, the editor and publisher of *The Progressive Farmer* was meeting with young Auburn graduate, Emory O. Cunningham of Birmingham, Alabama. The year was 1966 and amidst the racial strife and the Vietnam War, Cobb and Cunningham were poring over layouts for a dramatically new regional magazine -- a magazine whose purpose was to unite the hospitable ways of southern rural living for those offspring who choose to live in the new urban South.

The Progressive Farmer always contained a home and hearth section for the ladies, and it was this section of the agricultural magazine that was greatly enlarged in scope to become the framework for *Southern Living*. Of Emory Cunningham, the *Auburn Alumni News* remarked upon his death in January of 2000, "Emory O. Cunningham, age 78: publisher whose *Southern Living* magazine helped reinvent the image of the South. Frustrated that the region was stereotyped as an area mired in poverty and racism, Cunningham established his magazine to gracefully highlight the charm of the South. The magazine is known for its recipes and articles about traditional Southern crafts, music, and lifestyle. Time Inc. acquired *Southern Living* and its parent company, Southern Progressive Corp., in 1985 for $480 million."

Emory Cunningham was a Kansas native who was an avid outdoorsman, and at the onset of World War II, Cunningham enlisted in the Navy and worked his way into a slot at naval flight school in Pensacola. After serving as a fighter pilot in the war, Cunningham completed his B.S. degree in Agricultural Science at Auburn, graduating in 1948. He went to work with Cully Cobb of *The Progressive Farmer* magazine, and the rest is now a part of southern journalism history.

Southern Living made sure that its pages were not devoted just to topics that would appeal to women. Grilling recipes for venison, tailgate barbeque sauces, Southeastern Conference football predictions, Wrangler Jeep ads, and a host of "guy-oriented" columns guaranteed universal appeal for this colorful pioneer of regional publications.

Emory Cunningham, like his colleague and former boss, Cully Cobb, became a powerful voice for the South as it emerged from generations of "Jim Crow" culture. Eschewing politics, the magazine focused on all the wholesome aspects of a gracious southern lifestyle. Cunningham was a guest lecturer at most of the South's great Land Grant universities, and he was inducted into the Auburn Agricultural School's Hall of Fame. He also served on the Board of Trustees at Auburn and was one of the leading citizens of Birmingham. Another obituary of Cunningham noted, "A philanthropist as well as a business and civic leader, Cunningham contributed financial support for scholarships, an eminent scholar chair, an environmental institute and other programs and activities at Auburn. Before joining the AU Board of Trustees, he served as a director of AU Foundation and on the College of Agriculture's advisory council. In recognition of Cunningham's state and national leadership in agriculture, education, publishing and civic affairs, AU presented him an honorary doctor of science degree in 1981."

Ever claiming authority on American cultural matters, Howell Raines of the *New York Times* said of Cunningham, "the 'relentlessly cheerful' magazine was 'devoted to depicting the region as one endless festival of barbecue, boiled shrimp, football Sundays and good old Nashville music.'" There may be a disguised compliment in there somewhere for Emory Cunningham.

This month's edition of *Southern Living* has the usual "before and after" restoration miracle and an article entitled, "101 Ways to Give your Home Southern Charm" We have come a long way since the phrase "too poor to paint, too proud to whitewash," was used by visitors to describe our genteel straits. However, without *Southern Living* how else would we southerners keep close with the things that unite us? For instance, who would know that Chef Frank Stitt of Birmingham was voted best chef in the Southeast in 2001 and that his Highland Bar and Grill has been a top five finalist for "best restaurant in the nation" for the last four years? How else would we know that Nick Saban, Gene Stallings, and Pat Dye will be signing autographs at the SEC Tailgate kickoff on Gulf Shores and Orange Beach, Alabama, August 23 through 26?

The late Emory Cunningham and his mentor, Cully Cobb, pointed the way up and out of a checkered past and gave us a forum to shout out all that's great about living below the Mason and Dixon line.

The proofreader of *History's Lost Moments,* Millie Bull Horton, enjoys relaxing with the latest edition of *Southern Living* and a glass of sweet iced tea.

fini

Made in the USA
Columbia, SC
28 December 2019